GOING TO SCHOOL IN OCEANIA

GOING TO SCHOOL IN OCEANIA

EDITED BY CRAIG CAMPBELL AND GEOFFREY SHERINGTON

The Global School Room
Alan Sadovnik and Susan Semel, Series Editors

GREENWOOD PRESS
Westport, Connecticut • London

370.995
Goi

10/08

Library of Congress Cataloging-in-Publication Data

Going to school in Oceania / edited by Craig Campbell and Geoffrey Sherington.
    p. cm. — (The global school room, ISSN 1933–6101)
    Includes bibliographical references and index.
    ISBN-13: 978–0–313–33950–9 (alk. paper)
    1. Education—Oceania—History. I. Campbell, Craig, 1949– II. Sherington,
Geoffrey.
    LA2201.G65 2007   (2) Schools – Oceania
    370.995—dc22   2007028651

British Library Cataloguing in Publication Data is available.

Library of Congress Catalog Card Number: 2007028651
ISBN-13: 978–0–313–33950–9
ISSN: 1933–6101

First published in 2007

Greenwood Press, 88 Post Road West, Westport, CT 06881
An imprint of Greenwood Publishing Group, Inc.
www.greenwood.com

Printed in the United States of America

The paper used in this book complies with the
Permanent Paper Standard issued by the National
Information Standards Organization (Z39.48–1984).

10 9 8 7 6 5 4 3 2 1

CONTENTS

SERIES FOREWORD

Over the past three decades, with globalization becoming a dominant force, the worldwide emphasis on schooling has accelerated. However, a historical perspective teaches us that global trends in schooling are by no means a recent phenomenon. The work of neoinstitutional sociologists such as John Meyer and his colleagues has demonstrated that the development of mass public educational systems became a worldwide trend in the nineteenth century and most nations' school systems go back significantly further. The Global School Room Series is intended to provide students with an understanding of the similarities and differences among educational systems throughout the world from a historical perspective.

Although comparative and international educational research has provided an understanding of the many similarities in school systems across nations and cultures, it has also indicated the significant differences. Schools reflect societies and their cultures; and therefore there are significant differences among different nations' school systems and educational practices. Another purpose of this series is to examine these similarities and differences.

The series is organized into nine volumes, each looking at the history of the school systems in countries on one continent or subcontinent. The series consists of volumes covering schooling in the following regions:

North America
Latin America
Europe
Sub-Saharan Africa
North Africa and the Middle East
South Asia

Central Asia
East Asia
Oceania

As the third volume in the series to be published, *Going to School in Oceania*, edited by Craig Campbell and Geoffrey Sherington, provides an important and timely examination of the educational systems in Oceania, including those in Australia, New Guinea, Fiji, New Zealand, and Samoa. Through the history of the educational systems in each country and an analysis of contemporary systems, the authors provide a rich description of how schooling is related to national culture; religion; identity; social, political, and economic structures; and economic development. Moreover, the book illustrates the importance of historical, philosophical, and sociological perspectives in understanding the similarities and differences among societies and their schools. Finally, the book provides everyday examples of what schools in each country are like and how curriculum and teaching practices reflect the larger cultural, social, religious, and historical patterns of each society. Through essays written by students, its "day in the life of" sections provide rich, experiential commentary on what it is like to go to school in these countries from the perspectives of students themselves.

The editors and authors of each chapter examine a number of important themes, including colonialism, the effects of Western educational models, the cultures, education and treatment of indigenous and Aboriginal peoples, the effects of development and globalization, the tensions between Western educational systems and indigenous conceptions of education, and differences among countries with respect to access and opportunity systems.

Going to School in Oceania is emblematic of the series in that it provides students with an understanding that schooling needs to be understood in the context of each local culture, rather than viewed ethnocentrically from a U.S. or Western perspective. We often tend to make broad generalizations about other continents and assume that culture and schooling are uniform across countries. This book demonstrates the importance of examining national systems to uncover differences, as well as similarities.

In *National Differences, Global Similarities* (2005), sociologists Baker and LeTendre argued that the purpose of studying another country's educational systems is to understand worldwide trends in education, as well as national differences. Merry White in *The Japanese Educational Challenge* (1987) argued that the purpose of studying another country's educational system is not necessarily to copy it but rather to learn from the lessons of other societies and, where appropriate, to use these lessons to improve our own schools but only in the context of our own culture and schools.

Going to School in Oceania provides important illustrations of worldwide trends and national differences, as well as many important lessons. However, it also cautions us to understand educational systems in the contexts of historical, national, and cultural differences. At a time when policy makers in the United States and elsewhere look to other countries, especially in Asia and Oceania, in order to improve student achievement and to remain competitive in the global economy, this book reminds us that national achievement trends must be understood in a historical, sociological, and cultural context.

We invite you to continue to explore schooling around the world—this time in Oceania and then the rest of the world, as subsequent volumes are published.

Alan Sadovnik and Susan Semel

REFERENCES

Baker, D. P., and G. LeTendre. 2005. *National Differences, Global Similarities.* Palo Alto: Stanford University Press.
White, M. 1987. *The Japanese Educational Challenge.* New York: The Free Press.

ACKNOWLEDGMENTS

All the chapter authors thank the writers whom they recruited to make chronologies of days in their lives. In every case, the narratives illuminated the intersections between school, family, individual, and the broader social and national contexts.

Chapter 1

INTRODUCTION

Craig Campbell and Geoffrey Sherington

This volume represents the first major effort to write an overview of the history of education in the South West Pacific. Establishing connections between the histories of schooling in countries as disparate as Australia, Fiji, New Zealand, Papua New Guinea, and Samoa is a difficult task. Certainly, there is the geographic connection: the countries under study all share South West Pacific locations, though Australia also belongs to the Indian Ocean. However, geography alone in a historical study of schooling is insufficient justification. There is another justification, but in a historiographical era marked by strong sensitivity to Eurocentricism, it can also be a problem. Most of the school systems, institutions, and educational practices discussed in this volume certainly arose as a result of mainly European or "western" economic, missionary, and imperial activity in this part of the Pacific world. As Britain, France, Germany, Japan, the United States, and eventually Australia and New Zealand (curiously, both colonized and colonizers) came into the South West Pacific—often following their nationals as explorers, scientific investigators, whalers, traders, labor recruiters, or missionaries, for example—they eventually found it necessary either to establish schools with the curricula and institutional forms of European education in mind or to support those previously established by Christian missionaries. This dissemination of European-style schooling in the South West Pacific countries becomes a necessary connection between the chapters in this volume. Particularly in Australia and New Zealand, this story of the dissemination of European-style schooling is closely associated with European settlement and the provision of mass schooling for nonindigenous children. The problem is that this story, with such a thematic connection across the Pacific, tends to marginalize indigenous cultures and the ways local people educated their communities before and after the introduction and adaptation of western forms of schooling. The authors of the following chapters are sensitive to the problem,

but sensitivity alone is not always enough. In societies that had radically different kinds of literacy (usually dominated by the oral and visual) and very different senses of what kinds of knowledge were worth preserving, the sources for
writing histories of indigenous education differed greatly from the literacies
and epistemologies developed by Europeans—at least those developed by the
eighteenth and nineteenth centuries. Some of the authors in this volume have
depended a great deal on anthropological literature. Others have devoted less
time to reconstructing precolonial education and spent rather more on
"contact history," which is the story of what emerged as indigenous peoples
and the colonial school promoters began to engage with one another.

The past half-century has seen a blossoming of South West Pacific historical
study, and this book owes a great deal to the literature it has generated. C.
Hartley Grattan, the American historian, was a pioneer in the field and remains
one of the few who has sought to integrate the study of the Pacific islands,
Australia, and New Zealand, and even Antarctica into one study.[1] The literature
has been rich enough to have developed historiographical traditions of considerable complexity, some of which are shared with colonial and postcolonial
approaches to history generally, but there are also elements that are highly
distinctive. Nevertheless, the tendency has remained, despite Grattan and
others, not to produce integrated histories of the region. Australia and New
Zealand both have long-term cultural associations and loyalties, which have
made it difficult for their peoples, and in many cases, their historians, to consider the Pacific as a primary site of understanding for the historical experience
and associations of their peoples. In recent times, and especially since the
United Kingdom joined the European Community, New Zealand has had a
new tendency to imagine itself as part of the Pacific. However, the parallel
tendency in Australia has been to imagine itself as "part of Asia."

For the "South Seas," there was a highly significant period in which roman-
ticism overwhelmed European writing. This occurred from the mid-eighteenth
century to the early twentieth century and remains alive today in the tourist
brochures of the twenty-first century. Louis-Antoine de Bougainville, traveler
in the Pacific in 1767 and 1768, and whose published journals proved highly
popular, is often attributed with the beginnings of the trend. In Tahiti, he
wrote: "The chief offered me one of his wives, young and fairly pretty, and the
whole gathering sang the wedding anthem. What a country! What a people!"[2]
The theme of paradise on earth was taken up by many future visitors, writers,
and artists. In his precocious discussion of European imaginings of the South
Pacific, Bernard Smith in 1967 pointed to the issues that postmodernists and
others would elaborate many years later: such representations and imaginings
had dubious connection to the "realities" of South Pacific societies but, nevertheless, could be extraordinarily powerful in many different ways.[3]

This romantic period in South Pacific writing and historiography does not
quite fit the situation in Australia. There, the tendency to idealize Aboriginal peoples was quite short-lived. William Dampier's unfortunate seventeenth-century

depiction of the lives led by indigenous peoples was in the "nasty, brutish and short" tradition, and it persisted a very long time. Of course, in the islands of the South West Pacific, there had also been a tradition of writing that occurred before the great idealization. This often concentrated on the supposed barbarism and warlike qualities of the local peoples. Similarly, the New Zealand historiography regarding Maori was early tempered by the experience of vigorous resistance to European colonization, and indeed by a series of wars between Maori and pakeha (Europeans or "white" people). In both countries, indigenous culture and education were subject to either neglect or hostility while efficient forms of schooling for the nonindigenous populations were developed. Even in the countries where indigenous populations were in the majority, European settlers' general view usually was to "see education for islanders as a waste of money, if not politically dangerous."[4] This phase changed with World War II when white supremacy clearly waned.

The works of pioneering anthropologists, some of whom helped establish anthropology as an academic discipline, have provided a major source of understanding of indigenous peoples in the South West Pacific. Margaret Mead's Samoan studies consolidated both her reputation and her discipline in the social sciences. However, the challenge to her work in recent times has taught us that anthropologists themselves were not necessarily "objective" reporters despite the "science" in their research methodologies. The argument over the reliability of Mead's studies of the lives of young Samoan women is not over yet, but it did point to the probability that misleading "noble savage" views of Pacific peoples, with their apparently innocent freedoms and promiscuities, lasted well into the twentieth century.[5]

Readings of papers and books left behind by missionaries and amateur anthropologists with missionary backgrounds rarely fell into the same traps. The sheer difficulty and the tortuous politics of persuading indigenous peoples towards Christianity led to views of indigenous societies of a very different character. The problems in less politically cohesive Melanesian and Australian Aboriginal societies were very great indeed, and costly in terms of European and indigenous lives. This is in contrast to the Polynesian experience, where the "conversion" of one great chief could see a general conversion of his people and the rapid establishment of missionary schools.[6] The traditions of European scholarship that neatly divided indigenous peoples of the South West Pacific into Polynesian, Melanesian, Micronesian, and Australian with very clear lines on maps are increasingly contested.[7] For example, they especially fail to take into account the migrations of individuals and groups in the colonial eras associated with missionary and labor-recruiting activity. "Native" missionaries from Polynesia ended up in Melanesia. "Black-birding," appalling recruiting practices in the islands, saw a substantial Kanak population working plantations in Queensland, the Australian colony north of New South Wales.[8]

One of the historiographical movements that developed with a retreat from the chauvinist and imperial traditions (of which the romantic approach was a part) was the "fatal impact" school. It produced an overdue corrective—in many cases, correctly identifying the devastating impact on indigenous peoples of the economic and cultural practices of European missionaries, traders, administrators, and settlers.[9] In many parts of the South West Pacific, severe indigenous depopulations occurred following "contact." Nor is there any doubt that schooling along European lines assisted in the damage done to indigenous societies. Nevertheless, there have been at least two correctives to this approach to South West Pacific history. The first is along the lines that indigenous peoples are cast too much as powerless victims of overwhelming forces. Such an interpretation may not only undervalue narratives of resistance and successful adaptations by indigenous peoples to the external forces imping-ing but also fail to take the longer view: invasions, cultural crises and chal-lenges, and colonizations were a continuous feature of South West Pacific histories before—and after—the high point of European, Asian, and American contact and imperialism in the region. Moreover, the fatal impact approach tends to silence the voices of the survivors and, more importantly, the continu-ing cultural and social traditions of indigenous societies. Nowhere is this more evident than in the story of the Tasmanian Aborigines whom "fatal impact" historians incorrectly considered had suffered complete genocide.

The second corrective has resulted from the sensitivities of European settlers, especially in Australia, but also in New Zealand, and to a degree in New Caledonia. Fatal impact theory cast European settlers in a very bad light, such a bad light that in Australia, particularly, both from within the historical profession and the centre-right of politics, "black arm band" history has been condemned as dis-honoring brave European explorers, pioneers, and settlers. It is argued that such historical writing performs a disruptive role in both civics education and the development of national pride and loyalty. This debate continues and is often at the heart of a struggle to control and write new curriculum for civics, social stud-ies, and history in several parts of the South West Pacific region.[10]

Not all of these issues are equally present in the following histories of school-ing in Australia, Fiji, New Guinea, New Zealand, and Samoa. However, in one way or another they frame many of the subtexts and should certainly inform readers' questions as they read the chapter texts.

As is common with all the volumes of this series, The Global Schoolroom, the authors in this volume have arranged their texts in certain time periods with attention to actual schooling practices. In the process, they privilege the social history of schooling. Therefore, what happened to the variety of diverse cultural groups, the different populations marked by caste and class, gender, ethnicity, and "race" is the focus of the volume. Yet it is impossible to ignore the developing institutions, structures, and policies associated with education as they developed in each country. Each chapter devotes time to making sure that what happened in South West Pacific schoolrooms is given a broad context. Unlike a number of other volumes in this series, there are only four broad time periods to divide the chapters: before the nineteenth century, the nineteenth and then the twentieth century, and the present. This allows more depth of description and analysis though concentrating on the eras of European and American influence in the region.

A feature of the chapters is the specially commissioned "day in the life of" sections. A range of young people—children to young adults, those in elementary schools to a university college—were asked to write about a typical day in their lives. Each essay is revealing in its own way: one is certainly the recognizability of the schools as familiar organizations—regardless of them being situated in apparently exotic sites; another is the real differences between how families operate, how leisure time is used, and how daily lives occur. The considerable differences between the wealth of families and schools in different places is apparent not only in these sections but also within the stories told by the chapters. In some of the "day in the life of" sections, the problem is finding enough time to watch DVDs and play video games. In others, it is finding enough time to assist parents with all the jobs required to keep a family fed and together. In Samoa and New Guinea, education policy and funding are often associated with the targets of the World Bank and other agencies working in "developing" or "poor" countries. For Australia and New Zealand, the global interests are different. In those countries, the struggle to remain globally competitive through advanced education and training is revealed by the ways that the Organization for Economic Cooperation and Development (OECD) educational and economic data is studied and used. This is about the different agendas of "developed" rather than "developing" countries.

Another way of organizing these studies of schooling in the South West Pacific could have been to attach them to the periods of precolonial, colonial, and postcolonial (independence) status, but such divisions do not usually coincide with the periodizations associated with educational reform. It is very clear that the persistence of long-standing institutions and the ways that young people are schooled is often stronger than sporadic reform efforts or changes in colonial or national status. In terms of policies and assumptions, such as those that allocated indigenous peoples throughout the Pacific in the nineteenth and early twentieth centuries, the boys to work as agricultural or pastoral laborers, or girls as servants or mothers, resisted a variety of reform attempts. In Fiji, the continuing differences in employment patterns, status, and wealth between Indian-origin Fijians and the indigenous population, let alone the smaller European community, also demonstrate this.

In the twenty-first century, the countries of the South West Pacific inhabit very different spaces regarding educational policy and achievement. New Guinea continues to have great difficulty in providing universal elementary education. The struggle in Australia and New Zealand is to complete the transition of the final 20 percent to 25 percent of young people to full secondary school retention and to universalize some form of tertiary or postschool education. This includes the embracing of the indigenous population, much of which still fails to complete secondary school, let alone attend university or tertiary colleges. In the Solomon Islands, there is the problem of a "failing state," which consequently cannot organize schooling in ways that international organizations such as the United Nations Educational, Scientific, and Cultural Organization (UNESCO) consider highly desirable. Fiji and New Guinea also demonstrate fragilities in terms of state consolidation and state building, and the provision of what are now considered essential educational services across populations.

This volume in The Global Schoolroom series demonstrates the diverse educational experiences and histories of the countries of Oceania, but it also points to the eventual dominance of western institutions, practices, and epistemologies in schooling and education. This is not to deny some of the more exciting curriculum developments in recent times in most countries of the region where the attempts to restore and sensitize schooling to indigenous languages and knowledge are both constant and strong. However, the adoption and maintenance of the "school," the "teacher," the age-graded learner, the textbook, the test and examination, and certain pedagogic practices as essential for national development point to a western-based and globally sensitive imperative.

NOTES

1. C. Hartley Grattan, *The Southwest Pacific since 1900: A Modern History: Australia, New Zealand, the Islands, Antarctica* (Ann Arbor: University of Michigan Press, 1963); C. Hartley Grattan, *The Southwest Pacific to 1900: A Modern History: Australia, New Zealand, the Islands, Antarctica* (Ann Arbor: University of Michigan Press, 1963).

2. John Dunmore, ed., *The Pacific Journal of Louis-Antoine De Bougainville 1767–1768* (London: Hakluyt Society, 2002). See also Malama Meleisea and Penelope Schoeffel, "Discovering Outsiders," in *The Cambridge History of the Pacific Islanders*, ed. Donald Denoon et al. (Cambridge: Cambridge University Press, 1997), 128.

3. Bernard Smith, *European Vision and the South Pacific*, 2nd ed. (Sydney: Harper and Row, 1985). See also Jocelyn Linnekin, "Contending Approaches," in *The Cambridge History of the Pacific Islanders*, ed. Donald Denoon et al. (Cambridge: Cambridge University Press, 1997), 11.

4. Stewart Firth, "Colonial Administration and the Invention of the Native," in *The Cambridge History of the Pacific Islanders*, ed. Donald Denoon et al. (Cambridge: Cambridge University Press, 1997), 286.

5. Margaret Mead, *Coming of Age in Samoa* (New York: Penguin Books, 1943). The debate on Mead is reviewed in Hiram Caton, ed., *The Samoa Reader: Anthropologists Take Stock* (Lanham: University Press of America, 1990).

6. Ian Campbell, *A History of the Pacific Islands* (Brisbane: University of Queensland Press, 1990).

7. Linnekin, "Contending Approaches," 8.

8. On labor recruiting practices and capitalism in the South West Pacific, see, for example, K. Buckley and K. Klugman, *The History of Burns Philp: The Australian Company in the South Pacific* (Sydney: Burns Philp & Co., 1981); Frank Clune, *Captain Bully Hayes: Blackbirder and Bigamist* (Sydney: Angus and Robertson, 1970); William

T. Wawn: *The South Sea Islanders and the Queensland Labour Trade* ed. Peter Corris (Canberra: ANU Press, 1973).

9. Jocelyn Linnekin, "New Political Orders," in *The Cambridge History of the Pacific Islanders*, ed. Donald Denoon et al. (Cambridge: Cambridge University Press, 1997), 185–217.

10. Stuart Macintyre and Anna Clark, *The History Wars* (Melbourne: Melbourne University Press, 2003).

Chapter 2

SCHOOLING IN AUSTRALIA

Craig Campbell

Educational activity recognizable to those of European origin has only occurred in Australia since the very late eighteenth century. Before then, and the archaeological evidence regularly suggests an ever more distant past, indigenous occupation of the Australian mainland stretches back some sixty thousand years. The oldest rock carvings and paintings yet discovered on this planet are in Australia. Their evidence alone suggests a culture of some subtlety and, therefore, a culture requiring the systematic education of young Aboriginal persons to survive and live effectively in their families and language groups. The evidence of Aboriginal myth and poetry in the oral tradition through to the present day also suggests a rich and complex spiritual life in harmony with daily life. Such myths and legends learned by the young, which became part of their individual identities and the source of their daily culture, were avidly collected and written down by a small number of nineteenth- and early-twentieth-century anthropologists, missionaries, and scholars of various kinds. They demonstrate a "dreaming" of great diversity for Aboriginal people, the existence of languages capable of great mythic, poetic, and practical statement. Thus, "education" in Australia is many thousands of years old, though "schooling," as most readers of this text know it, proceeds only from 1788.[1]

As a continent, Australia is a very large place. It is almost the size of the continental United States of America, yet it is positioned geographically in latitudes that make much of the land quite arid. There are several large deserts and while there is constant controversy over the population that Australia potentially might support, even at the current twenty million persons, water shortages and land degradation are quite severe. There are several large cities in the early twenty-first century, mainly along the better-watered eastern and southern coasts. In the arid zones and agricultural areas, towns tend not to be large. The small population is spread over great areas. This low population density was clearly the case for Aboriginal Australia as well. Indigenous peoples were spread over a vast area. The diversity and number of Aboriginal social groups was very great. The number of actual languages and dialects is unrecoverable now, but there were well over two hundred language groups that have been identified.

When Australia was eventually invaded and colonized by Europeans, the character of the land, its great area, and the spread of its population would make for great challenges in the establishment of government over its land and populations. The "tyranny of distance," a popular metaphor invented by the historian Geoffrey Blainey, explains a great deal of the peculiarities of economic, governmental, and educational development in Australia.[2] However, environmental determinism is only a small part of the story. Once Britain had claimed Australia as part of its second empire, having lost its thirteen American colonies, and once British and Irish peoples began arriving in substantial numbers, it was also inevitable that the educational institutions and practices of the Australian colonies would resemble those of Britain and Ireland. Indeed, the very naming of the new Australian colonies and its regions portrayed an insistence on reproducing its institutions, its cultural, and social life. There was New South Wales, the first of the colonies, with New England, one of its northern regions. There were the colonies of Queensland and Victoria, named after the long-lived nineteenth-century queen and empress of India. Capital cities of the colonies, Adelaide, Sydney, Perth, Hobart, and Melbourne, celebrated individuals from the English aristocracy and royal family.

The story of Australian education then is a story of a long-lived indigenous tradition, and the beginnings of European traditions of schooling. It is a story of local adaptation and invention, as the peculiarities of Australian geography, developing economy, and populations asserted themselves. In 1901, the colonies of Australia federated to form a nation—perhaps not absolutely independent of the United Kingdom until 1942 when Australia ratified the Statute of Westminster, an Act recognizing that the dominions such as Canada and South Africa, as well as Australia, were no longer subject to laws passed in the United Kingdom without their consent. The story of Australian education is about the effect of the colonial origins and the nature of Australian nationhood and federation. No power over education was formally given to the new national government by the Australian constitution of 1901, yet that was hardly the end of the story. The federal government would eventually become the dominant influence in very many respects. And finally, the story of Australian education is also the story of the young people who have experienced its institutions and practices. This final story is also the story of its education workers—the teachers, administrators, and policy makers—who made the systems work.

BEFORE THE NINETEENTH CENTURY

The educational traditions of the different Aboriginal groups spread across the Australian mainland, Tasmania, and islands, especially to the north in the Torres Strait, separating Australia from New Guinea, were diverse. Indigenous peoples in each area had differing languages, spiritual and material cultures, and social organizations. Consequently, the content of the education of the young differed, yet all were similar in that institutions such as schools, or persons whom we might recognize as teachers, were absent from the educational process. There was also a similarity in that gender and the age of a young person were preeminent in their power to determine what would be learned when, and how a young person would learn his or her culture. The supremely important preparation for and fact of "initiation" into adult life was only part of the deliberate educational process.

The likelihood that men would be far more involved in hunting animals than the women, and the likelihood that women would be much more involved in the care of young children, and the gathering of vegetables, fruits, nuts, and herbs, also led to differing forms of practical education. In some parts of Australia, there were different technologies associated with managing the land and the produce that ensured continuing life. In southern Australia, there is evidence of fish trapping associated with tidal movements; in many parts of Australia, there is evidence of the deliberate burning of the scrub or forests, creating and maintaining open pasture on which certain animals, especially kangaroos, might graze, and be more amenable to tracking and hunting. In the north, there was long-lived seasonal contact with traders from Indonesia (Macassar in Sulawesi). Even in the most remote and arid parts of central Australia, trade and trading routes existed. Minerals of importance, such as different colored ochres used for decorative and ritual purposes, as well as specialized tools, woven bags, foods, and ritual objects could all be, and were all, traded. To maintain such economic and cultural exchange, education of the young was required.

In the territories of each Aboriginal social group, there were places for meeting and camping, and for hunting and gathering certain foods, often on a seasonal basis. There were also places of great spiritual power, perhaps dangerous places for the uninitiated, perhaps forbidden places to persons of a particular gender or family background. Besides these geographies of the spirit and the body, there were also the special totemic significances of certain animals to certain individuals and families to be learned. There were the dances, music, and poetry of their peoples—a culture which stretched back into the dreamtime when the activities of great animals, amazing men and women, and powerful spirits shaped the land, water-courses, cultural traditions, and lives of those who came after them. All of this knowledge was essential knowledge for Aboriginal peoples. Without it, they could not survive, culturally, or materially. Education was an essential part of social life, and the schooling that the Europeans brought with them to late-eighteenth-century Australia would have been regarded as a very narrow affair. The literacies essential to social life were to be replaced with the mean literacies of the slate and book—and initially at least, characterized by their powerful irrelevance to the conditions of daily life.

Why the British decided to send out the First Fleet to Australia, arriving in 1788, remains subject to argument. Each of several theories has its defenders. The fact that until the 1840s many of the ships were crowded with convicted felons must surely give some precedence to the idea that New South Wales, and Botany Bay, in particular, was to be a penitentiary-colony, a place where the convicts of England, and fractious Ireland, could be sent, far from the homeland. This penitentiary-colony was for the most part going to be a place of confinement without walls. Very early on, the governors and elements of the governing group gave earnest consideration to the punishments and incentives—and educational arrangements—that might be needed to keep order in such a place. Rebellion and lawlessness was never a distant threat or fact in the early colony. A period of very active government was required to ensure not only the material survival of the colony in alien territory but also an orderly future for the populations, nearly all of which, convict or soldier, had been very unwillingly transported. The colony's isolation made the creation of an orderly British society especially hard. There was also the problem of unrealistic attitudes towards the indigenous population, quickly converted from Enlightenment representatives of the "noble savage" into plain savages, especially those who organized and resisted the encroachment of the Europeans on their territories. The First and succeeding fleets to the colony brought rigid class, religious, legal, and ethnic divisions and hierarchies which created divisions between aristocracy and gentry, and middle and laboring classes. These divisions were intensified by religious and ethnic differences: Protestant and British, or Catholic and Irish, and within the Protestant group, established church or dissenting. Then there was that other layer: whether a person had come to the colony as convict or free.

Each of these divisions and hierarchies would profoundly affect the education of the young and their chances in life for a century to come, but it is time to move on to the education arrangements in the first few years.

The first thing to realize is that even from the earliest times of European settlement in Australia, government had little direct responsibility for schooling. In contrast with general European experience, England in particular was quite late in entrusting the state with direct educational responsibilities.[3] Essentially, the schooling of the young was a responsibility for family and church. For poorer families, there was often the possibility of a few neighbors collecting their children for a little school usually conducted by a local woman who promised to teach them their "letters" for a few pennies. Dame schooling was a popular option because it gave parents a great deal of control over when and where they would release their children for schooling. There was also the church and its gospel propagation societies, which could provide charity—"ragged" schooling of one sort or another.

In fact, Rev. Richard Johnson, the official colonial chaplain, arrived on the First Fleet in what became Sydney in 1788. As a clergyman of the Church of England, the established church, he was given official responsibility for making educational arrangements for convict children and the children of convicts. For many years to come, and excepting for some special cases, the Church of England and then the churches in general would be expected by government to take the main responsibility for organizing education in the new colony. It was not that government was uninterested in education; it was that government was not the traditional provider of popular education. Johnson was not particularly successful in his efforts, especially after the return to England of the first colonial governor, but we do know something of his intended curriculum. Johnson brought with him a number of tracts to be distributed and used for educational purposes. These are some of their titles and the numbers brought to the colony:

Exercises against Lying (200)
Cautions to Swearers (50)
Exhortations of Chastity (100)
Dissuasions from Stealing (100)
Religion made easy (50).[4]

It is pretty clear that a concern by the state and the established church for children, youth, and their education was, in very great part, a concern to control them. The great fear in the early convict colony was the fear of disorder and rebellion. A governor of the very early nineteenth century expressed the problem bluntly. Governor Bligh of "mutiny on the Bounty" fame was especially concerned with the rising tide of children in the colony, especially those whose unmarried parents gave them "natural" or "bastard" status. The discrepancy in numbers between adult males and females and the tendency of the officer class to monopolize the services of those women who were available led to a considerably impaired conventional family formation process in the colony. Nevertheless, very many children were born. They usually were expected to be as criminally inclined and as morally corrupt as their parents were assumed to be. Bligh believed it was only by the education of such children that they might "overbalance and root out the vile depravities bequeathed by their vicious progenitors." Even if government itself was not to be the direct agent of their reformation, it would certainly take an interest in them: "Remote, helpless, distressed, and young, these are truly children of the State."[5]

Johnson's difficulties in the first decade of the colony are well expressed in his own hand in a letter to the secretary of the Society for the Propagation of the Gospel in 1792. Teachers were in short supply: they were usually unsatisfactory, being either convicts themselves or of the wrong sex for the intended learners. Nevertheless, two schools were established, one in Sydney and one in

Parramatta (now incorporated into greater Sydney), yet the needs were barely met. Few texts were available to assist with instruction, promised teachers had not been sent, and there was a great need to establish Sunday schools, all in the interest of the "Reformation of these miserable & deluded people, & that they may be brought to a sense of their duty both to God & Man."[6] Then, there was the problem of the Aborigines:

A Number of the Natives, both Men and Women & especially Children are now every day in the Camp—two Native Girls I have under my roof—I hope in times that these ignorant & benighted heathen, will be capable of receiving instruction, but this must be a work of time & much Labour. It wd be advisable & is much to be wished that some suitable Missionary, (two wd be better) was sent out for this purpose.[7]

Johnson's attitudes towards the education of Aboriginal and convict children were not necessarily dominant attitudes among the governing class. They represent the evangelical bent of Johnson's religion, but there were sufficiently powerful successors in the Church of England in New South Wales with similar attitudes to make them powerful for the future. Such approaches anticipated great trouble for Aboriginal peoples as their social, economic, and cultural lives were progressively disrupted, their traditional knowledge and education neither valued nor taken into account. Their construction as fit subjects for the efforts of Christian missionaries would have consequences for their education and lives in general through to the present day. Johnson's letter also prefigured the destructive practices of the nineteenth and twentieth centuries, which designated too many Aboriginal parents as unsatisfactory parents and led to the removal of children to orphanage and other training institutions.[8]

Such attitudes towards Aboriginal people were not much different from attitudes towards many children and parents of convict, emancipist, and laboring class status and origins. Despite a reliance on churches for instruction, early colonial governors, even in the first few years of the colony, did establish institutions for the control, care, and education of children. The first of these was the "Orphan Institution," established on Norfolk Island in 1795. Shortly afterwards, the Female Orphan School (1801) and The Native Institution (1815) were established. Government, as can be seen, was not directly interested in all children, only those in most "danger," or those most likely to become unruly and the most trouble. Though the term "orphan" was used to describe the aims of some of these institutions, many of the children brought into these institutions had living parents. However, parents had either surrendered the children to the institutions through incapacity to provide for them, or they were regarded by church- and state-formed committees as too irresponsible or vicious to raise their children satisfactorily.[9] The emergent colonial state in Australia had begun a long tradition that would see children of the lower classes and those of the Aborigines as in potential need of rescue and reform. Girls from "unsatisfactory" families, European or Aboriginal, were of special interest. The argument was that their potential for promiscuous sexual activity could lead to untold future generations of unruly or vicious children and adults.

Having spent time on the interest of church and state in the education of young people, readers are reminded that in late-eighteenth-century Australia, the very great number of children, Aboriginal children, were still being educated traditionally, and the many fewer European children of the foundling colony either had no schooling at all or were involved in unstable and infrequent efforts to teach them their letters, religious duty, and morals. In fact, as for the Aboriginal children of Australia, the main forms of education for European children were associated with the economic, social, and cultural activity of their parents or adults of significance in their lives. Boys learned their fathers' or uncles' trades—or more likely went laboring with or without family support, and girls learned women's work, either in domestic service or other emerging rural and town industries. Apprenticeship in various forms was an early means of practical and vocational training, which was soon apparent in the colony. From earliest times, boys and girls of the governing and emerging merchant class had family-based educations, sometimes with governesses or tutors, but more often with their mothers. Governesses and tutors were not in plentiful supply, and it caused many families some grief that they were reliant on convict servants or emancipists to act as tutors and governesses for their children.[10] For a few, there was the prospect of a proper schooling when their families returned to England. Some boys went back to England for their education without their families.[11]

NINETEENTH CENTURY

The nineteenth century saw the development of Australia from one tiny European colony on the margin of a vast Aboriginal Australia to six very substantial British colonies on the verge of nationhood. Over the century, Australian wheat, wool, copper, and gold became significant commodities in the world economy. Even if the population remained small and dispersed, not quite four million in 1901, there were at least two metropolises, Melbourne and Sydney, which had made substantial progress towards reproducing the feel and amenities of substantial English and Scottish cities like Birmingham or Glasgow. By the end of the century, there were three public universities; technical and agricultural colleges; public, private, and corporate secondary schools; great centralized education departments controlling state primary schools and administering education acts and regulations—the most significant of which made it compulsory for all children to attend school, usually until they were thirteen or fourteen years old. In this century, both the modern teacher and the modern school child were invented in Australia. All the curriculum technologies and controls that typified similar educational developments in the United Kingdom and North America appeared with them. By the end of the century,

Australia had also been affected by the New Education or progressive education that had affected those other places.

Primary Schools

Throughout the nineteenth century, dame schooling survived, especially in the poorer parts of the larger cities. Such schooling came under great pressure, especially from the 1870s, as governments in most colonies established education departments organized on bureaucratic lines. "Efficiency" became a great cult in advanced educational circles, and its pursuit allowed the development of strict and articulated regimes of teacher training and certification; school and teacher inspection and regulation; the production of a multitude of regulations addressing everything from celebrations of the monarch's birthday through to Empire Day; the uses of certain punishments for different children; the orderly recruitment, promotion, and payment of teachers; the grading of schools; and the mandating of certain textbooks, examinations, and student promotion procedures. The ambitions of the great centralized "systems" of state education in each Australian colony were unique to Australia in comparison with North America and the United Kingdom where the local ward, city, or shire retained far greater autonomy than in the Australian colonies—even at the end of the nineteenth century.

In the first half of the century, the situation was more chaotic. An early assumption that the Church of England would be the chief agent of government to assist in the education of the laboring classes was contested. Along with New South Wales, the colonies and settlements formally established in the early nineteenth century, Hobart (1804), Brisbane (1824), Perth (1829), Adelaide and Melbourne (1836), had diverse though mainly British and Irish populations. Presbyterians, Wesleyans, Congregationalists, Unitarians, Quakers, Baptists, and the Roman Catholic Church would not accede to the Church of England hegemony. The Roman Catholic Church posed a particular problem for the governing groups in most colonies. Because the communicants of the Roman church were mainly of Irish and convict origin, and because Ireland itself was in a spasmodic state of near rebellion or "disloyalty" through the nineteenth century, suspicion and a desire to suppress Irish religion, culture, and incipient nationalism were taken up early in the Australian colonies.

The religious and ethnic diversity of the British Isles and Ireland was reproduced in Australia, but peculiarly. Where Scottish, Irish, English, and Welsh were often separated at home by region, they were often flung together in the same urban and rural communities in Australia. This had a powerful effect on the emergence of a distinctive Australian society and ensured that the way England organized its educational system, for example, could not be reproduced mechanically in the colonies.

Irregular subsidies of various school providers, all under the supervision of the Church of England, though ultimately responsible to the governor, came to an end in 1826. This included the short-lived provision of a Catholic teacher to a group of Catholic pupils in 1806. A Church and School Lands Corporation was established under the direct control of the Church of England in 1825. This solution was highly unstable given the religious rivalries of the colony. The next step was towards a system of direct subsidy to the different churches and denominations, including the Catholic. For many, the dominant characteristics of colonial school organization were inefficiency, sectarianism, and general messiness. There was no guaranteed coverage of the population. Attendance rates were usually low. The religious denominations fought any attempt to rationalize resources and facilities. The fitness of teachers to teach was highly variable, and curriculum, inevitably based on religious catechism and elementary literacy skills, may or may not have met emergent colonial needs.

The year of 1848 was a breakthrough year along the eastern coast colonies and settlements in New South Wales and what would become Queensland and Victoria. A system of schools was invented and a curriculum was adopted that provided the possibility of a "national" education. The model was the National system in Ireland, which was designed by the occupying Protestant power to provide nondogmatic Christian, rather than Catholic, education to the greater part of the Irish population. It had obvious attractions to the legislators and governors of New South Wales. The chief of these attractions was a curriculum that was arguably inoffensive to any of the main Christian denominations, and an opportunity to rationalize and improve schools, teachers, and teaching on a community basis, and around a defined series of textbooks, or readers at the least. In 1848, a National Schools Board and Denominational Schools Board were established, the former to develop the emergent National schools, the latter to organize the distribution of funds to the continuing church schools. This solution was not universal across the Australian colonies. In South Australia, which was founded as a free (nonconvict) colony with very high proportions of dissenter and other Protestant denominations (Wesleyan, Baptist, Congregationalist, and Lutheran, for example), and lower numbers of Catholics and members of the Church of England, any government assistance to religious institutions was viewed with suspicion. State aid to denominational schools was abolished there in 1852, and a Board of Education established to subsidize nondenominational schooling only.[12]

The founding of Australia's first public or common schools was a heroic affair. William Rusden was appointed agent of the National Schools Board, with special responsibility for encouraging the establishment of schools in the rural towns and villages of rural eastern Australia. A. G. Austin's story of the life of Rusden outlines the great journeys he made on horseback, on terrible roads and through all kinds of weather, talking with hastily convened village and town community meetings along the way. Did those communities want to establish a National School? Invariably the answer was "Yes!" despite the sermons preached against such institutions in the Anglican and other churches. National schools were established from Moreton Bay (Brisbane) through the Hunter

Valley and central and southern New South Wales. Getting as far as the coastal area of the western district of the colony, Rusden also organized in rural Victoria.[13] Despite the particular opposition of the Church of England, a public school system was established. However, it was a parallel set of schools to those of the churches, and there was no direct threat to such schools as was occurring in South Australia.

Another thing the National Schools Board intended was the establishment of a model school for the training of teachers; this was achieved in 1850 at the Fort Street School above the Rocks on Sydney Harbour. From England, William Wilkins was brought out to establish the training scheme. Though little affecting the majority of teachers or teaching for some time, a start had been made to the systematic instruction of school teachers.[14] Wilkins was an early graduate of the Battersea Training School for teachers in England where he was influenced by the work of the eminent educator, James Kay-Shuttleworth, an advocate of more modern forms of pedagogy.

Following the traditional individual method of teaching involving substantial rote learning, monitorialism had been introduced to New South Wales in the early nineteenth century. This introduction of modes of school organization and pedagogy deriving from the works of Andrew Bell and Joseph Lancaster proceeded in part from the recommendations of Thomas Bigge, commissioner of inquiry into Governor Macquarie's administration of the colony during the period from 1810 to 1821. Monitorialism was considered a cost-effective and highly efficient means of elementary education, especially for children of the convicts and laboring classes. There were few fully fledged examples of large monitorial schools to emerge in the Australian colonies, but "monitors" and many of the pedagogical devices and practices of monitorialism were certainly developed. By Wilkins's time and the 1850s, monitorialism was looking old-fashioned and not well-suited to the many small schools of the colonies. A related "pupil teacher" system was developed in its place.

In the 1850s, there were important events that would allow for the rapid transition of schooling from its early colonial basis to more modern systems. The first of these, and following the rush in California, was the discovery of gold, especially in what became the separate colony of Victoria. There was extremely rapid economic and population growth there, but also to a lesser extent and a little later in neighboring colonies. Contemporaneous with this expansion came the granting of responsible government to most of the colonies, except Western Australia, which unlike the others, was introducing rather than refusing convict transportation. The sharing of power by governors and legislative councils resulted in the development of democratic governments based on majority support in legislative assemblies. Power over education policy was finally in the hands of elected representatives of the people. These colonies were also pioneers in the introduction of manhood suffrage, the secret ballot in elections, payment of members, and even voting rights for women. The combination of a series of unstable but nevertheless democratic governments, combined with the success of National schools, and the gradual diminution of the power of churches, for a variety of broad social and cultural reasons, allowed the probability of further reform.

In the 1850s, whether national, denominational, or private, colonial schools had yet to give the impression of either efficient, economical, or systematic effort in Australian education. The enrollment of Catholics into the National schools was increasingly resisted by the Roman Catholic bishops who were in accord with the growing alienation of the Vatican from various aspects of modernity. Modern capitalism, democracy, liberalism, and socialism, as well as the waning of religious authority in the growing industrial cities, and many of the ideas espoused by modern science, all caused great anxiety. The bishops reflected the source of their training. The peculiarities of the Irish church, with its particular approaches to faith and asceticism, to discipline and authority, would lead, for them, to a sharp and unpalatable solution to the problems of religion and public education in the colonies. Compromises that sought to solve the problems in other parts of the British Empire, whether in England itself or Canada, would be rejected in Australia.[15] Like the United States, the Australian colonies would reject state-supported churches and church schools. Unlike the United States, this project was not dependent on Enlightenment philosophies but the pragmatic desire for economy, and a distrust of the Irish in general and the Catholic Church in particular.

Thus began the century of "no state aid" to private and church schools, born of struggle between churches and colonial states to control popular education. The Education Acts that brought in this change are usually referred to as the "free, compulsory and secular" Acts. Yet the phrase is misleading. It took many years for all the colonies to abolish school fees completely. More will be said about compulsion later. However, the word "secular" is also misleading. There was still a great desire to construct the public schools of the Australian colonies as friendly to "common Christianity," and the Acts usually allowed some time for bible-reading or the visits of clergy to instruct children during school time. The Catholic bishops viewed the developments with distrust: for them, the new public schools that were to emerge under the Public Instruction and Education Acts in each colony were simultaneously "godless" and full of Protestant bias.[16] Bishop Goold of Melbourne was in no doubt: "They boldly and defiantly tell you it is their determination to do away with your schools, and substitute for them Godless schools, to which they will compel you, under penalty (or imprisonment) to send your children.... [T]hey threaten the Catholics of this Colony ... with religious persecution in the shape of a Godless and compulsory system of education."[17] On the other side were genuine secularists such as one of Australia's great nineteenth-century novelists. Marcus Clarke wrote:

The temples are still full of worshippers, the offerings still tinkle in the plates, the confessionals are still thronged with breast-beating penitents.... But go out in the world.

Where is your religion then? Does it inspire the politician, assist the man of science or aid the physician? No, it embarrasses them all.... The measure of the people's knowledge is the measure of the people's religion. Educate your children to understand the discoveries of Tyndall, Huxley, and Darwin, and you will find them pleasantly laughing at the old fables of Jonah, Balaam, and Lazarus.[18]

Table 2.1 shows when the Education Acts were passed that produced the nearly free, nearly secular, and nearly compulsory public school systems of the Australian colonies.

The decision to make elementary education compulsory, usually to include children from the ages of six or seven to thirteen, was a major intervention into the control of parents over their children, the control of children over their labor and leisure time, and the very character of childhood itself. Yet it takes more than laws to really change long-standing social and cultural practices. The new laws allowed considerable room for absences. Lawmakers knew that the labor of children, especially on small and struggling farms, was vitally needed by parents. One historian has argued that it took well into the twentieth century for children to be clearly and decisively detached from paid labor.[19] Other interpretations have been keen to reject the idea that the new laws were simply either humanitarian or progressive in their focus. A group of historians influenced by the revisionism of American and English scholars from the late 1960s through the 1980s argued that the laws producing compulsion were either about the social control of potentially unruly populations, the preparation of populations for emerging regimes of industrial work, or the containment of potentially dissident groups marked by age (the young), gender (women), or race (nonwhites) under new patriarchal institutions.[20] There is evidence to support aspects of all of these arguments, but little evidence to suggest that any one of them should simply replace the others.

It was from these Education Acts that the final steps were taken towards "efficient" and bureaucratically organized education departments. The little dame schools and many of the parochial schools of the different churches were

Table 2.1
Dates of Passing the Mainly Free, Compulsory and Secular Education Acts in the Australian Colonies and States

	Free	Compulsory	Secular
Victoria	1872	1872	1872
New South Wales	1906	1880	1880–1882
South Australia	1892	1875	1852
Tasmania	1908	1868	1854
Queensland	1870	1900	1875–1880
Western Australia	1901	1871	1895

Source: Alan Barcan, *A History of Australian Education* (Melbourne: Oxford University Press, 1980), 151.

increasingly condemned as "inefficient." New, expertly graded curricula appeared in schools, taught by the new army of trained teachers, many of whom were young single women and whose emergence as the most desired primary schoolteachers destroyed the careers of older married women. The new regulations controlling the promotion and grading of teachers encouraged careers for men rather than those for women, except for the few who could manage their way into the leadership of newly popular infant schools or schools for girls only.[21]

In the wake of the Education Acts establishing public primary schools, the Protestant churches mainly closed their elementary schools. The new public schools became acceptable to most. The major exception was the Lutheran churches, mainly in South Australia, Queensland, and western mallee area of Victoria. The language of instruction in Lutheran schools, through to World War I at least, was usually German and helped maintain the cultural traditions of migrants who had arrived for the most part from the 1840s. However, for more children, the refusal of the Roman Catholic Church to be reconciled to the new systems of public education was more significant. The new and eventually perennial crisis of funding parochial schools without state aid was transferred to parishes and dioceses. Bishops were especially active in recruiting orders of brothers and nuns from Europe to take over and develop Catholic schools. An age of heroism in the face of adversity had set in. Mary McKillop and Tennyson Woods established one order of teaching sisters in Australia. The Order of the Sisters of St. Joseph of the Sacred Heart spread nationally from South Australia and was particularly effective in the more isolated country towns and poorer areas of the cities. Sometimes, other orders, such as the Mercy and Dominican sisters and Marist and Christian Brothers, opened schools for Catholics of the middle class, but the justification for high fee-paying schools was often the revenue it would generate for schools or classes for the poor. Sometimes, high and low fee classes existed in the same school. Where this was the case, the segregation of children and the curriculum usually followed.[22]

Sometimes, such differentiations and separations could occur in the new public schools. Some public schools, either surreptitiously or with official approval, responded to growing middle-class demand for the teaching of "higher" subjects. Fort Street was such a place in New South Wales, as was the Grote Street Model School in South Australia, but such efforts were viewed with suspicion by the nonpublic schools which offered a "superior" education at a fee to the middle and upper middle classes. In both colonies, such schools also offered a postelementary curriculum in order to support the pupil teachers being trained to become teachers in the public schools. In Victoria, the hostility of private and corporate schools to superior education being offered in state elementary schools was rewarded when an effective campaign forced public schools to remain elementary schools.[23] In New South Wales, there would be a very different approach, where some public schools would become Superior Public Schools, and they would provide opportunities not only for middle class children but also for some working-class children to gain the certificates

earned by public examination success. They could lead towards occupational advantage, and even to the university.[24]

This development of compulsory primary education by the end of the
century was undoubtedly a great achievement by colonial governments and,
under duress, the Roman Catholic Church. The older dame schools were close
to being wiped out as school registration schemes allowed governments to
close schools that could not meet certain standards following inspection. Yet
the new public schools were often rigid in their approaches and somewhat dis-
dainful of the populations they were expected to serve. Many working-class and
poorer rural families found the demands of the new public schools difficult to
meet. Corporal punishment quickly followed, especially for boys who breached
behavioral or punctuality standards. Failure to pass tests meant failure to be
promoted with one's peer group. Anxiety associated with performing amazing
feats in spelling and mental arithmetic followed from the pressure of a curriculum that was designed for easy testing and teachers who were subject to highly
intrusive and critical state inspection, sometimes two to three times a year.
"Payment by results" existed for short periods; it tended to narrow the curriculum to those activities that teachers knew would be tested of their classes and
would lead to their salary determination.

Nor, in the end, was there much romance associated with the small Australian bush school. In the smallest of them, the teachers were young, provisional,
and female, fighting the culture of the surrounding few families with the offi-
cially sanctioned culture of the school—the source of which was always the
head office of the Education Department and its grand men, collectively known
by the streets in the capital cities where the public education empires had their
main offices—Flinders Street, Bridge Street, and so on.

There was certainly little romance associated with the schooling of increasing
numbers of Aboriginal children as the nineteenth century progressed. Each
colony organized differently, but missions of the different churches often
retained educational responsibilities long past the time that the churches were
considered acceptable providers for the majority European population. The
formation of public education systems did not necessarily allow for the inclusion of Aboriginal children. For example, in New South Wales, the conditions
of exclusion were clearly written into the regulations, and they remained there
until the mid-twentieth century. The separation of children from their parents
commonly occurred through the nineteenth century. In South Australia, the
Church of England ran a boarding school, Poonindie, hundreds of miles
distant from where most of the students' families lived. Yet this was the less
common experience. For the most part, children lived with their families, but
Aboriginal families were decreasingly mobile or economically independent.
Confinement to missions or government-run settlements became common,
and the schooling available was usually very limited indeed. Imagined occupational futures for Aboriginal children often meant no more than domestic service for girls and some kind of agricultural labor for boys. This justified a mean

Long multiplication "sum" in a late-nineteenth century Australian government elementary school (1888). Arithmetic was a "core" subject, not only useful for improving mental capacity, but directing students towards the real business of living. Reg Butler, *Lean Times and Lively Days: Hahndorf Primary School 1879–1979* (Adelaide: Investigator Press, 1979).

curriculum, and sometimes a curriculum, which on the grounds of vocational utility, involved plenty of practical domestic and agriculture labor from which the missionaries and runners of settlements undoubtedly benefited.

In some parts of Australia, right through to the end of the nineteenth century, especially in northern and central Australia, indigenous peoples remained largely unaffected by European settlement. For others closer to the European expansion, the patterns from early colonization were quickly repeated: resistance, disease, and the loss of livelihood. Often, the survivors gathered in camps on the edge of country towns where running water, health care, and education for children was mainly inaccessible. Across the century, racist theories gained power, especially the more virulent forms of Social Darwinism which maintained Aboriginal people as lesser forms of humanity, and which regarded the nonsurvival of the less fit as an inevitable process. By the end of the nineteenth century, there was an obsession in many government and scientific circles with degrees of pure-bloodedness and the necessity to socially administer the children of "miscegenation." Many Aboriginal children designated half- or quarter-caste were removed from their mothers, raised, and trained, if not educated, in institutions of the churches or state.

Writing dictation from the teacher in a late-nineteenth-century Australian government elementary
school (1887). Developing concentration, testing
spelling, and good handwriting—and reinforcing
loyalty to the monarch—all in one lesson. Reg Butler,
*Lean Times and Lively Days: Hahndorf Primary School
1879–1979* (Adelaide: Investigator Press, 1979).

In 1901, the first year of the new century and the year that the Australian
colonies federated as states incorporated into a nation, the Commonwealth of
Australia, a remarkable speech was delivered to the educational establishment in
Sydney. Its speaker was Francis Anderson, a Scottish-educated professor at the
local university. His criticism of the way that primary education had developed
in New South Wales was devastating. His main argument was against the rigidi-
ties of a state education department that conceived the process of education as
systems and mechanisms. Neither the human spirit nor true learning was served
by such a system where a hundred children would learn their geography like
parrots: "New Guinea—North of Australia—birds of Paradise—gold."[25]
Anderson railed against the enslavement of teachers to pedantry, inspection,
examination, and apprenticeship modes of training.[26] The scene had been set
for the struggle for progressivism in education, or the New Education, which
would occupy much of the succeeding century.

Secondary Schools

If the nineteenth century was the age of the elementary or primary school in
the Australian colonies, assuredly the growth of advanced education was

considerably slower and certainly less spectacular. If public education had tri-
umphed in the provision of elementary education by 1901, the private entrepreneurs and eventually churches remained very much in control in postelementary
schooling. However, the picture is mixed from colony to colony. There are difficulties in developing a coherent analysis of secondary education in the nineteenth century. Even at the end of the period, there remained remarkable
confusion about exactly what "secondary" education was—even among those
who were supposed to know. Answering to a Royal Commission in 1911, Frank
Tate, one of the great men of public education administration in Australia had
this to say when asked what he meant by intermediate or secondary education:

It is very difficult to say. I think the term "secondary education" has usually been applied
to preparation for a future professional training in the University. There has been no name
given to the kind of training between the elementary school and the technical school....
[W]e have kept the term "higher elementary" ... and we are trying to popularize the term
"intermediate" education.... That would be a short secondary course ... it would not be
a grammar school course.... [And then] we are using "continuation school" to describe
evening work, and "high school" for more elaborate work during the day.[27]

Much of the problem was caused by the fact that modern articulated levels of
education associated with the age of young people were still in the process of
being invented in Australia. "Adolescence" as a distinctive stage in the life of a
young person had only recently been identified.[28] This discovery of adolescence,
as it had occurred in the United States and elsewhere, would encourage the creation of more schools specifically devoted to the adolescent, with clear age divisions between the steps of an emergent educational ladder. No longer the
"elementary" school, the first school for children would be the "primary"
school, then for adolescents, the "secondary" school, and finally for late adolescents and young adults, "tertiary" schools or colleges. The emergence of a
modern system of schools based primarily on the age of the young person represented a revolutionary challenge for the institutions, practices, and curriculum
traditionally associated with nonelementary, advanced, or superior education.

Even to reach this emerging situation in 1901, we must collect together a
wide variety of schools and educational practices from the nineteenth century.

Unlike the situation in elementary education, the coeducation of boys and
girls in nonelementary schools and classes was most unlikely in the nineteenth
century. There was not only the moral discourse about the dangers to the
virginity and respectability of girls, but for much of the century, the curriculum
needs of girls and boys were considered to be very different indeed. The stories
of girls' and boys' emergent secondary education are somewhat different, and
for a time, they can be discussed separately.

However, one thing of very great importance that they had in common is
the social class character of nonelementary schooling. For most of the century,
very few working-class or, for that matter, Aboriginal, youth had any access at
all. Many even called nonelementary schooling "middle-class education." It

was primarily the wealth, family, and class culture of parents that enabled this kind of education—it was not necessarily closely related to the intelligence or ability of the young people concerned. The idea that "merit" would have a role to play in the entrance to postelementary education came late in the nineteenth-century and, even then, it advantaged middle-class families in particular.

Girls

There were very few schools organized for middle-class girls early in the century. Many had governesses, especially as the wealth of some of their parents grew and more highly educated free migrants arrived from Britain. This pattern continued though the early twentieth century as can be seen from the educational experiences of Australia's foremost early feminist novelist, Miles Franklin, or the children of the very wealthy Robert and Joanna Barr Smith in Adelaide.[29] Girls with governesses were a minority, however. Very often, mothers had to do the work themselves, and a variety of handbooks on how to educate daughters properly had considerable popularity. Hannah Boyd's manual of 1848 was interesting for its insistence that sensible Australian girls did not need all the "ornamental" subjects that might be required for a girl of similar background in England.[30]

Nevertheless, there was some demand for a suitable education for young ladies apart from the elementary school or home education. Small schools run by women of hopefully untarnished respectability emerged early in each colony. How "respectable," in fact, some of the school entrepreneurs were varied. Reputations could be lost quickly, and schools often experienced drastic enrollment losses and closed as a result. The curriculum offered by such small private schools, called ladies' schools, seminaries, academies, and colleges, varied according to the proprietor's educational background and resourcefulness. Many of these schools were family affairs, with mothers and daughters providing and advertising a safe, close, family-based enterprise. Itinerant masters might be hired to teach "extra" subjects for a fee. The curriculum would often concentrate on elementary work, as girls could often enter these schools quite young. Usually, some opportunity existed to learn to play the piano—highly valued for middle-class girls in the nineteenth-century—and often some attempt at religious education, singing, sewing (fancy, rather than plain), and French language, but often some arithmetic, literature, and a variety of other subjects, for want of better terminology, either ornamental, academic, or practical.

Such a curriculum was a useful to many of the girls who experienced it. Despite George Eliot's and William Thackeray's devastating criticisms in their novels describing elaborate English versions of such schooling, they were "useful" in the following respects.[31] First, they gave the knowledge and skills to some girls, which, if they did not marry, allowed them the possibility of paid occupation and some economic independence. Becoming a teacher or governess, indeed establishing a private girls' school, could proceed from the mastery of such a curriculum. This was not to be despised in the nineteenth century when respectable paid work for middle-class women was virtually restricted to teaching. Second, where a suitable marriage was so crucial to the future security of middle-class women, such an education could provide a young woman with the cultural confidence and knowledge to become an acceptable marriage partner. Third, in the Australian colonies, where so many families had problems with establishing respectability, perhaps proceeding from convict or emancipist parents or grandparents, or even if free, having had to leave Britain or Ireland under less-than-happy circumstances, the buying of a suitable education could advance families towards upward social mobility and respectable social status.

Although concentrating on one of the more successful ladies colleges that was founded after the Victorian gold rushes, the historian Marjorie Theobald has added considerably to our knowledge of emergent secondary education for girls in the private tradition. The essay, *Mere Accomplishments*, argued that many private middle-class schools for girls did far more than prepare "husband hunters" with "useless" educations. In fact, private schools, such as that owned by the Paris-educated teacher Juliet Vieusseux, were well positioned to provide many of the early female graduates when girls were finally allowed to matriculate for the University of Melbourne in 1871. The education received by a girl in such a school was rigorous, with a range of subjects that addressed academic and broader cultural knowledge. Theobald is not so certain that something was not lost as the academic curriculum, strongest in some of the boys' grammar schools and especially valued by the new University (founded in 1852), eventually displaced the cultural subjects, especially those addressing the arts, in the soon to be established church ladies colleges.[32] A similar argument can be made for the work that occurred in the Catholic schools for middle-class girls, run as they often were by nuns from well-off families who had educated their daughters well enough.

The old "turning point" for the education of middle-class girls was usually taken to coincide with the establishment of corporate schools for girls by the churches and closely following the Education Acts from the 1870s. Though usually owned by churches, they were governed by councils. Their financing and government were established on the lines of the English day trust schools for girls and the boys' colleges or grammar schools established from the 1830s. One school in particular has enjoyed the prestige of being the first "modern" secondary school for girls in Australia. Presbyterian Ladies College in Melbourne was founded in 1875. Its first headmaster was Charles Pearson, sometime professor of history at King's College, London, and advocate for the higher education of women. The argument is that this school was the first to take the academic education of the middle-class girl seriously, introducing classical as well as modern languages, mathematics, and eventually the sciences into the curriculum core. However, we have already seen that this claim was too ambitious, given the work of some of the private girls' schools. Certainly, many of the female subjects associated with the arts continued within the school, though often as "extras." Moreover, as was the case of similar girls' collegiate schools that had emerged in England in the second half of the nineteenth century, the educational ideology did little to challenge women's roles in the family, labor market, and society in general. Nevertheless, there was some association with the rapidly changing development of families and the challenges that first-wave feminism would make to the activity of women in society.[33] Eventually, it was accepted that the way to become a more suitable middle-class wife and mother was to have an education similar to that of the proposed husband. There was also the example of the independent, usually single, women who taught in and operated such schools. Many were pioneers in the movements of first-wave feminism. Their pupils would often reap the benefits of increased access to higher education and the expansion of both the number of professions and white-collar occupations that were opened to women.

Some of the very first public high schools for girls also operated on such a basis. The Advanced School for Girls opened in 1879 in Adelaide and dominated the female matriculation lists for the University of Adelaide.[34] Only a couple of the girls' public high schools founded in 1883 in New South Wales were as successful.

Boys

In the early nineteenth century, there was an early demand for postelementary education from the families of certain boys. Various and usually short-lived private academies attempted to meet the demand. Christopher Mooney and others have traced the spare historical record of these in Sydney and Parramatta, in particular. He has shown that there was a demand for both commercial subjects as well as the classical languages, but the demand for the latter was not strong enough to cause the foundation of any substantial grammar school until the 1830s and 1840s.[35] The age of the private academies lingered on through the nineteenth century, though in the second half much more substantial foundations by the major churches signaled a period of decline.

The situation was rather similar in each of the colonies. In South Australia, the Rev. Thomas Stowe established his short-lived Classical Academy almost as soon as the colony was founded. Two of the most prestigious schools in the late nineteenth century in South Australia remained private academies: Lorenzo Young's Adelaide Educational Institution and John Whinham's North Adelaide Grammar School for boys. In particular, Young's academy operated on the basis that colonial boys were most likely to need the English or commercial subjects rather than the classics-centered curriculum. Such a school and its curriculum arose from the popularity of the various academies in England and Scotland from the eighteenth century, which often offered sets of subjects more responsive to the knowledge needs of modern occupations and the development of modern scientific knowledge. In Australia, in early-nineteenth-century Sydney, Henry Carmichael and his proposed Normal Institution of 1834, or the Presbyterian leader and radical, J. D. Lang, and his Australian College

(1831–1854), were early proponents of this tradition, which had also been responsible for the foundations of popular higher education in the United States.[36]

Nevertheless, a demand for the classical subjects, Latin of course and sometimes Greek, was present in the Australian colonies as well.[37] As the universities of Sydney, Melbourne, and Adelaide were established from 1850, there was an inevitable valuing of these subjects. What was this curriculum good for? There was some continuing role for it in the professions, such as law, medicine, and the church, but perhaps it inevitably signified cultural and social distinction and the process of consolidating upward movements in class, status, and social power. Nor should one be too sociologically hard-edged about the reasons. There were many who believed with some justice that the classics were the basis of the best in western thought and cultural achievement. Nevertheless, the study of the classics also signified the existence of family wealth through the ability to release boys from paid or unpaid labor in the pursuit of the knowledge and status appropriate to the gentleman. Leisure, and the ways that it was used, was significant for social status across the nineteenth century. William Wentworth, the great patriot, had an interesting education in relation to these forces. From a dubious past, in terms of respectability (his father had been convicted for a criminal offense in England before emigration), Wentworth was sent back to England at age thirteen for a classically based education and later, in his thirties, attended Cambridge University.[38]

The oldest of the church grammar schools surviving in Australia is The King's School at Parramatta (1832–). Other foundations, early and late in the nineteenth-century, included the Presbyterian-supported but short-lived Australian College (see above), and the longer-lived Scots (1893–) and Scotch (1851–) colleges in Melbourne and Sydney. Wesleyan churches founded Newington (1863–) in Sydney, Wesley College (1865–) in Melbourne, and Prince Alfred College (1867–) in Adelaide. The most richly endowed of all boys' corporate schools was the Anglican St. Peter's Collegiate (1847–) in Adelaide. Such schools, including the Roman Catholic colleges catering to the proportionately smaller Catholic middle class in the nineteenth century, taught not only the classics but usually a range of commercially relevant, modern subjects. In terms of curriculum, these were hybrid schools compared to the great public schools of England at much the same time. Virtually none could survive without very considerable numbers of day students either. If not in the capital cities, they needed to be within relatively easy commuting distance from or sited within substantial regional centers, such as Geelong or Bathurst. Efforts to escape the population centers and cultural imperatives of middle-class school enrollment saw failure for rural schools, such as the Stanley Grammar School, the Hahndorf Academy, or the Jesuit's school at Sevenhills in South Australia. However, the first two of these were private schools and they shared the decline of similar schools, whether based in the town or country.

An early-nineteenth-century reminiscence of life for a boy in The King's School, Parramatta, gives some flavor, literally, of the life there:

We walked to church two-and-two.... What would I not give to hear the old bugle-call again that used to summon us at nine o'clock at night to leave our lessons and go to bed.

School opened at seven A.M. and closed at nine P.M., but morning, noon, and night we had to learn the everlasting Eton Latin Grammar—parrot-like, as we learnt the Church Catechism. Of course there were some boys that read the Greek and Latin classics, but ... I had not advanced so far.

We paid only £28 per annum.... For breakfast and tea we had merely dry bread, with tea in large basins containing about a quart apiece ... a liberal supply of brown sugar ... and a dash of milk, made it into a kind of syrup. Two or three basinfuls were considered necessary to wash down the dry bread, and the consequence was that small boys became like podgy calves.... For dinner we had roast beef one day, and boiled the next ... sometimes mutton, and "duff", that is suet puddings—with lumps of suet an inch in diameter, and not very nice, either.[39]

Following the wealth generated by the gold rushes from the 1850s, and the ever more frequent connection of the Australian economy to world markets, there were both the money and appetite among middle- and upper-middle-class families for an education of substance for their boys. Boys might only last at a school like Geelong Grammar for one or two years, but the work was done. They had a smattering of Latin. They could say they had been to college. The connections they had made there could provide possible marriage partners from the sisters of their friends. The schools contributed towards middle-class formation in the colonies.[40]

The numbers of corporate school foundations for the boys of the colonial middle class rapidly grew after the 1850s, as Geoffrey Sherington and co-authors have shown. The site of most activity was in Victoria.[41] These authors also show the fair growth of girls' corporate schools following a short time after. By the 1870s, these church schools for boys were almost as much in need of reform as were the schools in England on which they had been modeled. As early as the 1850s in New South Wales, their failure to produce students who knew much Latin, or sometimes anything else, had led to the founding of Sydney Grammar School. A foundation of the colonial government rather than a church, it promised better teachers and teaching and a steady supply of scholars for the University of Sydney, which in its earliest years had buildings and professors, but precious few students.[42] Smaller, but similarly conceived, state grammar schools were founded in Queensland, though no university was founded in Brisbane until the twentieth century.[43]

More significant reforms to the schooling of boys of the middle and upper middle classes began to occur in the 1870s. This involved a very substantial transformation in the purposes and culture of such schools. The reforms, which are often given the name "Arnoldian," came to the colonies through report, but more significantly, English masters who had experienced the changes personally. The corporate and larger private schools for boys developed new cultures and technologies of middle-class education. Of great significance was the new role for "games" in the moral and physical education of the boy. For example, through cricket, the boy learned both the importance of leadership and team play, respect for the rules, to play fairly, and to deal with both defeat and victory with a gentlemanly demeanor. The culture of games could become the culture of the school. Boys would be happier, the books would continue to have their place, but the "whole boy" was now the object of a broad education. Other practices entered the school to make it a community to which middle-class parents might happily entrust their sons. School uniforms and colors, Saturday sports, and other activities such as military cadets, old scholar associations to keep old boys attached, songs and school magazines, and even chapel somewhat displaced from the center of school life, conspired towards the making of a school culture which engaged boys more. Middle-class masculinity itself was in the process of transformation, as reforms earlier mentioned with the girls' schools had changed middle-class femininity.[44]

Such reforms were occasionally resisted. A clear example occurred at St. Joseph's, a middle-class Marist college at Hunters Hill in Sydney. At this Catholic school for boys, the French headmaster resisted the pressure of an Irish sports master, and no doubt many boys, for sports grounds, more games, and entrance to football and cricket competitions with other schools. The sporting obsessions of the Australian schoolboy of the late nineteenth century were not encouraged by Brother Emilian. His retirement from the school headship saw a rapid reversal of policy and the games, which were increasingly seen as making the British Empire strong, were paradoxically assimilated into a Catholic school where most families were of Irish origin.[45] This school eventually became known for its ruthless rugby culture and a prime example of the problem of athleticism; that is, the domination of a school culture by sport, sporting prowess and sporting heroes, and narrow frames of acceptable masculinity, consequently making the lives of teachers and students interested in other things a misery.

At the End of the Century

By 1900, the genuinely private schools and academies offering secondary education were in decline. Their proprietors often sought the continuation of their schools through sale to the clearly emerging dominant providers of secondary education—the major churches. The large church school offered stability; it could survive a period of low enrollments, a scandal, or the reign of a poor headmistress or headmaster, whereas private schools could not. There were more resources available to deal with the growing demands of the public examinations boards operated by the universities for the teaching of certain subjects to a certain standard. They could pay for better-qualified teachers.

They managed to develop cooperative relationships with the universities that validated a curriculum with a strong academic orientation. That very many of their students failed to stay long or gain much worth from it was compensated for by the cultural, sporting, and social opportunities that such schools also provided. Secondary education was in the process of emerging as a somewhat elitist set of practices and very class-exclusive, with strong ideas about what characteristics should be encouraged in the personal and social development of both boys and girls.

This was not the whole story, however. Through the last quarter of the nineteenth century, there was an increasingly urgent debate about the competitiveness of the British Empire, especially in relation to the new industrial powers, Germany and the United States. Some of that debate affected education and the role that technical and scientific education, in particular, might play in correcting what increasingly appeared as a commercial and industrial decline for the Empire. The Australian colonies shared in the debate, and there was some effect on the conceptualizing of postelementary education.

One of the effects was to give greater status to academic merit as tested by public examination. This in turn led to bursaries and scholarships made available by governments to encourage bright children. Moreover, colonial governments found it increasingly difficult to resist the movement towards public secondary schools. In modern-day terms, secondary education was increasingly seen as a public concern, the more systematic organization of which might produce public good as well as the satisfying of private interests.[46]

It was a struggle to develop public secondary schools. The sector had been too long in the hands of private interests and churches, despite a number of the Education Acts of the 1870s allowing for the possibility of public high schools. Secondary education had been seen for so long as a middle-class education that the possibility of schools being opened to working-class youth was intolerable to many. Both South Australia and New South Wales were nineteenth-century pioneers in the development of public high schools. The high schools of both were only accessible on the basis of competitive examination; they also charged fees. The Advanced School for Girls in South Australia had met a demand for the academic education of middle-class girls that the private market had failed to exploit. Significantly, at the end of the century, when the Methodist Ladies College began, this school immediately attracted many middle-class enrollments, and the numbers of working-class girls who went into the Advanced School increased.[47]

In New South Wales, eight public high schools, four each for boys and girls, were founded in the years 1883 and 1884. Two were in Sydney, but the other six were in large country towns. The schools in Sydney and Maitland survived, unlike those at Goulburn and Bathurst, which quickly collapsed. There was hostility from nearby private and corporate schools which sought to attract potential high school pupils with fee reductions and scholarships. The New South Wales situation was complicated by the existence of Superior Public

Schools, which taught towards public examinations, charging quite low fees. In Victoria, there was no public high school founded in the nineteenth-century; private and church lobbies were too strong.

Unlike Scotland and the United States, where public high schools were substantially developed by the end of the nineteenth-century, they were very few and those that existed were rather weak in Australia. This was the case, despite the atmosphere of anxiety developing throughout the British Empire, to educate more efficiently and with an eye to produce the engineers, scientists, and managers required for the coming world competition. Very few working-class youth, and virtually no Aboriginal youth, had access to prolonged postelementary education.

Post-secondary Education

As for secondary education, it took some time for post-secondary education to be both broadly conceived and developed. For ambitious civic leaders in the wealthier Australian colonies, the establishment of universities was seen as highly desirable for a number of reasons. First was the prestige they would bring to both their founders and the cities in which they were situated. Second were the professional and other educational opportunities they would provide to boys, and eventually girls, from families that valued such an education. Third was the possibility of linking such isolated colonial societies to the center, a deeper engagement with the scholarship, debates, culture, and knowledge-exchange, which was apparently required to maintain both Empire and civilization itself. Much of what was considered the basis of the best in British and even western civilization, in general, was dependent on the higher culture preserved, disseminated, and generated in the universities and by university men. From quite early times, schemes existed to create universities. Some schemes were occasionally attached to plans for Church of England grammar schools for boys, which were seen as the first stage towards the development of universities imitating Oxford and Cambridge.[48] Other schemes were influenced by the development of the University of London and its creation of a secular curriculum.

The earliest plans for such foundations in Tasmania and South Australia came to nothing. Plans for universities were stayed until there was sufficient interest by colonial governments perhaps encouraged by promises of substantial private bequests. Even after foundations were achieved, the impact was low for a number of years, as might have been predicted given the parlous state of secondary education in the colonies.

Nevertheless, both the University of Sydney and the University of Melbourne were founded in the early 1850s. Despite wishing to appear architecturally as institutions similar to Oxford and Cambridge ("sandstone" universities exploiting the recent popularity of neo-Gothic architecture), their historians have shown that they often took their organizing characteristics from Irish and

Scottish universities as well as the University of London. Neither allowed residential colleges to compose the heart of tutorial teaching or university governance. Both were clearly public and secular universities, not beholding to any church, Church of England, or otherwise. Neither allowed theology to form the basis of a faculty, nor were degrees in theology allowed. These were universities for general cultural purposes—and increasingly interested in educating for the professions. Arts first, then law and medicine were early faculties to be established, with science not far behind in contrast to the efforts of the oldest English universities. The University of Adelaide, founded a little later in 1874, sought the possibility of female matriculation from the beginning but was forced to wait by the British government. Nevertheless, each of the colonial universities were British Empire pioneers in terms of female admissions and graduations. Women's College, University of Sydney (1892–), was an important centre for the dissemination of first-wave feminist ideas in Australia.

Perhaps a more productive beginning for post-secondary schooling might be found in other colonial institutions, though the term "post-secondary" ill fits many of them. One such set of institutions was the Mechanics Institutes and the Schools of Arts. Founded along the lines of similar institutions in Britain, these were popular institutions, and sometimes the smallest and least promising of villages had an Institute building and committee to run it. The better organized of them would include a small library and run occasional lectures and classes. Such organizations may be thought of as predecessor institutions to the various technical colleges and schools of mines and industry that were organized later in the century, although in a few places the Institutes and Schools of Arts survive to the present day. The institutes were often places that foreign and intercolonial newspapers and journals might be read; they are credited by some with the introduction of relevant and quickly applied knowledge in the interests of agricultural improvement. Better breeding of animals and the improvement of crops through the introduction of rust-resistant wheat occurred as a result of such knowledge dissemination. The institute movement lost its "worker improvement" bias in its adaptation in the colonies. No doubt, it was middle-class subscribers who used the libraries the most and won the battle for novels, as well as improving factual works, to rest on the shelves. Nevertheless, this movement was highly significant in its own right and was a pioneer of adult education and, sometimes, post-secondary initiatives in the late nineteenth and twentieth century.[49]

Other institutions of importance that might be considered post-secondary were those responding to the increased anxiety about vocational, technical, and applied scientific education towards the end of the century. In each of the colonies, great technical colleges were established, sometimes with branches in the largest of colonial rural towns, such as Ballarat or Bendigo in Victoria. They offered day and evening classes and rewarded their graduates with a certificates and diplomas. Engineering, dressmaking, technical drawing, boat-building, bookkeeping, and mechanics—all of these and dozens more subjects provided self-improvement opportunities to "go-ahead" young men and women in industry and commerce. Other institutions included the pioneering Roseworthy Agricultural College (1883–1991) devoted to the improvement of South Australian agricultural and pastoral production through the application and dissemination of scientific knowledge among farmers.

In the same year that the University of Sydney was founded, 1850, Fort Street School began to operate as a model and normal school for the training of teachers, especially those in the National schools. It took a very long time for elementary schoolteachers to win the right to a post-secondary education or even a secondary education of more than a year or two, for that matter. Nevertheless, the possibility of training in an institution beyond that to which a young person was appointed as monitor, pupil, or junior teacher had occurred. Such additional training was built up gradually from a few weeks to months and, by the end of the century, perhaps a year or two. In the United States, some normal schools developed into universities by the end of the nineteenth century, but that did not occur in the Australian colonies.

The situation was different for teachers in the boys' grammar schools. There, teaching staff were expected to have a university degree, and if there were labor shortages, then some university subjects at least. Men from English and Scottish universities initially took the work; but after the 1850s, there was the possibility of degree work in the colonial universities. For women, the situation was quite different. Excluded from universities for most of the nineteenth century, female secondary teachers often gained their education in well-regarded ladies schools and colleges. When opportunities for women to attend the colonial universities were allowed, they were well subscribed. Madeline Rees George, the last principal of the Advanced School for Girls and the foundation headmistress of Adelaide High School, from an educational background in ladies' colleges and governessing, was quick to take up the new opportunities for degree work. She was not alone. No modern teachers colleges as such had been founded in Australia by the end of the nineteenth century, although there were specialist-training institutions that provided courses of lectures to the few who entered them.

The contrast between the beginning and end of the nineteenth century was therefore quite amazing. Public, corporate, and private institutions devoted to higher education along European lines barely existed at the beginning of the period. At the end, there were institutions and cultural practices which would have been instantly recognizable in the great industrializing societies of Europe and North America. However, there were also unresolved tensions. Should public institutions be extended beyond the elementary level? Also, did the advanced forms of democracy developing in the Australian colonies require more accessible educational institutions—the most prestigious of which, both public and private, catered best to the private interests of some sections of the colonial middle and upper middle class? There was also the fact of growing rivalries in Europe, commercial, industrial, military, and imperial. How was

The School of Mines and Industries in Adelaide, founded between 1889 and 1892. One of the great technical colleges founded in late-nineteenth-century Australia in response to the growing awareness that economic and national development were increasingly reliant on modern technical and scientific education. G. S. Browne, ed., *Education in Australia* (London: Macmillan, 1927).

education to be improved to ensure that the Empire and its colonies were fit for the coming struggle? Additionally, there was the rarely voiced question about the educational conditions required to improve the lot of Aboriginal people. Charity and "protection," removal and training for laboring work often remained the answers, and the attitude began to set in that all that could be done was to "smooth the pillow" for a "dying race." Such sympathetic attitudes masked the violence, discriminations, and racially justified economic exploitation that often marked the day-to-day relations of Aboriginal peoples with white.

TWENTIETH CENTURY

In 1901, the Australian colonies came together to form a nation. The racial attitudes of the new citizens had been a major argument in favor of federation. Very early, the Parliament passed an Immigration Restriction Act (1901) that excluded nonwhite people from migrating to Australia. In an attempt to appease British ally, Japan, and an embarrassed Colonial Office in London, the White Australia Policy was administered as a "language known policy"—it fooled no one and was quickly adapted to exclude foreigners with questionable political attitudes as well as undesirable racial characteristics. If an undesired migrant presented for immigration, he or she was presented with a dictation test in a language he or she was expected not to know. Nor were Aboriginal people considered citizens in this new white Commonwealth in the antipodes; they were even excluded by the constitution from being counted in the national census. In this new Commonwealth, the attitude towards education was essentially that of assimilation. Regardless of national, ethnic, or racial background, the new Australian subject, for the Australian citizen remained a subject of the British monarch, was expected to leave aside difference, and schools would contribute to the formation of the ideal Australian. This was especially apparent as many of the old Lutheran schools, in which the language of instruction was German, either were closed down or subject to new controls during World War I.

By the end of the twentieth century, the White Australia Policy had gone, and assimilation had been displaced by a recognition of the diverse national and ethnic origins of the Australian peoples. Curriculum development and school provision were radically transformed under the new policies of multiculturalism, especially in the latter part of the century.

It is important to discuss briefly the operation of federalism as it relates to education in Australia. The makers of the constitution left education as a "residual power" of the newly formed states of the Commonwealth. Though not a specific power of the federal government, there were other powers which, if creatively interpreted, could lead to the Commonwealth influencing educational policy. However, there was little interest by the Commonwealth to interfere in the prerogatives of the states for over half a century. Where initiatives occurred, they were usually related to other powers of the Commonwealth, over defense for example.[50] In each of the six states of the Commonwealth, schooling developed in roughly parallel ways, though different school starting and leaving ages, different points of transition between primary and secondary, different curricula and syllabuses, and timings for the sitting of public examinations played havoc in the lives of young people whose parents dared to migrate from one state to another. Even in the twenty-first century, the struggle goes on, in a nation with as few as twenty million people, to establish common curriculum and assessment standards across the country. For much of the century, the responsibility for education in the major territories of the Commonwealth, the Australian Capital Territory, and the Northern Territory with its large Aboriginal population was allocated respectively to New South Wales and South Australia. Control was asserted by the Commonwealth in 1974.

The 1950s to the 1970s produced the great transformation. In this period, the states lost large portions of their educational autonomy to the Commonwealth. The way this occurred is simple to explain, though more complex were the motivations of the national government for its interventions. During World War II, the High Court of Australia gave the Commonwealth the primary power to raise the most lucrative of taxes: personal income tax. When the population rapidly expanded through natural increase and large-scale immigration programs, the combination of a reduced state taxation base and the crises in the provision of government services following the war left the states increasingly dependent on Commonwealth grants. Successive Commonwealth governments found it in their interests to not only make grants for nonspecific purposes but to offer "tied" grants; that is, to mandate the programs on which money could be spent. Through the latter mechanism and the rapid growth of independent Commonwealth programs administered by a burgeoning Commonwealth Department of Education, the Australian approach towards educational provision and control was transformed.

Following World War II, there was a period of national reconstruction in which the great powers of the state, liberated in order to defend Australia from the threat of Japanese invasion, were turned towards the development of national infrastructure and social services, in particular. The development of universities was one of the first problems to arrest the attention of federal governments in education. Schemes developed during the war to fund students were expanded in the reconstruction period. Following the foundation of the Australian National University in 1946 with a strong focus on scientific and medical research, the public universities in each state capital city were subsidized permanently by the Commonwealth from 1950, and by the end of the decade almost wholly funded through a semiautonomous Australian Universities Commission. The interventions in primary and secondary school education would be more controversial.

The decision by the Commonwealth to intervene in the school sector is incomprehensible without understanding its political context, ultimately based in the domestic effects of the Cold War. The advance of communism in Asia, through China, Korea, French Indochina, and with the associated emergency in Malaya and the instability of the newly independent Indonesia, transformed Australian foreign policy. The "domino theory" pointed to the possibility that unless the advance of communism southward through Asia was checked, a view also argued by the anticommunist foreign policy of the United States, Australia might be one more "domino" to fall. This pressure was complemented by serious conflict in the Australian labor movement and Labor Party. The Communist Party in Australia was small, but in the 1940s and 1950s it made some progress in winning control of several strategic labor unions. These successes, aligned with the Cold War threat, exercised the anxieties of sections of the Roman Catholic Church and laity. In Victoria, in particular, under the inspired leadership of B. A. Santamaria, effective strategies were developed that would contest communist leadership in unions and more ambitiously challenge the socialist left in both unions and the Labor Party itself. This activity caused great dissension, and the Labor Party, which had led Australia through the darkest hours of the war, split, most disastrously in Victoria.[51]

The alienation of many Roman Catholic families, working and middle class, from Labor presented non-Labor, the federal Liberal Party–led governments of

Robert Menzies (1949–1966) with a very great opportunity. The potential existed to win a substantial Catholic vote over to a side of politics that had generally been associated with the middle class—and Protestantism. Certainly, a vigorous anticommunist foreign and domestic policy would help secure the vote, but the century-old settlement of "no state aid" to church schools might also be revisited. One of the things that might be done, at both state and federal levels, was to offer state aid to Catholic schools. The Cold War provided very favorable circumstances. The alarming progress of the Soviet Union in developing its own atomic bombs, missile delivery systems, satellites, and the putting of human beings into space generated new educational anxieties, specifically concerning the adequacy of science education in the West. In Australia, the science curriculum was backward, school science laboratories, where they existed, were poorly equipped. Many secondary schools did not have useful libraries. The federal government made its move offering huge grants to government and nongovernment schools, including Catholic, in order to provide science laboratories (1964), and later libraries (1968), and scholarships to clever students regardless of who owned or controlled their schools. State governments also began offering nongovernment schools grants at the same time. These offers were mainly accepted with joy by the nongovernment sector, and the old settlement was overturned. Once Liberal-Country Party governments had begun offering state aid to nongovernment schools, the Labor Party and Labor governments could hardly afford not to do the same.[52]

From 1972 at the federal level, through the Schools Commission chaired by Peter Karmel, the old settlement finally ended. Funding for all schools would occur on the basis of need rather than religious status. That a very large number of the poorest schools were Catholic meant that through one scheme or another, Commonwealth government funding rapidly became the primary source of all funds for Catholic systemic schools. How the needs of a school were calculated changed with successive federal governments. An organization of supporters of the old settlement, Defend Our Government Schools (DOGS), mounted a High Court challenge. There was reasonable evidence that the constitution never imagined that the national government had a role to play in school education and, like the United States Constitution, the use of public taxation revenue to subsidize churches and their schools was contrary to its intent. The High Court challenge failed in 1981.[53]

By the 1960s, the state governments could barely afford to meet the demand for the expansion of their public school systems. The children of the baby boom and the new suburbs their parents were living in demanded a rapid increase in the numbers of schools and teachers. Thus, political, taxation, and demographic factors all conspired to give the Commonwealth a leading role in the provision of schooling. A major consequence of the way that it occurred was that the federal government increasingly funded church, independent, and other nongovernment schools, while the states retained broad responsibility for public schools. By the 1980s, as the new neoliberal policies affected all public services, including education systems, the creation of school markets and the encouragement of active school choice by parents became a major goal of the Commonwealth. The earlier period when, through a Commonwealth government-funded Schools Commission, the emphasis had been on producing fair access and equity to all through schooling was succeeded by a desire to produce school markets, a policy somewhat detached from social justice considerations.[54]

The change in the ways that Australian governments have funded and developed schools contextualizes the following discussion concerning primary, secondary, and post-secondary education in the twentieth century.

Primary Schools

At the beginning of the twentieth century, the greatest force promising rapid departure from the patterns of the previous century were the ideas of the New Education.[55] Its advocates had been active in the colonies from the 1880s, but little was achieved until the first decade or so of the new century. In a number of the Australian states, a new generation of educational leaders became directors of the various education departments, and their influence was powerful. In Victoria, there was Frank Tate; in South Australia, Alfred Williams; Western Australia had a long-time advocate of the New Education, Cyril Jackson. In New South Wales, there was Peter Board. Like Tate and Williams, Board made government-sponsored journeys to Europe and North America in search of new educational ideas. One of his many projects was a revision of the primary school syllabus for all public schools in New South Wales. (It must not be forgotten that the public school systems in the Australian states were highly centralized and bureaucratically organized whole state systems of education.) The statement began thus:

The school aims at giving to its pupils the moral and physical training and the mental equipment by which they may qualify themselves to meet the demands of adult life with respect to themselves, the family, society, and the State.... With regard to the material of instruction, the character of the teacher's lessons is determined, not by the quantity of the subject-matter that enters into his teaching, but by the fitness of the subject-matter for the powers and needs of the pupil, and the selection of it is regulated, not by what is possible for the child to learn, but by what he most needs to know.[56]

There followed the headings by which the topics of study in the new primary syllabus would be organized. English and mathematics were predictable, but then came "Nature Knowledge," "Civics and Morals," "Art and Manual Work," and "Music and Physical Education."[57] This approach was new because it elevated the character and needs of the child as the central focus of educational activity. The child's intellectual development was not even the first aim—more important was the child's moral and physical training. There were new subjects to be considered besides the old staples of reading, writing, and arithmetic. Nature study not only included the romantic vision of children made sensitive to the natural world, but the development of science study through observation and even experiment. The "object lesson" of the late nineteenth century was thus developed. Civics was appropriate in a new nation, especially one that highly valued both democracy and active national and Empire loyalty. At the heart of the art, music, manual work, and physical education of the twentieth-century child in the modern primary school was the image of an engaged, interested, and active learner. The dead hand of monitorialism and the pedagogic techniques wittingly or unwittingly encouraged by the "payment by results" system were to be left behind forever.

Of course, they were not completely left behind, and change was very slow. The most progress was seen in the classes and schools devoted to infants. There, the influence of the New Education and its predecessor schemes and philosophies had been evident enough in the last quarter of the nineteenth century. Attempts at the kindergarten, the implementation of the views of Pestalozzi, and the organization of schooling around the Froebelian "gifts" (educational apparatus encouraging experiential learning by young children) are well documented in Australia.[58] Nursery school associations, and later, the Kindergarten Union, were established. Independent of government through to the 1970s, the latter became the primary organizer of early childhood education. Over the century, and this was equally true in some other countries, some of the early thrust of this education towards the improvement of the lives of poorer children was lost to a more comfortable middle-class kindergarten movement. By the end of the twentieth century, had Maria Montessori been unnaturally long-lived, she would have been amazed to discover that in Australia a pedagogy, which was invented to meet the needs of slum children in Rome, had become a signifier of middle-class privilege. The kindergartens with the highest fees were often Montessori schools in middle-class suburbs.

The idea that schooling might positively affect the lives of children from poor families had certainly existed in the nineteenth century, but for a long period the most useful means of explaining the subsequent activity was the concept of "social control." Sometimes, there was not that much confidence that Aboriginal children or those of the laboring classes could be improved at all. More important was the need to control the unruly children of the unruly classes or races. By the early twentieth century, there was a new social theory advocating a new set of strategies for the improvement of "unsatisfactory" groups within the population. Eugenics can have malign as well as rather positive forms. "Improving the race" took more malign forms in parts of Europe and the United States where the castration of male criminals or the mentally defective had their seasons as part of public policy. The more positive forms were more influential in Australia, though Aboriginal persons might be less likely to agree. Nevertheless, slum clearance, the development of garden suburbs, and in terms of schooling, a concentration on improving the architecture of schools and classroom furniture, providing playgrounds large enough for adequate physical development, new curricula encouraging better nutrition and hygiene—all of these became influential in the early twentieth century. By the 1920s and 1930s, schools were being used to enable mass medical inspections as part of the wars against tuberculosis and other diseases, and from the 1950s, very effectively against poliomyelitis, rubella, and dental problems.[59]

One of the very significant changes to the primary curriculum was the introduction of the variably named "domestic arts" or "domestic science." Senior primary school girls in particular were the targets of this new curriculum. As the argument went, the working-class family could not be improved unless the girls who were to be future mothers could be improved. The argument depended on a profound lack of sympathy with the character and actual conditions of working-class life and culture, and its relationship to the conditions of production, their ownership, and control. Apparently, according to the eugenicists, who often were also the new liberals, the old profligacy, promiscuity, dirtiness, and drunkenness of the worst slum wives and mothers, necessarily leading to ever renewed cycles of larrikinism and unsatisfactory families, could be combated by a new curriculum devoted to cooking, laundry, and perhaps, baby care. That this curriculum was also advocated by middle-class women's organizations increasingly desperate, given the shortage of girls willing to enter domestic service, should not be forgotten either.[60]

The gendering of the curriculum in public primary schools in the nineteenth-century had not been as severe as in the secondary schools. Nevertheless, girls had lost time in the curriculum to the useful art of plain sewing, for example. Now there was domestic science as well which entered both public primary and secondary schools.

At least three reasons account for the relative failure of the New Education to have much impact in either the middle or senior primary school years before the 1960s. One was the continuing systems of inspection and central syllabus and textbook prescription, which tended against experimentation and the freeing of teachers and children from well-tried practices. The authoritarianism of the system, including its patriarchal nature, where inspectors and heads were almost universally older men, and the teachers, often younger, usually single women, militated against implementation of the progressive ideas of their leaders, even if they were a Board, Tate, or a Williams. Second was the continuing low impact of teacher education, even if teachers' colleges were well established in this period. Courses remained short, and apprenticeships in the classroom, the necessity that young people quickly learn the authoritarian skills required for survival in the large classes of the typical primary school, were more influential than any exposure to the ideas of Rousseau, Herbart, or Dewey. Third was the relative poverty of public education in this period. One crisis after another was cause for denying teachers wage justice or more professional autonomy, for denying progress in reducing class sizes, supplying adequate buildings and equipment, or professional development experiences.

After the educational "renaissance" of the early-twentieth-century years, described as such by early historians of education in New South Wales, came World War I and then the collapse of agricultural prices in the late 1920s. Then came the consolidation of that crisis in the Great Depression of the 1930s, and well before employment had risen again to early 1920s levels was World War II. In all states during the Depression, teacher salaries were cut, and in some states, the teachers' colleges closed. In some states, fees were reintroduced to the public high schools.

One of Australia's novelists who spent a little time working as a school-teacher in the 1920s captures some elements of the culture of primary school-ing in this period, though Christina Stead may have been exaggerating for artistic purposes:

"I hate it, I hate it," said the fair woman, rocking herself. "If I can only keep the kids down, I don't care if they never learn a line. That Milly Brown came in with a note from her mother again this morning about ink on her dress. I wish some of the mothers had to take care of my class for a whole day."
"I wish that too," said Mrs Keeling. "They'd wake up."
Teresa burst out with: "Why do you stay in it if you hate it so much?"[61]

There were occasional schools in which experimental activity was recorded, more in the nongovernment sector than the public. The Dalton Plan had brief moments in some places. Attempts to develop curricula that trusted teachers and encouraged the free movement of children, including trusting children to learn in naturalistic surroundings and "at their own pace," were few and far between. The educational historian R. C. Petersen has done most to explore instances of educational experimentation and progressivism in the early and mid-twentieth century. For example, his record of work in the Theosophical and Steiner schools showed their dependence on highly idiosyncratic semireli-gious philosophies and practices.[62] The poverty of educational renewal in the Australian states, and the unmet demand for educational progress, was exposed in the great traveling conference sponsored by the New Education Fellowship (NEF) as it appeared in Australia in 1937.[63]

Conferences were convened in state after state, where public schools were occasionally closed for a day or two to allow ordinary teachers to attend the lectures. Luminaries such Isaac Kandel and Harold Rugg from the United States, Susan Isaacs, William Boyd, and Beatrice Ensor from England, and many others lectured and hectored their audiences on the necessity for child-friendly education, on the need for teachers to be children's friends, on the contribution education could make to an improved social order, on the neces-sity to consider the emotional development of the child as well as the mental, on the need for health education and social studies, and of assessment plans which neutralized their threatening nature—and the need for arts activity and arts education. Even if scales did not fall from the eyes of the most hardened of educational leaders, the conference helped establish a climate which, in the period following World War II, would allow for more vigorous reform.

The kind of progressivism that was most active in the prewar years, in the phrase of the American historian, David Tyack, was "administrative progressivism." Schools were good places for the social administration of large populations. In the first years of the twentieth century, the new educational discipline, educational psychology, put huge effort into understanding, describing, and testing the intelligence of children. Intelligence testing promised an informed base from which new scientifically based teaching might occur. Children might only be extended as far as their intelligence quotient (IQ) suggested they were capable. Children with both very low and very high IQs might be removed from the ordinary classroom and given instruction appropriate to their "ability" and "capacity." In New South Wales, Harold Wyndham, a future director of education, made his reputation by developing expertise in the linking of child ability to appropriate groupings and pedagogies. "Opportunity classes" were introduced to some schools, and schools and classes for the mentally deficient, already an object of interest from the late nineteenth century, were developed for others. An understandable obsession by the administrative progressives for refining the technologies of testing, selecting, sorting, and allocating different populations of children according to their intelligence, abilities, and capacity rapidly developed.[64]

For most children, the primary school maintained a predictable routine. Reading through the graded readers, the learning of spelling lists, the taking of dictation, the chanting of multiplication tables and the doing of "sums," including the dreaded "long division" at a certain age, and performing the much-feared mental arithmetic which was thought to have a very positive effect on strengthening the brain as a mental "muscle." Then, there would be some kind of civics or social studies, perhaps a little history and geography. Too much of it was still taken up with learning the history and geography of Britain, especially the deeds and lists of royalty and British Empire heroes, such as Drake, Raleigh, Clive, Wolfe, Nelson, and Wellington. Those relevant to Australia were another set of Empire heroes. Supreme among them was Captain Cook, the great discoverer, then Bass and Flinders, and the various explorers of the land and rivers, Sturt, Stuart, Mitchell, Hume, Hovell, and Eyre, and the tragic ones who died in the wilderness, Leichhardt, Burke, and Wills. The efficacies of such study for the primary schoolchild were multiple. Empire loyalty could be encouraged through the study of its heroes, the legitimation of European claims to the land at the expense of Aborigines could also occur—great sacrifices had been made to win the harsh land that was Australia. Also, there was all the training in map drawing as dotted lines traced the explorers' routes across and around the continent. There was also the literature and song: sturdy verses read and learned by heart about all this heroic activity. The primary schoolchild of the 1900s to the 1950s hardly needed the flag-raising ceremony and the loyalty pledge: "I am an Australian, I love my country,

I salute the flag," as well. Dorothea Mackellar's poem, My Country (1904), became a standard in the curriculum. One verse at least usually was learned by heart:

I love a sunburnt country,
A land of sweeping plains,
Of ragged mountain ranges,
Of droughts and flooding rains.
I love her far horizons,
I love her jewel-sea,
Her beauty and her terror
The wide brown land for me![65]

If nationalist images of Australia were based on the romance of rural life and outback exploration, the wildlife, and landscape, the reality over the twentieth century was rural depopulation, as poor agricultural prices led to farm consolidation, and especially after World War II, employment opportunities were best found in the industrializing cities. In rural areas, one and two teacher schools began to close, and the school bus ferrying students to "district," "area," or larger primary schools became a perennial of rural life. Not all children in the outback could be dealt with in this way. Correspondence schools had been developed much earlier in the century, delivering lessons to isolated families. Successive technological innovations allowed "distance education" to occur, continuing to the present day with the introduction of Internet services based on satellite delivery systems. A. R. Welch begins his historical discussion of distance-based bush education with the Traeger pedal wireless, developed in the years following World War I:

Alfred Traeger, a farmer's son, developed a pedal-powered radio, based on German military field radios. The pedal wireless was not merely adopted widely as the basis for communication in the new Royal Flying Doctor Service, but also became a key element in the development of distance education.... More than 3,000 pedal wirelesses were built and Traeger travelled the outback, teaching radio operation and repair, and Morse Code, at least until he adapted a typewriter keyboard for use with the wireless set, in 1933. For the first time, Traeger enabled remote families and communities to communicate with each other via wireless, and via the School of the Air, which, established in Port Augusta in 1958, pioneered a powerful alternative to the older correspondence school model of distance education.[66]

With the post–World War II baby boom and the development of new suburbs in the expanding cities, new primary schools could not be built fast enough, nor could sufficient teachers be found. Under such circumstances, some of the last of the discriminatory employment regulations forcing married women to leave permanent teaching positions were revoked. Older schools were disfigured by great collections of transportable classrooms as they added to schools' enrollment capacities, and the number of children in each class also rose. In many places, any progress made towards a more child-centered curriculum was undermined. The old curriculum and its practices were also deficient in coping with the great influx of new immigrants, an increasing number of whom coming from Italy and Greece, in particular, were not English language speakers.

By the late 1960s, there was increasing talk of an education crisis in Australia.[67] It was in this decade, as already discussed, that the federal government began its halting steps towards the funding of ordinary public and nongovernment schools. In 1972, after twenty-three years of conservative national governments, the Labor Party took power. Its time in office was short-lived (1972–1975), but its impact on all levels of schooling was dramatic.[68] The inspiration for its educational reforms came in part from the United States where President Johnson had dramatically increased spending on education through his Great Society program. Along with this, there was a homegrown educational discourse which was very sensitive to educational inequality and the disabilities of certain groups in society. Such groups had their inequalities described and explained in terms of class, gender, race, and ethnicity.[69] Commissioned by the Labor government, a committee led by Peter Karmel produced a document proposing radical reform. It led to the establishment of a Schools Commission, which then proposed and administered a series of programs meant to correct the inequalities of the past.[70]

Some of the programs that profoundly affected primary schools were those targeting the "disadvantaged." New funding was poured into schools with such students, and teachers were encouraged to develop new curricula meeting the local needs of students. Among those identified as disadvantaged were Aboriginal children, and the children of non-English speaking parents. New school equipment was bought, class sizes were reduced, teacher assistants were hired, centralized and decentralized curriculum support units were funded in each state, and extensive teacher professional development programs undertaken. New schools were built with the federal money; some like the Parks Community School, in one of the poorest areas of Adelaide, experimented with drawing in the surrounding community, making the school facilities and services serve a wider group than the schoolchildren alone.

Allied with such activity were public policy changes that substantially modified the older assimilationist aims of education. In particular, the policies of multiculturalism demanded that Australian schools recognize the differing cultural origins of its students, and the rights of children from such communities to have their cultural identities sustained rather than ignored by the work of the school. Funds went into community language maintenance and teaching. Programs to involve parents from all backgrounds in schools were developed. Teaching English as a Second Language became a new focus in very many schools, especially in urban areas.[71] The more primitive or superficial attempts at multiculturalism, such as through "international day" where children dressed in their national costumes and brought "strange food" to share, were overtaken by more substantial programs. Though not completely left behind, the old voluntary Saturday schools, organized by Greek and other communities for language and cultural maintenance, could be wound down, as public and new private schools developed new curricula.[72]

The popularity in the 1970s of School-Based Curriculum Development (SBCD) in many of the states, especially strong in South Australia and Victoria, and less so in New South Wales and Queensland, supported many of the Schools Commission programs. Indeed, this was a period in which much of the promise of the New Education and the turn-of-the-century ideas of John Dewey finally had a chance to flower. Pedagogy remained based on the "class" system of teaching, but it was substantially modified. Some schools were built without internal walls; this was the experimental "open" classroom where the "resource centre" (rather than the library) stood at the center, receiving and dealing with steady streams of children on educational missions associated with their most recent "worksheet" or project. The textbook as such did not disappear, but there began to be many of them, often collected in repositories, which could be lent out on a topic-by-topic basis. Different schools made their own judgments about which books to buy. Many teachers and teachers' college lecturers turned their hands to writing innovative texts, suggesting new ways of teaching the material they contained. In all schools, the spirit duplicators, and eventually in the 1980s, the photocopiers became machines central to the work of teachers. In some places, the overhead projector and whiteboard began to subsume the central function of chalk and blackboard.

Associated with all this activity was an increase in the numbers of years that were devoted to teacher training, more likely to be called "teacher education" from the 1960s. Full bachelor degrees in education began to replace the older certificates and diplomas. Curriculum studies, as well as the education "foundations," soaked up the new time for training. The primary schoolteacher, often thought to have no need for a degree, let alone a more culturally based tertiary education, developed a new level of professional status associated with the reformed teacher education curriculum in the new teachers' colleges, and later in colleges of advanced education and eventually in the universities during the 1980s.

No doubt, most primary pupils benefited from all this activity, although the skeptics were soon active. The Australian debate resembled that of other countries experiencing similar turmoil and reform. By the late 1980s, new versions of human capital and national efficiency theories demanded a new accountability from school systems. The primary school came under scrutiny as insufficient regarding teaching of "the basics"—reading, writing, and arithmetic. New approaches to literacy and numeracy education were distrusted by the new conservatives. Certainly by the 1990s, the Commonwealth was using its financial muscle in education to impose new regimes of standardized testing at different levels of the primary school. At the beginning of the new century, the process had intensified, with the primary school being looked to for a "value-added" education if it received various educational grants. Various sanctions were suggested for schools and teachers that were seen to be failing.

In some respects, the new regimes of school and teacher surveillance and measurements of success and failure hearkened back to the practices of the late nineteenth century, with the centralized education departments so vigorous in their attempts to test and measure, to reward duty done, and punish failure. However, the spirit was different a century later. Now, each school was expected to be entrepreneurial in its practice, not to work as a mere efficient cog in a vast machine, but to develop independently: in fact, to work within a market of schools where the needs and demands of its "clients" or "consumers," parents and children, might be met by corporate school plans developed by school leaders knowledgeable in the ways of consumer survey and innovative managerial techniques.

At the end of the twentieth century, the modern primary school little resembled that of 1901. The primary schools belonging to Catholic and other churches had made a remarkable comeback. Each school was far more "self-managed," though the common criticism in the public sector was that such self-management was more about managing declining resources, and perhaps enrollments, than anything positive. The curriculum and pedagogic practices had very much changed as well. Teachers usually had far more control over what they did and when they did it. Nevertheless, there were still problems. Primary schools in poor areas, rural and urban, still found it difficult to attract experienced teaching staff willing to stay substantial periods of time. By 2005, primary students were distributed across the different sectors in the following pattern. (See Table 2.2.)

The period of additional funding, staffing, and intensive curriculum development had not solved many of the problems that Aboriginal children experienced in ordinary public schools. Research by scholars, such as Merridy Malin, had at last revealed some of the basic cultural differences between Aboriginal and European-Australian communities leading to school difficulties.[73] At the beginning of the early twenty-first century, some of the encouragement towards government-funded, self-managed solutions in Aboriginal communities was being criticized for their waste, encouragement to corruption, and the making of Aboriginal people "welfare-dependent." At least the twentieth century had witnessed some progress in other areas. Aboriginal people were no longer dependent on church missions for their education, nor were they confined to reservations. They had assumed full citizenship following changes to the Australian constitution, supported overwhelmingly by the Australian people in the 1960s. Regulations and laws, especially those of New South Wales, that had discriminated against the enrollment of Aboriginal children in public schools had been repealed.[74] There were bilingual schools and language programs valuing Aboriginal languages in a number of states. Nevertheless, Aboriginal children remained much less likely than other children to make a successful transition to secondary education. The poverty of many of their parents, especially in rural areas where employment opportunities were close to nonexistent, profoundly affected the health, let alone the potential for

Table 2.2
Primary Students Enrolled in Australian Schools by School System or Type, 2005: N, %

	Government	Catholic	Independent	Total
N	1,370,384	368,845	192,940	1,932,169
%	70.9	19.1	10.0	100.0

Source: Australian Bureau of Statistics, *Schools 2005*, Series 4221.0.

educational success, of their children. At the same time, there was a growing middle class among Aboriginal people and some educational success stories, but the legacies of the past and poverty remained powerful inhibitors to full access and equality of educational outcome.[75] One legacy, the damage caused to Aboriginal families, culture, and community by child removal strategies during the twentieth century was fully exposed in an inquiry by a federal government agency. Its report, *Bringing Them Home*, was published in 1997.[76]

At the end of the century, there were new anxieties. An earlier discovery in the late 1960s that girls suffered disadvantages in schools compared with those of boys, which led to well-funded Schools Commission programs, was replaced by the "boy crisis" in the 1980s. Some argued that the primary curriculum was oriented to the learning styles of girls, especially those dependent on language arts rather than the more boisterous activity-based learning styles of boys. Some blamed the primary schoolteachers themselves: there were too many women, and a consequent shortage of male "role models" for boys. Much of the argument was theoretically shallow and rested on precious little empirical evidence, especially that which showed social class and poverty were far more significant than gender in producing school failure and early school-leaving.[77] The problems associated with gender politics in the primary school were complicated by a new attention to the dangers of childhood. Moral panics about pedophilia appeared to discourage men in particular from becoming primary schoolteachers, yet for some, the overrepresentation of females as teachers had led to the boy problem.[78] Such new fears associated with children connected with other fears. As many parents developed closer supervision and surveillance regimes over their children, protecting their children, the children often became less active. This, combined with ever-increasing consumption of processed food, and their voluntary or involuntary confinement to the television set or computer-based entertainment, created the obese child and children with eating disorders. Then, there was a new set of issues around bullying at school.

Australian primary schools, government and nongovernment, shared the public and media scrutiny which had previously been more often experienced by secondary schools. With rapid economic and social change, childhood and the institutions that managed it, such as the primary school, could expect continuing and frequent policy-making attention.

Secondary Schools

Very early in the twentieth century in each Australian state, educational lead-ers began to argue that as universal elementary education had been achieved, so should universal secondary be developed. The complex curriculum and schooling traditions of post-elementary education militated against any easy achievement of this aim. Some of the same characters who reformed the primary school in the first decade of the twentieth century were active again. Peter Board, Frank Tate, and Alfred Williams, and William McCoy in Tasmania, and Cecil Andrews in Western Australia laid plans for more accessible public secondary education.

The new wave of public high schools just preceding World War I was not always achieved easily. In Victoria, the church and private school lobbies were very strong. Tate had to argue that the new schools would provide tuition in cur-riculum areas, such as agriculture, not well served by the existing schools and col-leges.[79] Nevertheless, Melbourne High School (1905–) was founded, as were a group of country high schools. There was a similar pattern in South Australia with Adelaide High (1908–) collecting the students of previous schools, the Advanced School for Girls, the Continuation School, and the Pupil Teacher School.[80] In Perth there was the Modern School (1911–) and in Tasmania the Hobart and Launceston High Schools (1913–). The most recalcitrant of the states to introduce a network of free public high schools was Queensland. A combination of factors led to this, not the least of which was a desire by some to protect the older grammar schools, foundations of the state, as well as the church schools.[81] The political party of the working class, Labor, was less supportive of secondary education for all than its sister parties in other states. It was not until the 1960s that high schools in Queensland became generally accessible.

The desire for universal secondary education was not compatible with the desire that high schools be academically selective, allowing entrance only through the passing of a series of examinations. "Merit" took precedence over universality. In his report recommending the opening of high schools in South Australia, Alfred Williams had argued that the proposed high schools would meet the social and psychological needs of the newly discovered adolescent. (Williams was an early publicist for the ideas of the American, Stanley Hall, on adolescence.) They were very appropriate schools for a new democracy, where citizens were expected to be educated enough to take informed decisions for the national good. Such schools would combat the low ideals arising from modern urban and industrial life.[82] Yet all of these arguments only produced academically selective schools, which would barely touch the lives of most working-class, let alone Aboriginal, children for another half century.

Schools based on meritorious entry were radical enough, however. They certainly were an improvement on the existing secondary schools to which entry was based on the means to pay fees or church affiliation, or ability to win either scholarships or state bursaries based on merit—and such opportunities were few. Research based on the analysis of the first cohorts of students in the new high schools in New South Wales and South Australia points to the fact that youth from social class groups previously excluded indeed found new opportunities. Young people from the "new middle class" were those to do best from the opportunities. In particular, their fathers were the white-collar employees in the growing sectors of the economy—government and business. Except for the youth from families headed by fathers in the old professions, youth from the old middle class (farming and small business) were less persuaded towards prolonged stays at secondary school and the single-minded pursuit of public examination success.[83]

The ability of the older church corporate and private schools to dominate the matriculation and graduation lists of the universities was challenged by the new state high schools, but such schools could easily be criticized as being overly focused on examination success. The new high schools sometimes looked with envy to the confident church schools and their now well-developed Arnoldian institutions and cultures. One historian of the new high schools, Bob Bessant, tended to dismiss them as far too imitative and respectful of the church schools, disappointing those who expected a new accessibility to working-class youth and a democratic culture.[84] The founding headmaster of Adelaide High School criticized another tendency by the high school boy who "too often looked upon [the school] as a place merely for the preparation of a boy in order that he may by and by become the possessor of £1000 a year and a motor car."[85]

Yet the occasional materialism of the high school boy was to be expected. Such schools had commercial courses as well as general; they were often vocationally oriented, quite directly in relation to the production of state schoolteachers. The new certificates gained by success in public examinations, such as the Intermediate and Leaving, were valued by the "city" and could be the foundation of successful careers in business and the public service. The notion that secondary schooling could exist at one remove from modern capitalism and modern government was increasingly archaic. Indeed, the public examination reforms of the early twentieth century led by Peter Board, for example, in New South Wales were all about making secondary school curricula and students more useful and decreasing the control of universities over public examinations. The curricula promoted had too narrowly suited the interests of the university, rather than the broad potential relations between secondary schools, families, local communities, and employers.[86]

The development of the public high schools was only one step towards the universalization of secondary education. As the rate of new foundations of church corporate schools slowed, especially after World War I, and as the remaining private schools rapidly diminished in number, the expectation was that the state would need to do more if universalization was to be taken seriously. The argument for the increase in school-leaving ages to fourteen, and eventually fifteen, and in one or two states to sixteen over the century had to be matched with new institutions. The discourse surrounding the idea that adolescents had special social and psychological needs made the simple solution, simply adding classes to the primary school, unlikely.

The problem was this. Could a form of secondary schooling be brought to working-class youth—a form that they would find useful, and governments would find efficacious in the pursuit of their goals for national and economic development?

Traditionally, the secondary curriculum was hostile to working-class youth. The old, middle-class curriculum for girls had emphasized middle-class gentility and accomplishments, while the male curriculum was often based around classical languages and mathematics. Clever working-class boys could be persuaded into such a curriculum, but the granting of bursaries, or the encouragement of the few, could not bring about universalization. The old division between elementary and "secondary" schooling had, after all, not been based on age, but different curricula. The differences between them were simultaneously intimidating and exciting to students entering the academic state high schools for a large part of the new century. As one new student of Adelaide High School wrote in 1914: "Some of the work has been rather strange to us, as we have done no Latin, Euclid, or Algebra before."[87] Such visionary statements as the Cardinal Principles of Secondary Education generated in the United States (1918) were deeply perplexing to Australian policy makers, as they were to the men of influence in English education—the educational policies of whom the Australians usually turned for guidance.[88] It was too early to imagine a comprehensive secondary school for all with a common curriculum, at least in the junior years, and the junior high school or campus as a partial solution was not taken up until late in the century.[89]

The curriculum of the new high schools was modern in the sense that "modern" subjects were displacing the older classical orientation, but Latin, for example, retained a central place in some systems until the 1960s. A high school course in the first half of the twentieth century could be constructed around modern languages, usually French or German, Latin, modern history, and geography, and the sciences such as physics, chemistry, botany, and physiology. There were also commercial subjects such as economics, commercial arithmetic, bookkeeping, economic geography, and sometimes, typing and shorthand.[90] Despite all this modernity, the curriculum content, the methods of teaching, and the means of assessment all contributed to very high rates of failure and school leaving. Working-class children, if they gained entrance in the first place, inevitably left school earlier than middle-class children.[91] We can say that early in the century, even the public high school system contributed to the social reproduction of inequality in substantial ways. The best that could be said for it was that it could reward some working-class children and their families if they were persistent enough. With senior high school qualifications, the rewards could be substantial.

It became very clear, very rapidly that the new high schools had not solved the problem of the working-class adolescent. Nor had they achieved the potential contribution that further education of the population could make to national defense, economic prosperity, and technical and industrial advance. In Victoria, the early argument that agricultural science would be an important subject in the rural high schools was not carried through. It was not just the weight of the school organizers who tended towards offering courses based on languages and mathematics but also the pressure of parents, who sought a curriculum for their children equivalent to that found in the corporate grammar schools. Then, there were the views of the politically active labor movement to be taken into account. It desired the provision of equal educational opportunities for working-class children in general but also a demand for a useful technical education for working-class boys in particular.

Such perspectives and pressures were unlikely to lead to common or comprehensive secondary schools. Several post-primary or "secondary" curricula were required if all the pressures were to be satisfied. Inevitably, the solution would be the establishment of separate courses and schools for youth not clever enough to win their way into a high school. Intelligence testing would eventually play an important part in such a process, but that only veiled the reality that secondary education in the twentieth century would continue as responsive to and an engineer of class difference.[92]

A suitable solution that would enable universal though differentiated secondary schooling was found in an amalgam of ideas suggesting that the likely vocations of working-class children should help mould the curriculum. Technical education, in which the high schools were very little interested, would form the basis of new secondary curricula, supported by the simple idea that the basics of the primary curriculum, practical English language use, arithmetic, and the equivalent of social studies or civics could be consolidated and worked on at a higher level. In the process, alternative credentials to those of the public examination boards in the various states would have to be developed under the aegis of the state departments of education, rather than the universities. It was clear rather quickly that the new forms of secondary education being invented would have problems regarding status. There had long been a difficulty among sections of the English middle and upper class that had regarded manual work, and therefore technical education, and anything to do with "trade," as low status. In Australia, the attitudes were perhaps not quite as virulent, yet they were powerful enough. Another of the problems for the development of a different secondary education for the "less clever" was obviously caused by merit-based selection. Academically selective secondary schooling was superior because only clever children were allowed to do it! Another problem was caused by, to use modern terminology, the restriction of post-secondary pathways. Even though education directors such as Peter Board put much energy into the creation of pathways which could lead any post-primary student to higher education in a technical, teachers', other college, or the university, the fact was that most such secondary schools provided "dead end" courses. There was little to do in further education, having completed the third or fourth year.

The transformative power of the early state high school! In this cartoon from an early-twentieth-century Australian high school, a girl is transformed by the subjects she studies and the extracurriculum into a modern young woman—in this case, a 1920s flapper. *Unley High School Magazine*, 1926. (The cartoonist, Joshua Hall, was a teacher at this high school in South Australia.)

Despite all these problems, the provision of such courses and schools was the obvious answer to the pressure to universalize secondary education. Across the different states, different mixes of central, junior boys' and girls' technical, and girls' domestic science and other post-primary schools were founded. They were often founded with enthusiasm. The director of Technical Education, then Education, in South Australia from 1916 to 1946, Charles Fenner, and Donald Clark in Victoria (chief inspector of technical schools, 1911–1930) were great advocates for technical education, both for "ordinary" and clever boys and girls. The new schools could encourage curriculum and pedagogic innovation unthinkable in the status-conscious corporate schools and the public high schools—always willing slaves to the demands of the public examinations. The Dalton Plan and "educational freedom" were introduced at Thebarton Technical School in South Australia. Some of the promise of the New Education could be met in such schools; there could be a new meeting of hand, eye, and brain in the workshops and classrooms of the technical schools as woodwork, metalwork, technical drawing, and other subjects were developed. There could also be a more direct connection between the skills and knowledge gained at school and preparation for the taking of an apprenticeship in a trade, and the successful completion of the demands of the various trade schools and technical colleges.

At the girls' technical and domestic science schools, the problems associated with female participation in the Australian workforce were probably reinforced. In 1906, the tendencies of the previous century regarding women and work had been reinforced by the Harvester Judgment, a determination of the new Commonwealth Court of Conciliation and Arbitration. The Australian basic wage would be a male wage, based on the expectation that women and children would be dependents of the male breadwinner.[93] Men should be paid more than women, and women, if working at all, should leave the workforce upon marriage, or not complain if they were paid less. For this and other reasons, the curricula of the girls' technical and domestic science schools concentrated on preparing women for the work of motherhood, and the low-paid work that was most likely in the years they remained unmarried. Domestic science was important, as were the commercial subjects. During the early twentieth century, women were delivered control of the typewriters and shorthand-writing in the modern office. Curricula were often utilitarian and narrow.[94]

For all the problems however, such schools were often popular schools as a recent social history of technical schools has clearly suggested.[95] When the time eventually came in the 1970s for the last of them to be closed down in favor of comprehensive high schools in Victoria and South Australia, there was a sense of great loss for many.

The exact enrollment effects of the Great Depression on public secondary education were mixed. In some places, youth unemployment increased enrollments. In others, the combination of government hostility to the cost of secondary education and the subsequent introduction of fees, combined with the necessity for young people to be on the streets, alert to any opportunity to earn some money, had the opposite effect. The combined effects of Depression and World War II depressed population growth. It was the young people who grew up in this period who would become the high and technical school teachers of children of the early stages of the postwar baby boom. In secondary schools, these were often difficult years. Teacher shortages, wage depression, and lack of curriculum innovation all led to the prevailing spirit.[96] In the late 1940s, and for much of the 1950s, little changed in secondary education. In visits from the 1930s through the 1950s, visitors, especially from the United States, were highly critical of conservatism and atrophy in Australian secondary education. Isaac Kandel (professor of education, Teachers College, Columbia University) spoke at the 1937 NEF conference mentioned previously. He underlined the need for the "all-round" education; he criticized the role of the public examination in Australia and the domination of centralized public school bureaucracies and university matriculation requirements. He asked the question: "Do the schools, especially the secondary schools, introduce the pupils to things that they will love and admire throughout their lives, or are they dominated by traditions which no longer have psychological justification and by the demands of the universities."[97] In the 1950s, Freeman Butts, also of Teachers College, Columbia, would develop such criticisms further.[98] There were local critics also.[99] It was becoming increasingly obvious that a new kind of secondary schooling was required for Australia, and the grammar school, or selective academic tradition, was clearly not the answer, nor was a separate set of junior technical schools, in the end objectionable for their limited curricula that limited opportunity.[100]

The creation of the Australian public comprehensive secondary school after World War II was sometimes presented as expanding educational opportunities on the basis of "secondary education for all." In effect, the outcomes were more complex. By the early 1950s, comprehensive education had been introduced in Western Australia and New Zealand. In New South Wales, the Wyndham scheme, later recognized as a national model for the introduction of the comprehensive principle, was argued for in terms of postwar modernization, producing social integration. It would support coeducation. Though promising new opportunities for all, in effect, it preserved an academic curriculum; nor did its implementation secure the closure of all the previous academically selective high schools. Significantly, the Wyndham scheme retained the principle of externally controlled public examinations. The failure to create thoroughly comprehensive secondary school systems in Australia led to renewed criticism in the 1960s and 1970s of the secondary school curriculum from the point of view of social justice.[101]

The pace of reform sped up in the 1970s. As previously discussed for the primary schools, the Schools Commission established during the time of the

Labor government (1972–1975) was a crucial agent of change. Programs based around disadvantaged schools, the education of girls, Aborigines, and recent migrants from non-English speaking countries all produced curriculum, school organization, and teacher education reform. They incorporated Catholic and other nongovernment schools into the new programs. Queensland did away with public examinations altogether, while in other states the Intermediate and Leaving were abolished. Very often, they were replaced with fewer examinations and more inclusive regimes of assessment. They could include "school-based" assessments, perhaps "moderated" on a statewide basis, by statistical or other means involving sample work being sent to central committees. At Year 12, an examination of some rigor usually remained, but new secondary school assessment boards were asked by government to increase the number of subjects available to students, and to make sure that subjects were available that students who were not necessarily university-bound could do.[102] A period of unceasing assessment reform and politicking set in. The old players were added to, as vocational educational and training subjects (VET) could also be taken by students. These could come from a variety of providers, including the TAFE (Technical and Further Education) education sector in each state.

As had occurred in the primary schools, there were critics of the process, but the pressure of youth unemployment dramatically increased from the 1970s, ensured that secondary schools remained mindful of increasing retention. The numbers of young people remaining to the end of high school, avoiding "drop-out," became a continuing concern of educators and governments of all political persuasions. There was special concern for Aboriginal students whose retention rates remained well below those of other groups.

As far as the contemporary history of secondary school systems was concerned, the late twentieth century was marked by continual restructure. Continual reform at all levels became an embedded feature of the system. From the return of state aid in the 1960s, but especially from the 1970s, a gradual decline of the nongovernment sector was arrested, and a period of growth ensued which has yet to slow. In the process, public high schools lost their share of enrollments. As Table 2.3 shows, nearly 40 percent of students were in the nongovernment sector. This figure had nearly doubled from the mid-1970s.

The decline of the ordinary government high schools was of great concern. They were the schools, which by being open to all, regardless of the wealth or religion of enrolling families, showed increasing evidence of social residualization; that is, they were increasingly enrolling unrepresentative shares of the poor and recently arrived non-English speaking migrants. Richard Teese has written about the consequences of this. He has argued that educational "failure" is exported to the public high schools as the nongovernment schools tend to specialize in students experiencing fewer economic, social, or language

Table 2.3
Secondary Students Enrolled in Australian Schools by School System or Type,
2005: *N*, %

	Government	Catholic	Independent	Total
N	875,703	304,137	236,130	1,415,970
%	61.8	21.5	16.7	100.0

Source: Australian Bureau of Statistics, *Schools 2005*, Series 4221.0.

difficulties. Within the additional context of the new school markets, Teese argues that the future for many local comprehensive schools is bleak:

In comprehensive high schools, residential segregation brings together many students with multiple disadvantages—low esteem, poor basic learning, language handicaps, poverty and family breakdown. Instead of a mass of cultural and economic resources being concentrated on one advantaged site and applied to the high end of the curriculum—as happens in private schools—there is an accumulation of liabilities at the one site. This weakens the instructional effort and risks severe retribution against those students who stray into the more academic subjects.[103]

As scholars Campbell and Sherington have shown for New South Wales, evidence of this phenomenon is highly specific to different regions.[104] In Central West New South Wales, the public high schools that seem to be in best shape were those that were somewhat isolated in reasonably prosperous country towns, such as Young, West Wyalong, and Cootamundra. This may seem surprising in view of the perceived economic crisis in rural and regional Australia. However, in many of the towns with reasonably prosperous economies, the local comprehensive high schools appear to be fulfilling their original mission of providing a good range of secondary options to local children. There is substantial evidence that the parents and "community" actively support these schools. What is also significant is the relationship with the "private" sector. In some of these places, there are Catholic schools which terminate at Year 10 and send most of their postcompulsory students to the local public high school, giving a boost to senior school enrollments.

In other parts of regional and rural New South Wales, the patterns of success for the local comprehensive high school are mixed. Two issues are important. One is the proximity of a large regional center (especially, if less than 40 kilometers away) with bigger public high schools and low-fee Catholic and Anglican schools. The second and related issue is the provision of subsidized transport for students, which may enable access to a larger school. In this respect, there is competition for students even within the public sector across regional boundaries. Under these circumstances, the smaller country comprehensive high schools can be vulnerable not only to competition from larger regional centers but from critical incidents within their own precincts (e.g., incidents associated with drugs, violence, antagonism between local school decisions, and the views of parents), thus leading to loss of students. Such losses in already small schools may dramatically affect their staffing entitlement and curriculum offering, making them "comprehensive" schools only in name.

At the same time, there is evidence that the smaller country comprehensive high schools are now using and benefiting from a range of other educational providers. This has allowed more senior school subject choice in some circumstances. Large regional centers, such as Coffs Harbour on the northeast coast and Dubbo in the central west, are now looking increasingly similar to parts of the larger Australian cities, with a range of public and private secondary schools. In cities like Sydney and Melbourne, there is an immense diversity of relationships between public comprehensive high schools and communities. There are a large number of issues that can affect a particular school in distinct ways. In summary, the following issues appear to have a major effect on the success of public comprehensive high schools in particular regions. First is the social class relations in a region, associated with property values. This is readily seen in the prosperous eastern suburbs of Sydney where very few public high schools survive. Of variable importance are ease of physical access via public transport, the frequency of critical incidents, the proximity of selective public high schools, and low-fee Roman Catholic, Anglican, and other low-fee schools, and the quality of school leadership.

At the end of the twentieth century, Australian secondary schools are increasingly segmented into serving different populations of students. Although all young people now have access to secondary education, the dream of a common secondary school for all, even most, has rapidly receded. The secondary schools have been restructured dramatically as neoliberalism and the new managerialism have dominated public policy in the last decades of the twentieth century. Opportunities for all young people to experience good teaching, fair educational facilities, and access to a broad and useful curriculum are retreating before the desire to create markets within and between public and nongovernment school systems and groups. Undoubtedly, the new school markets have benefited many, but for the large groups dependent on residualized schools, the outcomes are bleak.[105]

Post-secondary Education

Over the twentieth century, there was an ever-growing awareness by governments and others that post-secondary education was a crucial area requiring expansion. The second half of the century saw the sector assume such national importance that the states of the Commonwealth lost almost all effective control as the federal government took responsibility first, for its funding through various commissions, but towards the end of the century, through ever-increasing levels of direct micro-management. The policy discourse of higher education changed, especially as the potential of the system to attract overseas and domestic fee-paying students was realized, and governments became reluctant to provide the great majority of the funding required by the sector as a whole. In the process, the thinking that had led in the 1950s to providing government-funded places to poorer Commonwealth countries at that time, such as Malaya and Singapore, through the Colombo Plan, or the abolition of university fees to domestic students, was reversed.

Initially the university sector was slow to grow. New foundations following those of the nineteenth century included the University of Queensland (1909) and Western Australia (1911). In Tasmania, the small university there floundered, according to its historian writing in 1903, regarded by many as a "luxury" and "costly toy."[106] It would prove its worth much later as the university became a site of importance supporting great hydroelectric schemes and Antarctic studies. Yet, even as late as the 1950s, it had real problems with notions of great significance to universities in the western tradition, such as managing the "academic freedom" of its staff.[107] All of the Australian universities until the 1980s were public universities, and in the period to the 1950s and 1960s, there were paradoxes because of this. The universities were clearly places for the education of a small elite, those usually bound for the professions. They were public institutions serving, for the most part, the private interests of a small number of citizens. In the 1940s, an economics lecturer at the University of Adelaide had shown the links between university enrollments and the private and corporate schools, and the monopolization by the students from those schools of degrees in medicine and law, in particular. Arts and science degrees were a little more democratic, enrolling fair numbers of students bound one way or another to the state Education Departments, and doing university subjects as part of their teacher training.[108]

The universities supported student unions that provided a range of cultural and sporting associations. Full-time university graduates were changed by the experience; they knew they were part of a small and well-educated group in Australian society. This has been particularly well documented for early women graduates.[109] A few women, and many more men, could expect to become leaders in the professions, at least, and over the century, increasingly in government service and business. Earlier in the latter two areas, the university graduate might be treated with suspicion, as being somewhat incapable of practical administrative and business activity. Certainly, in public service, for example, recruitment was from secondary schools and then came career-long climbing of public service promotion ladders, beginning as a junior clerk, and for a tiny few, finishing forty years later, as the head of a department. Direct graduate entry was not common until after World War II.[110]

As was the case in some of the English universities, research was not always seen as a high priority in the early twentieth century. The research degree, the Doctor of Philosophy, was not introduced until World War II, and many academics spent useful careers concentrating on teaching rather than publishing research. The universities were usually conservative places, wary in the making of appointments. Brian Fitzpatrick, the author of a number of highly regarded books on the economic and social history of Australia, never found work in a university as a result of his radical, labor-oriented politics.[111]

For the scientific research that the Commonwealth valued most highly, a quite separate institution was established. The Commonwealth Scientific and Industrial Research Organization (CSIRO) was established in the period from 1916 to 1920. Where the Commonwealth showed little interest in the universities for some time to come, this organization devoted to applied scientific research was liberally funded, only coming under neoliberal pressure to generate more of its own income in recent times. In 1936, the first grants were made by the federal government to universities, especially for the training of researchers associated with the CSIRO. Such grants in the last decades of the twentieth century would be made competitively available to all areas of university research, though those associated with national development, science, and medical research tended to receive the major share.

World War II was of great significance for the universities. Under pressure of potential Japanese invasion, and the fact of Japanese bombings of Darwin and Broome in the north of Australia, the Commonwealth government requested the universities to assist in training personnel and researching possible war-winning science and technology. The interest was maintained after the war as the government funded many places for discharged servicemen. This period in the late 1940s and early 1950s was regarded as a golden age for the Australian universities. The student body was more socially diverse, many undergraduate students were men with broad life experience, especially as a result of the war. Political and cultural clubs blossomed, and tutorials were marked by engaged debate.[112] Nevertheless, this period was relatively short-lived, and there was no guarantee that the universities would not revert to a rather less-engaged role in Australian social life, nor that the student body would not be dominated by the same old private and corporate school crowd as had been the case in the past.

During the first half of the twentieth century, the technical colleges also experienced growth. Again, World War II was of great significance with a Commonwealth Technical Training Scheme, then Commonwealth Reconstruction Training Scheme, providing many places and the establishment of new institutions. Between 1939 and 1950, the number of technical colleges in Australia grew from 94 to 141, the number of students doubling, from 89,000 to 162,000. The colleges usually offered courses at three levels: apprenticeship for potential tradesmen and women, certificate courses for technicians, and diploma or associateship courses for higher-level technicians and engineers.[113] In the late 1940s, the process that would lead to the splitting of technical education began—one group advancing towards concentration on the higher-level diplomas and eventually, degrees, and the other, maintaining the work in supporting trades apprenticeship education. In 1949, a New South Wales

University of Technology was formed on the basis of higher-level courses in the Sydney Technical College. The story of this institution is a useful illustration of the evolution of one aspect of higher education through the nineteenth and twentieth centuries.[114]

This new university which became one of the most successful research universities in Australia could trace its origins back to the Sydney Mechanics Institute founded in 1843. It sought inspiration from institutions such as the Massachusetts Institute of Technology and the Berlin University of Technology. The focus was on "new knowledge, a new way of encountering, explaining and improving the material world." Its mission recognized that Australia needed to keep abreast of the diversity of challenges associated with World War II: "Its core concerns were teaching and research in science and technology, but courses included humanities and commerce components in recognition of the need to educate the full human being." The university achieved an enrollment of 15,000 students in 1968 and its staff was recruited both locally and overseas. It conducted research that established an international reputation. The new university spawned colleges at Newcastle (1951) and Wollongong (1961), which eventually became independent universities (1965 and 1975, respectively). The Australian Defence Force Academy in Canberra became a college of the university from 1981. "In 1958 the University name was changed to the University of New South Wales, and in 1960 it broadened its scholarly, student base and character with the establishment of a Faculty of Arts, soon to be followed, in 1961 by Medicine, then in 1971 by Law."[115]

The role of federal government funding in the expansion of the university sector has already been mentioned, especially in relation to the foundation of the Australian National University in 1946. There were further university foundations through the 1950s and 1970s. Often, their main campuses were sited in the outer suburbs. Such campuses presented a very different feel to those of the nineteenth- and early-twentieth-century foundations. Surrounded by gum trees and car parks, with spread-out buildings two to three stories high, at some distance from large population centers, they were pleasant enough during the day. After 5 P.M., they usually felt deserted. Few had residential colleges of any size attached to them. However, they did experiment with new academic structures. Arts tended to be replaced by social science and humanities; there were experiments with interdisciplinary groupings. Some of the universities in this group of foundations were Monash (Melbourne, 1958), Macquarie (Sydney, 1964), La Trobe (Melbourne, 1965), Flinders (Adelaide, 1966), Griffith (Brisbane, 1971), and Murdoch (Perth, 1973). Another small group was established in regional centers: New England (Armidale, 1954), James Cook (Townsville, 1970), and Deakin (Geelong, 1974). The federal government, as part of its decolonization strategy, established a university in Papua New Guinea (Port Moresby) in 1965.

This activity was only a beginning, however. Again, from the time of the Labor government of the 1970s and a few years before, the pace of change only accelerated. First came the major attempt to increase access, with university fees being abolished altogether, and the encouragement of women and mature-age students into higher education. The pressure increased to make post-secondary education a natural next stage in the life cycle of the young person. The Australian tradition in relation to this was very different from that of the United States. The effect was dramatic increases in numbers of students and staff, foundations of new universities, and the development of colleges of advanced education. The latter were formed out of the old teachers' colleges and institutes of technology as the federal government took over the funding of nearly all higher education from the states.

The period from the mid-1960s through the 1970s saw another period of student activism. The Commonwealth government's decision to conscript eighteen-year-old male youth to support the Australian forces in Vietnam, along with a revival of the Left, the New Left with its various Marxist, feminist, anarchist, and other strands, and the development of mass demonstrations against the war and conscription, helped lead to a radical questioning of what universities were for and for whom they existed. In some places, such as Flinders and Monash universities there were student occupations of university administrations.[116]

The next phase of radical activity in relation to the higher education sector was not student-led, however. In the 1980s, as the neoliberalism pioneered by the governments of Ronald Reagan and Margaret Thatcher also became the foundation of government policy in Australia, a new wave of restructuring began; nor is it a wave which has been exhausted in the first decade of the twenty-first century. The education minister in the Labor government of the 1980s and early 1990s was John Dawkins, and it is his name that gives the early reform phase its name. Included in these reforms was the decision either to elevate or amalgamate colleges of advanced education into the university sector. Also involved was the creation of private universities. The decision to abolish fees for students was wound back with the introduction of a loan system to assist students to pay for their courses. Research and other public funding was made more competitive, at the same time as the Commonwealth sought to wind back its share of higher education funding. Universities were expected to become more entrepreneurial, to develop different sources of funding, to establish partnerships with industry, and to attract overseas, full-fee-paying students. Under all this pressure, degree structures and subject offerings changed quite dramatically at times. The struggle increased as the best students were competed for. The work of the academic also changed. Each academic was expected to develop entrepreneurial qualities as he or she was rewarded for attracting external research grants and publishing in quantity if not always quality.[117]

Such reforms were continued by the succeeding Liberal-National Party governments led by John Howard. Initiatives included the abolition of compulsory student unionism (2006) and a strong attempt to replace collective employment awards for academics with individual contracts.

All of this activity brought on considerable resistance from the left, the conservative right, from students and academics, and sometimes the university vice-chancellors as a collective group, but the victories of the resistance were few. The justifiers of reform pointed to the forces of globalization. Australia's educational institutions and practices had to operate and compete effectively in a world marketplace, in which students, corporations, governments, and others would act as consumers, weighing up what was on offer, and the losers would bear the consequences. In Australia, it was the smaller regional and outer suburban universities which began to show the signs of strain, with reduced enrollments and a variety of other troubles.

THE PRESENT

By the beginning of the twenty-first century, schooling had transformed the lives of young people. An increasing group could expect to be in schools, including those of higher education into their mid- to late-twenties. Entry into the labor market was delayed. In 1901, most boys at age fourteen were working, and girls were also, though fewer were in paid work. The extreme differences in access by young people to different kind of schools, based on their social class, gender, and ethnic-race origins was modified considerably over the century, but there were continuing major problems for Aboriginal, and poorer Australians, rural and urban, in gaining fair access. In the twenty-first century, with declining government commitment to public schools—and public health, transport, and social services—the evidence was that unequal, and socially differentiated, schooling was again on the rise.

At the same time, it was true that Australia was prospering in the most recent phase of globalization, and its schools continued to produce high levels of literacy and numeracy—and education, in general. The regular reports of the Organization for Economic Co-operation and Development (OECD) did not always support the educational panics inside the country in terms of supposed falling standards and other crises. Its teachers were well regarded internationally, if not always at home. At the same time, this kind of assessment did not lead to complacency. Where the emphasis had once been on producing fair average quality for all in education, fewer young people now experienced the average. The extremities were more pronounced; some institutions were world class and some were failing.

Within its region, at both secondary and higher education levels, Australian schools and universities attracted many students from China and Southeast Asia. There was real evidence that, in its educational institutions, Australia had finally begun to meet the challenge that its geography had posed from the beginning. Its closest neighbors, other than New Zealand and the small Pacific island nations, were the great population centers of South, Southeast, and East Asia. Building on its continuing western traditions in education, there was an adaptation to the needs of its regional neighbors who increasingly became partners in economic, cultural, and educational enterprise.

In just over 200 years of European settlement, the developments had been remarkable. However, the main group of casualties from the beginning, the Aboriginal peoples, had by no means benefited equally in what the new circumstances had to offer and this certainly included education.

A DAY IN THE LIFE OF AN AUSTRALIAN PRIMARY SCHOOL STUDENT

Oliver Slamer was in Year 6 at a government primary school in inner Sydney in 2007. He is twelve years old and wants to go to a performing arts high school in 2008. His parents are also thinking about a nongovernment school for his secondary education. His parents are university teachers, especially in the area of English as a second language.

I woke up really early between 5 A.M. or 6 A.M. My legs were numb! About an hour or so later, my Mum slid the door open, came in, and said, "Okay, time to get up. It's 7 o'clock." I walked slowly to the breakfast table. There were two glasses of orange juice, one for me and one for my brother. I walked over to the table and took one of the juices and drank; then, I went and had three weetbix with milk and sugar. My Mum and Dad had to leave early for work so they gave me the keys and told me to leave for school by 8:30 A.M.

I walked to school. I don't really like walking to school and I often ask my Mum to drive me but she says, "No! It's good for your health to walk." When I got to school, I could see my friends in the distance playing handball. I went over and asked if I could play. They said, "Yes." I was seventh reserve. When I finally got in, Blake passed the ball to me and I did a slog and got William out. Then, William got me out and we kept up this pattern for four or five times until I slogged him and got him in to "dungs," which is the worst court. Then, Lachlan finished him off. I came second in this game. That's okay, nothing special.

Afterwards, we went into class and my teacher gave one of her boring lectures again. I can't remember what it was about. The way our seats and tables are arranged is that our teacher gives everyone a number and then we have to sit in that order. We had a fifty-word spelling test, then library. During library, we had a quiz and I got seventeen out of twenty, which was good, but the best was nineteen. Then, the recess bell rang. Recess isn't really that much fun because there aren't any running games allowed. So, as usual, I just made everyone laugh. I tell jokes.

We got back into class and we did some English, which was fairly easy, and then we did some geography and mapping. My friend William got Tyler's pen rubber and waved it around pretending it was something rude. We laughed and didn't finish our work. I got into trouble because of what he did and I had to sit in the corner. It was only for five minutes because the bell rang for lunch.

We ate our lunch. Our eating time only goes for 15 minutes; then we play soc-cer. My favorite sport is soccer. I scored five goals, but three of them were not allowed because they were too high. But, they were in the goals and I thought they should have been allowed.

Then, for the end of the day, our teacher asked us to do silent reading, and a speed test. Then, school finally ended. My big brother came and picked me up. Lachlan wanted to come over but he couldn't. So, another friend came over instead and his little brother was crying for most of the way while we walked home. He was scared that his Mum wouldn't know where he was. When we got home, we rang her to tell her where we were. It was a hot afternoon and luckily my Mum had bought some ice blocks. We played on the computer and my brother showed us some funny videos. For dinner, my Mum cooked Indian food. I watched two movies with my Dad and my brother. My Mum tried to wreck the fun by sending me to bed but I went to bed very late.

TIMELINE

To 1800	Dominant mode of education is traditional indigenous (from c. 60,000 before the present).
To c. 1950	Traditional indigenous education survives.
1788	First European settlement; Rev. Richard Johnson (Church of England) responsible for educational provision for children.
1789	Hut school established in Sydney with convict Isabella Rosson in charge.
1791	Hut school established in Parramatta with convict Mary Hutton in charge.
1799	London Missionary Society begins opening schools.
1801	Female Orphan School opened.
1803	Ephemeral private academies promising post-elementary education begin to appear in Sydney.
1805–1806	Hut schools run by convict teachers open in Tasmania (Van Diemen's Land).
1811	Crook's private academy introduces monitorial system to New South Wales.
1813	First recorded Sunday School in Sydney.
1815	Native Institution for education of Aboriginal children established by Governor Macquarie.
1817	Short-lived first Catholic school established.
1819	Orphan School for boys established.
1822	First government subsidy to a Catholic school.
1824	A director general of Government Public Schools appointed.
1826	Church and School Corporation proclaimed, providing for an Anglican hegemony over public schooling.
1826	Corporation school established in Brisbane (the new Moreton Bay colony).
1827	First Mechanics' Institute founded in Australia (Hobart, Tasmania).
1829	Native Institution abandoned; Aboriginal families do not support it.
1830–1831	Early schools in new colony of Western Australia (established in 1829) fail.

1832	Proprietary school opens in Perth (Western Australia).
1832	The King's School, Parramatta, established: oldest surviving collegiate school in Australia.
1833	Church and School Corporation dissolved. Economic factors as well as hostility from liberals and dissenting denominations achieve a victory over Anglican domination.
1834	Henry Carmichael opens a short-lived Normal Institution for teacher training (Sydney).
1837	State aid to church schools, eventually Anglican, Catholic, Presbyterian, and Wesleyan.
1838	South Australian School Society establishes its first school in new Colony of South Australia (established in 1836).
1848	Board of National Education established by Governor Fitzroy to introduce Irish National system to developing public elementary school sector. Parallel Denominational Schools Board founded to administer continued government funding to church schools.
1850	Fort Street Model School opened.
1851	Gold rush in New South Wales and Victoria.
1852	State supported schools in South Australia to be secular.
1852	University of Sydney opened.
1853	University of Melbourne established.
1854	Sydney Grammar School opened as a state foundation.
1864–1901	Victoria introduces payment of teachers according to the "results" gained by their pupils.
1867	Sisters of St. Joseph order founded to open and staff parochial Catholic schools.
1870–1880	Most colonies introduce laws providing for compulsory, secular, and free elementary public schooling; also, the abolition of state aid to church (or denominational) schools.
1875	Queensland establishes state grammar schools.
1878	Sydney Technical College opened.
1879	First state high school: Advanced School for Girls in South Australia.
1899–1901	Fink Commission establishes basis for reform of Victorian public education.
1900	Melbourne Teachers College opened.
1901	Federation of Australian colonies: education a residual state, not federal, responsibility.
1903–1904	Knibbs-Turner Commission establishes basis for reform of New South Wales public education.
1905	Sydney Teachers College opened.
1912–1914	Montessorian methods introduced to kindergartens and kindergarten training.
1937	New Education Fellowship conference in Australia.
1941	New South Wales raises school-leaving age from fourteen to fifteen.
1946	Australian National University established in Canberra.
1947	Commonwealth Reconstruction Training Scheme encourages new university enrollments.
1950–1970	Postwar baby boom leads to massive expansion of primary and secondary public education.

1950–   Federal government begins to establish its own schools in federal
               territories.
1957   Comprehensive state secondary schools recommended for New South
               Wales by the Wyndham Report.
1957   Murray Committee recommends the expansion of the university sector,
               to be funded substantially by the federal government.
1962   Goulburn strike (NSW)—Catholic schools closed by church to force gov-
               ernment assistance.
1963   State and federal governments begin to restore state aid to private and
               church schools.
1966   Colleges of Advanced Education as a new higher education sector to be
               funded by the federal government.
1968–1975   Period of student unrest coincident with conscription for Vietnam War.
1972   Interim Schools Commission established by Whitlam Labor Government
               beginning a new period of reform and federal funding for Australian schools.
1973–1974   Kagan Report recommends reorganisation of Technical and Further Edu-
               cation (TAFE) sector (federal initiative).
1974–   Disadvantaged Schools Programme established (School Commission
               project).
1974   Fees for university tuition abolished.
1975   Girls, School and Society report (Schools Commission project).
1975   Curriculum Development Centre established (federal initiative).
1987   Plan to create new universities from colleges of advanced education
               announced (federal initiative).
1987   Retention of students to final year of secondary school reaches 50 percent
               plus (boys: 49.4 percent, girls: 57.0 percent).
1989   Fees for university tuition reintroduced with a loan scheme (HECS).
2000   Federal funding for nongovernment schools increased, to be based on the
               assumed socioeconomic status of parents of students in such schools.
2002   Retention of students to final year of secondary school reaches 75 percent
               plus (boys: 69.8 percent, girls: 80.7 percent).
2006   Retention of Aboriginal students to final year of secondary school reaches
               40.1 percent (nonindigenous rate: 75.9 percent).

NOTES

Craig Campbell thanks the Faculty of Education and Social Work at the University of
Sydney for the gift of five months apart from teaching and administrative duties in which
to research and write. He is especially grateful to colleagues and friends, Kay Whitehead
and Geoffrey Sherington, who heard, read, and commented on early drafts of this chapter. He also thanks Reg Butler of South Australia who agreed to illustrations from one
of his excellent school histories being reproduced in this book.

1. D. J Mulvaney and J. Peter White, eds., *Australians to 1788* (Sydney: Fairfax,
Syme & Weldon Associates, 1987). See also bibliography in James Jupp, ed., *The Australian People: An Encyclopedia of the Nation, Its People and Their Origins*, 2nd ed. (Cambridge: Cambridge University Press, 2001), 868–76.

2. Geoffrey Blainey, *The Tyranny of Distance: How Distance Shaped Australia's History*, rev. ed. (Sydney: Macmillan, 2001).

3. Andy Green, *Education and State Formation: The Rise of Education Systems in England, France and the USA* (London: Macmillan, 1990).

4. Alan Barcan, *A History of Australian Education* (Melbourne: Oxford University Press, 1980), 7.

5. Ibid., 14.

6. Rev. R. Johnson to Rev. W. Morice, March 21, 1792. Reproduced in Clifford Turney, ed., *Sources in the History of Australian Education: 1788–1970* (Sydney: Angus & Robertson, 1975), 7–9.

7. Ibid.

8. Jan Kociumbas, *Australian Childhood: A History* (Sydney: Allen & Unwin, 1997), chap 1.

9. John Ramsland, *Children of the Backlanes: Destitute and Neglected Children in Colonial New South Wales* (Sydney: New South Wales University Press, 1986).

10. John F. Cleverley, *The First Generation: School and Society in Early Australia* (Sydney: Sydney University Press, 1971); Elizabeth Windschuttle, "Educating the Daughters of the Ruling Class in Colonial New South Wales, 1788–1850," *Melbourne Studies in Education* (1980).

11. "William Charles Wentworth," in *Australian Dictionary of Biography*, ed. Douglas Pike (Melbourne: Melbourne University Press, 1967).

12. On the emergence of a distinctive history of school education in South Australia, see Pavla Miller, *Long Division: State Schooling in South Australian Society* (Adelaide: Wakefield Press, 1986); and Malcolm Vick, "Schooling and the Production of Local Communities in Mid-Nineteenth-Century Australia," *Historical Studies in Education* 6, no. 3 (1994).

13. See A. G. Austin, *George William Rusden and National Education in Australia 1849–1862* (Melbourne: Melbourne University Press, 1958); and A. G. Austin and R. J. W. Selleck, *The Australian Government School 1830–1914* (Melbourne: Pitman, 1975).

14. B. K. Hyams, *Teacher Preparation in Australia: A History of Its Development from 1850 to 1950* (Melbourne: ACER, 1979); C. Turney, "William Wilkins–Australia's Kay-Shuttleworth," in *Pioneers of Australian Education: A Study of the Development of Education in New South Wales in the Nineteenth Century*, ed. C. Turney (Sydney: Sydney University Press, 1969); and Clifford Turney, *William Wilkins: His Life and Work* (Sydney: Hale & Iremonger, 1992).

15. See Ronald Fogarty, *Catholic Education in Australia, 1806–1950*, 2 vols. (Melbourne: Melbourne University Press, 1959); Patrick James O'Farrell, *The Catholic Church and Community: An Australian History*, 3rd ed. (New South Wales University Press, 1992); Geoffrey Sherington and Craig Campbell, "Middle Class Formations and the Emergence of National Schooling: A Historiographical Review of the Australian Debate," in *Transformations in Schooling: Historical and Comparative Perspectives*, ed. Kim Tolley (New York: Palgrave Macmillan, 2007).

16. There is a considerable historiography devoted to this question. Key texts include: G. V. Portus, *Free, Compulsory and Secular: A Critical Estimate of Australian Education* (London: Oxford University Press, 1937); A. G. Austin, *Australian Education 1788–1900: Church, State and Public Education in Colonial Australia* (Melbourne: Isaac Pitman, 1961); A. G. Austin and R. J. W. Selleck, *The Australian Government School 1830–1914*; Denis Grundy, *"Secular, Compulsory and Free": The Education Act of 1872* (Melbourne:

Melbourne University Press, 1972); Pavla Miller and Ian Davey, "Family Formation, Schooling and the Patriarchal State," in *Family, School and State in Australian History,* ed. Marjorie R. Theobald and R. J. W. Selleck (Sydney: Allen & Unwin, 1990).

17. Bishop J. A. Goold (1872). In A. G. Austin, *Select Documents in Australian Education: 1788–1900* (Melbourne: Isaac Pitman, 1963).

18. Marcus Clarke, 1879, in A. G. Austin, *Select Documents in Australian Education: 1788–1900* (Melbourne: Isaac Pitman, 1963), 220.

19. Dianne Snow, "Transforming Children's Labour through Schooling," in *Culture and the Labour Movement,* ed. John Martin and Kerry Taylor (Palmerston North: Dunmore Press, 1991).

20. See especially work which includes the following: Bob Bessant, ed., *Mother State and Her Little Ones: Children and Youth in Australia 1860s–1930s* (Melbourne: Centre for Youth & Community Studies, Phillip Institute of Technology, 1987); Pavla Cook, Ian Davey, and Malcolm Vick, "Capitalism and Working Class Schooling in Late Nineteenth Century South Australia," *ANZHES Journal* 8, no. 2 (1979); Pavla Miller and Ian Davey, "The Common Denominator: Schooling the People," in *Constructing a Culture,* ed. Verity Burgmann and Jenny Lee (Melbourne: McPhee Gribble, 1988).

21. See Kay Whitehead, *The New Women Come Along: Transforming Teaching in the Nineteenth Century* (Sydney: Australian and New Zealand History of Education Society, 2003); and Marjorie Theobald, *Knowing Women: Origins of Women's Education in Nineteenth-Century Australia* (Cambridge: Cambridge University Press, 1996).

22. Helen Northey, "Saint Mary's Convent Schools," in *William Shakespeare's Adelaide 1860–1930,* ed. Brian Dickey (Adelaide: APH, 1992).

23. Carole Hooper, "Opposition Triumphant: Against State Secondary Schooling in Victoria, 1850–1911," in *Toward the State High School in Australia: Social Histories of State Secondary Schooling in Victoria, Tasmania and South Australia, 1850–1925,* ed. Craig Campbell, Carole Hooper, and Mary Fearnley-Sander (Sydney: ANZHES, 1999).

24. See Alan Barcan, *Two Centuries of Education in New South Wales* (Sydney: NSWU Press, 1988).

25. Francis Anderson, *The Public School System of New South Wales* (Sydney: Angus & Robertson, 1901), 10.

26. Ibid., 22–28.

27. First Progress Report of the Royal Commission on the Adelaide University and Higher Education, p. 184. *South Australian Parliamentary Papers,* 1911, no. 27.

28. Craig Campbell, "Modern Adolescence and Secondary Schooling: An Historiographical Review," *Forum of Education (Australia)* 50, no. 1 (1995); Selwyn K. Troen, "The Discovery of the Adolescent by American Educational Reformers, 1900–1920: An Economic Perspective," in *Schooling and Society: Studies in the History of Education,* ed. Lawrence Stone (Baltimore: Johns Hopkins University Press, 1976).

29. Miles Franklin, *My Brilliant Career* (Sydney: HarperCollins, 2001); M. I. Legoe, *A Family Affair* (Adelaide: Author, 1982).

30. Hannah Villiers Boyd, *Letters on Education; Addressed to a Friend in the Bush of Australia* (Sydney: W. & F. Ford, 1848).

31. See William Thackeray's fictional description of accomplishments in education in *Vanity Fair,* 1848 (any edition, chap. 1), and George Eliot's version of accomplishments in *Middlemarch,* 1874 (any edition, Book I, xi).

32. Marjorie Theobald, "'Mere Accomplishments'? Melbourne's Early Ladies Schools Reconsidered," in *Women Who Taught: Perspectives on the History of Women and*

Teaching, ed. Alison Prentice and Marjorie Theobald (Toronto: University of Toronto Press, 1991). See also Marjorie Theobald, *Knowing Women: Origins of Women's Education in Nineteenth-Century Australia* (Cambridge: Cambridge University Press, 1996).

33. Key works in the historiography of this topic include, for PLC: Kathleen Fitzpatrick, *PLC Melbourne: The First Century, 1875–1975* (Melbourne: Presbyterian Ladies' College, 1975); Marjorie Theobald, "The PLC Mystique: Reflections on the Reform of Female Education in Nineteenth Century Australia," *Australian Historical Studies* 23, no. 92 (1989). See also the remarkable novel by Henry Handel Richardson, *The Getting of Wisdom*, 1910 (any edition). On the broader question of girls' education: Ellen Jordan, "'Making Good Wives and Mothers'? The Transformation of Middle Class Girls' Education in Nineteenth Century Britain," *History of Education Quarterly* 31, no. 4 (1991).

34. See Alison Mackinnon, *Love and Freedom: Professional Women and the Reshaping of Personal Life* (Cambridge: Cambridge University Press, 1997); Alison Mackinnon, *The New Women: Adelaide's Early Women Graduates* (Adelaide: Wakefield Press, 1986); Alison Mackinnon, *One Foot on the Ladder: Origins and Outcomes of Girls' Secondary Schooling in South Australia* (Brisbane: University of Queensland Press, 1984).

35. Christopher Mooney, "Securing a Private Classical Education in and around Sydney: 1830–1850," *History of Education Review* 25, no. 1 (1996); Geoffrey Sherington, R. C. Petersen, and Ian Brice, *Learning to Lead: A History of Girls' and Boys' Corporate Secondary Schools in Australia* (Sydney: Allen & Unwin, 1987).

36. On Carmichael, see C. Turney, "Henry Carmichael: His Advanced Educational Thought and Practice," in *Pioneers of Australian Education: A Study of the Development of Education in New South Wales in the Nineteenth Century*, ed. C. Turney (Sydney: Sydney University Press, 1969). On academies in the United States, Nancy Beadie and Kim Tolley, eds., *Chartered Schools: Two Hundred Years of Independent Academies in the United States, 1727–1925* (New York: Routledge Falmer, 2002).

37. Christopher Mooney, "Securing a Private Classical Education in and around Sydney: 1830–1850," *History of Education Review* 25, no. 1 (1996).

38. "William Charles Wentworth," in *Australian Dictionary of Biography*, ed. Douglas Pike (Melbourne: Melbourne University Press, 1967).

39. J. S. Hassall, *In Old Australia: Records and Reminiscences from 1794* (Brisbane: R. S. Hews, 1902); Turney, ed., *Sources in the History of Australian Education: 1788–1970*.

40. On how these patterns continued into the early twentieth century, see Peter Gronn, "Schooling for Ruling: The Social Composition of Admissions to Geelong Grammar School 1930–1939," *Australian Historical Studies* 25, no. 98 (1992).

41. Sherington, Petersen, and Brice, *Learning to Lead: A History of Girls' and Boys' Corporate Secondary Schools in Australia* (Sydney: Allen & Unwin, 1987).

42. Clifford Turney, *Grammar: A History of Sydney Grammar School 1819–1988* (Sydney: Allen & Unwin, 1989); Clifford Turney, Ursula Bygott, and Peter Chippendale, *Australia's First: A History of the University of Sydney 1850–1939* (Sydney: University of Sydney, 1991).

43. Rupert Goodman, *Secondary Education in Queensland, 1860–1960* (Canberra: Australian National University Press, 1968).

44. On the reforms, see both Martin Crotty, *Making the Australian Male: Middle-Class Masculinity 1870–1920* (Melbourne: Melbourne University Press, 2001); and Sherington, Petersen, and Brice, *Learning to Lead: A History of Girls' and Boys' Corporate Secondary Schools in Australia*.

45. Michael Naughtin, *A Century of Striving: St. Joseph's College, Hunter's Hill, 1881–1981* (Sydney: St. Joseph's College, 1981); Geoffrey Sherington and Mark Connellan, "Socialisation, Imperialism and War: Ideology and Ethnicity in Australian Corporate Schools 1880–1918," in *"Benefits Bestowed"? Education and British Imperialism*, ed. J. A. Mangan (Manchester: Manchester University Press, 1988).

46. Geoffrey Sherington, "Public Commitment and Private Choice in Australian Secondary Education," in *Public or Private Education? Lessons from History*, ed. Richard Aldrich (London: Woburn Press, 2004).

47. Helen Jones, *Nothing Seemed Impossible: Women's Education and Social Change in South Australia 1875–1915* (Brisbane: University of Queensland Press, 1985); Alison Mackinnon, *One Foot on the Ladder: Origins and Outcomes of Girls' Secondary Schooling in South Australia* (Brisbane: University of Queensland Press, 1984).

48. For the Adelaide example, see John Tregenza, *Collegiate School of St. Peter Adelaide: The Founding Years 1847–1878* (Adelaide: The Collegiate School of St. Peter, 1996).

49. P. C. Candy and J. Laurent, eds., *Pioneering Culture: Mechanics' Institutes and Schools of Arts in Australia* (Adelaide: Auslib Press, 1994).

50. A. D. Spaull, "The Constitution, the 'Nationhood Power' and Education before 1950," *Change: Transformations in Education* 4, no. 1 (2001).

51. Ross Fitzgerald, *The Pope's Battalions: Santamaria, Catholicism and the Labor Split* (Brisbane: University of Queensland Press, 2003).

52. W. F. Connell, *Reshaping Australian Education 1960–1985* (Melbourne: ACER, 1993), 105.

53. Australian Council for the Defence of Government Schools, "D.O.G.S. and the High Court Case." http://www.adogs.info/dogs_high_court_case1.htm.

54. Bob Lingard, John Knight, and Paige Porter, eds., *Schooling Reform in Hard Times* (London: Falmer, 1993); Simon Marginson, *Education and Public Policy in Australia* (Cambridge: Cambridge University Press, 1993).

55. For the best study, see R. J. W. Selleck, *The New Education* (London: Pitman, 1968).

56. Peter Board, "Preface to Primary Syllabus of Instruction (1905)," in *Sources in the History of Australian Education: 1788–1970*, ed. C. Turney (Sydney: Angus & Robertson, 1975), 232.

57. Ibid., 233.

58. Deborah Brennan, *The Politics of Australian Child Care: From Philanthropy to Feminism* (Cambridge: Cambridge University Press, 1994); Ruth Harrison, *Sydney Kindergarten Teachers College 1897–1981* (Sydney: KTC Graduates Association, 1985); R. C. Petersen, "The Montessorians: M. M. Simpson and L. De Lissa," in *Pioneers of Australian Education*, ed. C. Turney (1983).

59. Kociumbas, *Australian Childhood: A History*; David McCallum, *The Social Production of Merit: Education, Psychology and Politics in Australia 1900–1950* (London: Falmer Press, 1990).

60. Bob Bessant, "Domestic Science Schools and Woman's Place," *The Australian Journal of Education* 20, no. 1 (1976); Jill Matthews, "'Education for Femininity': Domestic Arts Education in South Australia," *Labour History* 45 (1983).

61. Christina Stead, *For Love Alone* (Sydney: Angus and Robertson, 1990), 113.

62. M. D. Lawson and R. C. Petersen, *Progressive Education: An Introduction* (Sydney: Angus and Robertson, 1972).

63. John Godfrey, "'Perhaps the Most Important, and Certainly the Most Exciting Event in the Whole History of Education in Australia': The 1937 New Education Fellowship Conference and New South Wales Examination Reform," *History of Education Review* 33, no. 2 (2004).

64. John Hughes, "Harold Wyndham and Educational Reform in Australia 1925–1968," *Education Research and Perspectives* 29, no. 1 (2002); David McCallum, "Knowledges, Schooling, Power: Questions about the Eugenics Movement in Australia" (paper presented at the ANZHES, Adelaide, 1992); Pavla Miller, *Long Division: State Schooling in South Australian Society* (Adelaide: Wakefield Press, 1986).

65. Dorothea Mackellar, *My Country: A Poem* (Sydney: Angus & Robertson, 1990).

66. Anthony Welch, "The City and the Bush," in *Education, Change and Society*, ed. Connell et al. (Melbourne: Oxford University Press, 2007).

67. Ian Cathie, *The Crisis in Australian Education* (Melbourne: F. W. Cheshire, 1967); John McLaren, *Our Troubled Schools* (Melbourne: Cheshire, 1968).

68. See Connell, *Reshaping Australian Education 1960–1985*, 263ff.

69. For example, Tom Roper, *The Myth of Equality*, 2nd ed. (Melbourne: Heinemann Educational Australia, 1971).

70. Peter Karmel (Chair), "Schools in Australia: Report of the Interim Committee of the Australian Schools Commission," (Canberra: AGPS, 1973).

71. Mary Kalantzis et al., *Cultures of Schooling: Pedagogies for Cultural Difference and Social Access* (London: Falmer Press, 1990); Uldis Ozolins, *The Politics of Language in Australia* (Cambridge: Cambridge University Press, 1993); Anthony Welch, *Australian Education: Reform or Crisis?* (Sydney: Allen & Unwin, 1996).

72. Paul Kringas and Frank Lewins, *Why Ethnic Schools? Selected Case Studies* (Canberra: Australian National University Press, 1981).

73. Merridy Malin, "The Visibility and Invisibility of Aboriginal Students in an Urban Classroom," *Australian Journal of Education* 34, no. 3 (1990); Quentin Beresford and Gary Partington, eds., *Reform and Resistance in Aboriginal Education: The Australian Experience* (Perth: University of Western Australia Press, 2003).

74. J. J. Fletcher, *Clean, Clad and Courteous: A History of Aboriginal Education in New South Wales* (Sydney: the author, 1989).

75. Dennis Foley, "Aboriginal Education and Pedagogy?" in *Education, Change and Society*, ed. Connell et al. (Oxford: Oxford University Press, 2007).

76. National Inquiry into the Separation of Aboriginal and Torres Strait Islander Children from their Families, "Bringing Them Home: Report of the National Inquiry into the Separation of Aboriginal and Torres Strait Islander Children from Their Families," (Sydney: Human Rights and Equal Opportunity Commission, 1997).

77. R. W. Connell, *The Men and the Boys* (Sydney: Allen & Unwin, 2000); Linda Doherty, "The Matter with Boys Is That There Are Not Enough Blokes in Schools," *Sydney Morning Herald*, January 1, 2003; Rob Gilbert and Pam Gilbert, *Masculinity Goes to School* (Sydney: Allen & Unwin, 1998); Jane Kenway and Sue Willis, *Answering Back: Girls, Boys and Feminism in Schools* (London: Routledge, 1998); Wayne Martino, "Disruptive Moments in the Education of Boys: Debating Populist Discourses on Boys, Schooling and Masculinities," *Discourse: Studies in the cultural politics of education* 20, no. 2 (1999); S. O'Doherty (Chair), "Challenges and Opportunities: A Discussion Paper: Report on the Inquiry into Boys' Education" (Sydney: NSW Government, 1994); Margaret Vickers, "Gender," in *Education, Change and Society*, ed. Connell et al. (Oxford: Oxford University Press, 2007).

78. Linda Doherty, "The Matter with Boys Is That There Are Not Enough Blokes in Schools."

79. R. J. W. Selleck, *Frank Tate: A Biography* (Melbourne: Melbourne University Press, 1982).

80. See Craig Campbell, "Inventing a Pioneering State High School: Adelaide High, 1908–1918," *Journal of the Historical Society of South Australia*, no. 29 (2001); Selleck, *Frank Tate: A Biography.*

81. Martin Sullivan, "Fifty Years of Opposition to Queensland's Grammar Schools," *Melbourne Studies in Education* 1974 (1974).

82. Craig Campbell, "Pioneering Modern Adolescence: The Social Significance of the Early State High Schools of Adelaide," in *Toward the State High School in Australia: Social Histories of State Secondary Schooling in Victoria, Tasmania and South Australia, 1850–1925*, ed. Craig Campbell, Carole Hooper, and Mary Fearnley-Sander (Sydney: ANZHES, 1999); Alfred Williams, "Preliminary Report of the Director of Education Upon Observations Made During an Official Visit to Europe and America 1907" (Adelaide: Education Department, South Australia, 1908).

83. Craig Campbell, "Secondary Schooling, Modern Adolescence and the Reconstitution of the Middle Class," *History of Education Review* 24, no. 1 (1995); Helen Proctor, "Gender, Merit and Identity at Parramatta High School, 1913–1919," *History of Education Review* 31, no. 1 (2002).

84. Bob Bessant, "The Influence of the 'Public Schools' on the Early High Schools of Victoria," *History of Education Review* 13, no. 1 (1984); Bob Bessant, *Schooling in the Colony and State of Victoria* (Melbourne: La Trobe University, 1983).

85. Report of the Minister of Education 1913, p. 56. *South Australian Parliamentary Papers*, no. 44.

86. A. R. Crane and W. G. Walker, *Peter Board: His Contribution to the Development of Education in New South Wales* (Melbourne: ACER, 1957); P. W. Musgrave, *From Humanity to Utility: Melbourne University and Public Examinations 1856–1964* (Melbourne: ACER, 1992).

87. *Adelaide High School Magazine* 6, no. 1 (1914), p. 15.

88. National Education Association, "Cardinal Principles of Secondary Education," (Washington: U.S. Bureau of Education, 1918).

89. Craig Campbell and Geoffrey Sherington, "A Genealogy of an Australian System of Comprehensive High Schools: The Contribution of Educational Progressivism to the One Best Form of Universal Secondary Education (1900–1940)," *Paedagogica Historica* 42, nos. 1, 2 (2006).

90. See the tables of subjects, Miller, *Long Division: State Schooling in South Australian Society*, 142.

91. Campbell, "Pioneering Modern Adolescence: The Social Significance of the Early State High Schools of Adelaide."

92. Craig Campbell, "Class and Competition," in *Education, Change and Society*, ed. Connell et al. (Melbourne: Oxford University Press, 2007); Miller, *Long Division: State Schooling in South Australian Society.*

93. Jocelynne A. Scutt, "Inequality before the Law: Gender, Arbitration and Wages," in *Gender Relations in Australia: Domination and Negotiation*, ed. Kay Saunders and Raymond Evans (Sydney: Harcourt Brace Jovanovich, 1992), 267–68.

94. Jill Blackmore, "Schooling for Work: Gender Differentiation in Commercial Education in Victoria 1935–1960," *History of Education Review* 16, no. 1 (1987).

95. Erica Jolly, *A Broader Vision: Voices of Vocational Education in Twentieth-Century South Australia* (Adelaide: the author, 2001).

96. For public high schools there are relatively few detailed histories, but see Craig Campbell, *State High School: Unley, 1910–1985* (Adelaide: the author, 1985).

97. I. L. Kandel, "Impressions of Australian Education," in *Education for Complete Living: The Challenge of Today*, ed. K. S. Cunningham (Melbourne: Melbourne University Press, 1938), 659.

98. R. Freeman Butts, *Assumptions Underlying Australian Education* (Melbourne: Australian Council for Educational Research, 1957).

99. W. F. Connell, *The Foundations of Secondary Education* (Melbourne: Australian Council for Educational Research, 1961).

100. Craig Campbell and Geoffrey Sherington, *The Comprehensive Public High School: Historical Perspectives* (New York: PalgraveMacmillan, 2006), 36–37.

101. R. W. Connell et al., *Making the Difference: Schools, Families and Social Division* (Sydney: George Allen & Unwin, 1982).

102. Antonio Mercurio, *Questions as Answers: Understanding Upper Secondary Selection and Certification Practices in South Australia, 1950–2000* (Adelaide: SSABSA, 2003).

103. Richard Teese, *Academic Success and Social Power: Examinations and Inequity* (Melbourne: Melbourne University Press, 2000), 189.

104. Campbell and Sherington, *The Comprehensive Public High School: Historical Perspectives.*

105. Pat Thomson, *Schooling the Rustbelt Kids: Making the Difference in Changing Times* (Sydney: Allen & Unwin, 2002); Margaret Vickers, "Markets and Mobilities: Dilemmas Facing the Comprehensive Neighbourhood High School," *Melbourne Studies in Education* 45, no. 2 (2004).

106. E. V. Piess (1902), as quoted in Turney, ed., *Sources in the History of Australian Education: 1788–1970*, p. 366.

107. For example, the Orr Case: Cassandra Pybus, *Gross Moral Turpitude: The Orr Case Reconsidered* (Melbourne: William Heinemann Australia, 1993).

108. J. A. La Nauze, "Some Aspects of Educational Opportunity in South Australia," in *Australian Educational Studies*, ed. J. D. G. Medley (Melbourne: Melbourne University Press, 1940).

109. Alison Mackinnon, *The New Women: Adelaide's Early Women Graduates*; Alison Mackinnon, *Love and Freedom: Professional Women and the Reshaping of Personal Life* (Cambridge: Cambridge University Press, 1997).

110. Gronn, "Schooling for Ruling: The Social Composition of Admissions to Geelong Grammar School 1930–1939."

111. Don Watson, *Brian Fitzpatrick, a Radical Life* (Sydney: Hale & Iremonger, 1979).

112. Alan Barcan, *Radical Students: The Old Left at Sydney University* (Melbourne: Melbourne University Press, 2002).

113. Turney, ed., *Sources in the History of Australian Education: 1788–1970*, 376.

114. See http://www.unsw.edu.au/about/pad/history.html, retrieved September 14, 2006. See also Patrick O'Farrell, *UNSW, a Portrait: The University of New South Wales, 1949–1999* (Sydney: UNSW Press, 1999).

115. Ibid.

116. Graham Hastings, *It Can't Happen Here: A Political History of Australian Student Activism* (Adelaide: Students' Association of Flinders University, 2003); Mick Armstrong, *1, 2, 3, What Are We Fighting For? The Australian Student Movement from Its Origins to the 1970s* (Melbourne: Socialist Alternative, 2001).

117. See Peter Coaldrake and P. Stedman, *Academic Work in the Twenty-First Century: Changing Roles and Policies* (Canberra: Dept. of Education, Training and Youth Affairs, 1999); Simon Marginson and Mark Considine, *The Enterprise University: Power, Governance and Reinvention in Australia* (New York: Cambridge University Press, 2000).

BIBLIOGRAPHY

Austin, A. G. 1961. *Australian Education 1788–1900: Church, State and Public Education in Colonial Australia*. Melbourne: Isaac Pitman.

Austin, A. G., and R. J. W. Selleck. 1975. *The Australian Government School 1830–1914*. Melbourne: Pitman.

Barcan, Alan. 1980. *A History of Australian Education*. Melbourne: Oxford University Press.

Beresford, Quentin, and Gary Partington, eds. 2003. *Reform and Resistance in Aboriginal Education: The Australian Experience*. Perth: University of Western Australia Press.

Butts, R. Freeman. 1957. *Assumptions Underlying Australian Education*. Melbourne: Australian Council for Educational Research.

Campbell, Craig. 1999. *Toward the State High School in Australia: Social Histories of State Secondary Schooling in Victoria, Tasmania and South Australia, 1850–1925*. Sydney: ANZHES.

Campbell, Craig, and Geoffrey Sherington. 2006. *The Comprehensive Public High School: Historical Perspectives, Secondary Education in a Changing World*. New York: Palgrave Macmillan.

Candy, P. C., and J. Laurent, eds. 1994. *Pioneering Culture: Mechanics' Institutes and Schools of Arts in Australia*. Adelaide: Auslib Press.

Cleverley, John F. 1971. *The First Generation: School and Society in Early Australia*. Sydney: Sydney University Press.

Connell, R. W., D. J. Ashenden, S. Kessler, and G. W. Dowsett. 1982. *Making the Difference: Schools, Families and Social Division*. Sydney: George Allen & Unwin.

Connell, W. F. 1993. *Reshaping Australian Education 1960–1985*. Melbourne: ACER.

Fogarty, Ronald. 1959. *Catholic Education in Australia, 1806–1950*. 2 vols. Melbourne: Melbourne University Press.

Hyams, B. K. 1979. *Teacher Preparation in Australia: A History of Its Development from 1850 to 1950*. Melbourne: ACER.

Kalantzis, Mary, Bill Cope, Greg Noble, and Scott Poynting. 1990. *Cultures of Schooling: Pedagogies for Cultural Difference and Social Access*. London: Falmer Press.

Kenway, Jane, and Sue Willis. 1998. *Answering Back: Girls, Boys and Feminism in Schools*. London: Routledge.

Kociumbas, Jan. 1997. *Australian Childhood: A History*. Sydney: Allen & Unwin.

Lingard, Bob, John Knight, and Paige Porter, eds. 1993. *Schooling Reform in Hard Times*. London: Falmer.

Mackinnon, Alison. 1986. *The New Women: Adelaide's Early Women Graduates*. Adelaide: Wakefield Press.

Marginson, Simon. 1993. *Education and Public Policy in Australia*. Cambridge: Cambridge University Press.

Marginson, Simon, and Mark Considine. 2000. *The Enterprise University: Power, Governance and Reinvention in Australia*. New York: Cambridge University Press.

McCallum, David. 1990. *The Social Production of Merit: Education, Psychology and Politics in Australia 1900–1950*. London: Falmer Press.

Miller, Pavla. 1986. *Long Division: State Schooling in South Australian Society*. Adelaide: Wakefield Press.

O'Donoghue, Thomas A. 2001. *Upholding the Faith: The Process of Education in Catholic Schools in Australia, 1922–1965*. New York: Peter Lang.

Selleck, R. J. W. 1968. *The New Education*. London: Pitman.

Selleck, R. J. W. 1982. *Frank Tate: A Biography*. Melbourne: Melbourne University Press.

Sherington, Geoffrey, R. C. Petersen, and Ian Brice. 1987. *Learning to Lead: A History of Girls' and Boys' Corporate Secondary Schools in Australia*. Sydney: Allen & Unwin.

Teese, Richard. 2000. *Academic Success and Social Power: Examinations and Inequity*. Melbourne: Melbourne University Press.

Theobald, Marjorie. 1996. *Knowing Women: Origins of Women's Education in Nineteenth-Century Australia*. Cambridge: Cambridge University Press.

Thomson, Pat. 2002. *Schooling the Rustbelt Kids: Making the Difference in Changing Times*. Sydney: Allen & Unwin.

Windschuttle, Elizabeth. 1980. "Educating the Daughters of the Ruling Class in Colonial New South Wales, 1788–1850." *Melbourne Studies in Education*, 105–33.

Chapter 3

SCHOOLING IN FIJI

Carmen M. White

Fiji is an archipelago of roughly 330 islands, primarily volcanic in origin. It straddles the southwestern and eastern Pacific Ocean and comprises a total area of 806,000 square miles of ocean with a land surface area of about 11,367 square miles. While 106 of the islands in the Fiji group are inhabited, the greatest land mass and total population is found on the two major islands of Viti Levu and Vanua Levu. Vanua Levu literally translates as "great/large land" in Fijian and makes up 30 percent of the land area while residence to 18 percent of the population. Viti Levu, which means "great/large Fiji" in Fijian, is the largest island and has one of the most urbanized infrastructures in the region, including the site for the two major cities of the archipelago—Suva, the capital, and Lautoka. Viti Levu constitutes 50 percent of the archipelago's land area and is where 75 percent of the population resides. Other sizeable islands include Kadavu and Taveuni. Fiji also includes the Polynesian outlier, Rotuma, located approximately 248 miles north of Viti Levu. Most of Fiji's population lives along coastal areas and, in the case of the largest islands, near the river deltas and valleys of the interior as well.[1]

Agriculture comprises roughly 17 percent of Fiji's gross domestic product while about two-thirds of the country's population is employed in the agricultural sector. Through a combination of favorable trade terms and aid provided by the European Union, Fiji's sugar industry has thrived, supporting roughly 25 percent of the population. Other exports include gold, fish, and timber. The garment industry has also gained increasing importance in Fiji's economy. It is tourism, however, that has become the largest single source of foreign exchange earnings, constituting about 30 percent of foreign revenue.[2]

Fiji's population is currently enumerated at about 840,000 people, representing a tapestry of ethnic, linguistic, religious, and cultural diversity. The two major ethnic groups are Fijians, who make up roughly 54 percent of the population, and Indians, who make up about 38 percent of the population.[3] The remaining 8 percent includes Chinese, Rotumans, Solomon Islanders, Europeans, Part-Europeans, Banabans, and Tuvaluans.[4] While Fiji's official language is English, Fijian is the first language of most Fijians and Solomon Islanders and Fiji Hindi for a majority of Indians, with both languages recognized in commerce, mass media, and as languages of instruction for the first few years of schooling for Fijian and Indian children. Other languages spoken by Indians include Urdu, Telegu, Tamil, and Gujerati. Rotuman, Chinese (Cantonese and Mandarin), Gilbertese, and Tuvaluan are also spoken by Rotumans, Chinese, Banabans, and Tuvaluans, respectively.

The development of an educational system that serves a relatively small island population spread across such a wide geographic expanse, and as varied and complex in its ethnic, "racial," and linguistic composition and cultural diversity as Fiji, has been intimately linked with broader social, political, and economic developments that began in nineteenth century colonial Fiji and which continue in the independent Republic of Fiji into the twenty-first century. Throughout Fiji's history of formal schooling, addressing quantitative and qualitative differences in access to schools and qualified teachers, and the relevance and fit of school curricula for Fiji's population, have been fundamental areas of concern. However, before the establishment of a system of mass education following the arrival of Europeans, there were the original settlers of the archipelago who had institutionalized forms of learning already in place.

BEFORE THE NINETEENTH CENTURY

Education is conventionally and broadly defined as the process by which values, knowledge, and skills are systematically transmitted often, but not exclusively, through intergenerational interaction and instruction. While it is a process that occurs throughout the lifecycle, much intensive learning occurs in various structured and unstructured contexts during the period that societies all over the world have recognized as the "formative years." In Fiji, prior to the nineteenth century, there were patterned similarities as well as variations in the values, knowledge, and skills transmitted across generations from area to area throughout the archipelago. These would have involved formal and informal, explicit and more indirect methods of teaching and instruction.

Archaeological data suggest that the Austronesian ancestors of indigenous Fijians began arriving from New Guinea and settling the archipelago between 1200 B.C. and 1000 B.C. These original settlers bore the Lapita culture, named after the red-stamped pottery style found at an archaeological site of the same name in New Caledonia. In addition to a distinctive pottery, Lapita culture in many areas was geared towards coastal rather than inland settlement and a corresponding emphasis on seafaring traditions and exploitation of marine resources, but also included such horticultural practices as terrace construction for irrigated taro patches as well as pig husbandry.[5]

As Fijian communities established themselves over the centuries that preceded European contact, the social, political, and economic landscape of the
archipelago was reproduced and transformed across generations through agents
of socialization that transmitted requisite knowledge and skills. Parents and
extended kinfolk were the most significant agents for passing on formal and
informal technical and social skills to the young, including enforcing compliance with standards of daily village protocol and behavioral roles and activities
related to age, sex, seniority, rank, and kinship. Traditional learning came with
the expectation that the young became skilled in, and knowledgeable of, their
respective roles and statuses within the social structure. Young people acquired
social and technical competence while enmeshed in the daily activities of the
patri-clan, or *mataqali*, into which they were born. *Mataqali* were related
patri-clans, which were further divided into *i tokatoka*, or extended families
with a male family head, or *vu*, and which resided in designated sections of villages. Polygamy was practiced while patrilineal descent and patrilocal postmari-
tal residence prevailed. Warfare between rivaling villages culminated in raids
where men and women were taken as tribute or slaves. Ritualistic anthropoph-
agy was also practiced to literally ingest the essence of enemies during wartime.

In the epoch that immediately predated the arrival of Europeans, the social
structure that had evolved throughout much of the archipelago was a pyramid-
shaped system with seven *mataqali* representing distinctive occupational clans,
collectively representing a *yavusa*. At the base were the warrior, fisher, and carpenter clans, who ranked below the heralds, deputies, and priests, who were, in
turn, positioned below chiefs at the apex. In this three-tiered system, the specialized knowledge and skills associated with occupational groupings were passed
on through a range of practices, including modeling and apprentice-type training by elder and more experienced community members. The *turaga mataqali*,
or chiefly clan that stood at the pinnacle of the hierarchical order, was the clan
from which the chief of the entire *yavusa* was formally installed by elders of the
sauturaga mataqali, or the deputy clan. Deputies also advised and acted on
behalf of the chief in his absence. Comparable in status to the deputies were
the *matanivanua*, or official heralds, and the *bete mataqali*, or the priestly clan.
The heralds were the spokespersons for, and companions of, the chief as well as
intermediaries between the chief and the commoners. Priests were the gate-
keepers of supernatural knowledge and had the power to summon the gods for
supernatural assistance in daily life. The warriors, or the *mataqali bati*, served
as bodyguards for the chiefs as well as guards for the *vanua*, or the people and
land of the *yavusa*. Members of the fishermen clan, or the *mataqali gonedau*,
sailed on the open sea, as well as in reefs and lagoons, for their catch and were
exclusively responsible for the chief's nourishment. Finally was the *mataqali
mataisau*, or carpenter clan, whose members cultivated skills in the creation of
refined handicrafts. Carpenters produced the utensils and eating vessels, ornamental hair combs, war clubs, axes and spears, oil dishes for body paints and
coconut oil emollients, wooden head-rests for sleeping, and a range of other

objects, often carving from special woods that were exclusively for the chiefs' use. The carpenters carved the chief's *tanoa*, or wooden *yaqona* bowl, which was always larger and more elaborately designed than other *tanoa*. The carpenters were also responsible for building the chief's canoes and for maintaining the chief's dwelling house.[6]

Throughout the archipelago, chiefly titles were transferred through patrilineal descent and primogeniture, with general consideration also given to leadership potential. In communities in the western and central regions of Viti Levu, the power and authority of chiefs was associated with less status differentiation in relation to commoners. In the more elaborately hierarchical structures of the eastern islands of the archipelago, chiefs were semidivine intermediaries between commoners and the ancestral gods, the latter bestowing chiefs with the high concentrations of *mana*, or sacred essence, that rendered them ritually powerful. Chiefly power, prestige, and sanctity were expressed through ritualized forms of protocol in daily social intercourse and ceremony that dictated the physical segregation and elevation of chiefs and all of their possessions, deemed *tabu*, or forbidden and ritually dangerous to commoners.[7] In addition to preparing the young to assume roles within this hierarchical system, the learning environment during the formative years included socialization into cosmological beliefs that permeated both the quotidian and more ceremonial aspects of life.

While the finer details in cosmologies varied across the archipelago, among the shared principles of these systems were that specific animate (e.g., birds) and inanimate (e.g., mountains) features of nature were invested with a living or supernatural energy and represented ancestral gods in relation to mortal humans. These ancestral gods were also bound together with ancestral spirits, chiefs, and mortal humans in relations of kinship. Children learned about the cosmos through the origin stories, related through *meke* and other forms of story-telling, which included the accounts of how the serpent god, or Degei, created man and woman. The young could also discern messages about the workings of the universe as they witnessed the erecting of shrines and temples where priests presented their offertories of first fruits, pig sacrifices, and whale teeth to the gods for protection and success in times of war with rivaling groups, or for productivity and prosperity during planting and harvesting seasons. The young learned about their kinship relation with, and proper treatment of, the animal totem of their clan and the totems of related clans. Children learned the necessity of observing the *tabus* on food consumption and other behaviors declared by chiefs and the supernatural consequences for failure to abide by them. They learned that all illnesses, misfortunes, and calamities of life were connected to the supernatural realm, be it through sorcery, witchcraft, or the will of aggrieved ancestral spirits. They learned, in turn, rituals of atonement to appease ancestral spirits and the precautions that were needed to provide protection from sorcery and witchcraft. Children learned that sacred sites were to be treated with respect. They learned, as well, about the concept of *mana* in all its complexity and the special role of chiefs as the closest descendants of the ancestral gods.[8] Fijian cosmologies also encompassed broader symbolic links between land, kinship, and personhood. For example, the distribution and consumption of feast foods during life crises or other ceremonial events, as well as more mundane forms of food-sharing integral to interaction between kin, were understood as generative processes; here, the collective ingestion of the fruits of a particular land rendered a common bodily constitution, solidarity, and an identification with the land among kin. A newborn's umbilical cord was buried in conjunction with the planting of a tree to reinforce the child's relationship to the land and guarantee future prosperity and productivity.

Other forms of early socialization reproduced a sexual division of labor in the production of material culture. Methods of teaching and learning included modeling as well as explicit instruction in the performance of relevant skills for male and female children. Hence, mothers and other elder female relatives instructed younger females in making the highly valued and durable sinnet cord from coconut husks used for binding in carpentry, making turtle nets, and a range of other industrial uses. Girls also received instruction in net-fishing, as well as in the construction of fish nets, basket-making, fan-making, and mat-making from the weaving of pandanus palm leaves and other vegetable fibers, the beating and hand-dyeing of strips of bark from the paper mulberry tree to produce *masi*, or Fijian bark cloth for male adornment, pottery-making, and other skills in the production of textiles and traditional wealth objects. From mothers, females also learned the making of *liku*, or the short, fringed skirts made from vegetable fibers adorned in the years just before puberty, and the longer *liku* skirts worn at puberty and after marriage. Fathers and other male elders instructed young males in building such thatched village structures as sleeping and dwelling units, spirit-houses or temples for ancestor worship, kitchens, and guest-houses. Males also made tortoiseshell hooks, spears, and arrows for fishing and hunting, while the building of outrigger, double-, and single-hulled canoes was a task originally relegated to the carpenter clans.[9]

Males and females were also instructed in the range of tasks associated with the cultivation and harvesting of the variety of *dalo* (taro), *kumala* (sweet potato), *tavioka* (cassava), and other tubers and crops grown as dietary staples throughout the islands. These tasks included instruction in terrace maintenance, weeding, and the use of digging sticks. Young males were expected to gain competence following the steps in preparing the *lovo*, or the underground earth ovens lined with heated stones and banana leaves, in which were placed the *magiti*, or feast foods, that accompanied all life-crisis events and ceremonies. Females learned their assigned task of maintaining the underground pits used to prepare and store *madrai*, or fermented breads made from yams, bananas, breadfruit and other starches—consumed in times of famine, or used for trade with groups residing in areas of limited productivity. Both males and females acquired skills in specific culinary arts commensurate with a sexual division of labor. Hence, while females learned the process of preparing *lolo*, or coconut cream through the scraping and hydration of the meat of mature coconuts, males assumed their own culinary role preparing baked foods and delicacies such as caramelized cassava puddings for ceremonial feasts. In some areas, a sexual division of labor also defined the ceremonial preparation of *kava*, or *yaqona*—the root of the *Piper methysticum* pepper plant. Here, instead of the pounding, hydration, and serving of *yaqona* strictly by males, girls chewed the *yaqona* root while young males hydrated the chewed root with water in the wooden *tanoa* and served it to their elders according to ceremonial protocol.[10]

Male and female children acquired skills in various *meke*, or action chants, including the *meke i wau* (men's club dance), *meke wesi* (men's fan dance), *sea-sea* (women's fan dance), and *vakamalolo*, performed by males and females seated in rows. In addition to learning these and other forms of expressive culture from parents, children found recreation through such games as pelting with ripened oranges, wrestling, sham fights, and throwing reeds akin to javelin-throwing. The young learned the importance placed upon the artistry of weaving the spoken word based on their communities' appreciation for refined oratory skills and story-telling. The sons and daughters of the untitled wore no clothing until about the age of seven, while children of chiefly descent went nude for slightly longer, with all leaving the carefree stage of childhood with the onset of puberty. Young manhood was signified by circumcision and the donning of the *masi* loincloth, or *malo*. Females were initiated into early womanhood by undergoing the tattooing of their inner thighs and buttocks with elaborate, symbolic geometric designs, along with donning a longer *liku*. By this age, young people were well initiated into the protocol of kinship relations between individuals and groups. This included the *vasu* relationship, where the young were indulged by their maternal uncles, the *tavale*, or cross-cousin relationship of camaraderie and marriage potentiality, and the sibling and parallel-cousin relationship of restricted and highly formal interaction or avoidance particularly with the opposite sex. There were also direct transcultural links, trade, intermarriage, and mutual borrowing between the people of Tonga and the most easterly islands of the archipelago, most notably between populations of the Lau group, and Tongan Va'avau island group, located about 43 miles immediately south of Ono i Lau. The results of such exchanges included Fijian influence on Tongan methods of body tattooing, canoe craftsmanship, and culinary practices.[11]

NINETEENTH CENTURY

Fiji's contemporary educational system has its most direct roots in precolonial and colonial developments of the nineteenth century that led to the importation and rapid dissemination of formally instituted types of schooling. This formal schooling was introduced by European missionaries arriving on the heels of a long line of explorers, beachcombers, traders in sandalwood and *beche-de-mer*, and whalers that descended upon the South West Pacific by the early 1800s. The introduction of mission schools heralded a type of education that differed as much in form as in content from anything that Fijians had before. It came with reading and writing for a population that had rich oral traditions, but no prior literary tradition. It came with regimented schedules where students focused on the teachings of a nonrelative instructor while seated inside the four walls of a schoolhouse for a population for whom traditional knowledge and skills were holistically integrated, occurred across a variety of social contexts, and involved kin. Finally, it introduced new knowledge as well as new skills that were intended to transform Fijians' conception of the cosmos and their place in it.

It was British Wesleyans, through their linguistic efforts, who established a religious foothold for the Methodists that withstood the challenges posed by French Marist Catholics by the mid 1840s and Anglicans and Seventh-day Adventists from Britain and Australia by the 1870s. Wesleyans propelled and cemented their influence as the first to establish mission schools and by promoting vernacular bible literacy. Once Britain declared Fiji a Crown colony in 1874, this would precipitate equally dramatic changes in the social, economic, and demographic structure of the archipelago in ways that transformed the shape and content of education in the Fiji Islands.

The first European missionaries to make inroads into the Fiji archipelago were David Cargill and William Cross, who arrived in 1835—operating under the auspices of the London-based Wesleyan Methodist Missionary Society—along with several Tongan pastor-teachers. The promotion of vernacular languages had facilitated the proselytizing objectives of Wesleyans elsewhere, including Tonga, where Cargill and Cross were stationed prior to embarking on a Fiji mission. Cargill and Cross were amply assisted in their preliminary study of the grammar and phonetics of the language spoken by an immigrant then residing in Tonga, but who originated from Lakeba in the Lau group of the Fiji archipelago. Once Cargill and Cross arrived in Lakeba, the collaborative assistance of the Tongan missionaries, Tongan immigrants residing in the Lau group, as well as Fijians who spoke Tongan, would ease the linguistic challenges of the British missionaries, who honed and refined their proficiency in Lakeban. Cargill and Cross came with a modest school primer already in hand that had been prepared with the assistance of the Fijian translator in Tonga. The first mission school was established on Lakeba within weeks of the mission party's arrival, with children and adults attending.[12] Following the 1838 arrival of another cohort of Wesleyans bearing a printing press, religious texts and other curricula materials were locally produced and distributed. In 1839, Cargill completed a manuscript on the "Fijian grammar" based on Lakeban. After engagement with speakers of other Fijian languages following relocation to Rewa on the island of Viti Levu, Cross made contributions that missionaries incorporated into revisions to the nascent Fijian orthography.[13]

Ultimately, the Bauan kingdom's reign of conquest and political supremacy—which was enabled by the provision of muskets by beachcombers—led Cargill, Cross, and other missionaries to promote the ascendancy of the Bauan language in the formulation of a Fijian orthography.[14] By 1847 one thousand complete and three thousand abridged copies of the New Testament, translated into Bauan, were in print. By 1850, another missionary, David Hazelwood, had compiled a new grammar and dictionary on the "Fijian language" based on Bauan. The acceptance and dissemination of Hazelwood's grammar secured the status of the Bauan language as the indigenous lingua franca of Fiji.[15] By 1865, ten years after the Fiji Wesleyan mission came under the jurisdiction of the newly established regional Methodist Missionary Society of Australasia based in Sydney, translated volumes of the Scriptures, hymnals, and other religious texts were printed in England and Australia and delivered to Fiji.[16]

Fijian nobles were the first to actively pursue the vernacular literacy offered by the Wesleyans, receiving private bible lessons as a mark of privilege. Early missionaries capitalized upon Fijians' early interpretations of novel and odd markings—which allowed communication between distant interlocutors—as inextricably bound to protections from strange new diseases and other tangible benefits bestowed upon those who accepted the missionaries' God. Hence, for chiefs, the initial appeal of bible literacy derived from anticipation that Christianity would facilitate access to such European material wonders as firearms, and insight into such puzzles as missionaries' medicinal treatments for various European-introduced illnesses.[17]

Wesleyans came to rely on mission schools with local vernaculars as a medium of instruction to facilitate their proselytizing projects. Meanwhile, for Fijian nobles and the commoners who followed their example, conversion to Christianity became secondary to a primary goal of attaining vernacular literacy.[18] Missionary desires to increase the supply of mission schools dovetailed with community demands as Fijian village residents vied to have mission schools located in their immediate communities. By the end of the nineteenth century, there were 1,453 Methodist mission schools with 25,610 registered Fijian students,[19] or roughly 21 percent of the estimated 120,000 Fijian population.[20]

The curriculum of the first mission schools consisted of two years of biblical instruction, complemented by provision of basic skills in reading and writing, and supplemented with instruction in arithmetic and hygiene. Reading and writing were particularly critical to the broader missionary enterprise of spreading the Gospel since Fijians had no prior literary tradition and needed to be initiated into the process of discerning an alphabet, grammar, and vocabulary of their language depicted in written symbols. In addition to providing instruction in written vernacular, missionaries drew from and incorporated other indigenous expressive forms into the instructional process to impart new knowledge and skills. One observer to an early mission school offered the following account of a "mass examination." The movements described are reminiscent of the *vakamalolo* dance form, or an action chant that involves raised arms, clapping, intricate hand gestures, and an upper body all vigorously animated, performed while seated and to the rhythmic beating of the wooden gong, or *lali*:

So they gave us a dance and pantomime all about the capture of Jerusalem, and very curious it was. Then they went through very creditable Scriptural examination and recitation, with some reading and writing, and finished off with a most extraordinary method of spelling and doing mental arithmetic. I cannot attempt to describe it, further than to say that though all the scholars as usual sat on the ground, the whole body was in perpetual motion, swaying from side to side, each row in opposite directions. There was incessant clapping of hands, now on one side, now on the other, now on the ground, now in the mid-air, and all in measured time; while the calculations were shouted aloud, and apparently produced a correct result.[21]

The wives of missionaries often assumed an instructional role for Fijian females. Their teaching objectives included transforming Fijian girls and women into proximate models of Victorian domestic femininity as homemakers, wives, and mothers. For this, they included instruction in such specialized domestic arts as needlework, sewing, the washing of the cotton clothing they encouraged all Fijians to wear and adorn to conform to missionaries' sense of modesty, and the adoption of missionary prescriptions in methods of childcare. Equally important to missionary wives was the discouragement of such practices as polygamy, separate dwelling houses for men and women, and the tattooing of pubescent girls.[22]

Mission school curricula were later extended to four years of schooling, including skills that placed Fijians in the role of producing the mission school infrastructure. Missionaries instructed Fijian males in their own methods of agriculture and animal husbandry to replace existing horticultural practices and methods of food production. They also taught Fijian males new carpentry and woodwork styles with imported tools to enlist their labor in the construction of schoolhouses, as well as printing and binding to garner their assistance with the production of bibles, teaching manuals, and other curricular materials. By 1857, Wesleyans established a central training institute at Mataisuva on Viti Levu for grooming Fijian males to work as pastor-teachers throughout the archipelago. Fijian teachers accompanied missionaries to serve in a similar capacity in mission stations in other parts of the South Pacific. The indigenization of the church provided cost-saving measures for the Methodist mission. Native teachers extended themselves far more for much less remuneration than missionaries. In addition to holding school three mornings a week for children and three evenings a week for adults in their district, pastor-teachers were expected to hold one weekday service, provide sermons for two Sunday services, hold prayer meetings, conduct morning and evening prayers in private residences, comfort the sick, provide personal counselling to community members, perform mortuary services, and to make weekly visits to the native minister.[23] Meanwhile, village residents were responsible for subsidizing the maintenance of Fijian teachers, with the provision of room and board a condition for a teacher's appointment to a village.[24]

Throughout the nineteenth century, Wesleyans moved increasingly towards an indigenization of the church hierarchy, and the mission system became a venue for Fijians to pursue an upward mobility that was particularly attractive to commoners. By the late 1800s, Fijians were being ordained as native ministers, regardless of rank. High-ranking chiefs were the least inclined to seek titles within the church hierarchy; the security of their status within the chiefly system precluded an orientation towards the church comparable to that of commoners.[25] Missionaries structurally undermined the authority of traditional priests but reinforced the authority of chiefs in the substance of their teachings by emphasizing the status of chiefs as ordained leaders, leaving much of their sanctity—including their *mana*—intact.[26] It was the ancestral gods of traditional religions who lost the most in the new teachings, as Wesleyans claimed the Christian God as the genuine source of the *mana* bequeathed to chiefs. This, coupled with the wonders already attributed to them, allowed missionaries to appropriate some measure of *mana* for themselves.[27] Still, missionaries ultimately remained reliant upon the goodwill and cooperation of chiefs for the smooth daily operations of mission life, particularly during the founding years as schools became entrenched institutions in villages.[28]

French Marist Roman Catholic missions arrived on the Fiji scene in 1844, disembarking on the island of Lakeba. While Marists were regarded as interlopers and rivals that posed a significant threat to established missions, precedence and their mission-style of localization proved to be of strategic advantage to the Methodists. By 1855, Marists had moved their major post to the bustling port town of Levuka on Ovalau island and were establishing few schools beyond central mission posts. While in 1882 three nuns arrived to assist in the establishment of several Catholic schools for girls and trained a congregation of Fijian nuns,[29] there was generally less indigenization of the church and generally less inclination toward gaining and promoting vernacular proficiency.[30] English was the medium of instruction in most Catholic schools, as well as in the less expansive Seventh-day Adventist and Anglican missions that arrived on the Fiji scene by the 1870s.[31]

By the 1870s, Wesleyans established the Training Institute for Natives at Navualoa on Viti Levu specifically for the sons of Fijian nobles, providing a relatively "advanced" level of agricultural training and an academic curriculum atypical of mission schools. In addition to reading, writing, and arithmetic, the curriculum included geography and English grammar. Lessons were conducted in English while the speaking of Fijian was prohibited during school hours.[32] The closure of the school seven years after its founding was prompted by the Australian principal appointed to the school; under the heightened influence of popular views of the day about the limited intellectual capacity of "native races," he concluded that Fijians were insufficiently endowed with the mental faculties necessary to grasp an academic curriculum to warrant the school's continuation.[33]

In the 1860s, while Wesleyans were establishing the foundation for a mission school system, Ratu George Seru Epenisa Cakobau, who hailed from the pre-eminent kingdom of Bau, was consolidating a constitutional government in Levuka. Under the advisement of European assistants, King Cakobau requested that Queen Victoria claim custodianship over the Fiji archipelago in the face of challenges to his own political reign from Australian planters, American whalers, rival Fijian chiefs, and Tongan Chief Enele Ma'afu who had attained political supremacy in Lau. By this time, Fiji was undergoing a steady demographic shift with an influx of settlers, most of whom were concentrated in and around Levuka. These included Chinese traders of *beche-de-mer* and laborers, many of whom married Fijian women. Most were Europeans pursuing such agricultural ventures as copra and cotton production, embarking on longer term settlement. Between 1867 and 1870, the European population increased from 830 to roughly 2,000.[34] This coincided with the emergence of a Part-European population, principally children from unions between Fijian women and European men, concentrated on Ovalau and Vanua Levu. While some Part-Europeans initially provided labor on copra plantations, a more plentiful labor source was established through deceptive recruitment and outright kidnapping of young men from coastal villages of the Solomon Islands and, to a lesser extent, New Hebrides (present-day Vanuatu) in the infamous practice that became known as "black-birding."

When Britain accepted Cakobau's offer to cede the territory making Fiji a Crown colony in 1874, the colonial administration initiated a number of "protectionist" practices and policies. The official rationale for protectionism was to minimize the deleterious impact that colonialists presumed would result from Fijians' rapid exposure to "civilization" and to "preserve" their way of life. Colonialists not only deemed Fijians a "primitive" population but—on the heels of a devastating 1875 measles epidemic that killed roughly one-third of the indigenous population—a "dying race." Hence, policies would be geared toward isolating a vulnerable Fijian population from the vagaries of modern institutions they were deemed unequipped to handle. The most auspicious of such policies for Fijians was one that would stave off foreign confiscation of indigenous land—that is, the declaration of all land not appropriated by the Crown at cession as inalienable. This provided for roughly 83 percent of the land in the archipelago to remain in Fijian hands. The *mataqali* was designated the standardized landholding unit, organized around village residence. With the rural village the defining unit for establishing the proprietary boundaries of rural land, Fijians were to become oriented toward the natal rural village as the core of existence while governed through a series of ordinances—the Native Affairs Regulations. To limit urban Fijian settlement, ordinances placed restrictions on temporary and more permanent Fijian migration, requiring evidence of urban employment even to venture into urban areas. Ordinances provided a blueprint for the conduct of village life, regulating every manner of behavior from the manner of disposing of refuse to mandating villagers' participation in such rural public works as road-building and contributing to communal labor to meet the agricultural produce tax levied on villages. Regulations also stipulated that all Fijians who lived within 3 miles of a school were required to enroll their school-age children.[35]

Protectionism included establishing a system of indirect colonial rule to facilitate the formulation and enforcement of native ordinances. This entailed the creation of a hierachically organized Native Administration as an auxiliary branch of the colonial administration comprising administrative and hereditary chiefs, with the Council of Chiefs at the apex, and administrative chiefs, or *turaga ni koro*, elected by and presiding over rural villages. Indirect rule followed from colonialists' definition of Fijians as generally incompetent in governing their own affairs independent of British patronage, but with the caveat that Fijian nobles were sufficiently able and competent to act as leaders of the Fijian masses and as liaisons between the Fijian masses and the colonial administration.

Protectionism was also expressed through the restrictions placed on planters and emergent industries in the use of indigenous labor in the territory. Once the colonial administration defined Fijians as ill suited for plantation work, European planters clamored for labor. The colonial administration assuaged the resident planters by encouraging alternative labor sources. While planters continued to turn to the Solomon Islands and New Hebrides for field laborers and domestic servants on their copra and sugar cane estates, by the 1870s there was relatively greater regulation that discouraged kidnappings; Melanesian laborers were recruited to work three-year contracts on the plantations of Ovalau and Vanua Levu for meager wages.[36] With prospects for a growing sugar industry in light of international demand and suitable conditions for cultivation on western Viti Levu and Vanua Levu, planters pushed for a more plentiful and steady labor supply, reissuing demands that indigenous Fijian labor be made accessible to them. The colonial administration determined, instead, that Fiji would join other territories in the British Empire in the importation of indentured labor from India. The first contingent numbering roughly 498 laborers arrived in 1879. About three-quarters of all laborers originated from the northern provinces of present-day Uttar Pradesh and the remainder from South India; roughly 80 percent were Hindus, primarily Sanatan Dharma, and approximately 20 percent were Muslim, largely Sunni. The ratio of women to men was roughly 40 to 100. For Hindus, ritual segregation and other observances associated with caste were untenable in the confines of ships, expediting the demise of the caste system. In Fiji, the contract—or *girmit* in Hindustani—provided for a nine-hour workday, five-and-a-half days per week for five years; for those who renewed their contract and opted to return to India, the government assumed the expenditures for repatriation—although most opted to remain. Living and working conditions on the expansive sugar cane estates were brutal.

Workers were housed in the "lines"—cramped, communal dormitory blocks devoid of privacy, where many struggled to create and sustain some semblance of family life. Men and women were beaten for failing to meet their labor quota while many women faced the additional horror of rape by European overseers and Indian sirdar. *Girmitiya* readily labeled the *girmit* experience as *narak*, or "hell."[37]

While Indians lived in the lines and labored in the cane-fields, Fijians were sequestered in their villages and living and laboring by the multiple dictates of the Regulations. Indian indentured laborers were designated wards under a loosely organized paternalism of the Australian-based Colonial Sugar Refining Company (CSR) that had established its monopoly over sugar by the early 1880s. Fijians continued to experience the more structured paternalism of protectionism. Ordinances ensured that the groups maintained disparate social and economic positions in the colony. Hence, Fijian villages that harbored Indian "deserters" from the cane-fields were punished with fines.

Colonialists did not regard missionary education designed to convert Fijians to Christianity as a threat to a protectionist agenda and so did not encumber mission schooling's spread across the rural Fijian landscape. The colonial administration, for its part, had limited interests in investing in formal education for the growing non-European population. CSR managers were particularly uninterested in channeling resources into schooling for indentured laborers and their children. A few Christian missions established schools that admitted Indians or were specifically designed for Indians by the 1890s. An Australian teacher who had lived in India established one of the first Methodist schools for Indians which consisted of a day school for children and night school for adults.[38] Also by the late 1890s, a few religious missions from India, such as the Arya Pratinidhi Sabha and Islamic associations, established temples and mosques where vernacular schooling was provided. The small contingent of local Europeans initially arranged for the education of their youngest children through Irish or Welsh governesses and nannies from Australia or New Zealand. There were small private schools such as the first "Ladies College" in Levuka in 1871 established by young female teachers, and private-tutoring by former teachers who married and provided instruction for their own children along with children from other households. Boarding schools abroad were additional options for the wealthiest Europeans.[39]

It was leaders in the local European planter community who were the first to effectively lobby for greater administrative involvement in local schooling on behalf of their constituency, culminating in the passage of two ordinances authorizing the establishment of two European schools—a primary school in the old capital of Levuka in 1879 and in the new capital of Suva in 1883.[40] The exclusion of non-Europeans was paramount, with concessions made only for select Part-Europeans deemed of the "highest class."[41] Like many similarly situated boarding schools throughout the Empire, the schools were modeled after English public schools, designed to create Victorian gentlemen through training in the classics, an emphasis upon discipline and dedicated study, patriotism toward the Empire, character-building through participation in such sports as cricket and football (rugby) or "muscular Christianity," and the enforcement of strict standards of comportment. Seven years after the founding of the public school in Suva, the Public Education Ordinance of 1890 was established stipulating a core academic curriculum in public schools for Europeans, comprising reading, writing, arithmetic, English grammar and composition, geography, British history, singing, and for female students, sewing and needlework. The list of electives included Latin, Greek, French, and German, as well as chemistry, physics, botany, geology, domestic economics, mechanics, bookkeeping, shorthand, and drawing.[42]

The other exception to the rule of colonial administrative lack of interest in local schooling pertained to educational provisions for the sons of Fijian nobles. With the implementation of a system of indirect rule, schools would be enlisted to groom future leaders and functionaries within the Native Administration. Particularly poised to become acquainted with the practical and symbolic functions of education, members of the Council of Chiefs turned to the colonial administration to affirm the privileged status of noble Fijian males, formally requesting that the sons of Fijian chiefs receive schooling that approximated that provided for the progeny of British colonial administrators—the highest ranked "chiefs" in the land. Council members looked to the elite academic schooling being arranged for European children in exclusive Levuka Public School for their model. The language of instruction was of particular symbolic, as well as practical, significance. Where vernacular instruction in Wesleyan mission schools signified the common status of the Fijian masses, English language instruction in "English ideas and habits" would be the cachet of prestige and distinction for a school serving Fijians of high rank.[43] At the 1878 meeting of the Council of Chiefs—on the heels of the closure of the Wesleyan Training Institute for Natives and the eve of Levuka Public School's opening—members forwarded their proposal to the colonial administration. Colonial administrators convinced Council members, instead, to settle for two upper-primary, boarding "industrial schools" providing training in practical trades in lieu of academic curricula, but with English as the medium of instruction. The ideal industrial school would "impart to the natives a thorough knowledge of modern agriculture" through training in manure fertilization, crop rotation, and other novel agricultural techniques as well as instruction in "the use of tools, how to work a saw, drive a nail, use a plane, and handle an adze."[44] It was projected that young Fijian nobles attending the school "will naturally become prominent and influential members of the native community, and it may be expected that the knowledge thus imparted to them will soon be extended to others."[45]

In 1880, the local colonial administration passed an ordinance mandating the establishment of industrial schools for Fijians, with the first opening in southeast Viti Levu that same year and named *Vulinitu*—"chief's learning" in Fijian. Vulinitu's staff comprised a European superintendent and carpenter and five Fijian elders, the latter representing each of the five provinces in eastern and southeastern Fiji from which students were selected. Fijian elders supervised students in the upkeep of gardens that supplied food for the hostels and in the general maintenance of the school grounds. As a prestigious institution for the indigenous aristocracy, the school also reinforced formal training in the intricacies of *vakaturaga*, or chiefly behavioral etiquette. The core curriculum included reading, writing, arithmetic, English, agriculture, and "care and management of stock" with electives in practical trades and skills such as carpentry, blacksmithing, boat-building, sail-making, rope-making, salt-making, soap-boiling, brick-making, printing, and road-making. The training of Vulinitu students was enlisted for road repair, the building of boats for sale, and the construction of buildings for a government post near the school. By 1890, an ordinance was passed that regulated the practical function of industrial schools. This included a provision that students, upon completion of their five years at the school, be granted a formal title of *matai taukei* or "carpenter of the land."[46]

Similar developments prioritizing the training of the Fijian nobility as the most skilled and learned in Fijian communities were occurring in the nascent field of medicine. The colonial administration established a "Medical School" in the Colonial Hospital of Suva in 1885 in response to the shortage of medical personnel available to address the devastating 1875 measles epidemic that claimed the lives of about 40,000 indigenous Fijians. The school was specifically designed to produce "native medical practitioners" trained in the rudiments of Western medicine. Three Fijian males commenced clinical training while working as nurses in the hospital wards, receiving formal medical instruction from the resident medical officer. Of the three students, two bore the honorific title, *Ratu*, signifying high chiefly rank. This first cohort of students completed a three-year course and upon their graduation in 1888 were formally registered as medical personnel following the passage of the Native Practitioner's Ordinance of 1888.[47]

Colonialists' conception of Fijians as a "dying race" had been propelled by the decline in the Fijian population following the measles epidemic. Fijian depopulation generated official concern well into the 1890s, spawning the convening of a Royal Commission to conduct a broader investigation into Fijian mortality. In its extensive 1896 report, the Commission implicated a range of factors, primary among them being alleged deficiencies in infant-feeding, weaning, and other care-giving practices of Fijian women. The administrative response included singling out Fijian women of childbearing age for special surveillance and for restrictions on their movements and activities during pregnancy. Methodists and Catholic sisters, for their part, made Fijian women the focus of "hygiene work," stepping up their programs to reconstruct Fijian womanhood in their own image through girls' schools.[48] One of the first such Methodist schools was Matavelo, established in 1899:

The aim of the school was, in addition to teaching English as a subject, to train and prepare Fijian girls for what is the happy lot of nearly every Fijian woman—motherhood; and to teach her how best she might help and succor the little life that God would entrust to her. It is impossible to exaggerate the influence of Matavelo in this respect.[49]

Methodist teachers extended their "hygiene work" to adult women in the villages. Colonial administrators, for their part, did not actively enlist schooling as an intervention strategy even to address their pressing concerns about Fijian depopulation. For the remainder of the nineteenth century, the colonial administration regarded provision of education for Fijian commoners, most Part-Europeans, Indians, Chinese, and Solomon Islanders, and—following the annexation of Rotuma to Fiji in 1881—Rotumans, as unnecessary and beyond their responsibility. This left Wesleyans, Catholics, Anglicans, and Seventh-day Adventists to continue their role in providing schooling in bible studies, the rudiments of reading, writing, arithmetic, and in the crafting of Victorian womanhood for the specific constituencies in which they took an interest.

TWENTIETH CENTURY

If the nineteenth century was the period when missionaries laid the foundation for Fiji's introduction to mass education, the twentieth century was the period when colonial policies, community initiative, and the government of an independent Fiji built from that foundation to expand and accelerate educational developments. By the turn of the nineteenth century, a mission school was an established fixture in the typical rural Fijian village. But even as the mission school became part of the rural landscape, it remained fundamentally a foreign institution, never functioning independently of synods based in Britain or Australia. Once the colonial government instituted a grant-in-aid system to encourage compliance with government curricular guidelines, there was a catalyst for an increasing shift of influence from the mission to the colonial administration. With the change in administrative control, the religious undertones that characterized mission schools gave way to a more explicit emphasis on agricultural and vocational skills in district and committee schools. Colonial administrators and Fijian leaders were united in their support for an overwhelmingly agricultural curriculum for Fijians. Such a curriculum meshed with colonial policies designed to orient Fijians toward a rural, agrarian existence of subsistence farming and cash-cropping in copra and other revenue-generating ventures—this to subsidize a colonial economy heavily reliant upon Indian labor in sugar production. Only Fijian males of chiefly descent primed as medical practitioners, lower-level civil servants, or members of the Native Administration were considered for any education beyond that which prepared for a settled life in a rural village. The colonial administration similarly supported an agricultural and nonacademic curriculum for Indians. However, Indians resisted a curriculum that differed markedly from that provided for Europeans, the most privileged segment of colonial society. As Indians lobbied for an academic curriculum, many local Europeans resisted in turn, alarmed by the "rascality" of former indentured laborers vying for equality with Europeans. While such struggles marked educational developments throughout much of the colonial period, the years immediately preceding independence were defined by the most dramatic and rapid changes in Fiji's school system.

There were no dramatic shifts in the colonial administration's policies or overarching philosophy in education at the turn of the century. Funding for the selective schooling of European children continued. By a 1916 ordinance, Levuka Public School formally became a government school and Suva Public School was converted into two schools—Suva Girls Grammar and Suva Boys Grammar schools.[50] Meanwhile the administration's supplementary funding of schooling for the sons of Fijian chiefs also continued. By 1900, the Fijian industrial school known as Vulinitu was closed. In 1902 the Council of Chiefs preempted plans to establish the second industrial school slated for development with a more pointed request that any new schooling for Fijian nobles develop comparable curriculas for Europeans, devoid of a vocational track.[51] The renewed requests from chiefs came at a time when colonialists were reassessing the functions and roles of the Native Administration. In some European quarters, there were calls to dismantle what was regarded as an arcane, isolated Native Administration and that such would be the first step toward transforming the Fijian masses into full British subjects.[52] While such recommendations were offered with the ostensible objective of "freeing" the commoner masses from chiefly tutelage, the argument for a form of direct rule was also favored by Europeans who saw in the Native Administration an impediment to access to Fijian land and labor. One of the administrative reforms of this period was the slating of two Fijian seats for the Fiji Legislative Council selected from nominees of the Council of Chiefs beginning in 1904.[53] The colonial administration shifted its orientation toward Fijian education in ways that served administrative reforms.

For the colony's new governor in 1904, Sir Everard Im Thurn, greater English proficiency and clerical training of Fijian nobles translated into a more cost-effective, efficient auxiliary administration of traditional bureaucrats—and if balanced with a hidden curriculum that fostered identification with the Crown, the cultivation of loyal bureaucrats as well.[54] In 1906, the colonial administration reopened Vulinitu and rechristened it Queen Victoria School (QVS)—an upper-primary boarding school starting at Class 3 and progressing to Class 8, admitting roughly 80 students. QVS more closely approximated the model of an English public school than its predecessor but still fell short of replication given its special mission. The new school was to prepare students for positions in the civil service as scribes, translators, clerks, and as high-ranking officials in the Native Administration. The official curriculum was delivered in English and included English literature, geography, chemistry, and bookkeeping, as well as instruction on the functions, roles, structure, and responsibilities of the ranked titles within the Native Administration. A hidden curriculum emphasizing British traditions and history proved as important as instruction in typing and stenography:

The result of Queen Victoria-type education was that Fijian children learned MacBeth by heart and "acted" it out in front of polite but non-comprehending Fijian audiences. They learned to recognise their "ancestors the Anglo-Saxons" and to consider the heroes of their own countries' resistance against the invaders as being sanguinary agitators. And when they spoke their mother tongue, they were put in the corner with the dunce's cap....From this arose a cultural schizophrenia and a mystification which inculcated a complex of racial inferiority in young indigenous Fijians. The bemedalled Sukuna[55] with his oversized decorations and tail-coat epitomised this inferiority complex with his attempt to become "more British than the British."[56]

Shortly after QVS was founded, the administration established provincial schools as a selective alternative to mission schools for Fijian males. Six such strategically positioned schools were created from 1909 to 1926, financed through the provincial tax imposed on Fijians and with matching grants from the colonial administration. These upper-primary boarding schools had average enrollments comparable to QVS. The first was Lau Provincial School, established on Lakeba in 1909. Provincial schools had rigid admission standards overlaid with more tacit exclusionary practices. Only Fijian males who successfully passed an entrance examination gained entry, while each school had a quota on the number of students that could originate from each province.[57] Moreover, particularly in the founding years of provincial schools, students of chiefly background tended to receive preference over commoners. Curricula were intended to approximate the academic orientation of the more prominent QVS. The typical weekly schedule included fourteen hours of English, five hours of arithmetic, and one hour each of vernacular, history, geography, agriculture, hygiene, manual work, and singing, with all subject classes meeting for one-hour sessions. As was common in Fijian boarding schools, "agriculture"—ostensibly a subject class providing formal agricultural training—constituted little more than the use of student labor in the planting and harvesting of crops on the school's farmland for sustenance.[58]

The curriculum of QVS and provincial schools reinforced a heightened quest among the Fijian nobility for a quantitative and qualitative advantage in education. And just as colonialists regarded the training of chiefs in the cultural capital of English ways as a pragmatic means to promote bureaucratic efficiency, chiefs pursued investment in higher levels of education as an instrument for meeting Europeans on their own terms. Fijians with English fluency and "European-style training" were needed to serve as spokespersons and representatives of the Fijian people in the Legislative Council where matters of importance to Fijians were being decided.[59] For many colonialists and chiefs alike, optimal training in "English ways" was attained directly at the source, which meant Britain or alternatively in the Commonwealth dominions of Australia or New Zealand. Shortly after the closure of Vulinitu, members of the Council of Chiefs proposed that the school's highest performing students receive scholarships to study in New Zealand. When colonial administrative support failed to materialize, Council members resolved to create a fund to which each province contributed 350 pounds a year to educate Fijians abroad.[60] The education of the most prominent and distinguished Fijian statesman and scholar of the colonial era and the first Fijian to be appointed to the Fiji Executive Council as Secretary of Fijian Affairs, Ratu Sir Josefa Lalabalavau Vana'aliali Sukuna, was financed through such provincial funds.[61]

In 1928, the extant Suva Medical School program was expanded with the founding of the Central Medical School, which was housed in the Colonial War Memorial Hospital established five years earlier in Suva. By 1929, the new medical school expanded opportunities in medicine for Indians as well as Fijians as the Fijian-language curriculum that dominated the Suva medical program was replaced with English. Enrollment was also extended to students from other island territories in the region. Locally, the school's tendency to favor Fijian students from QVS served to perpetuate its links with Fijian chiefs.

The Wesleyan mission system continued to dominate in the provision of primary schooling for the Fijian masses. By 1907, the Methodists had moved the central training institute to Davuilevu near Suva, expanding their operations into a campus with a high school, a technical school, and a theological college—the latter providing three years of formal theological instruction in English for Fijian males. Meanwhile, for the Indian population, during the first decade and a half of the twentieth century, there were minimal schooling options.

Throughout most of the indenture period, from 1879 to 1920, the roughly 65,000 Indians who arrived on Fiji's shores remained wards of the CSR. In 1912, an ordinance required the CSR to provide a modicum of formal education for the children of indentured laborers. Representatives of the CSR saw limited value in schooling for indentured laborers beyond creating a docile, loyal labor force. In offering his perspective on the type of education most suitable for Indians, the manager of the CSR at the turn of the century stated that Indian children should have teachers of Indian nationality, should be taught in their vernacular, and should not be converted to Christianity. As he contended, "professed Christianity and a knowledge of English are almost invariably associated with rascality in the classes of Indians that came to Fiji." He recommended that "in every state-aided school, a Union Jack be hoisted, and that this be saluted by the scholars each morning, as is done with the stars and stripes in America."[62] This appeared to be a reaction to a few schools founded by Methodist missions for former indentured laborers who established rural tenant farm communities as cultivators on land leased from Fijians. There they attempted to reconstitute and consolidate many cultural institutions that had been compromised under indenture, including the panchayat and patrilineal, patrilocal extended families. Indian Methodist schools addressed community demands for schooling among those who preferred an English-language curriculum. However, both Hindus and Muslims, eager to maintain the integrity of their respective religious, linguistic, and broader cultural practices, resisted Christian schools that embraced the most offensive forms of proselytizing and continued to be served by the few Hindu and Muslim missions with vernacular schools.[63] Some free laborers, who were among the literate few, having arrived with some education, also attempted to fulfill unmet demands for schooling through volunteer-teaching. Freelance teachers provided free and private tuition to children and adults from their homes on an ad hoc basis, often working around their students' and their own plowing and cultivation schedules. The curriculum was delivered informally in individual and small group sessions and in vernacular languages, emphasizing Vedic and Islamic sacred texts and such expressive forms as *bhajan*, or rhythmic Hindu devotional songs.[64]

The passing of the Education Ordinance of 1916 was a watershed moment in Fiji's history of formal education. While, on the one hand, it heralded an increased and more varied role for the colonial government in local education, it also precipitated the establishment and eventual dominance of community control of schooling and its attendant ethnic segmentation in the form of the committee school. Among the provisions in the 1916 Ordinance was the establishment of a Board of Education, a Department of Education, and a Superintendent of Schools. Communities that wished to found a school were required to submit a formal proposal to the Board of Education for approval. The Board of Education, in turn, allocated building grants for new schools and awarded grants-in-aid for teacher salaries and other expenditures. The Ordinance also called for the use of English as a medium of instruction and for at least four hours of "secular teaching." Only schools that complied with these curricular guidelines were eligible for grants-in-aid.[65] While this new system of "assisted schools" placed the fewer Catholic schools in good stead, Methodist schools in Fijian villages, with their legacy of vernacular instruction, were at a decisive disadvantage in staffing teachers who could teach in English.[66] The English language requirement was revoked in 1917 when most schools fell short of meeting it.[67] In 1926, an amended ordinance called for the use of Hindi and Standard Fijian (Bauan) as languages of instruction in Indian and Fijian schools, respectively, up through Class 3, and thereafter to be replaced with English.[68]

Indian education expanded gradually following the implementation of the grant-in-aid system, with many "assisted" Indian committee schools established through the continued efforts of the Hindu Arya Samaj and Sanatan Dharma organizations, and by the 1920s, the Fiji Muslim League. Early on, the religious and community associations that managed and financed these committee schools became cogent symbols of an Indian resolve to provide for their own children's education in the face of relatively minimal government interest in Indian education. While Indian committee schools proliferated in rural areas and the mill towns in response to a high demand for schooling following the end of indenture,[69] former indentured laborers weary of agriculture migrated to urban areas. Many *Girmitiya* ventured to Suva where they joined a few hundred Gujerati "free immigrants" who began arriving in the late 1910s to establish small businesses as tailors and retailers in small shops. There they established a niche among non-European clientele, including Indian and Fijian workers with disposable income and in need of a range of goods and services unavailable or inaccessible in the major retail establishments that catered to Europeans.[70] Marists, Anglicans, and Seventh-day Adventists established Indian schools in urban areas in response to the growing urban Indian population.[71] In addition to maintaining two primary schools for Indians with Hindi as the language of instruction, the CSR offered grants to Indian mission and committee schools. One Indian government primary school was established in 1919 in western Viti Levu, part of the sugar cane belt where Indian cane-farmers remained concentrated after indenture. A 1926 Education Commission Report identified the local government's relative neglect of Indian educational needs and noted that it was a problem that warranted redress. However, there were no proposed strategies for expanding Indian education and emphasis was placed, instead, upon upgrading existing schools. At this time, it was determined that roughly 2,485 out of approximately 14,000 Indian children, or about 17 percent of children from six to twelve years of age, were attending school. Meanwhile, of these 2,485 pupils, a mere 333, or 13 percent, were girls.[72] Comparable enrollment figures for the school-aged European and Fijian populations were 91 percent and 80 percent, respectively.[73]

The 1916 Ordinance would, meanwhile, precipitate major changes in Fijian education. Methodist mission schools faced mounting difficulties in meeting the standards stipulated in the Ordinance. Numerous schools began to consolidate into central or "group schools" to save costs. The government recommended assuming control over mission schools in lieu of increased funding. While Methodists initially resisted transition of control, by 1931 there began a process of voluntary relinquishing of control. Thus, while the number of mission schools reached its peak in 1909 with roughly 1,046 primary schools operated by the Methodist mission, there followed a steady decline, such that by 1925, there were 684 such schools. By 1934, a mere nine years later, the number of Methodist primary schools had plummeted to twenty four, twelve of which were Fijian and twelve of which were Indian schools.[74] There were also a number of "mixed English" schools run by missions in urban areas that admitted Fijian and Indian students.[75] For most Fijian mission schools, administrative authority was transferred to District Councils and local committees. Funding came primarily from district funds supplemented by grants from the government, the provincial tax levied on Fijians and fundraising by local communities.[76] As was the case for committee schools, the formal establishment of

District schools required the approval of the Board of Education while a local committee oversaw management of schools under the administrative guidance of a district officer.[77] The rapid transfer of administrative control from Methodist missions to inexperienced local committees compromised the overall management of most committee schools.[78]

By the 1920s, as the colonial government assumed greater structural control over schooling, curricular issues gained wider importance, particularly the question of what type of education the administration considered most relevant to the Fijian and Indian populations and the needs of the colony. The prevalent view among colonialists was that an emphasis upon agricultural and vocational skills was most suitable for the Fijian masses and Indians while the curriculum in schools serving Europeans and, to a lesser extent, the Fijian nobility, should maintain its academic emphasis.[79] The Education Ordinance of 1916 had originally proposed such courses as nature studies as well as manual trades as core subjects. An Education Ordinance of 1929 reenacted many curricular provisions of the 1916 Ordinance, while offering additional curricular guidelines proposed by the 1926 Commission Report.[80] Throughout this period, the Department of Education assumed a more proactive role in standardizing curricular materials, including textbooks, course prescriptions, and timetables. By this time, the Indian population was making pointed demands for an academic English-language curriculum as a vehicle toward civil service and professional employment, while suspicious that the incorporation of agricultural and vocational curricula was intended to perpetuate their subordinate status in the colony.[81] To local Europeans, such Indian "militancy" became a matter of concern at a time of heightened labor union activity among Indian cane-cutters, and active Indian lobbying for enfranchisement and representation on the Fiji Legislative Council for Indian males.[82] The Indian demand for more schooling in general, and a curriculum comparable to European schools in particular, further stirred local European angst about Indian "rascality" that had been earlier articulated by representatives of the CSR and the local colonial administration.[83]

The relative lack of local administrative initiatives for Indian education exposed in the 1926 Education Commission Report sparked the interest of officials in the Colonial Office in London, who demanded to be kept abreast of developments on the matter.[84] Queries, monitoring, and critiques from the Colonial Office propelled greater resource allocation toward Indian education.[85] There were protestations by local Europeans that government schooling for Indians was not financially viable, that the committee school system was better suited to Fiji's social and economic conditions, and that existing schools should instead be supported and enhanced. Local administrators, nevertheless, responded by creating a few government schools for Indians during this period. Hence, while, in 1926, there was one government Indian primary school, four years later the first government-run Indian secondary school, Natabua Secondary School, opened. By 1936, five more government primary schools were established that catered for Indians.[86] The CSR also responded by increasing subsidies to Indian committee schools. In 1936, Arthur Mayhew—a joint secretary of the Advisory Committee on Education in the Colonies—arrived in Fiji from London by invitation to tour Fiji's schools and to ascertain the general status of Indian education; he departed with a generally favorable impression of Indian committee schools and apparently satisfied that the colonial government was making strides in improving Indian education.[87]

While the colonial government channeled more resources into creating Indian government schools, many Indians remained supportive of a committee system that enabled some community autonomy. Indian communities had come to regard schools in general as vehicles to raise their social and economic status in Fiji society, to erase the humiliation of the indenture experience, and to achieve social, political, and economic parity with the European population—but additionally to promote and reinforce valued cultural knowledge.[88] By the 1940s, Indian males resisted joining the armed forces in protest against de jure and de facto discriminatory policies in the colony at a time when high chiefs were enjoining Fijian males to enlist in the Fiji Battalion. After their enfranchisement in 1929, Indians also lobbied for increased representation from the three seats on the Fiji Legislative Council in protest of the five seats allocated for the markedly smaller European population. Then in 1946, census data revealed Indians had become a numerical majority in the colony. By then, the Department of Education passed an amendment stipulating that the facilities of all government schools be reserved exclusively for teaching purposes. This was widely interpreted as a calculated, unnecessarily intrusive measure designed to stymie the activities of a large, increasingly politicized population. Indeed, for many Indian communities, school facilities served as social and cultural centers for ceremonial and other events outside of school hours.[89] Ultimately, the committee system allowed the varied institutionalized practices and, in some instances, contradictory philosophies of a heterogeneous Indian population to find representation in the schools. Hence, among Hindus, the Arya Samaj reformist minority tended to discourage certain practices of the orthodox Sanatan Dharma majority, including child marriage, which the Arya Samaj defined as antiquated, deleterious, and a contributing factor in lower rates of school enrollment and overall educational attainment for Indian girls. Many among the Muslim minority also desired that their schools reflect features of Islam and include recitation of the Quran, proper instruction in the reading and writing of Urdu, Arabic, and Persian script, and observance of female modesty through the inclusion of *hijab* headscarves as part of girls' school uniform.[90] Hence, there grew a contingent that supported the relative autonomy of committee schools that allowed communities to preserve the multiple functions of schools as institutions of cultural production and as community nerve centers.[91]

While Indians were seeking access to an academic curriculum and to maintain some measure of control over their schools, Fijian leaders concurred with colonial administrators that an agricultural education was most suitable for an indigenous population that had managed to retain title to most of the land in the archipelago. In 1944, eighteen years after the Education Commission Report of 1926, Fijian high chief and Secretary of Native Affairs Ratu Sukuna articulated his support for the maintenance of an agricultural-based education for the Fijian masses:

To raise his standard of living he should make every use of his inheritance and, to ensure this, education in the early stages should as far as possible be undertaken amidst native surroundings and native forms of life in order to accustom the child to its true economic environment.[92]

He also suggested the need for education to facilitate a gender-based division of labor in Fijian communities, providing for the training of "farmers, mechanics, boat-builders, men skilled in indigenous handicrafts; girls with a practical knowledge of house-craft—home cleaning, cooking, washing, sewing, nursing—as well as men with academic qualifications together with clerks, teachers and native medical practitioners."[93] Here, it was also understood that "men with academic qualifications" would constitute a select group of Fijian males. Ratu Sukuna would argue, further, that the acquisition of skills necessary to create this division of labor would require "a more or less sound knowledge of English" and criticized the majority of rural Fijian primary schools as having been "left entirely in the hands of bodies that either could not afford to pay for good teachers or give too much religious bias to education."[94]

The support that Fijian leaders and colonial administrators expressed for an agriculture-based curriculum in Fijian schools was in tandem with protectionist policies. Throughout Fiji's colonial history, the movement of indigenous Fijians outside of natal villages was regulated and circumscribed by the Native Regulations. When migration restrictions were relaxed for Fijian males in the early 1900s, members of the Council of Chiefs became alarmed by the potential loss of young males' productive labor needed to meet the produce tax and other labor requirements in the villages. Many chiefs were also troubled by purportedly "corruptive" influences that an urban existence devoid of structure and guidance was said to pose to young Fijians. The concerns of chiefs grew when the CSR began recruiting Fijian labor on a small scale following the end of Indian indenture.[95] Most Fijian migrants sought temporary wage employment merely to pay for various amenities and returned to their rural villages. Still, there were colonialists who shared the concerns of chiefs. In 1928, an absentee tax was imposed on Fijians residing outside their natal villages to compensate for the loss of their labor, and to stave off a massive Fijian exodus from rural areas.[96] Fijian males continued to pursue unskilled and semiskilled employment where there was selective recruitment of Fijian labor, particularly in the areas of shipyard labor, native constabulary service, and with the beginning of gold extraction by the Emperor Gold Mining Company at Vatukoula in the mid-1930s, underground mining.

Fijian leaders like Ratu Sukuna recognized the potential for an academic curriculum to channel the aspirations of average Fijians away from village life. And while the proselytizing in mission schools was regarded as relatively benign, Ratu Sukuna lamented the "religious bias" as a diversion from a practical curriculum. In either case, the schooling for the Fijian masses was distant from the selective academic education for which Fijian nobles lobbied and attained for themselves. In effect, qualitative deficiencies in Fijian rural schools followed, in part, from the inordinate proportion of provincial resources allocated toward the development of elite schooling for the sons of chiefs.[97] An expatriate who surveyed Fiji's educational system in the early 1940s noted that, "The standard of education in Indian Committee schools is much higher than in Fijian schools. The majority of scholars reach a good Class 4."[98] Surviving mission schools were also observed to have higher educational standards than Fijian District schools:

That the standard of education in District schools is very low is admitted on every hand—over 51% of the pupils are in Classes 1 and 2; 73% in Classes 3 and under, 89% in Classes 4 and under. European teachers in such Fijian schools as those run by the missions in Suva (the standard of which is much higher than that of the District schools) frequently receive scholars from District schools whose parents desire for them better schooling than provided by District schools. Such teachers maintain that practically all the children who come to them from District schools have to be put down at least one class lower than they were in the District school so that it would probably be correct to say...that Fijian children receiving primary education in District schools reach on the average a standard not higher than class 2.[99]

Meanwhile, the priority placed on developing selective Fijian schooling continued into World War II and the years that followed. In 1944, the colonial administration discussed plans to establish a sister institution to QVS, providing an exclusive intermediate-level boarding school education for Fijian girls of rank.[100] Christened after the grand-daughter of King Cakobau, Adi Cakobau School (ACS) opened its doors to the first cohort of 98 enrollees in 1948. While missionaries had established boarding schools for untitled Fijian girls, Fijian females of rank could attend Roman Catholic schools and other "mixed English" schools in urban areas for an academically oriented English-language curriculum.[101] Outside of limited opportunities for teacher-training and a more selective training in nursing, the education of titled and untitled Fijian girls, and Indian girls alike, was oriented toward grooming in the "home sciences" to prepare young women for roles as mothers and as helpmates to their husbands. ACS was to offer more specialized training in "refinement" for the "future educated wives" of Fijian leaders. The English-language curriculum emphasized academic subjects, traditional music, dance, and crafts as well as instruction in the intricacies of chiefly protocol.[102] By 1950, QVS advanced to matriculation level. That same year, the process of amalgamating provincial schools for Fijian males into a single vocationally oriented boarding school—Ratu Kadavulevu School—commenced.[103]

The colonial administration eventually ventured into regulating teaching standards. In addition to formally posting all principals and teachers to government schools, by 1920, the administration required all teachers to be registered in order to receive salary grants-in-aid, contingent upon meeting a stipulated set of standards based on their teaching qualifications and "moral character."[104] The expatriate European teacher was initially the embodiment of teaching quality for Europeans and non-Europeans alike. Initially, such teachers originated from Britain. Then, in 1924 the Fiji-New Zealand Scheme of Cooperation was launched. Teachers from primary and secondary schools in New Zealand served teaching stints in Fiji schools, commanding lower salaries than British teachers but higher than local teachers. The presence of New Zealand teachers also made its mark on the curriculum bringing in a specifically New Zealand influence into courses and examinations.[105] Yet the Scheme was costly and resources were increasingly channeled into developing local teachers.

Christian missions and government both invested in the expansion of teacher-training. In 1929, the colonial administration founded Natabua Teachers Training College to provide formal training of Indian and Fijian males as primary schoolteachers. Government establishment of a teachers' college was propelled by concerns that teacher-training increase in quantity, quality, and degree of standardization. Female exclusion from the major teacher-training institutions, including the Methodist Davuilevu Training Institute, received heightened attention by the late 1930s. In 1934, the Ballantine Memorial School for Girls was established by the Methodist Missionary Society near Suva to provide professional and vocational training for females, including grooming prospective Fijian and Indian female teachers. A smaller institution for preparing Indian girls as teachers was also established in Suva and relocated to Lautoka after World War II.[106] The Seventh-day Adventist mission had its own modest boarding school system for the teacher-training of Fijians and Indians, both male and female, beginning in the early 1900s and, by 1940, had amalgamated them into the Fulton Missionary Teachers College. In 1942, Davuilevu finally opened its doors to females.[107] In 1948, the second government-sponsored teacher-training college, Nasinu Teachers College, was founded. Meanwhile, in 1935 the Roman Catholic Archdiocese established a teacher-training college for Fijian males at Cawaci on Ovalau, and in 1958, founded Corpus Christi Teachers College for primary schoolteachers.

By 1942, there were 30 Europeans, 26 Fijians, and 23 Indians teaching in government schools. Europeans made up the majority of teachers at Catholic schools, with 92 teachers, compared with 36 Fijian and 13 Indian teachers posted at Catholic schools. For the surviving Methodist schools, there were a total of 11 European, 33 Fijian, and 51 Indian teachers. The 177 teachers based at Fijian district schools were exclusively Fijian while the 146 teachers at Indian committee schools were Indian. Meanwhile, Fijian District schools were characterized by exceptionally and exceedingly high student–teacher ratios, with roughly 84 students per registered teacher, leading to the phenomenon of teachers instructing multiple classes simultaneously.[108]

The divergent cultural trajectories and social interests that colonial policies fostered between the major racial groups culminated in the development of two distinct teachers' unions, originating with the European-dominated Fiji Teachers Union (FTU). By 1934, Fijian teachers established their own break-away union, the Fijian Teachers Association (FTA). In 1947, teachers in all government and some assisted schools were formally designated civil servants. By this time, teachers in government schools and committee schools experi-enced disparate working conditions and standards of employment. While teach-ers in government schools benefited from favorable terms of employment, including relative job security and a reliable salary with pay raises, grant-in-aid teachers in committee schools had to rely on committee management to provide most of their salary and could be terminated from their positions at the caprice of managing bodies.[109]

The legacy of a range of colonial policies was one of fostering myriad forms of educational disparity. In addition to disparities based on rank among Fijians was a gender gap in educational attainment across racial groups. Missions and colonial administrators were slow to develop either exclusively female or co-educational institutions in the face of exclusively male institutions for non-Europeans. This is reflected in the more marked enrollment disparities in the first half of the twentieth century. By the 1930s, gender disparities in educa-tion were relatively negligible among Europeans and most dramatic among Indians. Hence, in 1933, European females made up 644, or 49.6 percent, of the Europeans enrolled in school. Among the 15,098 Fijians enrolled that same year, 6,020 students, or 40 percent were female. For the Chinese, there were 22 females out of a total of 79, or 28 percent. Finally, of the 4,585 Indi-ans in school, 24 percent were female. While increased access to schooling in subsequent years contributed to a lessening of gender disparities at the primary level, a significant gender gap persisted at the secondary level throughout the colonial period, during which time access to secondary school-ing remained relatively limited for non-Europeans. Hence, in 1946 European females made up 50 of the total 116 European students attending secondary school, or 43 percent; by 1960, females constituted 45 percent of the 408 European secondary students in Fiji. For Fijians, there were a mere four females out of a total of 191 Fijian secondary students, or 2 percent of all Fijian secondary students in 1946; by 1960, Fijian female representation had increased to 37 percent, or 620 out of a total of 1,662 Fijian secondary school students. Among the 211 Indians enrolled in secondary school in 1946, only eight, or 4 percent were female; by 1960, the proportion of Indian female secondary school enrollees had increased, but at 912 out of 3,211, still consti-tuting a relatively meager 28 percent of all Indian secondary school students. For the Chinese population, one student out of the twelve enrolled in second-ary school was female in 1946; out of the 157 Chinese secondary students that were enrolled in 1960, seventy-one students, or 45 percent, were female.[110]

Among the ethnic groups that faced the greatest educational neglect were Solomon Islanders. Recruitment of laborers from the Solomons had ceased by 1911. About 4,000 of the original 23,000 "Melanesian" recruits remained in Fiji after leaving the copra and sugar cane estates, many of whom were marginally absorbed into Fijian communities. Since the specter of a precarious and landless status awaited members of the largely male Melanesian population following marriage into patrilineal, patrilocal Fijian communities, some former recruits established their own small villages with the assistance of the Anglican Church. Building from a prior mission presence in the Solomon Islands, Anglicans assumed a virtually singular role in establishing mission schooling for Solomon Islanders, founding the first small Melanesian school in Ovalau in 1888, another in Suva in 1924, and one each in Levuka, Savusavu, and Nasinu by the 1950s.[111] Chinese who began to arrive as merchants in a second wave of immigration after World War I were absorbed into Catholic and Anglican schools in Levuka and Suva, while members of the more established community on Ovalau were eventually admitted in small numbers into Levuka Public School. By the 1930s, the Chinese community established one committee primary school in Suva and another in Lautoka.[112] By then, growing numbers of children of Chinese descent claimed English and even Fijian as a first language, with a corresponding deemphasis upon Chinese culture. Part-Europeans navigated access to different schools, continuing to have variable experiences gaining acceptance into European institutions based on meeting the social standards set within European circles, but also attending mixed and Fijian schools. For Rotumans, primary schooling available on their island was made compulsory while many journeyed to the urban centers of Viti Levu for secondary school education and employment. By the end of World War II, populations from one of Britain's other Pacific colonies, the Gilbert and Ellice Islands, were relocated to the Fiji archipelago contributing to minor demographic changes in the colony. In 1945 the people of Banaba, or Ocean island—then classified as part of the Gilbert Islands (present-day Kiribati)—began settling onto Rabi island located 93 miles south of Vanua Levu, after the British had excessively mined Banaba of its phosphates rendering it uninhabitable. Then, in 1947, former residents of Vaitupu island—part of the Ellice Islands (present-day Tuvalu)—settled on Kioa about 5 kilometers from Taveuni. Hence, by the late 1940s, the provision of schooling now included several hundred Banaban and ethnic Tuvaluan children. Meanwhile, Europeans consistently enjoyed the largest amount of both public and private investment in their education and, hence, by all measures—including levels of schooling, degree of financial assessment and in quality of facilities—far exceeded all other groups in relation to their population size within the archipelago. Yet the source of disparity that generated the most official interest was that which would emerge between the two major racial groups—Indians and Fijians.

By the 1940s, there were recognized qualitative differences between Indian and Fijian committee schools at the primary level. Once the colonial administration moved towards increased development of postprimary schooling, disparities in educational attainment became more pronounced. "Native policies" and economic development, together, created the conditions that reinforced and widened existing educational disparities. Regulations restricting Fijian movement and migration became more strident in the years immediately following World War II with the reorganization and consolidation of a new Fijian Administration. This coincided with Britain's increased subsidization of its colonial economies, spawning a wave of development initiatives in Fiji that included the expansion of secondary schooling. In addition to establishing more government secondary schools, the colonial administration extended the grant-in-aid system to secondary schools.[113] Yet most rural Fijian villages were geographically isolated from these economic and educational developments. This was particularly the case for Fijian communities in the interior of Viti Levu and on the smaller islands of the archipelago. With roughly 80 percent residing permanently in rural areas,[114] a majority of Fijians gained little from the expansion of secondary schooling. Indian populations were concentrated in and around such mill towns as Nausori and Labasa and the port town of Lautoka; even rural settlements of the sugar cane belt were characterized by a relatively developed infrastructure and less isolation from major urban centers compared with rural Fijian villages. Indians not only benefited from the growth in government secondary schools and increased expenditure on secondary schooling in urban centers but also established committee secondary schools as well.[115] The Rama Krishna Mission, Fiji Muslim League, and Fiji Gujerati Society founded their own secondary schools to address the limited supply and growing demands for post-primary schooling among their Indian constituencies.[116]

Still, the local European population's privileged access to educational resources prevailed. Yet as Indians' educational status improved, the growing disparities between Fijians and Indians continued to generate the most concern among Fijian and European leaders. Qualitative disparities at the primary school level persisted into the 1950s. An annual colonial report for 1957 indicated that 100 out of a total of 155 Indian primary schools were providing schooling up to Class 8 while in only 35 out of 326 Fijian primary schools was this the case, with most Fijian primary schools only reaching Class 5.[117] The impact of post–World War II educational developments on disparities is demonstrated in the accelerated rates of Indian secondary school enrollment and a corresponding widening gulf between the groups from the early 1940s through the late 1950s. In 1942, there were 54 Europeans enrolled in secondary school, all of whom attended exclusive Suva Grammar School. That same year, there were five Fijian secondary students, all of whom were males attending Marist Brothers College, also in Suva. At this time, there were a total of 77 Indian students in secondary schools, all of whom were males, 36 of whom were attending Natabua Secondary and 41 of whom were enrolled at Marist

Brothers College.[118] Hence, Europeans, who constituted less than 1 percent of the population, made up 40 percent of all secondary school students in the colony. Two years later, there were 75 Europeans, 28 Fijians, 150 Indians, and 4 Chinese students attending secondary school.[119] In 1946, a total of 191 Fijians, 211 Indians, and 116 Europeans were enrolled in secondary school; the respective percentages of Fijians and Indians in the colony's population were 45 and 46 percent. That is, Europeans, who were still enumerated at less than 1 percent of the population, represented 22 percent of secondary school students while enrollment rates for Fijians and Indians were roughly at par. By 1955, there were 667 Fijians, 1,375 Indians, and 349 Europeans enrolled in secondary school, or an Indian secondary school enrollment rate slightly more than twice that for Fijians. The year 1959 was associated with a dramatic increase in the number of Indian secondary school students while Fijian numbers remained almost constant. Hence, there were 679 Fijian students, 2,542 Indian students, and 314 European students enrolled in secondary school.[120] In short, Indian secondary school enrollment was just under four times that of Fijian secondary school enrollment at a time when Fijians and Indians represented roughly 44 percent and 48 percent of the population, respectively.[121]

By the early 1960s, provisions in the Regulations restricting indigenous Fijian migration were rescinded, initiating a flow of Fijians from rural areas into urban centers largely in search of employment. However, qualitative deficiencies in Fijian rural district and committee schools first identified in the 1940s had made their mark as Fijian migrants found their employment prospects limited to unskilled labor. Many rural Fijian migrants also arrived for the express purpose of providing educational opportunities for their children, while nonmigrating parents who arranged for children to reside with urban relatives were similarly motivated. Low-income housing estates were erected to absorb rural migrants entering the unskilled labor force. The dramatic Fijian rural-urban drift that marked the late 1960s could not blunt the impact of persistent and striking disparities. Hence, Indian rates of secondary school enrollment were nearly double that of Fijians, while their participation in the professions and managerial and high-level positions in the civil service was nearly seven times that of Fijians, along with long-standing disparities in commerce participation. The proliferation of secondary schools, in conjunction with economic growth of the post–World War II period, had supported the development of a sizeable Indian middle class which pursued higher education, professional training, and employment in such areas as medicine and law. Indians also expanded their role in commerce as proprietors of duty-free shops and taxi businesses with the growth of tourism by the 1960s.

By this time, Fiji was in the throes of decolonization, and Fijian political leaders groomed for leadership positions in the polity were contemplating the wider implications of educational and economic disparities between Fijians and Indians. A Fiji Education Commission Report of 1969 devoted an entire chapter to causes of and attendant remedial measures for "the disparity in educational performance between children of the two major racial groups in Fiji."[122] Among the factors identified were rural poverty, physical fatigue of children traveling long distances by foot or punt to school, a shortage of quali-fied Fijian primary schoolteachers, and physical conditions compromising the quality and delivery of educational services for remote rural Fijian schools. The latter includes the unique challenges that issue from proximity to farming com-munities, where children are expected to contribute labor as their families meet the needs of rural subsistence. While more urban children have access to run-ning water, electricity, produce markets, groceries, and refrigerators, rural children must collect water from rivers and streams for washing, gather fire-wood for cooking, and assist in the gardening and harvesting of crops. More-over, when farming is the primary or sole source of income, families have been forced to weigh the financial and educational costs and benefits of keeping children in or out of school during harvesting periods.

With Fijian education equated with rural education, and with dramatic defi-ciencies associated with rural education, measures for improving rural educa-tion were widely conceived as critical to ameliorating the "Fijian education problem." Provisions included funding grants to upgrade extant rural primary schools. Additionally, to help relieve the financial burdens of rural and urban poor in meeting the basic costs of education, a fee-free tuition scheme was ini-tiated in 1973 starting with Class 1 students and extending to successive class levels in subsequent years. The Commission Report gave particular emphasis to government's need to address the growing demand for secondary school edu-cation among Fijians, the vast majority of whom were still residing in rural areas devoid of secondary schools. It was recommended that government estab-lish six strategically positioned junior secondary schools in rural areas. To accommodate the preponderance of rural Fijian primary schools ending at Class 6, junior secondary schools would begin admitting students at Class 7 or Form 1 level up through Form 4. Despite initial protestations from rural Fijian communities that anything short of full-fledged secondary schools advancing to Form 6 would disadvantage their children educationally, the process of establishing junior secondary schools commenced after political independence. From 1970 to 1976, the originally planned six schools had blossomed into 43 institutions as more rural Fijians lobbied for junior secondary schools in the vicinity of their villages. By the 1980s, the fears of many rural Fijian parents were realized; junior secondary schools were widely dismissed as deficient and "underdeveloped" secondary schools[123] that suffered the compounding bur-dens of rural location—including difficulties in the recruitment and retention of qualified teachers, substandard facilities, equipment shortages, physical isola-tion, and management problems due to the limited educational background and experience of school committee members.[124] As early as the mid-1970s, government had begun converting several junior secondary schools into com-plete secondary schools and pledged to assist with the conversion of more. By 1993, 22 junior secondary schools had been consolidated into complete secondary schools, with government vowing to "ensure that these schools are well equipped and fully staffed with trained teachers."[125] The development of rural junior and complete secondary schools, along with rural-urban drift, helped bridged the more striking educational disparities of the previous decades when rural secondary schooling was nonexistent. Additionally, urban centers responded to Fijian migration by revising the intake in secondary schools. A dual system emerged, widely referenced as the 6-6, 8-4 system. Some secondary schools commenced at Class 7, or Form 1, to accommodate Fijian students who attended primary schools that ended at Class 6. Other secondary schools continued the prevailing pattern of admitting students at Form 3, taking in students who attended primary schools ending at Class 8.

Students studying in a rural secondary school in the heart of the interior of Viti Levu. Carmen M. White.

In 1968, the regional University of the South Pacific (USP) was founded in Suva with United Nations' funding. The new tertiary institution made the legacy of disparities in access to secondary schooling particularly glaring, with markedly low rates of Fijian admission and matriculation. Affirmative action policies were implemented in line with recommendations of the 1969 Fiji Education Commission. Fijians were allocated 50 percent of Public Service Commission (PSC) scholarships with a lower minimum score requirement on qualifying examinations compared with non-Fijians. Then, in 1984, the Fijian Affairs Board (FAB) launched a Fijian scholarship scheme to address persistently high rates of attrition and lower rates of matriculation for Fijians at university level. FAB scholarships covered all of tuition, room and board, and a living and book allowance. Two years after the launching of the FAB scholarship, and roughly 14 years after the initiation of affirmative action PSC scholarships, 1986 census data revealed the persistence of Fijian underrepresentation in the professions—disparities that an increase in tertiary enrollments was intended to help address. At just over 48 percent of the population, Indians made up 69 percent of the upper-level professional and managerial sector, representing a decisive majority among doctors, engineers, judges, lawyers, and dentists and a significant percentage of general managers. Fijians, who represented 46 percent of the population, constituted a mere 17 percent of the upper-level professional sector, holding a slight majority as high-ranking state officials and as production managers in the Fijian-dominated Ports Authority. Among middle-level professionals, the respective percentages for Fijians, Indians, and the nebulously defined, but, in this case, largely European "Others" were 35 percent, 54 percent, and 10 percent, respectively. Here, Fijians constituted a marked majority only in the area of nursing, while they were significantly represented among primary schoolteachers, the clergy, service personnel in the tourism industry, and in positions throughout the Fijian-dominated Armed Forces.[126]

The root causes of Fijian underrepresentation in the professions, at the USP, and in overseas tertiary institutions were lost in the ensuing controversies surrounding Fijian tertiary scholarships; all of these indicators of lower Fijian socioeconomic status were preceded by disparities in secondary school enrollment—disparities that prevailed despite Fijians' increased access to secondary education. Two major factors contributed to the quandary of persistent imbalances at the secondary school level. First, rural Fijian migrants who attended junior secondary schools faced difficulties completing their secondary education up to Form 6, which was the minimum educational requirement among employers of skilled labor. An urban secondary boarding institution was established specifically to accommodate Fijian students from rural junior secondary schools, offering Form 5 and 6 classes.[127] Still, over 60 percent of the Fijian population was still residing in rural areas where secondary schooling remained limited. Second was the expansion of the secondary school curriculum. In 1987, Form 7 classes were introduced, replacing the previously instituted "foundation courses," or preparatory courses for entry into the university. Markedly higher numbers of Indians than Fijians were attaining schooling up to Form 7 and beyond. Very few rural secondary schools, either Fijian or Indian, were endowed with the resources to offer a Form 7 curriculum. In its first year, 29 Fijians and 311 Indians were enrolled in Form 7. By 1993, Indian enrollment was 1,766, or 62 percent while Fijian students made up 873 enrollees, or 31 percent of Form 7 students. At the time, Fijians and Indians represented 43 percent and 47 percent, respectively of the country's population.[128]

One factor that had been directly and indirectly linked to ethnic disparity and broader issues of equity in access to schooling was differences in teaching quality. Hence, proposals to improve rural education included recruitment drives for highly committed and qualified teachers to serve in rural schools. Typically lacking in such comforts as electricity, indoor plumbing, and treated water, and isolated from the entertainment and other amenities of urban centers, rural schools have historically represented "hardship posts" to urbanites, which has encumbered such recruitment efforts. Meanwhile, appointment to rural schools is widely interpreted as a form of punishment meted out to urban teachers for such "misdeeds" as failing to generate adequate results on external examinations. This has further contributed to the association between rural schools and less qualified teaching and an overall lower standard of education.

When the government of an independent Fiji established two teacher-training institutions to enhance and standardize teaching quality, the contention was that rural students would benefit by default. The first government teaching institution established after independence in 1977 was Lautoka Teachers College, for the training of primary schoolteachers. This became the sole government teacher-training college for primary schoolteachers following the closure of Nasinu Teachers College in 1982. By 1992, the government created the Fiji College of Advanced Education (FCAE) for the professional development of secondary schoolteachers. From its inception, the USP established an education program for secondary schoolteachers, offering bachelor's degrees in education, as well as two-year teacher's diplomas in a subject area of specialization. With the expansion of teacher-training, educators and administrators began to differentiate between the instructional quality of graduates of teacher-training institutions and university graduates devoid of formal training. The university was attributed with placing an inordinate emphasis on theory while devoting minimal attention to practical instruction in teaching, yielding teachers who transferred the pedagogical practices of the university into the secondary school classroom. Thus, while USP graduates were often described as arriving in classrooms with copious notes for students to copy from the chalkboard and "lecturing" to students, graduates of the FCAE were identified as trained in the psychology as well as mechanics of classroom teaching, thereby more effectively "teaching" students. By extension, primary schoolteachers—98 percent of whom were trained by 1999—came to epitomize "good teaching." At the end of the twentieth century, there were several venues to receive training to become a "good teacher." In addition to the two government teacher-training institutions, there were the surviving teacher-training institutions established by missions prior to independence—Corpus Christi Teachers College and Fulton Missionary Teachers College.

By the 1970s, teacher prescriptions prepared by the Ministry of Education began to actively encourage inquiry learning and experimentation with material supplementary to standard texts. However, educators and administrators in Fiji noted that very few teachers, particularly those having taught for years without teacher training, have felt confident enough to engage the curriculum as creative agents and innovators in the classroom.[129] Meanwhile, the resort to "traditional" classroom pedagogy, in the form of rote methods of teaching and learning, and a tendency to "teach to the test" in preparation for external examinations remains common in Fiji classrooms. The same script is played out daily in many classrooms where the teacher poses textbook questions to students from a specific lesson plan in the book; students then provide answers on cue from the text for that lesson, often using wording identical to the textbook. Administrators are widely conversant in discussions on rote-teaching as, at worst, stifling creativity and, at best, encouraging memorization of a litany of facts. They have increasingly looked to teacher-training to encourage alternative methods. Meanwhile, schools in Fiji, as elsewhere, are modeled upon an individualistic and competitive quest for high grades, high examination scores, placements in the most prestigious schools, scholarships, academic awards, praise, and other forms of academic recognition and distinction, which many observers argue is specifically in conflict with Fijian cultural values that place emphasis upon communalism and parity in access to resources. The transmission of skills in Fijian communities did not involve competition or ranking, as members of the same *mataqali* were all expected to attain the same level of competence in their skills as fisherman, carpenters, or in other roles. Schools have not been designed to bring all students up to a standard level of performance but, instead, encourage students to strive as individuals for positions of relative advantage. Some observers in Fiji contend that the chasm between the ethos of western-imported schooling and Fijian culture is one that has never been, and perhaps will never be, bridged.

The impact of the teaching enterprise on educational disparity and broader educational access dovetails with curricular issues. In the years following independence, much discussion centered on ways to make Fiji's school curriculum more socially, culturally, and economically relevant to local conditions. The question of relevance had been consistently broached since the inception of mass education, but the answers varied depending on the social location of those defining "relevance." During the precolonial period of mission schooling and throughout the colonial period under British rule, the majority of the "subject" population was excluded from any role in deciding the form and content of schooling. In the post–World War II era, the colonial government's emphasis upon developing post-primary education with an agricultural and vocational orientation, particularly for Fijians, prevailed—despite increased demands from the Fijian and Indian masses that access to selective academic schooling be broadened. Hence, by 1947 Ratu Kadalavu School strengthened its agricultural and vocational curriculum while agricultural and technical centers were planned in Vatukoula, Levuka, and Lautoka.[130] The Koronivia Farm Institute opened in 1954, renamed the Fiji School of Agriculture in 1962, offering diplomas in tropical agriculture. This was followed by the founding of Derrick Technical Institute in 1963 for training in manual trades.[131] By the 1950s, there were no local institutions of higher education. Only a select group of Fijians and Indians received scholarships from the local government, India, and through the Colonial Development Welfare Act to attend universities in New Zealand, Britain, and India.

With the shift in political power on the eve of independence, localization of curricula and expansion of schooling accelerated. This included responding to the demands for more academic schooling while also developing curricula in synchronisation with the economic, ecological, and social conditions of a budding multiracial, multilingual island nation. In 1968, the same year that the University of the South Pacific was formally established as a regional institution of higher education to meet local and regional needs for professional and technical training, the Curriculum Development Unit (CDU) was created as a division within the newly established Fiji Ministry of Education.

The charge of the CDU included initiating the creation and revision of courses, examinations, teaching manuals, textbooks, and other curricular materials. The CDU, in initiating the revision of curricula over a century in the making, commenced the labor of making education responsive and adaptive to the changing needs and demands of Fiji society. The CDU has strived toward reform where feasible while maintaining continuity where desired. Hence, English would remain the medium of instruction throughout secondary school, along with the policy of using vernaculars up through the first four years of schooling for the various ethnic groups, as established in the amended language Ordinance of 1926. Fiji's Ninth Development Plan included the recommendation to extend vernacular status to Tamil, Arabic, and Chinese in the schools. In 1986, the New Zealand University Entrance Examination was replaced with the Fiji School Leaving Certificate. Then in 1987, Fiji's legacy of divide-and-rule colonial policies reared its head when the electoral defeat of the Alliance Party precipitated two coups d'etat by the Fijian-dominated Fiji Armed Forces. The Alliance Party—a multiracial coalition representing European and Indian business interests and dominated by established Fijian leaders and which had held power since independence—had been voted out largely by Indian and urban Fijian voters who favored the more populist message of the newly elected Fiji Labour Party (FLP). Although the FLP had a Fijian prime minister, the cabinet was largely Indian. A Fijian nationalist movement emerged in opposition to the election of the FLP and in support of the military coups that followed. The 1970 constitution was rescinded and, by 1990, replaced with another calling for the office of prime minister, president, and a majority of seats in the House of Representative to be reserved for Fijians. In the immediate aftermath of the coups and the unprecedented political instability it generated, a sense of insecurity reigned in non-Fijian communities. Indians intermittently kept their daughters out of school out of fear of potential sexual assaults while many families migrated. The promulgation of the 1990 constitution spawned more waves of emigration among Indian teachers and other professionals. By the late 1980s, the Indian numerical majority of previous decades was undergoing a steady reversal.

Among the myriad responses to the coup crisis were retrospectives among civic leaders and educators about schooling's failure to instill Fiji's "unity in diversity" motto adopted after independence. The racial or ethnic, class, and ethno-regional underpinnings of the coups were expressed in the ways that opposition and support of the military intervention articulated with ethnic, class, and ethno-regional divisions within the Fiji population and suggested fissures in Fiji society that had been decades in the making. The curriculum was implicated as failing in the area of constructing a common national identity that could simultaneously embrace the cultural diversity of its population, underscoring educators' struggle to enlist primary and secondary education in nation-building.[132] Even by the mid 1990s, locally produced texts provided a rather uncritical interpretation of the country's colonial history.[133] Many parents, educators, and administrators also contended that the school curriculum had become abstract and removed from the daily experiences of rural students in particular, while many Fijians suggested that curricula were culturally discordant with Fijian communities, compounding other areas of educational disparity. In short, over 100 years after the introduction of formal education, schools in Fiji had become, at once, foreign and familiar.

The structure of Fiji's schooling system was increasingly implicated by some as, at best, perpetuating and at worst, actually fomenting cultural insularity and racial exclusivity. By the end of the twentieth century, schooling continued to be shaped by patterns of educational management and control initiated in the early twentieth century. Government schools remained in the minority while state-assisted committee and religious schools constituted the overwhelming majority. By 1999, among all primary schools, 529 were managed by committees, 130 by religious organizations, 36 by special cultural organizations, and 18 by other private or special institutes. Only 2 primary schools were government-run. Among secondary schools, there were 73 committee schools, 54 managed by religious organizations, 11 run by cultural organizations, and one each run by the Fijian Affairs Board, the Rabi Council, the Rotuma Council, and a private institute. There were twelve government secondary schools in 1999.[134] That is, most schools in Fiji were managed directly by committees and religious organizations serving a particular ethnic, religious, and/or residential community. Meanwhile, the ethnic and racial segmentation that characterized schools coincided with the bifurcation of teachers' unions that harked back to the colonial period, with the formerly European-dominated FTU now identified with Indians and the FTA sustaining its profile as a predominantly Fijian and, increasingly Rotuman, union. Critics of Fiji's current system have argued that multiracial schools are the key to building community across ethnic and racial boundaries. Pointing to the limitations of using English as the mediating language between communities, some have suggested, as well, that students be required to attain proficiency in Fijian and Hindi.

One way in which cultural and social bonds have been reinforced in schools is through ubiquitous fundraising. In the decades that the grant-in-aid system institutionalized the committee school, the fundraising enterprise had developed into a standard repertoire of activities held in government and committee schools alike. These include bazaars, *soli*, *gunupeni*, and other school events. The most labor intensive event is the annual bazaar. Here, food and handicraft stalls are erected on school premises, and floats are constructed and chaperoned by students and staff parading in the streets around the school. For *soli*, a feast is provided while feasters offer a monetary donation in the amount of their choice. For *gunupeni*, participants pay for each cup of *yaqona* consumed by fellow participants. *Soli*, *gunupeni*, and similar fundraisers are associated with the more regular and intensive fundraising of committee schools. During spell-a-thons, students petition sponsors to pay a stipulated amount of money for every word spelled correctly by the student during a spelling test. Additionally is "Mufti Day," when students pay for the privilege of wearing "colored clothes," or clothes other than the uniform, to school. Fundraising in both government and assisted schools is also assumed by other auxiliary institutions affiliated with schools. For example, many schools have a Parent Teachers Association (PTA). While its name recalls its equivalent in the United States, in Fiji, the typical PTA is confined to an institutional organ for parents to organize and shepherd fundraising activities. Another school organization that plays a fundraising role is the "Mother's Club," most widely known for preparing hot lunch meals for schools. Most secondary schools have alumni organizations, or "Old Students' Association," whose members may maintain active involvement in the fundraising of their alma mater. For the most prestigious secondary schools, these associations also serve social and professional functions for members, providing connections for graduates entering the job market, and cultural and social mentoring across generations.

While government schools are guaranteed financial assistance from the Ministry of Education in maintenance costs, the provision of textbooks, and subsidization of school fees, fundraising is still undertaken in government schools to finance projects, activities, services, or purchases not covered by the state. For schools run by committees and religious organizations, the grant-in-aid system subsidizes teacher salaries and other expenses. For religious schools, partial funding is also provided by respective religious organizations. However, most operating costs, including utilities, for nongovernment schools are garnered through fundraising, school fees, and "building fees" levied on parents. To ensure fee payments, committee schools have often resorted to such punitive measures as dismissal of individual students for unpaid fees. Meanwhile, in all schools, parents incur the costs for uniforms, textbook fees, and school supplies. By 1982, the tuition-free scheme launched in 1973 had expanded to Class 8 but was exclusive of Forms 1 and 2.

Another significant and prevailing legacy of the colonial era, despite increased localization of curriculum content, is Fiji's examination-orientated school system. With increasing centralization of Fiji's school system during the colonial period came more examinations as an expedient measure by which to assess and sort students. Some localization of the curriculum and examinations, after decades of imported British and New Zealand examinations, had commenced by the mid 1950s. A research committee was established and entrusted with formulating a new curriculum for primary schools, which included the production of new textbooks. The objective was to "produce a course which will develop good citizens, with an adequate standard of general knowledge, but which will also make special provision for requirements for a mainly agricultural society in the South Pacific."[135] A Secondary School Entrance Examination (SSEE) was instated by 1954 following the growth in post-primary schooling, while in 1955, the Cambridge Overseas Junior Certificate Examination was replaced with the Fiji Junior Certificate (FJC) Examination.[136] Following the replacement of the New Zealand School Leaving Certificate with the Fiji School Leaving Certificate in 1986, the Form Seven Fiji Examination (FSFE) was formally implemented in 1987, replacing the New Zealand University Entrance Examination.

By 1989, the secondary school curriculum consisted of three "courses," with three corresponding external examinations—the FJC, FSLC, and FSFE. The FJC course consists of Forms 3 and 4, concludes with the comprehensive FJC examination, and comprises the core subjects of English, mathematics, basic science, social studies, physical education, music, and art and crafts. Electives include accounting, economics, secretarial studies, technical drawing, metalwork, woodwork, home economics, and Fijian/Hindi. For the FSLC course in Forms 5 and 6, the number of subjects expand as classroom streams are divided into "general," "arts," and "science." Along with core requirements of English, mathematics, and physical education, students in Forms 5 and 6 general take history, Fijian/Hindi and geography. Forms 5 and 6 arts choose among commercial practice, economics, wood technology, technical drawing, clothing and textiles, and typewriting. Forms 5 and 6 science take biology, chemistry, and physics. The Form 7 curriculum comprises ten required courses: English, mathematics, economics, accounting, technical drawing, physics, chemistry, biology, geography, and history.

The examination-orientation of Fiji's school system is well entrenched and widely recognized, particularly at the secondary school level. The esteem and efficacy of teachers, the relative achievement of students, and the relative prestige of secondary schools are based on where students measure on the A-B-C grading scale of the FJC, FSLC, and FSFE papers. Local newspapers make examination results available for public consumption, publishing school names, students' names, and their respective grades in each subject, along with the overall pass rates for all schools. The reputation of the most selective secondary schools rides on high examination scores and grades; hence, the admission requirements of such "selective" schools include a minimum standard of performance on the SSEE, FJC, or FSLC to maintain the "good name" of such schools. Parents, in turn, aspire to have their children attain one of the limited number of seats for admission to prestigious, high-profile secondary schools with names like Yat Sen Secondary, Marist Brothers, Indian College, International School, Queen Victoria School, and Adi Cakobau School; meanwhile, such selection processes reproduce class inequities. Teachers are also implicated in the high or low performance of their students on examination results and so experience tremendous pressure to perform and "produce results." Mid-year examinations and end-of-year annual examinations administered to students in Forms 1, 2, 3, and 5—widely referred to as the "nonexam Forms"—are of less immediate interest to teachers, students, and parents. The high importance reserved for external examinations is also reflected in the devaluation of nonexaminable subjects, or the PEMAC classes—an acronym for physical education, music, and arts and crafts. PEMAC tend to be the most neglected classes characterized by the least structured curriculum and ad hoc teaching methods.

Perhaps the centrality and value placed on examinations makes its greatest impression upon students during the prize-giving ceremony held in all secondary schools and which commemorate the various achievements of students at the end of each academic year. There is no distinct formal graduation ceremony following the completion of Form 6 or Form 7. Passing marks on the FSLC and FSFE constitute certification that one has "graduated" or attained "academic qualifications" that potentially open professional and academic doors. Yet it is during the prize-giving ceremony where the rewards of plodding through examinations with high scores take on a particular immediacy for

Form 3 students in a rural school on the eve of an annual examination. Carmen M. White.

students as early as Form 1. Here students in each Form class receive first- and second-place awards for attaining the highest and second highest composite scores on external and annual examinations while a "progress award" is given to the student who attained the greatest gains in points in their composite score for their annual examination in relation to their mid-year examination. Additionally, "character awards" are issued to students in each Form class. Prizes for awardees may consist of textbooks, a set of school supplies, novels, or similar items. Certificates of merit are also awarded to students in each Form classroom who received the highest examination score in each examinable subject or the overall distinction in nonexaminable subjects. A large trophy, and in some schools, other major prizes are presented to the school dux, or the student achieving the highest score on the FSLC or the FSFE. Other awards include trophies for excellence in athletics, the annual oratory contest, and any academic competitions (e.g., "Chemquiz") in which students at a given school have participated and successfully distinguished themselves.

THE PRESENT

There remains recognition that Fiji's system of schooling, which has generated a population with a 92 percent literacy rate, must continue to evolve while meeting the varied and specific needs of a multicultural island nation in the twenty-first century. In addressing the diversity of Fiji's population, educators continue to stress the need for a school curriculum that fosters genuine, mutual understanding and respect between ethnic and racial groups and which also promotes the cause of gender and class equity.[137] This has taken on a particular urgency in the new millennium as the nation attempts to heal from two more coups d'etat. A civilian coup in 2000 was staged by Fijian businessman George Speight, ousting the country's first elected government with an Indian prime minister. Mahendra Chaudry's People Coalition Party (PCP) came to power in 1999 under a revised 1997 constitution that eliminated provisions mandating Fijian political dominance. The civilian coup that included the holding of PCP members hostage led to an intervention by the Fiji Armed Forces, the installation of an interim government, and new elections. In December of 2006, the military ousted the 2001-elected government led by Prime Minister Laisenia Qarase; Military Commander Frank Bainimarama staged the coup, charging the Qarase government with corruption and impropriety in pardoning the 2000 coup conspirators. Once again, there were ethnic fault lines in the expressed support and resistance to the coups, although they are less apparent in the most recent coup.

Formal schooling continues to stand at the center of disparities that contribute to societal divisions. The marked gender differences in enrollments of the colonial period have waned. Female educational attainment at primary and secondary school levels now slightly exceeds that of males owing to higher female retention rates, along with significant gains in higher education with women as likely to receive a scholarship for tertiary studies at the USP as males. However, males receive the majority of scholarships for tertiary studies overseas and continue to dominate overwhelmingly in math, the natural sciences, technology, and other fields still regarded as male domains.[138] Survey data for 2000 indicated high representation of women in the professions, but primarily in the area of teaching, with women constituting 57 percent of primary school-teachers and 48 percent of secondary schoolteachers. Meanwhile, only 14 percent of secondary school principals are female, while women constitute only 20 percent of legislators, senior government officials, and managers.[139] Hence, gains in education have yet to translate into access to the seats of power in the educational system and beyond.

In 2000 a ten-year strategic plan titled "Blueprint for the Protection of Fijian and Rotuman Rights and Interests and the Advancement of their Development" was launched, building upon prior affirmative action policies for Fijians. The Blueprint was to address persistent disparities in educational attainment and representation in the professions, despite significant Fijian gains in educational attainment in the last two decades, such as high rates of secondary school attrition and lower rates of Form 7 enrollment among Fijian students. Survey data for 2000 also indicated that Fijians, who constitute 54 percent of the population, represented 23 percent of legislators, senior officials, and managers while Indians, who made up 34 percent of the Fiji population, constituted 54 percent within the same professional sector even with migration of Indian professionals.[140] In addition to various loan schemes, the Blueprint includes increased allocation of funds for Fijian Affairs Board scholarships, additional resources, and other tactical support for pre-dominantly Fijian schools, as well as the construction of a Form 7 College for Fijian students.[141] Meanwhile, other educational disparities that warrant redress are generating increased attention. This includes ameliorating the lower educational status of marginalized groups classified as "other Pacific Islanders," particularly Solomon Islanders, but additionally Banabans and Kioans, as well as the disadvantaged status of those living in poverty across all ethnic and racial categories.

Deficiencies in education for the disabled have also been of heightened concern. Developments in schooling for the disabled are relatively recent, and the expansion of special education services and institutions continues. Schooling created to meet the various needs of disabled children commenced in the 1960s with the creation of the Crippled Children's Society in 1967. Additional schools were founded by the 1980s. There are currently seventeen schools in Fiji that cater specifically to children with disabilities. Such schools receive government support as well as charitable donations while many civic leaders and local celebrities contribute time and material resources as committee members of such schools. Lautoka Teachers Training College has embarked on a teacher-training course specifically for special education, but it is acknowledged that meeting the needs of special education, which falls under the primary school curriculum, will require more resource allocation in all areas, including the provision of adequate teacher-training and remuneration.[142]

Preschool education is another relatively new frontier in Fiji education garnering increasing attention. Preschools were first established as privately-run institutions by expatriates in the early 1940s by European parents for their own children, and regulations for such schooling were not established until 1962. By 1999, there were 9,223 children enrolled in preschools with 494 recognized schools.[143] Of particular interest is the identification of differential access to preschool and kindergarten as a new mitigating factor in future academic performance and educational attainment.[144] This has become of sufficient interest in recent years that, in 1998, the Ministry of Education began to provide salary grants to preschool teachers in rural areas.[145]

Schools are looked upon with heightened expectations to reflect the growing and global emphasis on information technology, both in terms of the official curriculum and in the delivery of educational services. Yet, while the Fiji government has provided some computer training for teachers since the late 1980s, it has yet to assume an active role in promoting information technology through schools. In the face of limited teacher-training in information technology, and marked imbalances between rural and urban schools in access to computers, relative access to information technology stands to become another arena of inequality. By 2000, roughly sixty out of 154 secondary schools provided instruction in computing and information technology, largely through the initiatives of school committees.[146]

Compulsory education was instituted at the dawn of the new millennium with the passing of the Compulsory Education Regulation in 1997, which calls for parents or guardians to ensure that children attend school from Class 1 up through Form 4, or up to fifteen years of age.[147] This was facilitated by government expansion of tuition-free education up through Form 4,[148] and more recent pledges to extend fee-free education up through Form 7. Promotion of tuition-free schooling up through Form 7 occurs on the heels of the founding of another tertiary institution as an alternative to the USP and FIT—the University of Fiji. Founded in 2005, the private institution located in Lautoka offers foundation courses, certificates, diplomas, and bachelor's degrees in fields ranging from business to the humanities with plans to expand into various post-graduate programs.[149]

CONCLUSION

Prior to the introduction of mass education to the Fiji Islands, families, clans, and apprenticeships were the institutions enlisted with the task of imparting behavioral prescriptions, relevant skills, and knowledge for the indigenous population of the archipelago. By the mid-1800s, these institutions were supplemented or syncretized with and, in some areas of knowledge, supplanted by the epistemology of the Christian missionary through the mission school.

Thereafter, local conceptions of what to learn, how to learn, and what was recognized as worthy of knowing in Fijian communities would change. Significant changes in education also accompanied the demographic shifts that followed once the archipelago was ceded to Britain as a Crown colony. Imported formal schooling in Fiji developed along a rapid trajectory in the twentieth century. This included the growth of community establishment; investment and control of schools through voluntary associations; rural committees and religious organizations; colonial administrative involvement in education through the creation of a grant-in-aid system; the development and attempted redress of quantitative and qualitative disparities in educational attainment based on gender, "race," rank, and region; the expansion of secondary education; and the push for compulsory schooling in tandem with the expansion of fee-free schooling.

DAY IN THE LIFE OF A FIJIAN PRIMARY SCHOOL STUDENT

Asenaca is a ten-year old Fijian female in Class 6 who attends a predominantly Fijian committee school in a semirural town near Suva. The following chronicles a typical school day for Asenaca from sunup until sundown. The year is 1997.

6:00 A.M.: Asenaca wakes up on a Tuesday morning, says her morning prayer, then washes her face before helping her mother lay out the morning breakfast, which consists of white tea—that is, black tea with milk, sweetened with locally produced sugar—and loaves of bread, purchased fresh from the corner store. Asenaca and her mother slice the bread and place it on two plates next to a container of margarine for spreading.

6:30 A.M.: Asenaca, her mother, father, and two brothers, Adriu and Mosese, sit down for their first meal of the day. Asenaca's father says, "Masu," or "We pray," and offers a prayer of thanks before they partake in their meal. As they enjoy a leisurely breakfast, the day's schedule and other small talk are the focus of discussion.

7:00 A.M.: After clearing the breakfast dishes, Asenaca goes to have a bucket bath with water warmed from the kitchen stove, then dons her school uniform of a maroon tunic and matching *sulu*.

7:30 A.M. Asenaca sits down with her mother to check her homework.

7:45 A.M. Asenaca grabs her backpack and sets off for school with her younger brother, Adriu, who is in Class 3, and her elder brother, Mosese, who is in Form 5 and attends a secondary school farther down the road. They meet some classmates along the way and walk together.

8:00 A.M. Upon arriving at school, Asenaca and Adriu go to their respective classrooms as Mosese continues on to his school. Asenaca, along with classmates who also arrived early, perform "morning duties," or various tidying operations to help prepare the school and their classroom for the school day that will formally commence in fifteen minutes. All of the children are

supervised in their task by the teachers assigned to "general duties" this morning, Mrs. Rokosoi and Mr. Chand. Asenaca and her female peers are most
actively involved in using *sasa* brooms, made of coconut fronds, to sweep the
sidewalks that border their concrete and wood classroom blocks. They also help
collect any stray refuse they find on the lawn and classroom floor, along with
any other debris and deposit it all in one of the two large metal trash barrels in
the school quadrangle. Anytime students are on the concrete paths bordering
their classrooms when a teacher or other staff member approaches, they
respectfully yield the path by stepping off and away from the sidewalk until the
teacher or staff member has passed. After taking wooden chairs down from
wooden desktops, students settle down in their seats in preparation for "Form
time." Asenaca takes her seat at a front desk on the lefthand side of the classroom where most of the girls are seated. Her desk is right next to one of the
windows that line the length of both sides of their classroom block. She enjoys
the breeze that streams in intermittently through the opened louver blades on
this warm morning.

8:15 A.M.: As the Form teacher enters the room for Form time, Asenaca and
her twenty-eight classmates rise briskly from their chairs.

"Good morning, class," Mrs. Naidu greets them.

"Good morning, ma'am!" the students recite in unison and remain standing
until Mrs. Naidu asks them to be seated. Her brief morning announcements
include telling the class how exciting the upcoming bazaar will be. After
announcements, Mrs. Naidu leaves the room, on her way out reminding the
students that since it is Tuesday, they will be having their weekly assembly; then
she relinquishes the classroom to the teacher of the first subject class of the day.

8:30 A.M.: The school siren shrilly rises and falls to sound the beginning of
the first class period. Students once again rise from their seats with the arrival
of Mr. Kadavu, the math teacher, whom they greet. He greets them in turn
before asking them to be seated. Before beginning the day's lesson, he reminds
the students that their first six class periods will be shortened from their regular
thirty-five minutes since they will be having their assembly today and so will
need to get through their lesson more quickly. Thirty minutes of math is followed by social science, then two periods of basic science, all in the same classroom as each subject teacher arrives and relieves the next subject teacher.

10:30 A.M.: The fifteen minute recess begins. As teachers head to the staff-
room for their morning tea, students emerge from their classrooms and pass
into the lawn quadrangle to participate in a range of merriments, such as touch
rugby, rock-paper-scissors, singing and dancing. Asenaca sits on the lawn having an intense conversation with three of her best friends from her class while
reviewing the homework assignment for their upcoming English class.

10:45 A.M.: The siren sounds to announce the end of recess and the beginning of the fifth class period. Asenaca and her classmates resume their seats and
wait for the arrival of their teacher for the next subject class, which is a double
period of Fijian today.

11:45 A.M.: Assembly begins in the multipurpose hall. Students arrive before the staff and are seated closely together on the floor, shoulder to shoulder, knee to knee, knees against backsides. They all face the two rows of chairs that will soon be occupied by the principal, assistant principal, and teachers. The staff strolls into the assembly hall. One of the teachers approaches the microphone positioned in front of the staff to offer the devotion, which, today, focuses on the importance of being humble and obedient and to place service to others over pride and conceit. This is followed by the address by the principal, who makes announcements and reminds students to do their part to make the school bazaar a rounding success. Students remain seated until all staff have left the assembly hall.

12:05 P.M.: Lunch time begins. As soon as students leave the assembly hall, they make a dash for the vendor with his portable "tuckshop," or the lunch canteen, which consists of a transparent trolley encased in glass and wood, positioned near the quadrangle of the school compound. The tuckshop vendor becomes the center of attention, and the quadrangle is bustling with activity as students congregate to purchase curry-spiced peas, *bhuja*, fried potatoes, and *gulagula*, or small, fried "doughnut-holes" sold in brown hand-sized paper bags. A myriad of other spicy, fried finger foods and Fijian and Indian delicacies are also available for purchase. There are also wrapped hot meals with generous helpings of curried chicken with rice, and chop-suey or baked chicken or pork with boiled *dalo* (taro) and *rourou*, or the green leaves of the *dalo* plant cooked with onions and coconut cream. The hot meals were provided by the Mother's Club, of which Asenaca's mother is a member. An ice cream vendor is also on the scene as usual selling ice cream cones and popsicles. The youngest children are assisted in their purchases by older children and teachers.

Asenaca already knows what she will eat today. On this day, she and two friends pool some money together to purchase a plate of chop-suey. They stretch out on the lawn, sharing their food while in intense discussion about a video that one of the girls saw at a neighbor's house on Saturday.

12:50 P.M.: Before the resumption of classes, students perform their afternoon cleaning detail under the supervision of teachers. Aseneca and a few other female classmates sweep the inside of their classroom while others sweep the classroom sidewalks.

1:05 P.M.: Students have resumed their classroom seats and are ready for the last three class periods of the day. For Asenaca's class today, this is a double period of English in the classroom followed by music in the multipurpose hall.

3:00 P.M.: Asenaca's class returns from music; and as Mrs. Naidu enters the classroom, she commands that the class settle down and clean up before they leave. Asenaca and her classmates help place chairs on desktops, collect pieces of stray paper, and generally tidy up the classroom. Once Mrs. Naidu dismisses them, they stream out excitedly in groups and head home absorbed in their conversations, singing and general merriment, glad to be retiring from a long school day. Adriu is waiting for Asenaca in front of his classroom.

3:15 P.M.: Asenaca, Adriu, and her friends walk home.

3:35 P.M.: Asenaca and Adriu set their backpacks at the entrance of their home, take off their shoes, and place them on a mat at the door's entrance. Mosese arrives within minutes. They all prepare to do chores around the house before their mother supervises Asenaca in a short math homework assignment.

5:00 P.M.: With homework and chores completed, Asenaca asks if she can go to their neighbor's house to watch an after-school children's program on television. Her mother consents but tells Asenaca that she must be home within an hour to help with dinner.

6:00 P.M.: Asenaca returns home hurriedly to help her mother prepare one of her favorite meals, chicken curry with *dalo* and for dessert, *vudi vakasoso*, or ripened plantain drizzled with coconut milk and grated coconut meat.

8:00 P.M.: Asenaca prepares her uniform for the following school day and places her completed homework in her backpack before saying her evening prayers and going to sleep.

TIMELINE

1200–1000 BC	Austronesian-speaking ancestors of indigenous Fijians begin settling the archipelago.
1835	British missionaries David Cargill and William Cross arrive in the Lau group in the eastern region of the archipelago, spearheading the introduction of vernacular bible literacy throughout the archipelago.
1857	Wesleyans establish a central training institute for male Fijian pastor-teachers at Mataisuva.
1874	Fiji is ceded to Britain as a Crown colony.
1879	The first contingent of indentured laborers are brought to Fiji from India to labor on sugar cane plantations.
1916	An Education Ordinance is passed making provisions for a Board of Education, a Department of Education, a Superintendent of Schools, and a grant-in-aid system to subsidize nongovernment schools.
1918	An ordinance is established requiring that all teachers be registered.
1920	Indian indenture officially ends.
1924	The Scheme of Cooperation Agreement begins between Fiji and New Zealand whereby New Zealand teachers are posted to teach in Fiji schools.
1928	The Central Medical School is established as a regional institution in Fiji.
1929	Natabua Teachers Training College is established as the first government teacher-training institution.
1947	Nasinu Teachers College is established.
1947	All teachers in government schools and some assisted schools are declared civil servants.
1955	The New Zealand Overseas Junior Certificate is replaced with the Fiji Junior Certificate.
1968	The Laucala Campus of the University of the South Pacific is established in Suva, through United Nations sponsorship, as a regional tertiary institution, officially opening its doors the following year.

1970	Fiji attains political independence from Britain.
1973	Tuition-free education is initiated beginning with students in Class 1.
1986	New Zealand University Entrance Examination is replaced with the Fiji School Leaving Certificate at the Form 6 level.
1987	Form 7 replaces the New Zealand-based Foundation course as preparation for tertiary programs.
1987	After the electoral defeat of the Alliance Party, the Fiji Armed Forces stages two coups d'etat, ousting the democratically elected Fiji Labour Party from office, precipitating an exodus of non-Fijian professionals from the country.
1992	The Fiji College of Advanced Education is founded as the first teacher-training institution for secondary school teachers.
1997	Schooling is formally made compulsory from Class 1 to Form 4.
1999	The People's Coalition Party is elected into office with Mahendra Chaudhry as Fiji's first Indian prime minister.
2000	A civilian coup d'etat is staged against the People's Coalition government by a Fijian businessman, generating a hostage crises. The impasse that follows leads to intervention by the Fiji Armed Forces and the establishment of an interim government.
2000	The ten-year affirmative action strategic plan, known as the "Blueprint," designed to promote the educational and economic advancement of Fijians and Rotumans, is launched.
2001	The United Fiji Party headed by Laisenia Qarase is elected into office.

NOTES

Carmen White would like to express her sincerest appreciation to all of the students, teachers, administrators, and everyone else in Fiji who, directly and indirectly, played a role in making her ethnographic research in Fiji possible. She would also like to recognize the U.S. Fulbright-IIE doctoral research grant that funded her dissertation research.

1. *Fiji Today* 2005/2006. http://www.fiji.gov.fj/uploads/FijiToday2005-06.pdf (accessed December 28, 2006).

2. Ibid.

3. Ibid.

4. In Fiji nomenclature practices, "Fijian" is used specifically to designate the indigenous people of the islands, while "European" refers to all "whites" or those of Caucasian ancestry regardless of national origins.

5. Patrick Kirch, *On the Road of the Winds: An Archaeological History of the Pacific Islands Before European Contact* (Berkeley: University of California Press, 2000).

6. Epeli Tagi, "Fijian Identity," (MA thesis, University of the South Pacific, 1991); and Thomas Williams, *Fiji and the Fijians, Vol. 2. The Islands and Their Inhabitants* (London: Paternoster Row, 1858).

7. Williams, *Fiji and the Fijians.*

8. Ibid.

9. Ibid.

10. Ibid.

11. Ibid.

12. J. W. Burton and Wallace Deane, *A Hundred Years in Fiji* (London: Epworth Press, 1936).

13. Albert Schutz, *The Fijian Language* (Honolulu: University of Hawaii Press, 1985).

14. James Calvert, *Fiji and the Fijians: Vol. 2, A Mission History* (London: Paternoster Row, 1858).

15. J. R. Clammer, *Literacy and Social Change: A Case Study of Fiji* (Leiden: E.J. Brill, 1976).

16. Ibid.

17. Burton and Deane, *A Hundred Years in Fiji*; and Clammer, *Literacy and Social Change*.

18. Clammer, *Literacy and Social Change*.

19. W. L. Allardyce, "The System of Education in Fiji," in *Educational Systems of the Chief Crown Colonies and Possessions of the British Empire, including Reports on the Training of the Native Races [1908]* (London: Dawsons of Pall Mall, 1968).

20. Clammer, *Literacy and Social Change*.

21. Ibid. 64.

22. Burton and Deane, *A Hundred Years in Fiji*.

23. Clammer, *Literacy and Social Change*, 90–91.

24. A. W. Thornley, "Fijian Methodism, 1874–1945: The Emergence of a National Church," (PhD diss., Australian National University, 1979).

25. Thornley, "Fijian Methodism."

26. Ravuvu, *Development or Dependence*. See also Christina Toren, "Symbolic Space and the Construction of Hierarchy: An Anthropological and Cognitive Developmental Study in a Fijian Village," (PhD diss., University of London, 1986).

27. Ravuvu, *Development or Dependence*; and Toren, "Symbolic Space and the Construction of Hierarchy."

28. Thornley, "Fijian Methodism."

29. Clammer, *Literacy and Social Change*.

30. Cecil Mann, *Education in Fiji* (Melbourne: Melbourne University Press, 1935).

31. Thornley, "Fijian Methodism."

32. Ibid.

33. Burton and Deane, *A Hundred Years in Fiji*; and Thornley, "Fijian Methodism."

34. Aloesi Suguta, "Squatting in Fiji," in *In Search of a Home*, ed. Leonard Mason and Pat Hereniko (Suva: University of the South Pacific, 1987).

35. J. D. Legge, *Britain in Fiji, 1858–1880* (London: MacMillan, 1958).

36. Aduru Kuvu, *The Solomons Community in Fiji* (Suva: South Pacific Social Sciences Association, 1974).

37. Ahmed Ali, "Fiji: The Fiji Indian Achievement," in *Pacific Indians: Profiles From 20 Countries* (Suva: University of the South Pacific, 1981).

38. Claudia Knapman, *White Women in Fiji, 1835–1930: The Ruin of Empire?* (Sydney: Allen & Unwin, 1986).

39. Knapman, *White Women in Fiji*.

40. Allardyce, "The System of Education in Fiji."

41. Desmond Lance Kelly, "The Part-Europeans of Fiji," (MA thesis, University of Wellington, 1966).

42. Allardyce, "The System of Education in Fiji."

43. Kenneth N. James, "Schooling in a Colonial Setting: An Account of the Government School for Fijian Boys, 1881–1900," (MA thesis, La Trobe University, 1981).

44. J. Horne, *A Year in Fiji: An Inquiry into the Botanical, Agricultural, and Economical Resources of the Colony* (London: Edward Stanford, 1881), 140–41.

45. Horne, *A Year in Fiji*, 141.

46. Allardyce, "The System of Education in Fiji."

47. H. Landers and V. Miles, *The Fiji School of Medicine: A Brief History and List of Graduates* (Kensington: University of New South Wales, 1992).

48. Margaret Jolly, "Other Mothers: Maternal 'Insouciance' and the Depopulation Debate in Fiji and Vanuatu, 1890–1930," in *Maternities and Modernities: Colonial and Postcolonial Experiences in Asia and the Pacific*, ed. K. Ram and M. Jolly (Cambridge: Cambridge University Press, 1998).

49. Burton and Deane, *A Hundred Years in Fiji*, 100.

50. Knapman, *White Women in Fiji*.

51. James, "Schooling in a Colonial Setting."

52. Deryck Scarr, *Ratu Sukuna: Soldier, Statesman, Man of Two Worlds* (London: Macmillan Education Limited, 1980).

53. Ibid.

54. Simione Durutalo, "Internal Colonialism and Unequal Regional Development: The Case of Western Viti Levu, Fiji," (MA thesis, University of the South Pacific, 1985).

55. Fijian high chief, scholar, and statesman of renown during the colonial period, Ratu Sir Josefa Lalabalavau Vana'aliali Sukuna was the first Fijian to serve on the Fiji Executive Council and as secretary of Fijian Affairs.

56. Durutalo, "Internal Colonialism," 159.

57. F. B. Stephens, *Report on Education in the Colony of Fiji*, Fiji Legislative Council Paper No. 18 of 1944 (Suva: Government Printer, 1944).

58. Stephens, *Report on Education in the Colony of Fiji*.

59. Scarr, *Ratu Sukuna*.

60. Ibid.

61. Ibid.

62. A. Ali, *Plantation to Politics: Studies on Fiji Indians* (Suva: University of the South Pacific, 1980), 30.

63. J. P. Bhagirathi, "The Education Ordinance of 1916: Its Impact on Subsequent Educational Developments," (MA thesis, Auckland, 1970).

64. Rajesh Chandra, *Maro: Rural Indians of Fiji* (Suva: South Pacific Social Sciences Association, 1980).

65. Bhagirathi, "The Education Ordinance of 1916."

66. Mann, *Education in Fiji*.

67. Bhagirathi, "The Education Ordinance of 1916."

68. A. I. Mayhew. *Report on Education in Fiji. Legislative Council Paper No. 3 of 1937* (Suva: Government Printer, 1936).

69. Stephens, *Report on Education in the Colony of Fiji*.

70. Brij Lal, *Broken Waves: The Fiji Islands in the Twentieth Century* (Honolulu: University of Hawaii Press, 1992); and Ali, "Fiji: The Fiji Indian Achievement." By 1936, Ali estimates the Gujerati population had increased to 2,500.

71. Mann, *Education in Fiji*.

72. Clive Whitehead, "Education in Fiji: A Study of Policy, Problems and Progress in Primary and Secondary Education, 1939–1973," (PhD diss., University of Otago, 1975).

73. Helen Tavola, *Secondary Education in Fiji: A Key to the Future* (Suva: University of the South Pacific, 1991).

74. Mann, *Education in Fiji.*

75. Mayhew, *Report on Education in Fiji.*

76. Ibid.

77. Stephens, *Report on Education in the Colony of Fiji.*

78. Mayhew, *Report on Education in Fiji.*

79. Education Commission 1926. *Report of the Commission. Fiji Legislative Council Paper No. 46 of 1926* (Suva: Government Printer, 1926), 17.

80. Bhagirathi "The Education Ordinance of 1916."

81. Clive Whitehead, "Education and the 'Indian problem' in colonial Fiji, 1920–1945," *Education Research and Perspectives*, 8.

82. Whitehead, "Education in Fiji."

83. Whitehead, "Education and the 'Indian Problem.'"

84. Ibid.

85. Ibid.

86. Mann, *Education in Fiji.*

87. Whitehead, "Education and the 'Indian Problem.'"

88. Ali, *Plantation to Politics.*

89. Bhagirathi, "The Education Ordinance of 1916."

90. Esther Williams, "A Study of the Education of Girls with Special Reference to the Education of Indian Girls," (BA thesis, Melbourne University, 1937).

91. Bhagirathi, "The Education Ordinance of 1916."

92. Scarr, *Ratu Sukuna*, 307.

93. Ibid. 340.

94. Ibid. 340.

95. Scarr, *Ratu Sukuna*, and Timothy J. Macnaught, "'We Seem to no Longer be Fijians': Some Perceptions of Social Change in Fijian History," *Pacific Studies* 1 (1977), 15–24.

96. Legge, *Britain in Fiji.*

97. Carmen White, "Historicizing Educational Disparity: Colonial Policy and Fijian Educational Attainment" *History of Education* 32 no. 4 (2001), 345–65.

98. Stephens, *Report on Education in the Colony of Fiji*, vii.

99. Ibid.

100. Colonial Office Annual Report on Fiji for the Year 1947 (London: Your Majesty's Office, 1949).

101. Williams, "A Study of the Education of Girls."

102. Mai Na Ruku Ni Veidakua: The Story of Adi Cakobau School (Videorecording, Pasifika Communications, 1998).

103. Colonial Office Annual Report on Fiji for the Year 1950, 36–37.

104. Bhagirathi, "The Education Ordinance of 1916."

105. Tavola, *Secondary Education in Fiji.*

106. Stephens, *Report on Education in the Colony of Fiji.*

107. Ibid.

108. Ibid.

109. Bhagirathi "The Education Ordinance of 1916."

110. Department of Education Report, 1960.

111. Kuva, *The Solomons Community in Fiji*; and Talalelei Tapu, "The Solomonis of Ovalau" in *In Search of a Home*, ed. Leonard Mason and Pat Hereniko (Suva: University of the South Pacific, 1987).

112. Colonial Office Annual Report on Fiji for the Year 1947.

113. Whitehead, "Education in Fiji."

114. N. McArthur, *Report on the Census of the Population*. Fiji Legislative Council Paper No. 1 of 1958. (1956).

115. S. Singh, "Trends in Secondary Education in Fiji: A Study of the Trends, Past and Present, and Programmes and Prospects of Future Development,"(MA thesis, University of Leeds, 1972).

116. Ali, "Fiji: The Fiji Indian Achievement."

117. Colonial Office Report on Fiji (London: Her Majesty's Stationary Office, 1958).

118. Stephens, *Report on Education in the Colony of Fiji*.

119. Ibid.

120. Department of Education, Annual Report for the year 1959, Legislative Council of Fiji Paper No. 15 of 1960.

121. Department of Education, Annual Report for the year 1960, Legislative Council of Fiji Paper No. 29 of 1961.

122. Fiji Education Commission, *Education in Modern Fiji*, vi.

123. Helen Tavola, "Secondary Education in Fiji: An Investigation Into School Effectiveness in a Changing Society," (PhD diss., London, 1990).

124. Tavola, "Secondary Education in Fiji."

125. Ministry of Education, *Annual Report* (Suva: Government Printer, 1993); and Fiji's Ninth Development Plan, 1986–1990, "Policies, Strategies and Programmes for National Development," (Suva: Government Printer, 1986), 139.

126. Social Indicators for Fiji, No. 5 (Suva: Government Printer, 1989).

127. Clive Whitehead, *Education in Fiji Since Independence: A Study of Government Policy* (Wellington: New Zealand Council for Educational Research, 1986).

128. Ministry of Education, *Annual Report*.

129. Francis Mangubhai, "Fiji," in *Schooling in the Pacific Islands: Colonies in Transition*, ed. R. M. Thomas and T. N. Postlethwaite (New York: Pergamon Press, 1984).

130. Colonial Office Annual Report on Fiji for the Year 1947.

131. This became the Fiji Institute of Technology in 1978.

132. Subramani, "Reinscribing Vision" in *Learning Together: Directions for Education in the Fiji Islands* (Suva: Government Printer, 2000).

133. Social science textbooks and English readers alike often contained explicit and implicit messages and themes that conveyed a culminating benevolence of missionary intervention and colonial rule. For example, texts granted relatively greater focus upon the celebration of missionaries and other primary architects of British intervention than upon the myriad forms of oppression and exploitation that followed directly and indirectly from indenture and protectionism. Meanwhile, locally produced texts on other societies often enlisted outmoded references, such as "Red Indians" and "Negroes" for the U.S. population.

134. Helen Tavola, "Status Report," in *Learning Together: Directions for Education in the Fiji Islands* (Suva: Government Printer, 2000).
135. Colonial Office Annual Report on Fiji for the Year 1953 (London: Her Majesty's Stationery Office, 1955).
136. Colonial Office Annual Report on Fiji for the Year 1957 (London: Her Majesty's Stationery Office, 1958).
137. Subramani, "Reinscribing Vision."
138. Helen Tavola, "The Education of Women and Girls," in *Learning Together: Directions for Education in the Fiji Islands* (Suva: Government Printer, 2000).
139. Tavola, "The Education of Women and Girls"; and Fiji Islands Bureau of Statistics, Key Indicators, Employment and Wages, December 2006, http://www.statsfiji.gov.fj/Social/paid_employment.htm (accessed March 12, 2007).
140. Fiji Islands Bureau of Statistics.
141. *Fiji Today.*
142. Helen Tavola, "Special Education," in *Learning Together: Directions for Education in the Fiji Islands* (Suva: Government Printer, 2000).
143. Suliana Siwatibau, "Early Childhood Education," in *Learning Together: Directions for Education in the Fiji Islands* (Suva: Government Printer, 2000).
144. Wadan Narsey, *Academic Outcomes and Resources for Basic Education in Fiji Disparities by Region, Ethnicity, Gender and Economic Background* (Suva: University of the South Pacific, 2004).
145. Siwatibau, "Early Childhood Education."
146. Esther Batiri Williams, "Information Technology and Distance Education," in *Learning Together: Directions for Education in the Fiji Islands* (Suva: Government Printer, 2000).
147. *Fiji Today.*
148. Tavola, "Status Report."
149. University of Fiji. http://www.unifiji.ac.fj/index.htm (accessed March 12, 2007).

BIBLIOGRAPHY

Books

Ali, Ahmed. 1980. *Plantation to Politics: Studies on Fiji Indians.* Suva: University of the South Pacific.
Clammer, J. R. 1976. *Literacy and Social Change: A Case Study of Fiji.* Leiden: E.J. Brill.
Fiji Education Commission. 1969. *Education for Modern Fiji: Report of the 1969 Fiji Education Commission, Fiji Legislative Council Paper no. 2.* Suva: Government Printer.
Fiji Islands Education Commission/Panel. 2000. *Learning Together: Directions for Education in the Fiji Islands.* Suva: Government Printer.
Lal, Brij. 1992. *Broken Waves: The Fiji Islands in the Twentieth Century.* Honolulu: University of Hawaii Press.
Mann, Cecil W. 1935. *Education in Fiji.* Melbourne: Melbourne University Press.
Mayhew, A. I. 1936. *Report on Education in Fiji. Legislative Council Paper No. 3 of 1937.* Suva: Government Printer.
Narsey, Wadan. 2004. *Academic Outcomes and Resources for Basic Education in Fiji: Disparities by Region, Ethnicity, Gender and Economic Background.* Suva: Institute of Education, University of the South Pacific.

Norton, R. 1990. *Race and Politics in Fiji*. Brisbane: University of Queensland Press.
Stephens, F. B. 1944. *Report on Education in the Colony of Fiji, Fiji Legislative Council PaperNo. 18 of 1944.* Suva: Government Printer.
Tavola, Helen. 1991. *Secondary Education in Fiji: A Key to the Future.* Suva: University of the South Pacific.
Whitehead, Clive. 1986. *Education in Fiji Since Independence: A Study of Government Policy.* Wellington: New Zealand Council for Educational Research.

Periodicals

White, Carmen M. 2003. "Historicizing Educational Disparity: Colonial Policy and Fijian Educational Attainment." *History of Education* 32, no. 4, 345–65.
Whitehead, Clive. 1981. "Education and the 'Indian Problem' in Colonial Fiji, 1920–1945." *Education Research and Prospectives* 8, 76–88.

Chapter 4

SCHOOLING IN NEW ZEALAND

Gregory Lee and Howard Lee

BEFORE THE NINETEENTH CENTURY

Given its distance from other lands it is not surprising that New Zealand was one of the last places to be settled by Polynesian migrants, probably sometime in the thirteenth century. European explorers sailed into the South Pacific in the mid-seventeenth century. Abel Tasman, the Dutch explorer, attempted to land on the South Island in 1642 and, later, on the west coast of the North Island but without success. It was not until 1769 that the Englishman Captain James Cook arrived on board the *Endeavour*. Cook returned to New Zealand in 1773 and in 1777. By the late eighteenth century, hundreds of seal hunters from Australia, North America, and Britain were landing on the southern coast of the South Island and slaughtering seals, the skins of which were then sold in China, America, and England. Whalers, along with flax and timber traders, were also regular visitors to New Zealand until the early 1830s.

Prior to the arrival of planned European settlement in the early 1800s, Maori youth were not formally educated in schools but in their homes and wider village communities. Parents accepted responsibility for teaching the language, oral traditions, and appropriate ways of behaving to each of their children. In their communities, Maori youth learned important survival skills such as cooking, fishing, gardening, house-construction, hunting, and weaving. Young men whose fathers were chiefs (*rangatira*) also received detailed instruction, often in a *whare wananga* (house of learning), in tribal law from expert elder males (*kaumatua*). These educational traditions continued well into the latter part of the nineteenth century.

NINETEENTH CENTURY

Colonial Education and Society

The style and content of primary, secondary, and university education in nineteenth century New Zealand society mirrored existing educational practices in England and/or Scotland. The British missionaries who survived the journey by ship between 1816 and 1840 brought with them the social characteristics and the desire for similar institutions of the society from which they came. The massive economic and social changes then occurring in Britain and Ireland led many citizens to consider emigration to the colonies as a remedy for their economic and social distress.

Between 1816 and 1840, formal education in New Zealand was provided by missionaries—in particular, Thomas Kendall—under the auspices of the Anglican Church Missionary Society (CMS). The Society's brief was to proselytize the Maori, an objective entirely consistent with contemporary British missionary practice in many parts of Africa and the East. Under the direction of the Rev. Samuel Marsden, then senior chaplain to New South Wales, Kendall opened the first mission school at Rangihoua in the Bay of Islands on August 12, 1816.[1] The early years of the CMS were dominated by Marsden. He believed that the missionaries' task was to introduce Maori to "western civilization" and Christianity. The mission schools were expected to facilitate "conversion" by providing Maori with access to the Bible. Schooling was intended to encourage Maori parents to let their children come under the missionaries' influence and thus to learn the English language. For those Maori in attendance at mission schools instruction was also provided in arithmetic, needlework, and domestic employment for Maori girls and carpentry and agriculture for boys.[2]

While the missionaries had wanted to delay colonization until "civilization" was attained and Maori were better able to cope with an influx of migrants, the colonizers were anxious for settlement to commence. By the late 1830s, official British policy toward New Zealand had switched from one of nonintervention to one of formal colonization.[3] Colonization, it was thought, was "inevitable" and could not be stemmed indefinitely. Accepting responsibility for their own subjects and Maori, the Colonial Office in London undertook to protect Maori and to introduce a system of self-government for British settlers. Following the signing of the Treaty of Waitangi by almost all Maori chiefs on 6 February 1840, and the beginnings of organized colonization thereafter, New Zealand was granted the formal status of a colony. In November the imperial government separated New Zealand from New South Wales. After the signing of the Treaty and the declaration of New Zealand as a Crown colony, the government became anxious to extend the work begun by the missionaries. In keeping with the requirements of an emerging nation, policy on Maori education became demonstrably assimilationist—the European culture was to be imposed upon and adopted by Maori in New Zealand.[4]

The assimilationist ideology was refined further by Governor Robert FitzRoy. He proposed a Native Trust Ordinance in 1844 that allowed endowments and financial assistance to be given to the three principal denominations (Anglican, Wesleyan, and Roman Catholic) to extend their native school endeavors. Having established the principle of introducing grants for educational purposes, the Ordinance allowed the trustees to allocate sites for building schools, to establish such schools, to appoint and pay teachers, and supervise all aspects of school life. However, the Ordinance failed to excite interest in either Maori or European communities, and with the perilous state of the colony's finances, it was not enacted. Nevertheless, the missionaries' educational achievements in New Zealand were noteworthy to the extent that some 20,500 children, aged between five and fifteen years, were attending day schools.[5]

FitzRoy's successor, George Grey, was convinced that by providing the "right" kind of education Maori would become "civilized" and form an integral part of New Zealand society. Grey's educational policy, therefore, was directed toward the "amalgamation" of the European and Maori races, thereby creating "one society." He enacted legislation to enable "civilizing" work among Maori by placing their children in boarding rather than day mission schools, thereby removing them from the "barbaric and demoralizing influences of the Maori villages."[6]

The resultant Education Ordinance of 1847 authorized the disbursement of public funds to establish and maintain schools, provided always that those schools taught English, included religious instruction and industrial training in their curricula, and were managed by a religious body in receipt of state aid. The governor appointed inspectors to survey the schools annually and provide reports to the Legislative Council. These reports were to contain a description of each school, the funds that supported it, attendance data, the teachers' salaries, the annual costs of educating each student, the discipline and management of scholars, and a precise description of the industrial training provided.[7]

The arguments for including English, industrial training, and religious education in the school curriculum were simple. Knowledge of the English language, Grey claimed, would not only facilitate a mixing of the Maori and European races but also, more importantly, would introduce Maoridom to the "superior, civilizing" European culture. The second subject, industrial training, introduced Maori (and European) to those practical skills, trades, and domestic arts considered indispensable in a European society. Special emphasis was placed on agriculture which would enable schools to become self-supporting. The inclusion of religious instruction was founded on Grey's personal view that it was an essential element in rescuing and uplifting the Maori race. The Education Ordinance, with some minor changes, governed Maori education through to the passage of the Native Schools Act in 1867.[8]

The rapid expansion in the European population and the increasing settler demand for independence was finally recognized by the British Parliament. It granted representative government to New Zealand, effective from 1853. New

Zealand adopted a federal system of government whereby the colony was divided into six provinces (Auckland, New Plymouth, Wellington, Nelson, Canterbury, and Otago), each with its own elected provincial council enjoying wide-ranging powers. Although the Constitution Act made no mention of education, it soon transpired that the provision of schooling would be left in the hands of individual provinces. Inevitably, the variety of approaches to education that came to be adopted in the provinces from 1853 reflected not only their geographical isolation but also the differences in their educational beliefs, natural resources, and educational endowments. In fact, throughout the entire provincial period (1853–1876) the South Island provincial governments prospered while the North Island provinces, by comparison, were economically impoverished. As late as 1870 only US$2,800 of the total colonial educational expenditure of US$44,800 was being spent in the North Island.[9]

By the early 1870s, a clear pattern had emerged. Regional differences in schooling practices should give way to the view that responsibility for education should lay no longer with the churches or voluntary societies but with central government. There was a general acceptance that the provinces had outlived their usefulness and that what was urgently needed was a strong central government that would fund and administer a nationwide primary education system. After four months of intensive debate the New Zealand parliament voted overwhelmingly to introduce free and compulsory primary schooling and to exclude denominational rivalry and controversy from state schools by making instruction "entirely of a secular character."[10] The Education Act of 1877, albeit modified over time, governed primary education until the late 1980s.

Looking back at the nineteenth century, it can be argued that the social class and occupational backgrounds of the early settlers shaped their educational experiences in profound ways. The majority lacked significant capital but were prepared to work hard to make a new society. That they had traveled some 12,000 miles to a country about which they knew little is testament to their commitment. Many settlers were anxious that their children received at least a basic primary education and, therefore, were prepared to contribute by paying school fees and donations. However, attendance came at a cost for many poorer families in terms of their children's reduced capacity to contribute to the family income through paid and unpaid work. This was a major problem in the predominantly rural New Zealand society of the nineteenth century. As more affluent times came and government support for families increased, more children began to attend school and more regularly.

The educational experiences of Maori youth in the nineteenth (and into the twentieth) century were shaped by exposure to western-style schooling. The vehicle for assimilation was the missionaries and the mission schools. As Maori began to retreat from these schools the government introduced legislation—the Native Schools Acts of 1858 and 1867—allocating state funds to those secular rural day schools where Maori were taught in the English language. In 1880, a native schools "Code" was published that emphasized the importance of less formal and more practical forms of instruction, with the schools being encouraged to offer instruction in agricultural, technical, and health subjects that would assist the survival of the villages.[11] The Maori population had declined rapidly through the nineteenth century, reaching a low point of 42,113 in 1896. By contrast, the European population had increased markedly to exceed 700,000 by the same year. Despite the high birth rate, disease and infant mortality exacted a heavy toll on the Maori population.[12]

The native school syllabus laid down in the Code was similar to that prescribed for Standards 1–4 (Years 2–6) in the ordinary public primary schools except that history, elementary science, and formal grammar were omitted. Maori children were taught reading and writing in the English language, arithmetic, geography, and "such culture as may fit them to become good citizens."[13] Although government scholarships were available to enable "bright" Maori scholars who had passed the Standard 4 examination to advance to Standards 5 and 6, in practice few Maori did. Only a handful went on to secondary schools such as Te Aute College before enrolling at university. Such an outcome should not be surprising. In an era where a Standard 4 pass marked a completed primary education most parents, Maori or European, saw little benefit in keeping their children at school any longer.[14]

A similar pattern can be observed for female students during the nineteenth century. Girls usually spent less time at primary and secondary school than boys. Their curriculum was oriented towards practical, often domestic-related, subjects regarded as being useful to them in their afterschool lives. Their education was generally regarded as little more than a brief interlude between childhood and marriage. Many girls who stayed longer were employed as primary schoolteachers and nurses. The fact that a gender-differentiated schooling experience existed in the first place owed much to nineteenth-century medical opinion about the damaging effects of strenuous academic study (in particular mathematics and some languages) on girls' development.[15] For their part, non-academically inclined school-age boys were liable to be viewed as future unskilled or semiskilled workers in a rapidly expanding economy and labor market.

Primary Schools

Students

Prior to the introduction of free, compulsory, and secular primary schooling in 1878, student enrollment and attendance patterns had varied greatly in line with parental attitudes towards education and families' economic circumstances. The impact of the 1877 Education Act on public primary school enrollments was obvious. Between 1878 and 1898, for example, the primary school rolls doubled (from 65,366 to 131,600) whereas the increase in the general population had been 41 percent.[16] Such data reveal a steady and consistent increase in the regularity of attendance during the last quarter of the nineteenth century.

From 1878, all children aged between seven and thirteen years, and who lived within two miles of a public school were required to attend one of the 748 public primary schools, unless specifically exempt, for at least half the time that the school was open. Exemptions were allowed on the grounds of efficient or regular instruction provided elsewhere: the child's state of health, the distance between the child's home and the school, impassable roads, and level of schooling achieved (set at Standard 4). However, the Act specified that the compulsory attendance measures be put into operation only at the discretion of individual school committees by majority vote.[17] These provisions represented a sensible compromise given that the New Zealand Parliament was not designing a primary education system for a country that had no need of child labor. New Zealand compulsory schooling legislation allowed a role for local committees as best able to judge local needs.[18]

Maori children were treated differently. Maori parents were free to decide whether or not to send their children to a public school. "Half-castes" who lived away from their tribe or community were judged to be Europeans and were unable to be exempted from the compulsory attendance provisions. Politicians, it seems, had approached the issue of compulsory school attendance prudently and cautiously; they delayed making attendance compulsory until such time as Maori in sufficient numbers became convinced that the schooling opportunities on offer were in their best interests.

Curriculum and Teaching Methods

Upon introducing the 1877 Education Bill into Parliament, the minister of Justice, Charles Bowen, declared that the Bill was designed to satisfy three important criteria: First, the primary education provided had to be freely available to all school-age (5–15-year-old) children; second, the control of education had to remain decentralized; and, finally, the public school curriculum was to be secular, except for the provision (later deleted) that schools could be opened every morning with a reading from the Bible and a recitation of the Lord's Prayer.[19]

Bowen also highlighted the social advantages of a state-provided nationwide primary education system. Without it there would be large numbers of school-age children "growing up in absolute ignorance" who posed a great danger to the state. Drawing upon his knowledge of educational developments in the United States, England, and Australia, Bowen pointed to the correlation between crime and the lack of formal schooling. Compulsory schooling in would "prevent the population from falling into the absolute brutishness into which an uneducated people have a tendency to descend."[20] After four months of debate the Bill became law and, from 1878, all primary schoolteachers were required to provide instruction in reading, writing, arithmetic, English grammar and composition, geography, history, elementary science and drawing, object lessons, vocal music (singing), military drill (for boys), and, for girls, sewing, needlework, and the principles of domestic economy.

The new regulations outlined an elaborate scheme of primary school "standards" that allowed the centrally prescribed curriculum to be delivered to all primary schoolchildren. Students were classified into one of six "standards," instructed in accordance with the syllabus laid down for that standard and then examined by a school inspector to check that the quality of education was being maintained. The advantage of this system, Bowen claimed, was that it provided a uniform mechanism both to evaluate the work of teachers and students throughout the country, in educational institutions funded by public money working for the public good.[21] It was in this climate that the relationship between the primary school curriculum and examinations became legitimized with the introduction of the annual standards examinations in 1878. In 1884, 1885, and 1891, the inspector-general of Schools (Rev. William J. Habens) introduced a series of regulations amending the 1878 requirements. From 1884, all primary school pupils had to be examined, including those children who had not yet passed Standard 1, and every child who passed a standard had to be presented for the next standard examination the following year.[22] In an attempt to reduce pupil absenteeism on examination day, the 1885 regulations required inspectors to record pass rates based on the total school roll rather than the number of candidates being formally examined.[23]

In many respects primary schoolteachers embodied the dominant Victorian attitudes towards children and their place in society. Classrooms were places where children were expected to work silently and efficiently on predetermined tasks under the firm authority, direction, and discipline of their teacher. In 1881 Robert O'Sullivan, an Auckland inspector, noted that children needed to be taught to walk quietly and to be "relegated to their proper and natural position of insignificance." However, a Nelson inspector, William Hodgson, saw the matter very differently and wrote in 1878 that schools should not be regarded as penal institutions and that children should be able to move freely about the classroom.[24]

Teachers' pedagogical skills and "efficiency" were evaluated formally by the inspectorate and by various ministers of Education who vigorously supported using the standards examination results to assess school and teacher efficiency. As early as 1879, for example, William Rolleston had argued that the "best" school was the one that passed a higher proportion of children than did any other in the district. Eleven years later, William Pember Reeves declared that the percentage pass rate constituted "evidence" of a school's educational progress. In practice, the demand for examination passes was so intense that Hodgson observed that teachers who had departed from the prescribed standards syllabus were not likely to repeat that mistake.[25] Curriculum and classroom reform therefore remained beyond the grasp of educational reformers until such time as the examination system was modified or abolished.

Everyday Life

Nineteenth-century public primary schools were places where "wild" children were to be "tamed" and, hopefully, educated. Classrooms were unattractive places where children sat on uncomfortable wooden furniture, facing the teacher who sat at the front of the class. In the weeks before examination day students and teachers engaged in an orgy of "cram," involving intensive preparation during and after school hours, additional homework, and harsh discipline for inattention, carelessness, and lack of academic progress. On the day of the inspectors' annual examination classrooms were brought alive with flowers, welcoming messages, and examples of students' work placed on classroom walls. The inspectors questioned the students on the curriculum, listened to them reading, read their written answers, and marked their arithmetical calculations. All questions were designed to elicit factual answers—geography, for example, required little more than the memorization of key capes and bays, mountains, rivers and lakes; history encouraged a strictly chronological approach with emphasis on the dates of succession of English sovereigns, and of battles and wars—and were marked with a tick or cross. The next day an "Inspector's Holiday" was observed, during which time the inspector marked the students' scripts, calculated the percentage of passes, and determined the classification of students for the following year.[26]

Although some inspectors and teachers desperately wanted the curriculum to be related more closely to students' interests and experiences, the primary school system was highly resistant to new ideas. Teachers were reduced to being mere technicians who were concerned with the control and instruction of the class as a whole rather than with the individual progress of each student.[27] A child-centered educational philosophy was not yet on the educational horizon.

Secondary Schools

Students

Prior to the introduction of free secondary education in 1903, noncompulsory attendance at a fee-charging secondary school was usually associated with privilege, prosperity, and familial ambition. These institutions were either private or church supported, or state assisted through denationalized public land endowments. The high cost of tuition (and boarding, at the eleven schools with such facilities) meant that enrollments were small.[28] The twenty-five single-sex and coeducational secondary schools in existence in 1900 collectively had only 1,800 boys and 1,000 girls in attendance, 95 percent of whom were over 12 years. This represented 39 students for every 10,000 residents in New Zealand. Seventy-five percent of these schools in 1900 each had fewer than 100 pupils. Only three high schools had more than 200 students on their rolls. There were four denominational secondary schools exclusively for select Maori youth with a combined roll of over 230 students, 34 percent of whom paid no tuition fees on account of winning a free place or gaining a scholarship.[29] The latter statistic compares favorably with the 24 percent of non-Maori students who attended public secondary schools free of charge in 1900. Students who won scholarships tended to remain at secondary school for two to three years, only becoming candidates for the University of New Zealand matriculation examination in their third year.[30] Of this group, some 45 percent were females.

In the absence of free places at secondary schools nationwide, a growing proportion of thirteen-year-old to fifteen-year-old primary school students from the 1880s chose to pursue secondary-level instruction in their own schools—in Standard 7 classes—rather than enrolling and paying fees at secondary institutions. In this way, ambitious, academically able working-class youth could access higher education at a substantially reduced cost. Because these senior primary schoolchildren bypassed their local secondary schools, the latter were starved of first- and second-year students. Relations between many primary and secondary schools in close proximity began to improve only after the government established a national free place system for secondary schools in 1903.[31] Until this time, curriculum boundaries between senior primary school and secondary schools remained largely unregulated.

Curriculum and Teaching Methods

Throughout most of the nineteenth century secondary school authorities maintained that their schools should operate entirely independently from district or provincial (pre-1877) and state primary schools (post-1877). This separation gave an automatic justification for the adoption and promotion of an academic, university-oriented curriculum that largely mimicked what was offered in the greater public schools in Britain.[32]

New Zealand's first state girls' secondary school, Otago Girls (OGHS), High School, was established at the same time as the nation's first university was founded, and in the same town, so it is hardly surprising to learn that this school quickly came to be seen as a natural "feeder" of students to the University of Otago and later New Zealand universities. The association between New Zealand's higher schools and the colony's universities was strengthened from the 1880s with the wider promotion of the University of New Zealand's Matriculation Examination in secondary schools.[33]

The governing authorities and principals of the six secondary schools that were operating by the late 1860s—and of the nine more established in the 1870s and a further nine through the 1880s and 1890s—were able to refer to the 1877 Education Reserves Act for external validation of their academic curriculum orientation. This legislation stated that the secondary schools' course of instruction was to consist of "the English language and literature, Latin and Greek classics, French and other modern languages, mathematics, physics, and other branches of science." Murdoch noted however that in the 1870s one secondary school had dropped Greek to allow more time for Latin, and that by 1900 only two secondary schools taught Greek.[34]

Nineteenth-century secondary school teachers usually taught their students for three hours in the morning and two in the afternoon, from Monday to Friday inclusive. A four-quarter, forty-two week year was generally adopted by the 1890s, as was a twenty-five-hour school week. Morning classes ran from 9 A.M. to 12 noon, or 9:30 A.M. to 12:30 P.M., while afternoon classes occupied a 1 P.M. to 3 P.M. or 2 P.M. to 4 P.M. slot. When school finished in the afternoon approved extracurricular and optional pursuits commenced. Saturday afternoon social events for senior students, hosted by a school principal and staff—sometimes in the principal's home—were commonplace.[35]

The methods employed by nineteenth-century secondary teachers were shaped largely by national examination syllabuses and by the perceived need to deliver "the good old fortifying classical curriculum." A former director of Education—reflecting on weaknesses in the secondary school curriculum in the late 1800s—lamented that "a slavish obedience to the tyranny of mechanical tradition and convention" was all too often evident. He believed that rigidity, formality, and "bookishness" were ill suited to the temperament of the great majority of adolescent boys and girl.[36]

The tendency to emphasize textbook-based learning and teaching rather than practical work and experimentation in science and mathematical subjects and in foreign languages, for example, was a product of the uncritical and inflexible pursuit of a traditional literary curriculum in most if not all secondary schools. It was also a response to rising parental and student demand for access to high-status school credentials through successful performance in the literary-oriented Junior Civil Service, University Matriculation, and Scholarship examinations. Mention is made frequently in the historical literature on secondary students being "drilled" by teachers who were merely repeating what they had experienced themselves as students.[37]

Corporal punishment was used extensively in boys' schools as the main "discipline" mechanism, alongside a system of fines, although a small minority of teachers recorded their opposition to physical punishment. A monological "chalk and talk" approach to teaching was used with some exceptions. Eileen Wallis noted that in the 1870s OGHS students did most of their work on slates. Desks had tins attached to them holding water, a sponge, and a duster for cleaning the slate during and after lessons. The material would then be memorized and reproduced for examination purposes. Transmission of what counted as valuable knowledge—almost always from a liberal or classical curriculum— usually involved a one-way monologue between the "teacher and the taught." Rote-learning was usually judged a fundamental ingredient to "effective" or "good" teaching.[38]

By 1900, the newly appointed head of the national Department of Education, George Hogben, was advocating greater adjustment of school curricula to match the realities of "practical life" so that students' innate manual, technical, and other aptitudes could be identified more accurately. Such adaptation ought to apply across school curricula in both primary and secondary schools, Hogben declared, even when the latter were presently enrolling only a small proportion of the nation's adolescent population. His was, for all practical purposes, a minority view.[39]

Teachers' work was often made more difficult by limited access to resources and apparatus. In some instances this concerned the supplying of slates and textbooks and at other times to obtaining charts, maps, globes, and microscopes for teaching geography, history, and science subjects. A shortage of classroom space was also a general concern, mostly in relation to science laboratory rooms, gymnasiums, school libraries and, in the case of various sports, too few outdoor courts and fields.[40] Pressure on space and resources increased significantly and unexpectedly in and from the first decade of the twentieth century on account of the government's introduction of the secondary schools' free place system for suitably qualified primary school leavers.

Everyday Life

As we have already seen, there is plenty of evidence to argue that the great majority of secondary schools from the mid-1850s were unashamedly academic. Surviving curriculum plans suggest that English, mathematics, French and/or Latin, and at least one branch of science were typically delivered to Form 3 to 6 (Year 9 to 12) students, for a substantial part of the school day. Some schools employed Frenchmen and other Europeans as language teachers.[41] Length of an individual student's intended stay at secondary school was seldom seen as the determinant of a boy's or girl's particular course of study. Whatever was studied was to have a general or liberal educational purpose. In the case of the four denominational secondary schools for Maori operating in 1900, only Te Aute College and Hukarere Girls' High School provided an academic curriculum comparable to that available in secondary schools for non-Maori boys and girls. The two other Maori high schools emphasized practical rather than academic instruction.[42]

From individual secondary schools we can gain insights into what happened inside and beyond classrooms. At Christchurch Girls' High School (CGHS) in the early 1880s, for example, fourth-year students were expected to devote three and one-half hours each evening to homework during the school week, after sitting in classes for five hours daily for five days a week. Languages occupied 50 percent of the timetable—Latin (six hours), English (four and one-half hours), and French (two hours)—and mathematics, 24 percent.[43] Because these girls were viewed as future university students, they needed a good grounding in traditional university subjects. This pattern was similar to that proposed by the New Zealand O'Rorke Commission in 1880, with the latter emphasizing language teaching and mathematics. But the Commission had suggested that Greek be available only in the classical stream of boys' secondary schools and not in girls' schools.[44]

A subject hierarchy was in operation at CGHS however. Geography, history, science, and singing were allocated only one hour each per week. Science was often seen as less important for girls than boys, but some girls' secondary schools emphasized the teaching of natural and physical science.[45] Drawing, however, received two hours per week. German and physical education were taught after regular school hours, later in the afternoon, and in other schools, as options.

In light of this "heavy" curriculum, it is noteworthy that the school's external examiner recorded his concern in 1883 about "the appearance of fatigue visible in the faces of nearly all the school girls," before concluding that senior girls especially "do very much more work than is good for them."[46] Preparation for high-status university entrance examinations was the chief culprit, he lamented, and this inevitably involved plenty of homework. Girls and boys in both state and private secondary schools were required to sit in their school assembly hall to hear, among other things, a daily Bible reading and to participate in prayers. Secondary school boarders had additional commitments.

Of the nineteenth-century youth whose secondary schooling experiences have been recorded, several acknowledged that they generally respected and admired their teachers. The discipline methods used by some teachers—including firm, sometimes harsh, rebukes and sarcastic comments to students in class—were not forgotten. Other forms of discipline involved staff recording misdemeanors in "black books," a fines' system, expulsion for "bad" oral and written language, expulsion for dishonesty, and students being required to mow school lawns and fields under a principal's instructions.[47]

Students who attended secondary schools in the 1800s were well aware of the importance attached to national examination performance. One principal remarked in 1893 that "if parents enter their [sons and] daughters for a race they must expect to see them hard-driven."[48] The often-cramped classrooms—sometimes steeply stepped and with high ceilings—with uncomfortable desks and forms, poor ventilation and lighting did nothing to improve matters. At least one principal complained that these dark, gloomy, and damp environments contributed to pupils' restlessness and inattentiveness, and to teachers' occasional irritability.[49]

Boarders at secondary school hostels fared little better. At OGHS they awoke at 6 A.M. in both summer and winter to the sound of a "get-up bell," then studied from 6.30 A.M. until breakfast at 8 A.M.—sometimes in cold rooms with smoky kerosene lamps and open fires, but no electricity. Classes ran from 9:30 A.M. (up to 1907) until lunchtime at 12:30 P.M. and resumed in the afternoon for two hours. The evening meal occupied the 6 P.M. to 7 P.M. slot, followed by two hours of homework then evening prayers before bedtime at 9:30 P.M. Breakfast alternated between bread and butter, fresh lobster and hot bread rolls, with tea as the main drink. The evening meal also varied, with bread and butter and blackcurrant jam some days, soup followed by a meat dish on others, and meat followed by a boiled desert with sauce on the remaining evenings.[50]

Post-secondary Education

Background

Prior to the first university being opened in Dunedin in July 1871 ambitious secondary school leavers were compelled to travel overseas—Melbourne was the closest university—at significant personal cost. Although a second South Island university had opened in Christchurch (Canterbury College) three years later, bitter interprovincial rivalry precluded the possibility of any degree of cooperation between the two universities. The way forward, the government of the day concluded, lay in introducing legislation to establish a single national university with colleges affiliated to it.

Following a period of oftentimes acrimonious debate, principally between Otago and Canterbury regarding where the University of New Zealand (UNZ) was to be located, Otago and Canterbury finally agreed to support the passage of the University of New Zealand Bill that became law in late August 1874. For the next eighty-seven years the UNZ, operating in strict accordance with the 1874 Act and subsequent amendments, was responsible for the curriculum content, academic standard, structure, and examination of all degrees issued under its name. It prescribed the staffing levels, salaries, and working conditions of academics; set the standard and appointed markers for its entrance examination; administered complex and sizeable budgets; and introduced and financed a scholarship system to support students' undergraduate studies. Such were the legal powers and dominant status of the UNZ that it came to shape, if not govern, the daily working lives of university students and staff throughout its lengthy and often tortuous history.

Students

The first chancellor of the University of New Zealand (1871–1884), Henry Tancred, was adamant that university education should be available to all students who passed an entrance examination and who sought access to higher education, irrespective of their social class backgrounds. Accordingly, he oversaw the introduction in 1872 of a system of competitive examinations in classics, mathematics, physical science, modern languages, history, and English literature. Of the thirty-eight candidates who entered that year, seventeen passed; they were each rewarded with an allowance for the duration of their degree. As generous as this might appear, the reality was that these scholarships were invariably won by youth from well-to-do families who could afford to send their sons and daughters to the "best" fee-charging secondary schools.

This was the pattern until "free place" secondary schooling and university bursaries were introduced in 1902 and 1907, respectively.[51]

Such was the success of the UNZ that by 1885 Sir Robert Stout (New Zealand's premier) could proudly boast that the nation had as many students receiving university education as any other country.[52] What Stout did not say, however, was that the quality of that education was impossible to assess. While some commentators publicly applauded the overall standard of the UNZ's degrees, others criticized not only the unevenness of teaching within and between the affiliated colleges but also the lack of any uniformity of standards by the various external examiners. The government appointed a Royal Commission in late 1878 specifically to investigate the conditions of university education in New Zealand and the relationship to existing secondary schools. The Commission's report argued the case for establishing additional university colleges in Auckland and Wellington where there had been rapid population growth. By the mid-1880s there were approximately 170 students enrolled in undergraduate arts, science, law, and medical degrees in the three affiliated university colleges.[53]

Most university students were males who enrolled for the BA degree on a part-time basis and attended late afternoon and early evening classes. The fact that very few lectures were scheduled before 2 P.M. reflected the predominantly parttime nature of university student life. Such was the popularity of the BA degree that of the 858 degrees conferred by the UNZ between 1876 and 1900, 86 percent were arts degrees; the remainder were spread evenly across science, law, and medicine.[54] While no statistics are available regarding the length of time taken from university entrance to degree completion, it is likely that few students graduated in the minimum time.

Notwithstanding the UNZ's confidence that it provided "as good an education as could be provided out of Europe," students quickly understood that a university college was where they went to distil from their lecturers and from a few carefully selected textbooks the information they needed to pass the annual external examinations administered by the University.[55]

Curriculum and Teaching Methods

While much of New Zealand's educational history demonstrates a close affinity with Scottish educational ideas and practices, the University of New Zealand Act of 1874 borrowed heavily from the University of London model of university administration and organization. Thus from the outset the UNZ functioned strictly as an examining body; the University Council would remain peripatetic; and its finances would be devoted to setting and arranging the marking of its own examinations, with additional funds used to support undergraduate scholarships.

In deciding the content of its various undergraduate degrees and setting the standard of its examinations the UNZ Senate looked at the level and academic standard of work expected in the nation's senior secondary school classes. Prior to 1875, for example, a BA candidate could graduate having passed, often with moderate success, in as few as three of the eight degree subjects, of which either classics or mathematics were compulsory. Thereafter it was decided that the BA degree standard would be equivalent to that for the pass examination at Oxford and Cambridge universities. Although the Senate was responsible for prescribing course textbooks, this was done without consulting university lecturers and professors. Moreover, no checks were made to ensure if these texts were available in New Zealand, and no attempt was made to monitor the academic quality of students' work from year to year.[56] The use of external examiners from overseas, it was widely believed, provided the necessary safeguard for the overall standard of degrees issued under the name of the University of New Zealand.

By the end of the nineteenth century the four affiliated colleges (Victoria, in Wellington, had opened in 1899) offered a variety of degrees—Bachelor of Arts, Law (introduced in 1877), Science (from 1883), Medicine (MB ChB at Otago from 1881), and Music (1876). Interestingly, the subjects listed for the new BSc degree were all but identical to those for the BA except for history, political science, and jurisprudence; applied mathematics and natural science (biology) were compulsory with Latin optional. The opportunity for students to undertake laboratory work in science subjects was practically nil. For years what masqueraded as experimental science in the university colleges was in reality taught entirely from textbooks.[57]

In formulating regulations for the MA degree the UNZ turned to the Melbourne University for inspiration. Accordingly, by the late 1870s candidates for the University of New Zealand MA degree were expected to locate their own books and to indicate to their examiners the specific line of enquiry they had pursued; the examiners, however, were free to choose whether or not to examine candidates in that area.[58] Although doctoral degrees were available in law, medicine, music, and science by 1883, the introduction of the PhD degree was some time away (1922).[59]

Most accounts of the early New Zealand universities reveal a very book-centered approach to teaching and learning, with little room for discussion and questioning.[60] Lecturers and students knew what textbooks the UNZ Senate prescribed and approved, knew what had to be covered in lectures, and were familiar with the content and style of past examination papers, bound copies of which were available in each university college library. Given the near impossibility of procuring textbooks from England, the teaching methods invariably were didactic with lecture material often quoted directly from the approved textbook. Much to their annoyance, lecturers and professors were unable to depart from the syllabus and present original ideas for fear that their students would be penalized by remote, faceless overseas examiners.[61]

Everyday Life

During the early years of university education there were few opportunities for students to socialize during the day because most were part-time and only attended evening classes. Despite the restrictions, groups of students nevertheless managed to organize parties, dances, and balls. In stark contrast to their late twentieth-century counterparts, these students did not live in university halls of residence or in student flats but instead boarded in private homes. A well-defined student community remained some time away.

Other Nineteenth-Century Post-secondary Institutions

By the close of the nineteenth century there were four teachers' training colleges operating in New Zealand, each responsible for preparing secondary school leavers to teach in the colony's primary schools. The more ambitious primary school trainees and certificated primary teachers increasingly sought access to university education as the route to senior teaching and headship positions, greater professional status, and a higher salary. At this point in time secondary schoolteachers were not required to have undergone any formal training—the only requirement was a university degree and a willingness to "learn on the job."[62]

Major Reforms

A variety of reforms were implemented in the nineteenth century. Very significant was the decision taken by government to intervene in schooling provision from the 1840s. This culminated in the state gaining substantial control over elementary schooling by 1900. Because Christian churches had been involved in educational activity for some thirty years before government intervention, their work could not be set aside by government, at least initially. The resulting system was neither free nor compulsory, because fees were levied and mandatory attendance was practically unenforceable. For Maori and "half-caste children" rather than the children of the settlers from Britain, a "civilizing," Christian orientation, evident from earlier missionary activity, was a fundamental ingredient of the schooling agenda. This shaped "Native" (Maori) schooling in particular from the late 1840s.

By the late 1860s, deficiencies in the effectiveness of provincial education led government towards "a thoroughly national and ... a purely secular system of public education," leading to the passing of the 1877 Education Act. The introduction of this statute represents perhaps the most significant turning point in the country's nineteenth century education history. By 1900, the national attendance rate at elementary schools was at an all-time high: 81 percent. Government intervention in the schooling domain was a proven success, and not likely to diminish in the coming new century.

TWENTIETH CENTURY

Type of Educational System

By 1900, the state was able to exercise almost complete jurisdiction over primary but not secondary schools. Its authority—mainly fiscal—extended to the administration of public schools via elected school committees and education boards, prescription of the primary school curriculum, and the power to make regulations to give full effect to the spirit of the 1877 Education Act, among other considerations. By comparison, gradual control over secondary schools was possible only with statutory intervention from 1903.

Private (denominational) school authorities had to wait until 1975 before they received public monies. Previously, they could only gain small-scale assistance in the form of school apparatus, books, and "grants-in-aid" from education boards at the latter's discretion. For much of the twentieth century the state's philosophy was that owing to their sectarianism private schools should not look for financial relief, given their decision to remove themselves from the mainstream school system. Government coined the term "state-integrated schools" for former private primary and secondary institutions that had been permitted by a minister of Education to change their name if not their orientation, and to receive full fiscal relief in the process. Nonetheless some private schools chose after 1975 to retain their name and identity, thus bypassing the opportunity to gain 100 percent government funding. By 1999, 11 percent of New Zealand schools were state integrated, with private schools constituting only 4 percent. Some criticism was leveled at the amount of government funding their government schools received: US$26 million in 1998 for 25,000 students.[63]

For most of the twentieth century, the tertiary education sector was a state one. But from 1992, private training establishments were set up alongside newly created *wananga* (Maori tertiary education and training providers) and the four established state colleges of education, twenty-three polytechnics, and eight universities. By 2000, 834 private providers had been registered within the New Zealand Qualifications Authority; 75 percent of them attracted some government funding and 20 percent were established by Maori. This private sector accounted for 25 percent of the total enrollments in 2000, receiving US$360 million in income that year from tuition fees and from student subsidies paid by government.[64]

Social Class and Education

With the introduction of the government free place system in the early 1900s the nature and composition of the secondary school population began to change. Very gradually these institutions ceased to be almost exclusively available to the social and intellectual elite of the country, with the result that "the children of the Dominion's upper social stratum were compelled to mingle with the juvenile Toms, Dicks, and Harrys of the humbler class."[65] It was easier for the sons and daughters of wealthy parents to remain longer at high school however, and, almost automatically, to gain prominence within and perhaps beyond them. They had the financial and other means to delay entry to the paid workforce. Nevertheless, the free place system was underpinned by a meritocratic ideal: the notion that able children from whatever social class ought to receive a specific period of secondary schooling free of charge.[66]

Not surprisingly, public examinations came to be used increasingly as a means for youth to have some, or more, upward economic and social mobility. The abolition in 1937 of the selective primary school Standard 6 Proficiency Examination led to more primary school leavers from working-class families entering post-primary institutions alongside the children of wealthier parents—unless the latter opted for private schooling. While the transformation of post-primary schools from selective to egalitarian institutions was an intended consequence of the Labour government's equality of educational opportunity policy post-1939, the youth who fared worst under this model were predominantly those of lower socioeconomic status. These children were unable financially or were less willing than were boys and girls of prosperous parents to continue their schooling much beyond the prescribed minimum entitlement.[67] By the mid-1970s there was growing official confirmation of a link between enhanced secondary school retention and higher socioeconomic status. A connection was also made between schools with large Maori and Pacific Island student enrollments and the lower socioeconomic status of these.[68]

Increasing sensitivity to allegations of social class privilege and of parental snobbery associated with private (independent) schools led to some spokespeople from the 1960s attempting to challenge the widely held belief that parents had to be wealthy to afford to send their children to these institutions. Nevertheless such institutions continued to be linked to ambitious middle-class parents seeking to secure an educational advantage in a competitive schooling market.[69]

For much of the twentieth century Maori youth generally stayed only briefly at school before leaving to take up working-class jobs. Low socioeconomic status Pakeha (European-origin) boys and girls were little different: the main determinant of school retention, school "success," and entrance to tertiary education was a person's social class rather than his or her ethnicity. In other words, social and economic disadvantage was, and is, not the sole preserve of Maori. Nonetheless, because more Maori than Pakeha have proportionately been working class it is more likely that poverty will militate against the fulfillment of their educational and vocational potential.[70]

One account from the mid-1940s, conveniently ignoring social class factors, sought to persuade readers that the underrepresentation of Maori in professions was attributable simply to "the inability or shortsightedness of some Maori parents in planning a career for their children."[71] By the early-1960s, growing official concern was being expressed about the poor educational and social prospects for Maori who were mostly of low socioeconomic status. Despite government advocacy of equality of educational opportunity for all New Zealand citizens, such policy had minimal impact on Maori.[72] Throughout the twentieth century the longer a student remained in the education system beyond the school-leaving age the better the outlook was for his or her upward social mobility. Males and females from high rather than low socioeconomic families were 60 percent more likely to enroll at a tertiary institution when they left secondary school in 1999.[73]

Race, Ethnicity, and Education

For a large part of the twentieth century, government sought to adjust primary and postprimary schooling to suit the perceived requirements of people of different ethnicity. This was scarcely surprising, given that the precedent for differentiation had been firmly established in the preceding century. It was also to apply later to Asian and Pacific people. The separate native (Maori) primary schooling system, for example, offered a curriculum since 1880 that was narrower and more practically and vocationally oriented than what was available in public primary schools. Three decades later, the native school curriculum began to resemble more closely that of the public school.

The movement to towns and cities that gained momentum from the late 1940s, and the compulsory introduction of a comprehensive common core curriculum for all high school students, led to significant changes in education policy making and practice for Maori and non-Maori alike. In 1969, the separate, predominantly rural, native schooling system was abandoned. Maori children had been absorbed into public primary schools increasingly since the early 1960s. This move was interpreted by some as assisting the integration of Maori and affording equality of educational opportunity and equal status. Later, in the 1970s prominent Maori began to establish their own institutions, with a view to placing the Maori language center-stage in all learning and teaching, reducing Maori students' disillusionment with—and therefore above average rates of expulsion and suspension from—regular state primary and secondary schooling. By 1990, six *kura kaupapa* Maori (Maori language immersion primary and secondary schools) had been created and by 1998 fifty nine of these schools were in operation.[74] Much the same thinking underpinned the creation of three *wananga* at the tertiary education level in the 1990s.

Almost invisible in the New Zealand education system until the 1980s, Asian students—primarily of Chinese but also of Indian origin—accounted for 6 percent of school enrollments and 9 percent of tertiary enrollments nationwide in 1998. They tended to be enrolled only in a few schools. They stayed at secondary school longer than non-Asians and were more likely to leave school with a Year 13 qualification and to complete a university degree. At the end of the twentieth century, Pacific students, by comparison, made up 7 percent of the school population and, like Asian learners, were concentrated in a small number of schools in New Zealand's largest city. Although they left secondary school on average with higher qualifications than Maori, these students made up only 4.7 percent of the tertiary population in 1999.[75] Finally, more Pacific than Maori tertiary students gained a diploma or a degree in 1999.

Gender and Education

By about 1910, Department of Education data demonstrated the different participation rates for girls and boys in primary schooling and beyond. More twelve-year-old to fifteen-year-old boys than girls were in senior primary standards, not because of superior intellectual ability but because girls were withdrawn from school at a younger age. Ruth Fry's study has revealed social attitudes about the respective worth of prolonged schooling for boys and girls. While the 1877 Education Act gave the appearance of offering equality of educational opportunity, this equality was not absolute. There were, on occasion, different classroom and examination requirements for some compulsory subjects, based for example on the premise that boys were "naturally" superior to girls in their arithmetical and geometrical understanding.[76]

The introduction of a Manual and Technical Elementary Instruction Act in 1900, with additional school funding available when certain "practical" and applied subjects were taught in schools, did little to break the relationship in the public mind between gender and "appropriate" fields of study. This relationship only began to lose force from the 1970s, when there was less inclination to view girls and women as a homogeneous group possessing identical needs, talents, and dispositions, and more of a tendency to focus on the "uniqueness" of each and every student—yet never entirely independent of his or her gender.

Parents appeared even less concerned about girls not entering a secondary school, especially prior to 1903. Nonetheless the presence of girls' schools that offered an almost identical curriculum to that available at boys' secondary schools helped promote the idea that females could study the same subjects as males and be candidates for the same high-status public examinations. But beliefs that women were physically inferior to men and were thus more vulnerable to stress and fatigue, and that as future wives, child-bearers, and child-rearers women had a special duty to be healthy proved next to impossible to overturn for most of the century. Given the strengths of these views, the Department of Education issued regulations relating to the "natural spheres" of males and females. Mandatory home science teaching for first- and second-year secondary school girls was introduced in 1918. Practical agriculture and dairy science were mandated for first- and second-year boys in district high school secondary departments.[77]

The perceived need to have some gender-based curriculum differentiation was still visible in the 1940s and 1950s, despite legislation having been introduced to add more compulsory subjects into the curriculum of state post-primary schools. The Labour government's policy implemented from 1939, that every youth was to receive "a free [primary and secondary] education of the kind for which he [or she] is best fitted"—while purporting to be non-selective—meant that differentiation on the grounds of gender (and perceived academic and practical ability) was retained.[78]

While there was compelling evidence to conclude that between 1950 and 1960 many more girls were gaining university entrance qualifications than previously, and that the percentage increase in that decade considerably outstripped that for boys (194 percent, 83 percent), far fewer qualified girls than boys proceeded to a university. Girls were far less likely than boys to study several sciences and mathematics throughout the 1950s. A national commission on education suggested in 1962 that many more senior girls should begin to specialize in mathematics and science and train as skilled technicians for new industrial positions.[79]

Finally, it will come as no surprise to learn that males and females accessed and then utilized the tertiary education sector differently throughout the twentieth century. Less than 5 percent of boys and girls leaving secondary school had entered a university directly in 1900. By 1938, the situation had changed only slightly, with 6.4 percent and 3.6 percent of male and female school leavers proceeding to university study. In the mid-1940s only 8 percent of boys and girls went on to university, the figure being low probably on account of World War II. By the mid 1960s, 11 percent of post-primary school leavers entered a university, but within a decade the proportion of males and females so enrolled was 30 percent. Different institutional preferences were apparent, with girls being four times less likely than boys to proceed to a university in 1965 but four times more likely than boys to enter a teachers' college. By 1990, 28 percent of secondary school leavers had enrolled immediately in a tertiary institution—a university (16 percent) or a polytechnic (12 percent).[80]

At the end of the twentieth century women made up 56 percent of university students, and 60 percent in *wananga* (Maori tertiary institutions). Only 45 percent of polytechnic and private training establishments' rolls were male, 21.5 percent for colleges of education. From 1993, male tertiary enrollments were overtaken by female for the first time. By 2000, males constituted only 43 percent of the national tertiary student population. Nonetheless, there were proportionately more female than male part-time students between 1994 and 2000 (45 percent, 39 percent).[81] This data points to the familial, fiscal, and vocational pressures encountered by females in their pursuit of tertiary education.

Primary Schools

Students

By the beginning of the twentieth century there were 130,742 students attending approximately 1,650 public primary schools in New Zealand. By 1950, 291,897 students were at primary school, and 403,513 in 2000. Five years later total primary school enrollments had dropped back slightly to 399,535.[82] Early-twentieth-century primary schoolchildren were confronted with an education system that embodied the rules, routines, and regulations of Victorian society. Such formalism was exemplified in the school architecture, classroom furniture, discipline, and ultimately, teachers' authority and conduct. Students attended school because they had to legally, not because they necessarily wanted to. Gradually, more attention was given to the students' physical well-being with school medical (from 1912) and dental (from 1920) officers appointed to monitor children's health. Nevertheless, as late as 1920, there were reports of children working long hours in farming communities before and after school and then being so exhausted as to be incapable of concentrating on their school work. The use of child labor declined as the economy improved and parents could afford to pay for outside labor.

With the abolition in 1937 of the standards examinations, and the Form 2 (Year 8) Proficiency certificate in particular, all primary school leavers were awarded a certificate that entitled them to free post-primary education. When the school-leaving age was raised from fourteen to fifteen years in 1944, all primary schoolchildren could expect to advance to a post-primary school where they would receive a "generous and well-balanced education." Freed now from the shadow of examinations, innovative primary schoolteachers quickly grasped the opportunity to design their own curricula and to assess students' progress formally and informally. Intelligence tests, widely used since the 1920s in New Zealand intermediate schools, gradually fell out of favor with educationists and were used but rarely by the 1980s.[83] Over the last thirty-five years students have been assessed in mathematics, listening and reading comprehension, and reading vocabulary using the standardised Progressive Achievement Tests (PATs), developed (and periodically renormed) by the New Zealand Council for Educational Research. More recently, teachers have had access to the online Assessment Resource Bank (ARB), designed to assess learning objectives in English, mathematics, and science, and to the Assessment Tools for Teaching and Learning (AsTTle) software that provides teachers with detailed information about their students' achievement and progress in mathematics, reading, and writing.[84]

The much greater diversity of students in New Zealand primary schools and the progressive inclusion of children with special needs (formerly sent to special schools) into mainstream state schools has been underwritten by a social commitment to greater equity of treatment for all citizens.[85] Today's students are encouraged to discover what they are capable of and to become independent learners who can utilize modern technology to research topics of interest and enhance their understanding of their place in the world.

Wellington Primary School Class in 1919. Professor Thomas Hunter's photographic collection, Alexander Turnbull Library, Wellington. Reference number 2816 MN2 1/4 (Private photographic collection, Professor Ian McLaren).

Curriculum and Teaching Methods

A radically new primary school curriculum, drafted by Hogben, was introduced in 1904. It was grounded in the Froebelian philosophy that children learn best by making things, by firsthand observation and experimentation, and by reflecting upon and explaining their experiences.[86] Copies of the syllabus were issued to teachers. The first part briefly outlined requirements for each of the six standards while the second part provided detailed content for each subject. English (reading, composition, writing, spelling, recitation), arithmetic, drawing, singing, physical instruction, moral instruction, nature study or elementary science, and health were compulsory subjects, with geography and history introduced for Standards 3 to 6. The number of additional subjects (handwork, needlework, military drill) taught depended on the size of the school. For the very first time primary teachers were allowed to plan their own courses in some subjects, either by selecting from a list of suggested topics or by devising, with the inspector's approval, their own curriculum.[87] Despite Hogben's best efforts, the fact remains that he overestimated the capabilities of most teachers at that time. Much of the criticism that followed the release of the syllabus centered on its overly comprehensive and prescriptive content.[88]

By the 1920s, there was widespread agreement among New Zealand educators that the benefits to be derived from a more child-centered approach were not achievable in a wholly examination-driven education system that ignored children's individual abilities and temperaments. Although New Zealanders had to wait until 1937 for the standards examinations to be abolished, educationists undertook ongoing syllabus revisions throughout the 1920s. Further progress towards recognizing the increasing professionalism of primary teachers came with the release of the 1929 syllabus (the "Red Book") that allowed teachers to make any alterations or amendments they thought desirable to meet students' needs.[89] However, the reformist zeal of the syllabus was subsumed temporarily by the continued presence of the standards and Proficiency examinations.

The practice of revising the curriculum in its entirety was abandoned in 1942 when the decision was taken to revise the primary school curriculum, subject by subject, over time. This process of "rolling revision" involved close consultation between teachers and the Department of Education, with separate representative committees responsible for drafting each subject. Over time these draft syllabuses were piloted in some primary schools before the final version was approved. By the late 1950s new syllabuses were in place for arithmetic, art and crafts, English, handcraft in wood and metal, health education, homecraft and sewing (for girls), mathematics, music, nature study and science, physical education, and social studies. In the early 1960s the Department established a permanent curriculum development unit that had oversight of the school curriculum until 1989.[90]

Throughout the 1960s and 1970s, primary schools increasingly organized their curriculum around unifying themes and matters of interest to students. By the 1980s, however, the curriculum was being criticized not only for failing to reflect New Zealand's contemporary and future cultural, economic, and social needs but also for disadvantaging female students, Maori, Pacific Islanders, and those with learning disabilities. A 1980s, attempt at curriculum reform failed to win government approval. In 1993, the National government launched the *New Zealand Curriculum Framework* that outlined in detail its curriculum expectations for all Year 1 to 13 students. It set out nine broad curriculum principles and specified seven essential learning areas (subjects) and eight groups of essential (and generic) skills that all students were supposed to acquire throughout their schooling. A series of tightly specified learning outcomes ("achievement objectives") accompanied these, describing what students should know and be able to do as they progressed through each of the eight levels.[91] By the year 2000, national curriculum statements had been formulated and published for all seven essential learning areas: mathematics (1992), science (1993), language and languages (1994), technology (1995), social sciences (1997), health and physical well-being (1999), and the arts (2000).

Many teachers have felt a distinct lack of ownership of the very curriculum they were charged with implementing owing to the new competitive contractual model adopted by the Ministry of Education in the 1990s. According to this model, tenders were invited for each curriculum area with a rigid timeframe for teacher and parent consultation. This signaled a radical departure from the former practice of lengthy discussion and negotiation between the Department of Education's curriculum development officers and teacher interest groups when syllabus revisions were being contemplated.[92] The pressure to produce the new curriculum also meant that there was little opportunity to trial it in schools. Not surprisingly, teachers began to complain about the increased workload associated with implementing the new *Curriculum Framework*. The *Curriculum Stocktake* report of 2002 acknowledged that the curriculum was overcrowded, that it sacrificed depth for breadth, and that it contributed to increased teacher stress and workload.[93]

Despite New Zealand's geographical isolation, some educationists were attuned to the increasingly liberal and student-centered approach that was at the forefront of "new" education thinking overseas during the 1920s. The publication of Percy Nunn's influential book, *Education: Its Data and First Principles* (1920), was significant for its advocacy of realizing the individual potential of students and the need for teachers to experiment with the curriculum and their classroom practice.[94] It became a key text in New Zealand teachers' colleges and universities by the time that the "Red Book" syllabus was published in 1929. Two years later, the Hadow Consultative Committee's report, *The Primary School*, was released in England and clearly embraced the spirit of "new" education when it recommended that the curriculum should be thought of in terms of "activity and experience rather than knowledge to be acquired and facts to be stored."[95] The impetus for reform was blunted by the economic depression from the late 1920s and the educational cuts that followed.

The election of the first Labour government (1935–1949) paved the way for a more student-centered educational focus. Once all primary school examinations were abolished in 1937 teachers were able to devise their own curricula to take account of the variation in students' needs and abilities in their classrooms. This liberal education philosophy was further reinforced by the educationists who spoke at the New Education Fellowship conference in July 1937. Such was the importance attached to this event that the government closed all primary schools so that teachers could attend.[96] Teachers left these meetings excited about the educational future and aware that New Zealand was embracing ideas that were commonplace in England, Europe, and the United States of America.

Notwithstanding the impact of World War II, New Zealand teachers have been keen to seize the opportunity for greater professional autonomy, to engage in less didactic teaching, to avoid rote-learning of meaningless and irrelevant facts, and to encourage children to take a more active role in their own learning and understanding. The fact that for many years teachers have been introduced to child development theories and educational psychology during their training has probably served to illustrate the importance of treating each student as an individual, thereby avoiding a "one-size-fits-all" pedagogy.

Everyday Life

Following the transformation of education initiated by Hogben in the early twentieth century, New Zealand primary school classrooms became much less formal. Students were encouraged to be more active in class, engage in more practical activities, participate in outdoor activities and organized sports, and, over time, to ask questions of their teachers in order to clarify their understanding. The catalyst for this shift from a formal, systems-driven education to one that is more holistic and student-centered was the decision taken in 1937 to abolish all primary school examinations. Twenty-first century New Zealand primary schools are certainly very different from the culturally starved "one-size-fits-all" institutions of the past. Today's teachers face different pressures, particularly the abundance of paperwork that results from increased student assessment, testing, and report writing, coupled with the ever-present need to comply with Ministry of Education and Education Review Office dictates. They also know that for any curriculum reform to be successful, teachers must be actively involved in its design and implementation and convinced that it will be workable and meaningful for their students.

Secondary Schools

Students

By the end of the nineteenth century, those few boys and girls who attended secondary schools normally paid substantial tuition fees for the privilege. Some won scholarships which allowed them to stay for up to three or four years, but these were few in number and were offered unevenly across New Zealand. Concern about the small percentage of students who proceeded to secondary school led the Seddon liberal (left of center) government to introduce a secondary school free place system in 1903 via the Secondary Schools Act.[97]

There is evidence that the free place scheme provided financial stability for several secondary schools that had been struggling to survive. It is also clear that the scheme brought students of a different kind into these institutions. Between 1903 and 1912, the number of females enrolling at secondary school had increased by 61 percent, whereas male enrollments for the same period increased by 41 percent. The expansion of secondary rolls was relentless: secondary enrollments rose by 400 percent for example between 1903 and the mid-1920s.[98] Length of stay data for all secondary schools reveal that by 1910, boys and girls on average remained for 2.6 years, and that 67 percent of boys and 70 percent of girls were to be found in junior (first- and second-year) classes. Little discernible change was evident in secondary school pupils' retention between 1920 and 1930. Nationally, there was a very slight increase in the proportion of senior to junior secondary students by 1930. Analysis of data for the period 1930 to 1950 shows that a steady stream of primary school leavers continued moving into secondary schools, culminating in a substantial 25 percent national roll expansion in the latter institutions over these two decades. From 1930 to 1940, the average stay at secondary school was 2.8 years.[99]

The growth in enrollments was more pronounced after 1944 on account of the elevated school-leaving age. In the period 1945 to 1960, state and private secondary school rolls increased by 115 percent, with a massive 63 percent expansion in the 1950s alone. By 1950, some 90 percent of primary school leavers entered secondary school compared with 69 percent 20 years earlier. However, this movement did not translate automatically into a significant increase in secondary pupils' length of stay. In 1955, for instance, the average duration of stay was 2.8 years—the same as for 1930 to 1940. Increased pupil retention was more visible though from the mid- to late-1950s: by 1960, 86 percent of the 1957 secondary school intake was in their third or fourth year compared with 76 percent five years earlier.[100]

While the retention of non-Maori pupils had increased substantially throughout the 1950s, the same was not true for their Maori counterparts. In 1960 for example, 56 percent of the latter had left secondary school in the first two years—64 percent in 1955—compared with 39 and 48 percent for non-Maori, respectively. Non-Maori enrollments in the third and fourth year at high school had increased by 272 and 245 percent, respectively, between 1950 and 1960, compared with 142 percent for Maori.[101] The tendency for students to remain longer at secondary school in the postwar era became more pronounced by the mid-1960s, even though twice as many boys as girls stayed to their fifth and final year. Nonetheless, a very small minority of secondary school leavers continued to enter a New Zealand university—8.5 percent of non-Maori and a minute 1.1 percent of Maori in 1965.[102]

The retention of students from Form 3 to 7 increased more markedly in the 1990s than in any previous decade through the twentieth century. By the mid-1990s the average length of stay was 4.5 years, up from 3.8 years in 1980. Asian students remained the longest at secondary school (4.8 years), followed by non-Maori (4.5 years), Pacific Island (4.4 years), and Maori students (4.1 years). This increase in retention is attributable primarily to government raising the school-leaving age to 16 years in 1993. With a larger group of primary school leavers moving on to secondary schools post-1995 than previously, state secondary rolls increased nationally by 3 percent between 1995 and 1999, while private secondary enrollments underwent a 7.8 percent rise.[103]

From the mid-1990s growing demand for school credentials, alongside government agitation for more secondary school leavers to pursue some kind of tertiary education or training, culminated in the longest length of stay at secondary school for students since the free place system was instituted in 1903.

Curriculum and Teaching Methods

In 1900, 195 teachers in twenty-five secondary schools delivered an academic, two foreign language (Latin and French) course to the great majority of their students. The enrollment of "free place scholars" post-1903 brought into the nation's secondary classrooms a new group of students, many of whom intended to remain fewer than two years before entering the workforce. For many years, if not decades, teachers continued to emphasize the special merits of studying an academic course almost irrespective of students' length of stay. Because the government's rationale behind the free place system was for more qualified primary school leavers to have access to a variety of courses besides a traditional academic secondary school offerings, it was not surprising to discover that curriculum criticism developed. From 1903, the capacity of secondary school authorities to ignore government agitation for curricular reform began to diminish with the government's offer of finance—often to struggling institutions with small enrollments.

The instruments government used to secure curriculum change, albeit gradually, were regulations for junior (Form 3 and 4/Year 9 and 10) and senior (Form 5 and 6/Year 11 and 12) free places, under a succession of Education Acts commencing in 1904. These regulations initially specified a small number of compulsory subjects for all incoming students, notably English and arithmetic. Students were also obliged to choose at least three other subjects from an extensive list (including French, German, Latin, mathematics, geography, and history).[104]

Between 1917 and 1920, Latin was studied nationally by an average of 47 percent of secondary school boys and girls compared with 88 percent of boys and girls for French. The compulsory study of the former subject for University Matriculation Examination purposes until 1944 guaranteed Latin a prominent place in the curriculum. At two of New Zealand's older single-sex secondary schools an academic course was studied by an average of 58 percent of boys and 70 percent of girls in the period 1921–1930. The French language also continued to occupy a prominent place in this decade, with an average of 86 percent of secondary pupils engaged in its study nationwide.[105]

A shift in the proportion of students pursuing an academic course became evident post-1930. Language-based courses were less popular on average. While secondary school authorities were not willing to dismantle their academic courses altogether, they were more prepared than previously to offer alterative courses, probably unenthusiastically in some cases. In the 1930s and 1940s, a commercial course was taken by an average of 19 percent of boys and girls and a home life course was chosen by 13 percent of secondary girls. Agriculture and industrial courses were unpopular. Given that secondary school authorities had *not* been compelled by legislation to offer more courses to their students, it was predictable that the creation of a range of courses besides the academic would take time.

A shift in popularity of some subjects occurred because secondary school authorities had begun to offer a wider range of courses and because the university matriculation qualification could be gained from 1944 by students studying one foreign language only. Furthermore, the Labour government had signaled in the early-1940s that the existing secondary school compulsory curriculum would be expanded to give more recognition to aesthetic subjects and to establish a more balanced general education program for all adolescents. This was deemed vital at a time when only 8 percent of secondary school entrants proceeded subsequently to a New Zealand university.[106]

The period from 1946 to 1999 and later was, in the main, one in which teachers endeavored to meet adolescents' widely varying educational and vocational interests and requirements. Early on, there was apprehension about the requirement that, nationally, high schools were to teach aesthetic subjects compulsorily (e.g., music, a craft, or a fine art subject), even if Home Crafts counted as a "craft" for girls under the new regulations. Secondary schools were legally obliged to teach "Social Studies" mandated for the first time, as a new integrated subject. The introduction of compulsory "General Science" as a second integrated offering led some teachers and others to speculate critically on the introduction of these "soft" or "frill" subjects and "amorphous alternatives" to "proper" established subjects such as geography, history, biology, chemistry, and physics. In short, there was suspicion towards those subjects that had gained optional status in the curriculum only since the late-1930s and early-1940s. A perception that academic standards were being lowered was predictable, especially from private secondary school authorities and many university professors.[107]

By the mid-1970s there was minimal evidence of much variety in course offerings besides academic/professional/general, agricultural, commercial, industrial, and home life options that had been in place since at least the 1930s.[108] Nonetheless a greater desire on the part of secondary teachers by and from this time to introduce new subjects such as urban studies; social, health, and family life education; interdisciplinary studies and human relationship studies was apparent. One consequence was that "academic" subjects were chosen by a smaller proportion of the national school population.

The trend towards—more students taking "vocationally relevant" subjects intensified post-1975, reflecting shifts in students' (and doubtless parents') perceptions of the worth of particular subjects. For predominantly vocational reasons, accountancy, computing, economics, and horticulture were chosen more often in the 1980s than in the 1970s. Variants of English, mathematics, and science were introduced for "low ability" students in senior forms as a response to greater pupil retention and fewer job market opportunities for lower qualified youth. Discrete courses—professional, commercial, and technical for instance—ceased to operate in the 1980s.[109]

From 1993, the national *New Zealand Curriculum Framework* was in place. Because senior students were permitted greater subject choice, the proportion studying core subjects declined with increasing seniority. The most popular language besides English for Year 11 and 12 was Japanese (5 percent), followed by Maori (4 percent), and French (3 percent).[110] In the late 1990s very few schools concentrated on a narrow range of traditionally recognized academic subjects—the great majority provided an extensive range of electives for senior students.

Throughout the nineteenth century, the great majority of secondary teachers had adopted more rather than less formal methods of curriculum delivery. As long as a curriculum–examination nexus remained firmly in place, there was little possibility of a wholesale shift by secondary teachers through the twentieth century to less formal teaching methods. There was not much incentive to make modifications as the public came increasingly to equate examination success with effective teaching. Despite having seen examples of teachers adjusting their methods to better accommodate the interests and abilities of their students, John Murdoch still found ample reason to complain about "[the] powerful hold on the public mind" of the Form 5 (Year 11) University Matriculation Examination, to the extent that "little beyond the examination subjects" was seriously entertained by students and teachers alike. He observed that in such a situation "considerable uniformity of substance and method is inevitable." Predictably, then, teaching was often dull and unimaginative and seldom fired students' interests and imaginations.[111]

From the late-1930s Murdoch detected a shift in geography teaching, away from students memorizing "capes and bays" toward a more humanistic approach to the subject. The same could not be said about history teaching though, for an "acts and facts" approach was still obvious. The situation was not helped by national curriculum regulations that allowed schools throughout New Zealand to offer history for as little as 1.5 hours per week compared with several hours for other "academic" examination subjects. Adolescents' interests hardly counted in the overwhelming rush to secure passes in the University Entrance Examination.[112]

The history of secondary education after World War II and for the rest of the twentieth century is, to a large degree, centered on the numerous difficulties teachers encountered and the strategies they sought to employ when presented with ever-increasing numbers of youth who entered their classrooms every year. Notwithstanding firm support from a government committee in 1944 for secondary teaching methods to be adapted to suit the widely varying needs, interests, and abilities of students, secondary teachers often struggled to translate official rhetoric into daily reality. The retention of an external examination—even in a modified form—provided little relief because teachers knew from experience that a race for examination passes generally discouraged experimenting with a variety of more adolescent-centered methods. "Tried and true" methods were still being used in the 1960s and 1970s. Clarence Beeby, director of Education for New Zealand (1940–60), reported that as a group secondary teachers were often conservative. He argued: "Paradoxically, the [secondary] teaching profession imposes the greatest restraint on major educational change, and yet offers the only means of bringing it about."[113]

A "wait-and-see" approach operated until the 1960s because the Department knew that secondary teachers could not be forced to adopt different teaching methods at a time when there was a chronic teacher shortage. Dissatisfaction with secondary school-teaching methods led a government-appointed committee in the mid-1980s to reemphasize the perceived merits of a child-centered approach to leaning and teaching. Because the learner was regarded as "the central focus of schools" it was held that all learning must be "interesting, stimulating, practical, and successful." Such sentiments were echoed in the 1993 national curriculum framework statement.[114]

Two broad schools of thought have emerged about the movement towards teaching and curriculum reform. One asserts that a holistic, student-oriented approach must be visible in every institution. The other maintains that the movement from the 1980s toward excessively individualistic, adolescent-centered, "relevant," teaching methods has led to reduced teacher professionalism and status and that such an orientation was patently miseducative.[115]

Everyday Life

The academic orientation of New Zealand secondary schools in and from 1900 heavily influenced the kinds of activities in which adolescent boys and girls were involved, both within and beyond classrooms. While this orientation changed as the century evolved, notably from the 1950s, adherence to "traditions" and the promotion by school authorities of a strong sense of pupil identity with their own institution affected students' lives in a variety of ways.

Many school principals encouraged students' regular involvement in sports and games, with differentiation based inevitably on gender: hockey, tennis, badminton, and athletics commonly for girls, and on occasion basketball, netball, and swimming. Boys' schools throughout New Zealand provided cricket, football, tennis, hockey, fives, rowing, boxing, shooting, and swimming, although not all were available at every secondary school. Some girls' schools had difficulty finding adequate space for these activities, so existing playgrounds frequently doubled as unofficial sports fields. Games for adolescent girls included sack races, thread-the-needle, and slow bicycle races. Some female principals actively encouraged their students to learn to dance because it developed grace, poise, rhythm, and aided deportment. Indoor games were also popular. When boys' and girls' secondary schools were located in the same town or city girls attended boys' sports days and special football matches regularly, but always under supervision.

It was common practice for students to cycle, walk, or catch a bus or train to and from school. Students who lived a substantial distance from school boarded at a school facility—initially for the school week but, later, full-time— or privately in the town or city. Regardless of where they lived, it was expected that day students and boarders alike would participate regularly in sports matches between schools, school "house" challenges, garden parties, concerts, drama performances, and such.[116]

Senior students could be selected as prefects, whereupon they were obliged to supervise games, uniforms, and other students daily, and, less frequently, to bank monies for the school and represent their institution at social and other functions. At the latter, senior female students were required to wear either a school or a Girl Guide uniform from the mid-1920s. A move to set up School Councils in secondary schools from the 1970s allowed for greater involvement of all students—not just prefects and seniors—in discussions about uniforms, timetables, and other school matters. The simultaneous appointment of Form Deans was intended to promote better student–teacher understanding.[117]

When the job market was buoyant it was common for principals to receive daily requests from employers for students to commence paid work immediately. This demand for workers resulted in class sizes fluctuating on a regular basis, especially before the school-leaving age was raised from fourteen to fifteen years in 1944. Although pupil retention improved from the 1950s employment opportunities remained plentiful for secondary school leavers.

Because of space restrictions in many institutions students and staff often used the assembly hall or gymnasium for dances, drama and music performances, and speech competitions besides using it for visiting speakers and, sometimes, for classes. Some principals insisted on a daily morning assembly, commencing with a hymn, a Bible reading followed by the Lord's Prayer, and finishing with a morning talk for about fifteen minutes on contemporary issues. These talks were not always enjoyed by students. Regular denominationally based religious observances were, of course, a feature of private—and, from 1975, state integrated—schools, because of these institution's affiliation with a particular brand of Christian or other religion.[118]

Beginning in the 1960s girls' and boys' schools began to implement joint recreational programs for senior students. Some subjects (e.g., music, woodwork, and life/social skills) were taught occasionally to senior boys and girls from single-sex schools together in the one institution from the 1980s. For most, if not all of the twentieth century the great majority of secondary schools began their day with a 9 A.M. whole-school assembly and the singing of the school song. But in recent years variations to this practice became increasingly apparent. A typical secondary school week in the late 1990s was thirty-four to thirty-five hours long, including a one-hour lunchtime and fifteen-minute morning and afternoon daily intervals. By law, the school year had to comprise a minimum of 380 half days—this number was specified by government from the 1920s. Classes usually ended at 3:15 P.M. or 3:30 P.M. daily, although after-school sports activities and school clubs extended the time spent at school.

By the late-1970s, the long-running practice of streaming classes according to perceived academic ability was losing favor nationally. Junior and senior students found themselves in mixed-ability classes at coeducational and single-sex schools. In some schools classes were created where two teachers taught students in the same Year/Form in the one subject, to allow for more individual tuition whenever problems were encountered.

Post-secondary Education

Students

The increase in university student numbers throughout the twentieth and into the twenty-first century was nothing short of remarkable. Analyzing enrollment data for each quarter century reveals that total student enrollments increased from 800 to almost 4,000 (1900–1925), from 4,000 to 10,333 (1925–1950), from 10,333 to 46,207 (1950–1975), and from 46,207 to 122,727 (1975–2000). The numbers have continued to climb thereafter—by 2005, 16,424 more students had enrolled at university than in 2000: an increase of 13.4 percent.[119] Clearly significant numbers of New Zealanders have availed themselves of the opportunity to study in what Tancred had envisioned earlier as being a nonelitist, open entry, low fee university system.

Further analysis of the New Zealand tertiary education sector over the period 1990–2005 shows that the number of students enrolled for tertiary-level study has trebled. The proportion of female-to-male students has increased from 48.4 to 55.2 percent, and Maori and Pasifika student enrollment has almost trebled. Between 1990 and 2005, the number of people graduating with a bachelor's degree or higher qualification increased by 145 percent. By 2005, 58 percent of New Zealanders aged 25–64 held a tertiary-level qualification (degree or diploma). Finally, the 2005 Census data revealed that people with a high school–level qualification had an unemployment rate of 7 percent, whereas the rate for degree holders was only 3.6 percent.[120]

Most tertiary students today understand the importance of studying full-time and are prepared to make significant financial sacrifices in order to gain their qualifications. This is in marked contrast to the experiences of past generations of university students and graduates who typically worked full-time and studied part-time. The progressive introduction of more generous bursaries throughout the twentieth century doubtless induced some students to switch to full-time study and, over time, helped to reduce the number of part-time students.

By the late-1950s, when the Hughes Parry Committee met, approximately 55 percent of full-time arts and science students took longer than four years to graduate. Not surprisingly the Committee turned its attention to the financial costs borne by the students, universities, and the community in general. They also investigated the standard of the University Entrance Examination but could find no evidence of lowered standards to explain the slow path to graduation. The Committee reiterated the need for more university staff to be appointed, the provision of better buildings and library facilities, substantially increased government funding for university education, and greater financial support for full-time students.[121]

While there is some contemporary evidence to suggest that the average degree completion time has decreased, albeit very gradually, since the 1970s, the greatest difference has occurred following the introduction of university fees and loans in 1992. Today's increasingly diverse student body (57.5 percent of whom are female, 51 percent of whom are Pakeha/European, 10 percent Asian, 10 percent International, 18 percent Maori, and 5 percent Pasifika) are well aware of the importance of successful full-time study and the significant personal impact of student loans on their finances, their career choices and their futures.[122]

Curriculum and Teaching Methods

Besides the mainstay bachelor's degrees in arts and science subjects, from 1905 students could enroll in new degrees in literature, veterinary science, public health, and naval architecture, and in five branches of engineering. Moreover, the four university colleges were by this time competing to establish special schools. The University of Otago set up a school of dentistry (1905), Auckland opened schools of engineering (1905), and mines (1906). By 1930, Auckland had established schools of architecture (1917), forestry (1924), and agriculture (1925), whereas Canterbury had its own school of forestry (1921) and the country's first school of engineering (1889). The University of Otago, for its part, founded New Zealand's first school of home science in 1911 while Victoria established a school of agriculture in 1923. When the latter amalgamated with Auckland University College's school of agriculture in 1926 the New Zealand Agricultural College was formed, based in Palmerston North. The following year this school was renamed Massey Agricultural College, later (in 1961) becoming Massey University. Canterbury had established its own agricultural college in 1880 that became known as Lincoln Agricultural College in 1896, reestablished as Lincoln University in 1990.

In many respects the four teachers' training colleges could also be viewed as special schools attached to the four university colleges, to the extent that a common entrance standard was required (i.e., a pass in the fifth form/Year 11 Matriculation Examination), and attendance at certain university courses was compulsory. The principal of the training college was usually a lecturer in education at the local university and a member of the professorial board of advice of the training college. In 1904, when the theory and history of education became an approved degree subject, the central (Wellington) Department of Education insisted that all training college students gain the theoretical part of their education by attending lectures at one of the university colleges. Over time, the training college/university department of education relationship became even closer, such that by the mid-1970s a jointly taught Bachelor of Education (BEd) degree was being offered at Otago and Waikato University.[123] Over the last fifteen years all six colleges of education (formerly teachers' colleges) have merged with their local university and all trainee teachers who graduate do so with a university degree.

By the early-1960s, students had a wide range of subjects and courses from which to choose. At the close of the twentieth century New Zealand universities were offering new degrees in Asian languages, business administration, communications studies, computer science, design studies, economics, finance, food sciences, gender studies, human nutrition, linguistics, management, Maori studies, marketing, media studies, microbiology, nursing, physiotherapy, sociology, and tourism.

Following the abolition of the UNZ in 1961 and the establishment of the UGC, universities were funded in five-year block grants (until the mid-1980s). In the wake of substantial but long overdue funding increases, more vigorous public and political criticism of the perceived "irrelevance" of universities to New Zealand society was voiced. Academics, however, by no means agreed what functions universities ought to perform. Some emphasized the value of studying arts and humanities subjects, others science and technology, others maintained that the universities' special schools were entitled to receive proportionally more money, resources, and staffing.[124]

The creation of a competitive environment within and between universities and other postsecondary establishments for comparatively scarce resources and "customers" was seen by some political groups as being the key to enhanced institutional efficiency. A major feature of this seemingly relentless drive to maximize efficiency was the belief that the allegedly profligate university sector needed to be brought into line with other tertiary education institutions and large-scale government enterprises. Not surprisingly therefore, support for introducing a market or business model (that would encourage competition rather than cooperation within the tertiary sector), the rhetoric of "provider capture," and the ongoing political fascination with predicting the types of skills and knowledge needed for New Zealand to be able to compete globally was evident in a raft of documents produced from the mid-1980s.[125]

To assist more students to attend tertiary institutions, a new government-funded "user pays" loan scheme was introduced in 1992 to cover tuition fees, course-related expenses, and living and accommodation costs. Approximately 70 percent of all full-time tertiary students have taken out student loans since 1999. By 1999, total tertiary student indebtedness had reached US$3.5 billion and was estimated to exceed US$6.3 billion in 2006.[126]

The long shadow cast by the UNZ over the four affiliated university colleges, the colleges' lack of any meaningful autonomy until the late 1950s, the difficulty students encountered in obtaining costly textbooks, the poorly resourced libraries, and the looming end-of-year examinations practically dictated the style (and content) of university lectures. Most lecturers presented copious quantities of information to their mainly part-time students who dutifully recorded as much as they possibly could on paper during their hour-long late afternoon or early evening lectures.[127] For many students attendance at evening classes was impossible. These students enrolled extramurally and typically obtained their university degrees by cramming from textbooks and from the typed notes provided by the college without attending any on-campus lectures. Many of these students were primary schoolteachers who had begun their university degrees as internal (on-campus) students but later moved to schools that were remote from university centers. By 1949 the University Senate felt compelled to act and declared that from 1951 extramural study would not be permitted beyond Stage II in arts and sciences, although no such barrier existed for accountancy and law. From 1941, each college was allowed to examine Stage I students in all BA and BSc subjects. The New Zealand Educational Institute (NZEI) promptly objected to the Senate's position and, following a conference between the University and the NZEI, agreement was reached about postponing the ban and ascertaining the demand for extramural study.[128] By the early-1960s Massey University had taken up the challenge of educating extramural students and today enjoys a reputation as the country's leading provider of extramural degrees.

Following the dissolution of the UNZ in late 1961, each college became a university in its own right. Enjoying this newfound autonomy, lecturers gradually began to experiment with different teaching methods and to utilize new technology as it became available. The introduction of overhead projectors in the 1970s, personal computers in the mid-1980s, and the Internet in the 1990s have provided tertiary teachers with the technological means to deliver their lectures in less didactic ways to on-campus and extramural students. By the late-1990s, increasing numbers of academics had embraced the pedagogical possibilities that electronic (e-) learning offered, beginning to provide their courses entirely online via computer terminals. Many tertiary-level institutions now use an electronic "blackboard" where lecture notes, tutorial topics, assignments, course readings, and other course-related information can be posted and updated regularly. Students can access this information using one of the many on-campus computers or from their home computers.

Everyday Life

The predominantly part-time nature of university study throughout the first half of the twentieth century made it very difficult for students to identify with the more cohesive (and different) experiences of full-time on-campus students, many of whom chose to live in the usually gender-segregated university halls of residence. Turner's detailed survey of this accommodation revealed that, by the 1950s, there was a pressing need for more residential halls to be built because the number of students who lived away from home had outgrown the available supply of housing near the universities. Many students were living in cramped and substandard housing that often led to illness and encouraged undesirable behavior. Moreover, given the small size of university libraries, students had few places where they could study quietly and work without interruption.[129]

Recognizing the urgent need to provide a dedicated place for students to congregate, each of the seven university students' associations in the 1960s introduced a compulsory annual levy that every student paid. This levy was used to fund the building of student unions where students could purchase food and alcohol, dine, and enjoy access to common rooms. The degree to which university students have chosen to participate in nonacademic, on-campus activities has fluctuated over time. One survey undertaken in the mid-1950s revealed that barely half (47 percent) reported being actively engaged in sports clubs and sporting events.[130] In the absence of more recent data, it is impossible to gauge the extent to which students have become more or less involved in such activities. Possibly the widespread adoption of semester-length courses from the mid-1990s and the virtual absence of year-long courses have further reduced students' discretionary time. What we do know, however, is that significant numbers of students have protested over such diverse issues as the Vietnam War, the Springbok Tour (1981), antiabortion legislation, changes to employment law, the introduction of tertiary education fees and student loans, tertiary education funding, and welfare benefit entitlements.

The introduction of tertiary fees and student loans in 1992 has created a level of student indebtedness unknown to older generations of tertiary students. In 2005, 154,411 students borrowed a total of US$680 million—an average of US$4,402 per student—to cover their tertiary course fees, course-related costs, and living and accommodation costs.[131] Many of these students have no option but to juggle the competing demands of full-time study with part-time work and struggle to find enough time to complete the multitude of internally assessed assignments, the marks for which count towards their overall course grade.

As in the past, the government's objectives for tertiary education will continue to shape the daily experiences and expectations of tertiary students and staff. The Labour government's current tertiary blueprint, *Tertiary Education Strategy (TES) 2002/07*, outlines six core goals and priorities for the tertiary sector until 2007—raising foundation skills so that all people can participate in the knowledge economy; developing the skills New Zealanders allegedly need for the knowledge society; strengthening research, knowledge creation, and uptake for our knowledge society; contributing to the achievement of Maori development aspirations; educating for Pasifika peoples' development and success; and strengthening the system's capability and quality. The imminent

Tertiary Education Strategy 2007/12 will prioritize as key tertiary education outcomes the achievement of greater equality, relevance, and value for money.[132] What this will mean in practice is yet to be determined.

Major Reforms

The twentieth century was a particularly busy period for education at every level. Numerous changes were instituted at regular intervals into the schooling system, often a response to the massive, unpredicted expansion in school enrollments in the primary and secondary schooling domains. From a potentially very long list we focus on the evolution of technical high schools and their later transformation into tertiary-level institutions and the provision of state financial aid to private schools.

Technical day (high) schools were established from 1905 as a direct reaction against secondary schools' resistance to government and Department of Education agitation for a wider range of subjects and courses to be introduced following the passage of the free place system. By attempting to redefine a "general education" in less academic, more vocational terms through persuasion and encouragement, with special financial grants available to schools that taught manual and technical or "applied" subjects, Hogben hoped that the New Zealand public would quickly embrace an alternative to the allegedly highly conservative secondary schools.

He was soon disappointed. The general public perception of these new institutions was that they suited less academically minded working-class youth who would remain at a postprimary school only briefly before they entered the paid workforce. Nevertheless they were not strictly vocational, unlike English technical schools. In a calculated effort to boost their status, technical authorities utilized the manual and technical instruction regulations from 1908—to which they were legally required to adhere—in highly creative ways. By the 1920s throughout the country, these schools had established academic courses (alongside several others) leading directly to the University Matriculation Examination.[133]

Both government and the Department of Education had chosen not to intervene overtly, because the education legislation had allowed technical (and other) school authorities to devise a wide variety of programs. While education officials expected that a very small minority of adolescents would opt for an academic offering at a technical school, they were surprised at its almost immediate and ongoing popularity nationwide. Because technical high schools were often located in centers where secondary schools operated, the latter became aware of the potential to compete for pupils at a time when attendance at a postprimary school was not compulsory (until 1945).[134] The result was a steady expansion in courses provided at secondary and technical high schools, to such an extent that ministers of education and other officials began complaining about the increasingly visible overlap between these institutions. This overlap meant that schools with different titles—"secondary" as opposed to "technical"—started to resemble one another more closely, especially from the 1930s.

A small number of education officials and policy makers however welcomed the emergence of one type of post primary school in New Zealand: a comprehensive, multilateral one. But they were not prepared to legislate immediately for the abolition of different types of post primary schools, preferring instead to let the comprehensive schooling model evolve over several decades. The introduction in 1946 of a compulsory core curriculum to be delivered in New Zealand's three kinds of post-primary institutions—district high secondary departments, technical high schools, and secondary schools—gave additional momentum to the transition process. By the mid-1970s technical high schools had ceased to operate nationally, their students having been distributed around secondary schools in the same center of population, or enrolled in new secondary schools. The "night school" component of technical schools, long associated with trade and allied training and separate from the day school, was retained. It was soon incorporated into a newly created tertiary-level institution—a polytechnic or institute of technology. This transformation was encouraged primarily because of the perceived need to train technicians and technologists from the 1960s for new types of highly skilled technical work with a strong applied mathematics and science foundation, and by the then director of Education's firm commitment to modernizing New Zealand's education system. In more recent years, a wide variety of degree, diploma, and certificate programs were developed in polytechnics—including doctorates—often in fields not covered by New Zealand universities. The twenty-three polytechnics that were operating in 2000, for example, tended to emphasize vocational preparation or career-focused learning to a greater extent than did most university faculties or schools.

Debate over whether partial, or full, government financial aid should be granted to nonstate private denominational schools—both primary and secondary—proved to be one of the more contentious issues for a large part of the twentieth century. State funding was to be available from the outset solely to secular (nondenominational) schools. Private school authorities had argued consistently that their total exclusion from state fiscal aid under the 1877 Education Act, an exclusion that remained in place for almost 100 years, was both unjust and discriminatory.[135]

Having received some aid for their schooling endeavors in the period 1847–1877 they maintained that their educational contributions were immediately devalued with the passing of the 1877 Act, effective from 1878. Their reasoning was that as long as private school rolls remained small in comparison to those of state schools, there would be little or no incentive for government to provide any direct fiscal relief. Once their rolls began to expand annually at an ever-increasing rate—and when they began exceeding private schools' capacity to accommodate students on account of the raised school-leaving age from

1944—then it was thought that private schools' demand for "natural justice" would finally be treated seriously. This thesis proved correct, especially for Roman Catholic school authorities who were far more critical than Protestant authorities about having to "surrender" their sons and daughters to "irreligious" secular state schools. By the early 1930s, private school pupils alone constituted 12 percent of the total primary school population, with Catholic boys and girls representing 84 percent of nonstate institution rolls. Since Catholic pupils made up the great bulk of the private school population, it is not surprising that Catholic school authorities were the most vigorous in pushing for financial relief to church schools. In the period 1910–1940, the number of Catholic primary and secondary schools increased by 47 percent and enrollments within them by 83 percent.[136]

The post–World War II era, with the elevated school-leaving age in place, was one in which Catholic authorities in particular, and other denominational authorities in general, vigorously pushed their agenda for reform. Lobbying for state aid was based on known increases in private secondary rather than primary school rolls. By 1970, Catholic school authorities actively publicized the fact that 75 percent of the nation's private primary schools were Catholic and that the insatiable demand for more places in these schools had resulted in some 40 percent of Catholic boys and girls attending state (secular) primary schools. Although the proportion of pupils attending private primary and secondary schools had declined slightly between 1945 and 1970, the joining together of Protestant and Catholic church authorities in the early-1960s helped to advance the private schools' case for 100 percent government funding.[137]

In 1975, full state aid for private primary and secondary schools, subject to certain conditions being satisfied, was granted. Under this legislation church authorities retain ownership of their school premises, although government monies are used to upgrade these former private schools to state school standards. In these institutions sectarian teaching takes place, which is specifically protected under the 1975 Act's "special character" clause. Such schools are obliged to adhere to national curriculum requirements, given that their teaching has to be comparable to that of regular state schools. Integrated institutions post-1975 have attracted considerable critical scrutiny. Many point to the high fiscal costs, the power a minister of education has to vary the proportion of students able to enter a denominationally specific state-integrated school who are not of that denomination, and the potential to indoctrinate students into a certain way of thinking and behaving. By the end of the twentieth century complaints about state-integrated schooling—the concept and its manifestation—had not diminished in either frequency or intensity. This was only to be expected perhaps, given the profile of these institutions. In 1998, there were 312 state-integrated primary and secondary schools nationwide, and they embraced almost 10 percent of students. Furthermore the extension of state-integrated schooling to Seventh-day Adventist, Jewish, Montessori, Muslim, and Steiner schools in the period 1988–1998, representing 24 percent of this sector by 1998, provided additional confirmation to critics of state integration that the 1975 Act was fatally flawed and ill conceived.[138]

THE PRESENT

Type of Educational System

The New Zealand schooling system is predominantly a state one. The smallest sector is that of home-schooled children, comprising less than one percent of six-year-olds to sixteen-year-olds. A small private (independent) schooling sector constitutes 3.9 percent of school enrollments nationwide and embodies 107 schools. State-integrated (former private, denominational) schools, by comparison, have undergone roll growth post-2002 in the primary/intermediate and composite school sectors. However, their secondary school enrollments, as a proportion of total state and private rolls, have remained constant at 13 percent since 2001. Nationally, state-integrated schools constitute 11 percent of compulsory school sector enrollments.

At the tertiary level, the extent to which the state is involved in and exercises control over tertiary education and training institutions has been slightly harder to ascertain in more recent years. While the present Labour government has invested heavily in the state and private tertiary sector, there is no doubt that it expects New Zealand's eight universities in particular to attract more external research income annually. With double the fiscal allocation to private tertiary educational activity in New Zealand, compared with the OECD average allocation for the period 2002-2004, alongside lower New Zealand expenditure than the OECD average for individual tertiary students and for institutions, it may be argued that the government is considering the extent to which it wants to direct state monies to support public tertiary institutions. This lower investment is reflected in the near steady-state of government tuition subsidies and in a slight decline in allowances paid to tertiary students from 2003.

Social Class and Education

Having identified a relationship between students' social class and their access to schools and achievements within them in the twentieth century, we shall now discuss the extent to which this relationship is also evident in the current education system. There is compelling evidence to conclude that, notwithstanding government efforts to actively promote equity policies—in an attempt to minimize the effect of students' lower socioeconomic status on their access to institutions and their retention and performance within them—socioeconomic status remains a powerful determinant of "success" in and beyond educational institutions. To this end the Ministry of Education acknowledged in 2003 that because "socioeconomic status is strongly correlated with achievement" it was fully committed to "raising achievement and reducing disparity."[139]

In relation to early childhood education, the most recent Ministry of Education data demonstrate that children from a high socioeconomic status background were slightly more likely to have engaged in this education before commencing primary school than were boys and girls from lower socioeconomic families (98 percent, 86 percent). Nevertheless the proportion of low socioeconomic status children involved in early childhood education since 2002 has increased slightly more than for boys and girls from high socioeconomic status families, but the latter still participate more consistently in this type of education.[140]

At the secondary school level, middle-class students were four times less likely to leave school at 15 years of age, by gaining an "early leaving exemption," than were boys and girls from a working-class background. Nevertheless a 52 percent increase in the proportion of working-class students gaining a Year 11, National Certificate of Educational Achievement (NCEA) Level 1, qualification was identified in the period 2002–2006.[141]

Race, Ethnicity, and Education

Currently in the schooling system, Pakeha (non-Maori) students form the largest ethnic group, with 59 percent of primary and secondary enrollments nationwide. Maori, Pasifika, Asian, and "Other" constitute 21.6, 9.1, 8.2, and 2.0 percent, respectively. In the senior secondary school, variations are evident in student retention according to ethnicity. A greater percentage of Pasifika youth (19 percent) than Pakeha (11 percent) and Maori (8 percent) were at secondary school as 18-year-olds in 2006.

Very few Asian students leave secondary school early (at 15) compared with Maori in particular, who make up by far the largest group of early leavers. A real concern though was the 25 percent of Maori who departed from school with no qualifications, even though this percentage has declined significantly since 2002.[142] Maori students who gain a first degree significantly enhance their income compared with non-tertiary-qualified Maori, and with Pakeha who hold a bachelor's degree. Completion by Maori (and by Pasifika people) at the tertiary level markedly reduces the widely recognized income disparity that generally exists between Maori, Pasifika, and Pakeha men and women.

Gender and Education

Some of the gaps observed in the twentieth century between males and females have closed slightly in certain respects, while others continue to be visible. The Ministry of Education for example recently claimed that, based on a large-scale national study, girls and boys vary substantially in their writing ability. Year 9 and 10 girls at secondary school in 2005 were one year in advance of their male counterparts in this respect. Furthermore, these girls were slightly ahead of Year 9 and 10 boys in their reading ability. The gap was noticeably larger, favoring girls again, in Year 11. Although the situation was reversed in the case of science, with Year 9 boys having performed on average better than girls, the biggest achievement gains were recorded for Asian and Pasifika girls in Year 9.[143]

Females in Year 11, 12, and 13 (the senior secondary school) in 2005 were slightly more likely than males to attain an NCEA qualification; the former also met the prescribed literacy and numeracy requirements for NCEA Level 1 more often (79 percent, 72 percent). It was to be expected, then, that more females than males would achieve a university entrance or higher qualification (38 percent, 28 percent) and that, as a consequence, fewer males than females would proceed to a tertiary institution (48 percent, 52 percent).

With reference to secondary school subjects there was a tendency for boys to achieve an NCEA credit more often than girls in 2005 in mathematics, science, and technology, and for more girls to gain credits in the arts, English, other languages, and social sciences. A very slight imbalance was detected in favor of boys for health and physical education, and favoring girls for Te Reo Maori (the Maori language). That the Ministry was alert to this reality is beyond doubt, since they reported in 2006 that "gender imbalances in curriculum choices continue."[144]

Two other areas where there was a difference between males and females concerned school stand-downs and suspensions, and early-leaving exemptions. Girls were 230 percent less likely to be "disengaged from school" but were no less likely in 2004 to have been a frequent or an infrequent truant from school. Males were considerably more likely than were females to gain an early-leaving exemption in 2005, mainly on account of being disillusioned with school for various reasons.[145]

Women demonstrated a slightly higher qualification completion rate than did men at all levels save for master's degrees. Women who gained a first degree or a higher qualification received a 140 percent increase on average in their median weekly income in 2005 over the average income for women who lacked such a qualification: the figure was 139 percent for men. But a large gap in men's and women's income remained for those possessing these tertiary qualifications, because men's median weekly income was still some 30 percent more than women's in 2005. This reality may have been offset partly by the realization that as a group, men who held at least a bachelor's degree in 2005 had a slightly higher rate of unemployment than had women: 2.8 percent and 2.5 percent, respectively.[146]

Recent Developments in the Secondary Sector, Teacher Workforce, and Curriculum

Education data for 2006 show that there are 269,659 students, including 7,170 foreign full fee–paying males and females, attending 335 state secular, state-integrated, and private secondary schools. With an average school size of

805 students these institutions are rather small by North American and British standards.

The New Zealand state secular, state-integrated, and private secondary schooling system presently employs some 21,000 teachers. These men and women work in 335 schools across the country, with nearly 270,000 Year 9 to 13 students. Although this means an average pupil–teacher ratio of 1:12.8, Ministry data do not distinguish between teachers with different levels of responsibility. The great majority of secondary teachers are classified as permanent employees (82 percent). Whenever vacancies arose and/or additional appointments were made, permanent teachers were twice as likely as nonpermanent candidates to be appointed. Over the last five years the age profile of secondary teachers has shifted noticeably, however. While the majority still belong in the forty- to fifty-four-year-old age band, with the average age having remained at forty-four years since 1998, the greatest decline has occurred in the forty- to fifty-four-year bracket. Now, more teachers are found in the thirty- to thirty-nine-year-old and fifty-five-years and over band than in 2001. The Ministry maintains that this decline in the proportion of teachers in "the mid-range of ages" has serious implications presently for recruiting and retaining "experienced middle management teachers."

Further insights into both the primary and secondary teaching profession—covering state secular and state-integrated, not private, schools—are gained from studying the Ministry's latest Teacher Census, undertaken in September 2004. This comprehensive survey had an 89 percent response rate from secondary teachers so it provided an accurate indication of the profile of the profession. Nearly 80 percent of secondary staff were non-Maori/Pakeha, while only 8 percent identified as Maori. Pasifika and Asian teachers were the least visible ethnic groups (2 percent and 3 percent, respectively). It was more likely that, on average, students would be taught by women than by men (58 percent: 42 percent), and by women aged between 40 and 49 years (57 percent) than by women under 30 years (16 percent).[147] Teachers usually hold a degree (75 percent) and, if not, have a recognized teaching diploma or certificate (19 percent). Degreed teachers also tended to be younger members of staff—under 40 years (79 percent).

In relation to the secondary school curriculum, only 11 percent of primary and secondary teachers indicated they had taught the national curriculum in either Maori or a Pasifika language; the Samoan language mostly in the latter instance. From the data a picture clearly emerged of secondary teachers as subject specialists: 70 percent taught two subjects while only 13 percent taught in four or more areas. There was a slight but steady drop since 2004 in the percentage of secondary students—Maori and non-Maori alike—who study their curriculum through a Maori language medium.[148]

Maori men and women make up only 7.8 percent of the secondary teacher population although Maori students make up 18.7 percent of the total state secondary school enrollments. The Ministry of Education freely concedes that there are major difficulties in trying to attract Maori to teach at any level in the New Zealand education system—especially those who are fluent in the Maori language—and they acknowledge that most Maori students opt for "mainstream secondary schooling" over *kura kaupapa* Maori.[149]

The New Zealand Curriculum Framework (*NZCF*, 1993–) prescribes the direction for teaching, learning, and assessment in all state secondary schools. While it is not compulsory for private (independent) schools, the great majority adhere to it. This document specifies nine curriculum principles—for instance, equal educational opportunities are to be made available to all learners through nonracist, nondiscriminatory, gender-inclusive programs. It also stresses that the increasingly multicultural composition of New Zealand society must be recognized and respected in schools, and that programs must be designed and delivered around children's perceived learning needs and community and societal requirements, economic and otherwise.[150]

English remains a compulsory school language, although learners can also choose to study Maori, European, and various Asian and Pacific Island languages.[151] In addition to the seven essential learning areas outlined in the *NZCF*, the Ministry and government expect a variety of "essential skills" to be taught in all classrooms. The authors of the *NZCF* boldly claim that the set of skills, and essential learning areas, outlined in the document prepare boys and girls for full participation in the world beyond school. Life outside the classroom is described as competitive, complex, and economically and technologically dynamic but demanding. It is also characterized allegedly by "some disturbing social trends" associated with violent crime, teenage pregnancies, youth suicide, and drug and alcohol misuse.[152] Since 2000 the Ministry has commissioned several inquiries into the national curriculum framework, with a view to ascertaining the effectiveness of the curriculum as a whole and determining where modifications should be made to designated learning areas.

In recent years there has been greater encouragement from the Ministry of Education for teachers to be more involved in curricular discussion at the national level. This is clearly evident in another phase of the review process known as The New Zealand Curriculum/Marautanga Project, since 2003. It aims to "reframe, refocus, and revitalize" the national curriculum mainly through clarifying curriculum outcomes, giving students and teachers a stronger sense of curriculum ownership, and by strengthening school-community and school-parent relationships.[153] Such principles lie at the core of a new draft national curriculum launched on July 31, 2006. Scheduled for implementation in 2008—probably in slightly amended form—the draft departs from previous practice by substituting "key competencies" for the *NZCF*'s eight sets of essential skills.

The current New Zealand national curriculum specifies learning areas, skills, principles, attitudes, and values in some detail but does not prescribe teaching methods for primary or secondary schools. Nevertheless, teachers are left in no doubt that they are expected to satisfy the aims and objectives of the *NZCF*, regardless of the methods they use. They are told they can choose to devise programs around subjects, opt for an integrated approach, or utilize thematic or topic-based methodology. Whatever choice they make, ultimately teachers are expected to devise programs that are "relevant to the learning needs of their students and communities"—always within the context of the national curriculum.[154]

At present, there are ten secondary education teacher providers operating in New Zealand. Six of them are based at a university college, school, or faculty of education, two are standalone teachers' colleges that are currently amalgamating with their local, neighboring university, and two are small-scale non-university affiliated institutions. Together, they offer a one-year, full-time graduate diploma of secondary teaching for applicants who already have a degree, or a four-year bachelor's degree program, in most instances (either a Bachelor of Education or Bachelor of Teaching). While it seems reasonable to presume that the methods trainee secondary teachers were exposed to in their preservice courses (in lectures, tutorials, and in practicums) will influence their subsequent classroom practice, there is little research evidence to describe the precise relationship between preservice secondary training or education and later practice.

Major Reforms

In the twenty-first century, numerous reforms have already been undertaken in the New Zealand education sectors. Initiated by a left-of-center national government, they have been introduced ostensibly to help promote New Zealand as a modern, dynamic, and global knowledge economy. For example, some have sought to overhaul the senior secondary examination system, and to reestablish differentiation between the various types of institutions that make up the tertiary education sector. Some of these reforms have attracted widespread criticism.

In the secondary school arena, the long-standing Year 11 School Certificate and Year 12 Sixth Form Certificate examinations were abandoned in late 2001. These qualifications were replaced by the National Certificate of Educational Achievement (NCEA) that spans Years 11–13 inclusive. When introducing the NCEA, the Labour government sought to eliminate the much-criticized rigid pass–fail norm-referenced system operating within the School Certificate by instituting at each certificate level a four-level grading scheme—Not Achieved, Achieved, Merit, and Excellent—in place of letter grades that coincided with a range of marks.[155]

Criticisms of the NCEA are that it has a demotivating effect on a substantial number of students because the same number of credits can be gained by students pursuing conventional academic subjects (English, chemistry, history) as for those studying other allegedly "easier" subjects (e.g., catering skills and call-center management). Moreover, there is evidence that students are increasingly avoiding difficult topics or sections in subjects because they have already gained enough credits to warrant an "Achieved" grade. With a record 160,000 "Standard Not Attempted" grades allocated in 2005, whereby students enrolled for an externally assessed standard but did not submit work for it, anxiety has mounted regarding the underlying philosophy of the NCEA. The government though is insistent that NCEA will remain the key qualification for senior secondary students.[156]

In its education manifesto for the 1999 general (nationwide) election, the Labour Party undertook to reintroduce school zoning if elected to government. The Party honored its pledge when elected in 2000 and argued that all students had the right to attend their local primary and/or secondary school, rather than allowing schooling authorities to select the students they wanted, as had been the case from the mid-1990s. Equity considerations were the main reason behind the Labour government's change in policy. Schools would no longer be able to "cherry pick" the brightest students and leave the remainder to be accommodated at other schools, the government declared. The Minister of Education Trevor Mallard declared in 2000 that almost 50 percent of Maori students, as opposed to 10 percent of non-Maori youth, were unable to attend schools that operated enrollment schemes under the previous regime. Critics of zoning argue that it artificially evens out enrollment variations between different state schools, that it militates against parental and student choice of schools, and that many parents cannot afford to live in the school zone of their choice. In short, zoning is seen to promote middle class interests. Opponents contend that zoning provides no guarantee of school quality: it represents an intrusion into what should be a highly competitive school market. Supporters respond with the claim that school choice is already a feature of the present New Zealand schooling system because parents can choose between state, state-integrated, and private institutions. Their claim has validity, because private schools enrollments increased nationally by 16.7 percent and those for state-integrated schools by 11.3 percent between 2000 and 2005. State school rolls, in contrast, grew by only 2.8 percent during that period.[157]

With reference to tertiary education reforms, greater differentiation between the various institutions that make up this sector is being encouraged by government, chiefly through progressively separating funding for teaching from funding for research purposes. All full-time academic staff are required to submit to a newly created government agency, The Tertiary Education Commission (TEC), "evidence portfolios" relating to their research activity, publications, graduate supervision, and peer esteem over a six-year period for the Performance-Based Research Fund (PBRF).[158] The second PBRF round was completed in mid-2006 and researchers received notification of their grades in April 2007. Although this recent move to a high-stakes national research assessment and accountability regime for tertiary education institutions has not been universally applauded across the sector, the government is committed to the PBRF system. Current predictions are that the Fund is likely to create a bigger gap fiscally and educationally between staff (and institutions) who research and teach and those who solely teach. The vice-chancellors of New Zealand's eight universities, as academic and administrative heads of their respective institutions, welcome this differentiation. They argue that all undergraduate and graduate degree courses must now be taught by staff who are actively engaged in research in institutions with proven research expertise and possessing high-quality research facilities.

The TEC is charged with implementing the government's 2002–2007 Tertiary Education Strategy that applies to tertiary education and training institutions. It also has responsibility for auditing these institutions to determine the extent to which they contribute to national economic and social goals, and for advising government about tertiary policies, priorities, and the performance of organizations. The TEC's powers are extensive, for it also funds industry and modern apprenticeship training, adult and community education, adult and workplace literacy programs, and e-learning initiatives. Furthermore it provides special supplementary grants for disabled, Maori and Pacifica students, along with contestable funding for polytechnics to strengthen relationships with local employers and organizations.

The government claims that the establishment of the TEC is a particularly important "reform," having proudly declared that "for the first time ever, New Zealand has an explicit, connected, future-focused tertiary education strategy that will directly contribute to broad national, economic and social goals."[159] Nevertheless, sheer breadth and complexity of activities with which the TEC is involved will doubtless prove challenging for the organization to manage and direct in the near future.

A DAY IN THE LIFE OF A NEW ZEALAND SECONDARY SCHOOL STUDENT

Katherine is a fifteen-year-old who formerly attended an all girls' secondary school in a large South Island city and is now in Year 11 (the fifth form) at a single-sex girls' school in a central North Island city. She moved north with her Mum, Dad, and two brothers at the start of 2007.

A typical day for me involves getting up about seven A.M., depending on how tired I am. Fortunately, I live quite close to my school so I can get up a little later, unlike my friends who live further out and have to catch the bus. I have breakfast, brush my teeth, do my hair and then walk to school which takes me about twenty minutes. I arrive at school just after 8:30 A.M. School starts at 8:45 A.M. One day, I slept in and got to school slightly late and was given a verbal warning. If I get another one, then I get a yellow card that is worth one week of detention after school. Before the bell rings for form time, I meet up with my friends and catch up with what has happened in the last twenty-four hours, what we watched on television, etc.

Form time goes for fifteen minutes and during this time, our teacher takes the attendance register and reads out important notices. Then, we are allowed to talk.

The bell rings and we go to our first lesson. We have a timetable so whatever I have at certain times of the day varies but on every Monday, I have Science (first period), PE Studies (second period), Mathematics (third period), English (fourth period) and, finally, French.

In general, my subjects are OK. In science, we are studying Chemistry at the moment. My teacher is really helpful and she is very good at explaining things. Sometimes, we do experiments but mainly we copy notes to prepare for our end-of-year NCEA (National Certificate of Educational Achievement) Level 1 external examinations.

PE Studies is fun. We don't get too much homework for this subject and it is practical. We are doing team-building skills at the moment, which is good for me because I can meet new people and make new friends. We are doing lots of different sports this year. We are also going to be doing kick-art, which I have never done before so that will be interesting!

Yeh! It is interval; the second best part of the day (lunch is best because it is longer!). I meet up with my friends again and we gossip and eat some of the lunch that Mum has made for me. I can't believe that I am at high school and Mum still makes my lunch! How sad is that?! I think Mum makes it because if I made it, then I wouldn't put sandwiches in. Interval lasts for half an hour.

It is now Maths, my most hated subject! I struggle with it and because I am bad at it, I really don't enjoy it. We are doing measurement at the moment and everyone else is practicing for their NCEA assessment. I sat the exam last year at my former school, so I don't have to do as much work. I sit next to a girl who is really good at maths, so if I get stuck or want to check my answers with hers, I always ask her. She's great to talk with and we get along well.

Next, I have English which is probably my favorite subject. It's pretty easy and that's probably why I like it. I sit next to one of my friends too. We are doing "wide reading" at the moment, where we read books and get three credits for doing this.

It is now lunch time and my stomach is growling loudly! My friends and I meet up, and if it's not raining, we sit outside on the grass. We chat about funny things that have happened and anything that hasn't been covered at interval.

Last, but not least, is French. My French teacher is such a crack-up! She's from Belgium and she's really funny. I don't think she realizes just how funny she is! We normally watch educational French programs (which is OK because we get to compare the French students' fashion and their way of life to ours) and practice writing in French. We also sing songs towards the end of the lesson. It's a great way to unwind. There was a real cool song called "Leon le chameleon." We all really get into it, sometimes going a bit over the top!

After school finishes at 3:20 P.M., I meet my friends outside the lockers and we walk home together. Some of my friends get picked up by their parents and others catch the bus home. I walk home and when I finally arrive, I blob out for about ten minutes and then do my homework (otherwise I'll get a yellow card). Then, I watch C4 on TV (a music channel with video clips and celebrity gossip). Most New Zealand teenagers watch it. I am always busy when I get home with lots of homework to do.

TIMELINE

1816	Thomas Kendall of the Church Missionary Society opened the first mission school in the Bay of Islands.
1840	Signing of the Treaty of Waitangi by Maori and non-Maori representatives.
1847	An *Ordinance for Promoting the Education of Youth in the Colony of New Zealand* (Grey's Ordinance) allocated resources to those mission schools providing instruction in English, religion, and industrial training, who agreed to annual government inspection.
1851	Christs' College opened in Christchurch. First rural District High School opened (in Otago).
1858	The Native Schools Act allocated $9,800 annually to educate Maori and half-caste children.
1869	University of Otago (in Dunedin) established under a royal charter (first classes held in July 1871).
1870	University of New Zealand Act passed empowering the University to examine students and to grant degrees.
1875	Abolition of the Provinces Act passed (effective November 1876).
1876	First New Zealand women (Kate Edgar) received a University of New Zealand degree.
1877	Passage of the Education Act—established free, compulsory, and secular primary schooling.
1879	O'Rorke Royal Commission on problems of secondary schools and the University.
1880	Native Schools Code released. Wellington (Teacher) Training College established.
1883	NZEI (New Zealand Educational Institute) founded—advocated uniform national salary scales and condition of service for primary school teachers.
1899	Standard 6 (Year 8) Proficiency Examination introduced.
1901	Free places introduced for rural District High School students. School-leaving age raised from thirteen to fourteen years.
1902	Free places introduced for urban secondary school students.
1905	First technical high school opens.
1912	School medical service established.
1914	Education Act created free places in all state post-primary schools.
1915	Alien Enemy Teachers Act passed—prohibited the employment of German-born teachers.
1920	School-leaving age to fifteen years (postponed until 1943).
1924	Terman Group Test of Mental Ability administered to every high and technical school entrant.
1925	Second (Reichel-Tate) Commission on university education.

1926	Massey Agricultural College established in Palmerston North.
1931	Native school regulations revised to align native school syllabus with that of the ordinary public primary school syllabus.
1932	School starting age raised from five to six years.
1934	School Certificate Examination (Form 5/Year 11) introduced.
1937	Abolition of primary school standards and Standard 6 (Year 8) Proficiency Certificate examinations. National milk-in-schools scheme launched.
1940	Dr. Beeby appointed Director of Education (1940–1960).
1943	Free textbooks issued for primary school students.
1944	Thomas Report recommends a common core curriculum for all post-primary school students.
1959	Free textbooks introduced for secondary school students. Hughes-Parry Report recommends dissolution of University of New Zealand and establishment of a University Grants Committee.
1960	Hunn Report recommends that schools become the "nursery of (racial) integration."
1961	Maori Education Foundation established to "lift Maori education standards."
1969	Control of Maori schools transferred to education boards.
1975	National Conference on "Education and the Equality of the Sexes." Private Schools Conditional Integration Act passed, allowing private schools to integrate into the state system.
1982	Maori Affairs Department establishes Te Kohanga Reo (Maori language) centers for preschool children.
1985	University Entrance Examination (Form 6/Year 12) abolished.
1990	Corporal punishment in schools became illegal.
1991	National Curriculum of New Zealand and National Qualifications Framework documents released for consultation.
1992	Access to student allowances tightened and tertiary fees set by individual institutions. Student loans scheme introduced.
1993	School-leaving age raised from fifteen to sixteen years. Wananga recognized as state Maori tertiary institutions.
1999	First polytechnic granted university status—Auckland University of Technology.
2007	Ministerial release of final *New Zealand Curriculum* report for schools (September).

NOTES

1. Timothy H. Beaglehole, "The Missionary Schools, 1816–1840," in *Introduction to Maori Education*, ed. John Ewing and Jack Shallcrass (Wellington: NZ University Press, 1970), 21–25.

2. Timothy H. Beaglehole, *Education* 20, no. 4 (1971), 5.

3. Kerry R. Howe, *Race Relations, Australia and New Zealand* (Wellington: Methuen, 1977), 283; Claudia Orange, *The Treaty of Waitangi* (Wellington: Allen and Unwin), 8.

4. John M. Barrington and Timothy H. Beaglehole, *Maori Schools in a Changing Society* (Wellington: NZCER, 1974), 36.

5. Ibid., 25–26, 40.

6. John Barrington, "Maori Scholastic Achievement," *New Zealand Journal of Educational Studies* 1, no. 1 (1966), 1, 21.

7. John Mackey, *The Making of a State Education System* (London: Geoffrey Chapman, 1967), 37–39.

8. Stephen J. Ball, "Imperialism, Social Control and the Colonial Curriculum in Africa," in *Defining the Curriculum: Histories and Ethnographies*, ed. Ivor Goodson and Stephen J. Ball (London: Falmer, 1984), 123–24.

9. *NZPD*, 1870, vol. VIII, 33.

10. Ibid., 1877, vol. XXIV, 35–36.

11. R. Openshaw, H. Lee, and G. Lee, *Challenging the Myths: Rethinking New Zealand's Educational History* (Palmerston North: Dunmore Press, 1996), 38–44, 46–47.

12. Ibid., 46.

13. *Appendices to the Journals of the House of Representatives [AJHR]*, 1880, H-1F, 1, Section II; 47.

14. Barrington, "Maori Scholastic Achievement," 4; Openshaw, Lee, and Lee, *Challenging the Myths*, 48.

15. Ruth Fry, *It's Different for Daughters* (Wellington: NZCER, 1985).

16. *AJHR*, 1902, E-1, 11.

17. Arthur G. Butchers, *Education in New Zealand* (Dunedin: Coulls Somerville Wilkie, 1930), 592; Education Act, 1877, Sections 86, 87 (1)–(4), 95.

18. J. David S. McKenzie, *Education and Social Structure; Essays in the History of New Zealand Education* (Dunedin: New Zealand College of Education, 1982), 5.

19. *NZPD*, 1877, vol. XXIV, 32–34.

20. Ibid., 32.

21. The Education Act, 1877, Section 84 (1); Regulations defining standards of education and for inspection of schools, *New Zealand Gazette*, 1878, vol. 2, 1309–1312; *NZPD*, 1877, vol. XXIV, 32.

22. John Lithgow Ewing, *The Development of the New Zealand Primary School Curriculum 1877–1970* (Wellington: NZCER, 1970), 17–18.

23. Ibid., 17.

24. Arnold E. Campbell, *Educating New Zealand* (Wellington: Department of Internal Affairs, 1941), 80–82.

25. *AJHR*, 1880, H-1A, 12; H-11, 22; 1891, E-1, v.

26. *AJHR*, 1883, E-1B, 7; J. Belich, *Paradise Reforged: A History of New Zealanders from the 1880s to the Year 2000* (Auckland: Allen Lane/Penguin Press, 2001), 356.

27. Campbell, *Educating New Zealand*, 88–89; Ewing, *The Development*, 48.

28. A. G. Butchers, *The Education System: A Concise History of the New Zealand Education System* (Auckland: National Printing Co., 1932), 122; Campbell, *Educating New Zealand*, 110.

29. Ibid., 241; John H. Murdoch, *The High Schools of New Zealand: A Critical Survey* (Wellington: NZCER, 1944), 23.

30. Ibid.

31. David McKenzie, Howard Lee, and Greg Lee, *Scholars or Dollars? Selected Historical Case Studies of Opportunity Costs in New Zealand Education* (Palmerston North: Dunmore Press, 1996), 99–114; Openshaw, Lee, and Lee, *Challenging the Myths*, 103–6, 207–9.

32. William J. Brittenden, "Foundations Well and Truly Laid," in *The Years Between: Christchurch Boys' High School, 1881–1981*, ed. Arthur Trevor Campbell (Christchurch: Christchurch High School Old Boys' Association, 1981), 19; Fry, *It's Different for Daughters*, 34–35; Murdoch, *The High Schools*, 3–20.

33. Brittenden, "Foundations," 22; Olga E. Harding, *One Hundred Years: A History of Wellington Girls' College* (Wellington: Wellington Girls' College Centennial Committee, 1982), 7, 24.

34. Ian Cumming and Alan Cumming, *The History of State Education in New Zealand: 1840–1975* (Wellington: Pitman Pacific, 1978), 112; Murdoch, *The High Schools*, 15, 30.

35. Brittenden, "Foundations," 22–23; Harding, *One Hundred Years*, 7.

36. Campbell, *Educating New Zealand*, 109; John Caughley, "The Development of the Curriculum," in *Fifty Years of National Education in New Zealand: 1878–1928*, ed. Ian Davey (Auckland: Whitcombe & Tombs, 1928), 38.

37. Butchers, *The Education System*, 153; Campbell, *Educating New Zealand*, 76–88, 108–17.

38. Brittenden, "Foundations," 23–24; Campbell, *Educating New Zealand*, 30, 117.

39. Openshaw, Lee, and Lee, *Challenging the Myths*, 102–4, 202–14; Herbert Roth, *George Hogben: A Biography* (Wellington: NZCER, 1952), 56–57, 88.

40. Harding, *One Hundred Years*, 10–19, 25–41.

41. Brittenden, "Foundations," 26–27; Murdoch, *The High Schools*, 3–37; Eileen Wallis, *A Most Rare Vision: Otago Girls' High School—The First One Hundred Years* (Dunedin: Otago High Schools' Board of Governors and John McIndoe, 1972), 47.

42. Barrington and Beaglehole, *Maori Schools*, 163–68.

43. Barbara Peddie, *Christchurch Girls' High School: 1877–1977* (Christchurch: Christchurch High School Old Girls' Association, 1977), 41–42.

44. Cumming and Cumming, *A History of State Education*, 117–19.

45. Fry, *It's Different for Daughters*, 42; Harding, *One Hundred Years*, 7; Peddie, *Christchurch Girls' High School*, 51–52.

46. Peddie, *Christchurch Girls' High School*, 42–43.

47. Brittenden, "Foundations," 25–30.

48. Wallis, *A Most Rare Vision*, 47–48.

49. Harding, *One Hundred Years*, 10–11; Wallis, *A Most Rare Vision*, 27–31, 54–56.

50. Wallis, *A Most Rare Vision*, 27–29, 44–45, 52, 66.

51. Hugh Parton, *The University of New Zealand* (Auckland: Auckland University Press, 1979), 98–100.

52. Campbell, *Educating New Zealand*, 154.

53. Hugh Parton, *The University of New Zealand* (Auckland: Auckland University Press/Oxford University Press, 1979), 20.

54. John C. Beaglehole, *The University of New Zealand* (Wellington: NZCER, 1939).

55. *University of New Zealand Calendar*, 1900–1901, 16; Campbell, *Educating New Zealand*, 159; Parton, *The University of New Zealand*, 26.

56. Beaglehole, *The University of New Zealand*, 115, 127; Parton, *The University of New Zealand*, 20.

57. Beaglehole, *The University of New Zealand*, 128; Parton, *The University of New Zealand*, 22, 60, 81.

58. Ibid.

59. Parton, *The University of New Zealand*, 185.

60. Beaglehole, *The University of New Zealand*; William. J. Gardner, Edward T. Beardsley, Tony E. Carter, *A History of the University of Canterbury* (Christchurch: University of Canterbury, 1973).

61. Beaglehole, *The University of New Zealand*, 134.

62. Ewing, *The Development of the New Zealand Primary School Curriculum*; A. H. W. (Bob) Harte, *The Training of Teachers in New Zealand from its Origins until 1948* (Christchurch: Simpson & Williams Ltd., 1972).

63. Gregory Lee and Howard Lee, "The State Aid and Integration Debate in New Zealand Education, 1877–1998: Policies, Problems and Possibilities," *Waikato Journal of Education* 4 (1998), 150–66.

64. Mark Harrison, *Education Matters: Government, Markets and New Zealand Schools* (Wellington: Education Forum, 2004), 300; Ministry of Education, *Tertiary Education Sector Report*, 66.

65. Butchers, *The Education System*, 201.

66. Roy Shuker, *The One Best System? A Revisionist History of State Schooling in New Zealand* (Palmerston North: Dunmore Press, 1987), 55–56.

67. Openshaw, Lee and Lee, *Challenging the Myths*, 156–57, 199–202.

68. Department of Education, *State Secondary Schools in New Zealand: A Baseline Survey* (Wellington: Department of Education, 1981), 86, 95.

69. Harry H. Hornsby, "The Independent Schools of New Zealand," in *New Zealand Education Today*, ed. Frank Mitchell (Wellington: A.H. & A.W. Reed, 1968), 105–11.

70. Openshaw, Lee, and Lee, *Challenging the Myths*, 78–80, 276; Cora Vellekoop, "Social Strata in New Zealand," in *Social Process in New Zealand: Readings in Sociology*, ed. John Forster (Auckland: Longman Paul, 1969), 253.

71. Historical Branch of the Department of Internal Affairs, *Introduction to New Zealand* (Wellington: Whitcombe & Tombs, 1945), 162.

72. Commission on Education in New Zealand, *Report of the Commission on Education in New Zealand* (Wellington: Government Printer, 1962), 417–18; Minister of Education, *New Zealand Schools 98*, 91.

73. David Bedggood, *Rich and Poor in New Zealand: A Critique of Class, Politics and Ideology* (Sydney: George Allen & Unwin, 1980), 103–4; Ministry of Education, *New Zealand's Tertiary Education Sector Report: Profile & Trends 2000* (Wellington: Ministry of Education, 2001), 16.

74. Barrington and Beaglehole, *Maori Schools*, 234–36; Alison Jones, Gary McCulloch, Jim Marshall, Graham Smith, and Linda Smith, *Myths and Realities: Schooling in New Zealand* (Palmerston North: Dunmore, 1990), 140–47.

75. Minister of Education, *New Zealand Schools 98*, 27–29, 93–94; Ministry of Education, *Tertiary Education Sector Report*, 103–4.

76. Fry, *It's Different for Daughters*.

77. Gregory Lee, "From Rhetoric to Reality: A History of the Development of the Common Core Curriculum in New Zealand Post-Primary Schools, 1900–1945," (PhD diss., University of Otago, 1991), 849–50.

78. Clarence E. Beeby, *The Biography of an Idea: Beeby on Education* (Wellington: NZCER, 1992), 188–89.

79. Commission on Education in New Zealand, *Report*, 65–66, 316–17, 394–95.

80. Butchers, *The Education System*, 133; James C. Dakin, *Education in New Zealand* (Auckland: Leonard Fullerton, 1973), 32, 62.

81. Ministry of Education, *Tertiary Education Sector Report*, 21, 101–3.

82. Butchers, *Education in New Zealand*, 590–93; Commission on Education in New Zealand, *Report*, 47; Ministry of Education, *Education Statistics of New Zealand* (Wellington: Ministry of Education, 2000), 39, Table 20; 2005, 47, Table 29.

83. Mark Olssen, ed., *Mental Testing in New Zealand: Critical and Oppositional Perspectives* (Dunedin: University of Otago Press, 1988).

84. Ewing, *The Development*, 270; ERO, *Assessment in Primary Schools: A Guide for Parents* (Wellington, June 2006), 14, 20.

85. Ian A. McLaren, *Education in a Small Democracy: New Zealand* (London: Routledge & Kegan Paul, 1974), 112–13.

86. *AJHR*, 1904, E-1C, 2.

87. Ewing, *The Development*, 104–9; *New Zealand Gazette*, 1904, vol. 1, 265–304.

88. Campbell, *Educating New Zealand*, 96.

89. Ewing, *The Development*, 167–75, 180–86.

90. Ibid., 208–254; David Philips, "Curriculum Development on New Zealand," *Educational Review* 45, no. 2 (1993), 156.

91. Ministry of Education, *The New Zealand Curriculum Framework* (Wellington: Ministry of Education, 1993), 4–9, 22–23.

92. Warwick B. Elley, "Curriculum Reform: Forwards or Backwards?" *Delta* 52, no. 2 (1996), 39–63; D. Philips, "Curriculum and Assessment Policy in New Zealand: Ten Years of Reforms," *Educational Review* 52, no. 2 (2000), 143–53.

93. Ministry of Education, *Curriculum Stocktake Report to Minister of Education* (Wellington: Ministry of Education, September 2002). www.minedu.govt.nz/index.cfm?layout=document&document=7823&data=1&goto=00 (accessed March 28, 2007).

94. Ewing, *The Development*, 152.

95. Board of Education, *Report of the Consultative Committee on the Primary School* (London: His Majesty's Stationery Office, 1931), 93.

96. Arnold E. Campbell, *Modern Trends in Education* (Wellington: Whitcombe & Tombs Ltd. 1938), xiii.

97. Butchers, *The Education System*, 123.

98. Howard F. Lee, "The Credentialled Society: A History of New Zealand Public School Examinations, 1871–1990" (PhD diss., University of Otago, 1991), 497.

99. Lee, "From Rhetoric to Reality," 40, 193–95, 292, 557.

100. Commission on Education in New Zealand, *Report*, 47–53, 204; Lee, "The Credentialled Society," 96.

101. Ibid., 405, 408.

102. Department of Education, *Educational Statistics of New Zealand, 1966, Part 2* (Wellington: Department of Education, 1966), 35–36, 49.

103. C. E. Beeby, "A Problem of Secondary Education Unsolved Worldwide," in *Looking Forward: Essays on the Future of Education in New Zealand*, ed. Geraldine McDonald and Alistair Campbell. (Wellington: Te Aro Press, 1984), 88–111; Ministry of Education, *Education Trends Reports: Primary and Secondary School Enrollment Trends to 1990 and Beyond* 4, no. 1 (January 1991), 2; Ministry of Education, *New Zealand Schools 98*, 17, 21, 24, 64.

104. Lee, "From Rhetoric to Reality," 826–35, 848–58, 869–77; Openshaw, Lee, and Lee, *Challenging the Myths*, 104–19, 132–76.

105. Lee, "From Rhetoric to Reality," 167, 205, 239.

106. Lee, "The Credentialled Society," 607; McLaren, *Education in a Small Democracy,* 119.

107. Openshaw, Lee, and Lee, *Challenging the Myths,* 184–88.

108. McLaren, *Education in a Small Democracy,* 131; Department of Education, *State Secondary Schools in New Zealand: A 1985 Follow-up of the 1975 Baseline Survey* (Wellington: Department of Education, 1986), 171–72.

109. Ibid., 1–2.

110. Department of Education, *New Zealand Curriculum Framework,* 8–9; Minister of Education, *New Zealand Schools 98,* 81.

111. Murdoch, *The High Schools,* 75, 77, 79–82, 89–90.

112. Ibid., 133, 136, 141–45.

113. Beeby, *The Biography of an Idea,* 179–80, 195–201; Department of Education, *The Post-Primary Curriculum,* 7; Murdoch, *The High Schools,* 390.

114. Department of Education, *The Curriculum Review,* 6, 14–15; Ministry of Education, *The New Zealand Curriculum Framework,* 6–7, 27.

115. Martin Hames, *The Crisis in New Zealand Schools* (Palmerston North: Dunmore Press, 2002), 40–55.

116. William J. Gough, "A Flowering in the 1960s," in *The Years Between: Christchurch Boys' High School, 1881–1981,* ed. Arthur T. Campbell (Christchurch: Christchurch High School Old Boys' Association, 1981), 49–68, 81–103; Peddie, *Christchurch Girls' High School,* 125.

117. Harding, *One Hundred Years,* 126, 145–46, 162; Muriel May, *St Hilda's Collegiate School: The First Seventy Years, 1896–1966* (Dunedin: St Hilda's Collegiate School, 1969), 18–19.

118. For example, Harry S. Baverstock, "A Great Headmaster Shapes His School," in *The Years Between: Christchurch Boys' High School, 1881–1981,* ed. Arthur Trevor Campbell (Christchurch: Christchurch High School Old Boys' Association, 1981), 50, 57.

119. Ministry of Education, *Education Statistics of New Zealand* (Wellington: Ministry of Education, 2000, 2005), 90; Ministry of Education, *State of Education in New Zealand* (Wellington: Ministry of Education, 2006); Parton, *The University of New Zealand,* 42, 167, 174.

120. Ministry of Education, *Education Statistics of New Zealand* (1990, 2005), 89; *Student Loan Scheme Annual Report* (Wellington: Ministry of Education, 2006), 13–14.

121. Parton, *The University of New Zealand,* 223–224; *Report of the Committee on New Zealand Universities,* 4, 25–36.

122. Ministry of Education, *Education Statistics* (2000, 2005), Tables 69, 78, 94, 103; *Students Loan Scheme Annual Report,* 13–17.

123. David Keen, *In a Class of its Own; A Dunedin College of Education Anniversary* (DCE and Longacre Press, 2000), 200.

124. D. McKenzie, "A Decade in the Life of New Zealand Universities," *Educational Research and Perspectives* 23, no. 1 (1996), 146–62.

125. Greg Lee and Howard Lee, "New Zealand Universities in Retrospect," *New Zealand Education Review* (December 14, 2000); McKenzie, "A Decade in the Life."

126. Ministry of Education, *Annual Report on the Student Loan Scheme* (Wellington: Ministry of Education, 2000 and 2006), Table 3, 14.

127. R. M. Burdon, *The New Dominion: A Social and Political History of New Zealand 1918–39* (Wellington: Reed, 1965), 88–89; Campbell, *Educating New Zealand*, 167; Parton, *The University of New Zealand*, 157, 229.

128. Burdon, *The New Dominion*, 88; Campbell, *Educating New Zealand*, 155; Parton, *The University of New Zealand*, 164, 189–90.

129. William J. Morrell, *The University of Otago: A Centennial History* (Dunedin: University of Otago Press, 1969), 175, 184, 193–222; Parton, *The University of New Zealand*, 228–229; Harold. W. Turner, *Halls of Residence* (Wellington: NZCER, 1953), 2–5.

130. Parton, *The University of New Zealand*, 52, 228.

131. Ministry of Education, *Student Loans Scheme Annual Report* (Wellington: Ministry of Education, October 2006), 1, 4–5.

132. Ibid. 8.

133. Openshaw, Lee, and Lee, *Challenging the Myths*, 105, 151–55.

134. Ibid., 117–19.

135. Ibid., 241–43.

136. Ibid., 242; Butchers, *The Education System*, 195; McLaren, *Education in a Small Democracy*, 57; Shuker, *The One Best System?*, 251.

137. Commission on Education in New Zealand, *Report*, 700; Dakin, *Education*, 81–82; McLaren, *Education in a Small Democracy*, 57; Openshaw, Lee, and Lee, *Challenging the Myths*, 244–45.

138. Ibid. Minister of Education, *New Zealand Schools 98*, 14–15, 21.

139. Ministry of Education, *Statement of Intent: 2003–2008* (Wellington: Ministry of Education, 2003), 16; See also Ministry of Education, *Briefing for the Incoming Minister of Education* (Wellington: Ministry of Education, October 2005), 43, 50–51.

140. Ministry of Education, *State of Education*, 11–12.

141. Ibid., 33, 42, 45–47.

142. Ibid., 33, 45, 51, 59.

143. Minister of Education, *New Zealand Schools 05*, 12–13, 41.

144. Ibid., 72; *State of Education*, 42.

145. Ministry of Education, *State of Education*, 28, 31, 33.

146. Ibid., 59–60, 71–72, 79.

147. Ministry of Education, "Teacher Census," June 2005, http://www.education-counts.edcentre.govt.nz (accessed February 23, 2007).

148. Ibid. Ministry of Education, "Maori Medium Education as at 1 July 2006," 2006, http://www.educationcounts.edcentre.govt.nz; Ministry of Education, "School Roll Summary Report."

149. Ministry of Education, *Annual Report on Maori Education, 2005*, 45, 51, 130; "Maori Medium Education."

150. Ministry of Education, *The New Zealand Curriculum Framework*, 6–7; Pat Snedden, Jo Ayers, Anne-Marie Cervin, and Maurice Cervin, *Excellence: New Zealand Education Directory 2005* (Auckland: Snedden and Cervin, 2005), 80–83.

151. Mathematics and science are not presently compulsory in Years 12 and 13.

152. Ministry of Education, *The New Zealand Curriculum Framework*, 1, 17, 28.

153. Ministry of Education, "The New Zealand Curriculum/Marautanga Project," 2003, http://www.tki.org.nz (accessed February 19, 2007); Ministry of Education, *Curriculum/Marautanga Project Issue 1* (Wellington: Ministry of Education, April

2004), 1; Ministry of Education, *Curriculum Update Issue 56* (Wellington: Ministry of Education, September 2005), 8.

154. Ministry of Education, *New Zealand Curriculum Framework*, 4, 6, 8, 23.

155. New Zealand Qualifications Authority, *NCEA Update, Issue 18* (Wellington: New Zealand Qualifications Authority, June 2003), 2, http://www.ncea.govt.nz (accessed February 23, 2007).

156. New Zealand Qualifications Authority, *AQ News*, no. 52 (April 2006), 3.

157. Amie Richardson, "School Wars," *New Zealand Listener* 202, no. 3430 (February 4, 2006), 17–19; Peter Shirtcliffe, "Lessons to Learn," *New Zealand Listener* 197, no. 3378 (February 5, 2005), 32–33.

158. Jonathan Boston, "The Performance-Based Research Fund," in *Punishing the Discipline—The PBRF Regime*, ed. Richard Smith and Joce Jesson (Auckland: AUT University, 2005), 173–85.

159. Steve Maharey, "Foreword: Facing Our Knowledge Future," in *A New Tertiary Landscape*, 4–5.

BIBLIOGRAPHY

Alcorn, Noeline. 1999. *To the Fullest Extent of His Powers: C. E. Beeby's Life in Education*. Wellington: Victoria University Press.

Barrington, John M., and Tim H. Beaglehole. 1974. *Maori Schooling in a Changing Society: An Historical Review*. Wellington: New Zealand Council for Educational Research.

Beeby, Clarence E. 1992. *The Biography of an Idea: Beeby on Education*. Wellington: New Zealand Council for Educational Research.

Campbell, Arnold E. 1941. *Educating New Zealand*, Wellington: Department of Internal Affairs.

Commission on Education in New Zealand. 1962. *Report of the Commission on Education in New Zealand*. (The Currie Report). Wellington: Government Printer.

Department of Education. 1944. *The Post-Primary Curriculum: Report of the Consultative Committee Appointed by the Minister of Education in November, 1942*. (The Thomas Report). Wellington: Government Printer.

Department of Education. 1986. *State Secondary Schools in New Zealand: A 1985 Follow-up of the 1975 Baseline Survey*. Wellington: Department of Education.

Department of Education. 1987. *The Curriculum Review: Report of the Committee to Review the Curriculum for Schools*. Wellington: Government Printer.

Ewing, John. 1970. *The Development of the New Zealand Primary School Curriculum 1877–1970*. Wellington: New Zealand Council for Educational Research.

Fry, Ruth. 1985. *It's Different for Daughters: A History of the Curriculum for Girls in New Zealand Schools, 1900–1975*. Wellington: New Zealand Council for Educational Research.

Jones, Alison, Gary McCulloch, James Marshall, Graham H. Smith, and Linda T. Smith. 1990. *Myths and Realities: Schooling in New Zealand*. Palmerston North: Dunmore Press.

Mackey, John. 1967. *The Making of a State Education System*. Great Britain: Geoffrey Chapman.

McKenzie, David, Greg Lee, and Howard Lee. 1996. *Scholars or Dollars? Selected Historical Case Studies of Opportunity Costs in New Zealand Education.* Palmerson North: Dunmore Press.

McLaren, Ian A. 1974. *Education in a Small Democracy.* London: Routledge & Kegan Paul.

Ministry of Education. 1991. *Education Statistics News Sheets.* Wellington: Ministry of Education.

Ministry of Education. 1991. *Education Trends Reports: Primary and Secondary School Enrollment Trends to 1990 and Beyond.* Wellington: Ministry of Education.

Ministry of Education. 1993. *The New Zealand Curriculum Framework.* Wellington: Ministry of Education.

Minister of Education. 1995. *New Zealand Schools 1994: A Report on the Compulsory Schools Sector of New Zealand.* Wellington: Learning Media.

Ministry of Education. 1999. *New Zealand Schools 98: Report of the Minister of Education on the Compulsory Schools Sector in New Zealand 1998.* Wellington: Ministry of Education.

Ministry of Education. 2001. *New Zealand's Tertiary Education Sector Report: Profile and Trends 2000.* Wellington: Ministry of Education.

Ministry of Education. 2002. *Curriculum Stocktake Report to Minister of Education.* Wellington: Ministry of Education.

Ministry of Education. 2005. *Annual Report on Maori Education, 2005.* Wellington: Ministry of Education.

Ministry of Education. 2005. *Making a Bigger Difference for all Students: Schooling Strategy 2005-2010.* Wellington: Ministry of Education.

Ministry of Education. 2005. *New Zealand Schools 05: A Report of the Minister of Education on the Compulsory Schools Sector in New Zealand 2005.* Wellington: Ministry of Education.

Ministry of Education. 2006. *A Changing Population and the New Zealand Tertiary Education Sector, 2006.* Wellington: Ministry of Education.

Ministry of Education. 2006. *State of Education in New Zealand 2006.* Wellington: Ministry of Education.

Murdoch, John H. 1944. *The High Schools of New Zealand: A Critical Survey.* Wellington: New Zealand Council for Educational Research.

Openshaw, Roger, Greg Lee, and Howard Lee. 1993. *Challenging the Myths: Rethinking New Zealand's Educational History.* Palmerston North: Dunmore Press.

Chapter 5

SCHOOLING IN PAPUA NEW GUINEA

John Cleverley

Papua New Guinea faces unique challenges as it seeks to achieve the UNESCO target of education for all by 2015, given the nation's rugged geography, scattered settlements, and diverse cultures. The country's physical shape was determined some six thousand years back when the land mass of New Guinea was separated from the north of the Australian continent by a cataclysmic inflow of waters. This newly isolated country comprised a spine of mountain ranges densely forested and cloud covered, and cut across by great rivers like the Sepik and the Fly, with their surrounds of swamp and grassland. Around the upward thrusting mainland are low-lying coastal regions and clusters of islands in coral shallows subject to earthquake and violent volcanic eruption.

The great New Guinea Island today is divided into an eastern half, Papua New Guinea (PNG), which became an independent nation in 1975, and a western half, previously, Netherlands New Guinea, that was formally declared an Indonesian province, Irian Jaya, in 1969. PNG's population of around six million Papuan and Melanesian people is split into near 1,000 clans speaking over 800 separate languages known as Tok Ples, and among this population are Polynesians, Asian, and European people dispersed in the many small townships across land and ocean. Traditionally, PNG clans had no written language, however, all had strong oral traditions for the transmission of culture and knowledge. English was selected as the official language on Independence and now Tok Pisin, a Melanesian pidgin, and Hiri Motu, a Papuan lingua franca, are recognized and continue to be widely spoken.

Despite about one million children in school in a range of institutions from pre-school to university, the country has been unable to meet the demand for school places from its rapidly increasing population (which has more than doubled since 1980).[1] Education remains a desired commodity among parents and young people—both the well-to-do and poor. After meeting with the urban disadvantaged in the capital, Port Moresby, in 2006, a UNICEF coordinator reported: "I have had opportunities to speak with many ex-convicts, 'raskols' and prostitutes who share the same concern. Most would like to complete their education and find a decent job."[2]

BEFORE THE NINETEENTH CENTURY

Humans reached PNG by island hopping from the north 60,000 or more years ago, where they sustained themselves at first by hunting, fishing, and food gathering, and by agriculture and extended trading later. Over time, the country sustained waves of new arrivals who maintained small communities and cultures suited to their needs, material and spiritual. Millennia before the nineteenth century, long-recognized social practices bound these communities together laying down the prescriptions of childhood and adolescence.

Traditional Education in the Highlands and the Coastal Regions

Significant differences arose in the detail and in the timing of educational activities across PNG, especially between the people who lived among gardens, huts, and fortified hamlets in the central Highlands, and the coastal and island dwellers whose small settlements were reliant on the sea, garden cultivation, and trading.[3] While there were different customs across Highland regions and Islander communities, the practices of days long past, named *Kastom* in pidgin, continue to provide an underpinning for national sentiment.

The children of the Highlands shared a land of small valleys surrounded by forest, river, and escarpment, and a network of gardens where sweet potato and other crops were cultivated along with pig rearing. Both sexes lived in their mother's hut close to their garden and their pigs' foraging area: they were breast fed up to five years of age or so and remained closely attached to the mother throughout her working day, the very young carried on her hip or in a knitted string bag greased with pig fat. By contrast in coastal and island regions the children grew up in a world of sea and sand with huts built on the shoreline frequently over water, the rise and fall of the tide lapping below. Unlike the Highlands clans, coastal people lived as families although younger boys could stay for a period with their older brothers or uncles.

The First Stage of Learning

For Highland boys this stage occurred at around five or six years when they began imitating the activities of their older brothers and male role models. Mostly they went naked, their hair plaited, or they wore a bark belt and strings, a bark wrist shield and a necklace or two. On special occasions, the male would be decorated in spectacular color with feathers, ochre, shell, and tooth ornaments. Given bows and arrows of small size stimulating learning through play, they tried their hand at hunting birds of paradise, and small animals like possums, cuscus, fish, and reptiles. They found opportunities to learn drumming, to make fire and torches, and engage in mock warfare.

A Highland girl grew up in a more circumscribed world. Her learning began inside the hut where her mother taught her to mind the fire and tend the pigs shut in overnight, and where she joined in making ornaments and preparing twine for the net bags. Her garb was similar to a boy's: nakedness and hair plaiting, or a bark belt with strings holding leaves at the front and back. Later she would wear a distinctive bark cloak on her shoulders. On special occasions, a girl would be bedecked with bird of paradise feathers, possum skins, shell ornaments, face painting, and tattooing in an unrivalled display of color and wealth.

Girls were the ever-present observers as their mothers responded to the spirit world around them learning the taboos that bound them and the common medical remedies. By the time a girl reached eleven or twelve years, she was a significant helper in her family. Using a sharpened digging stick, she would join her mother in the garden, planting, weeding, and harvesting the sweet potato, yams, and greens. She also collected wild plants and fruits, prepared sago, distributed cooked food, gathered firewood, and carted water.

The first learning stage for boys in the coastal regions saw them in and out of the water from four years with their sisters and friends, learning to swim without conscious effort. At age six or seven, a boy's dress was little more than a belt, an armlet, and a necklace perhaps of dogs' teeth; otherwise, he went naked. Young males were soon piloting miniature canoes getting the feel of paddle and water, trying their hand at ferrying the family around. Spear throwing was practiced, as they learned to spike fish and kill turtle, and they went reef-fishing using nets and baskets. As they grew older, boys would sail at night with their kinsmen, helping with the catch and tending to the bamboo torches. In some places, they helped catch crocodiles unless a clan totem applied, enjoying the succulent meat. The young men soon moved from the spearing of fish to throwing spears at each other, testing themselves in weaving and dodging. In their early upbringing, boys were more likely pampered than girls, being allowed to chew their father's red betel nut and lime and given guardian spirits drawn from the ranks of their dead ancestors.

Girls' early education in coastal regions differed from that of boys as the girls grew older. Up to the age of three or four, a girl mostly went naked or could wear a small grass skirt as a sign of difference. During this first stage of learning, she played freely with boys until eleven or twelve, when she began helping her mother in preparing sea food, smoking fish, cooking taro, maintaining the fire, and weaving fish traps and baskets. Both boys and girls learned the clan's dancing and singing in preparation for the ceremonies and other rituals. Theirs was a world of good and bad magic, and both sexes learning how sorcerers' powers influenced their lives and how to detect spells and, hopefully, overcome them.

The Second Stage of Learning

For boys in the Highlands, the second stage occurred when they were thought ready for ear lobe and nasal septum piercing, a preinitiation ceremony when bone and pig tusk was inserted. Now approaching puberty, boys were secluded for a period, joining their fathers and kinsmen in separate men's house where strong male bonding occurred. There, plans were laid for the ceremonies, warfare, and trade exchanges. Also, cult secrets were revealed and transmitted: the totems and taboos of the clan passed from old to young.

In coastal regions, boys underwent similar ear and nose piercing by sharpened wood skewers preparing them to carry ornaments of coconut ring and crescent of pearl shell. Large ceremonial feasts were held before and after this second stage. It was around this time that the female companions of childhood became taboo, a major break in the routine of the boy's life. By now, both males and females were usually tattooed.

The second stage of a girl's learning in both Highland and coastal regions, the equivalent of initiation, occurred in a cycle of menstruation, betrothal, and marriage. On menstruation, a Highlands girl was sent away to a special hut with some female companions for several weeks. Betrothal and, sometimes, marriage, which could happen before menstruation and was common by age fifteen, was accompanied by a great show of wealth from the husband and his family. Afterwards, the young woman was sent to her husband's family, sometimes becoming the second wife of a "big man." Some young women fled from these arranged marriages to older men or were known to commit suicide.

With arranged marriages the norm, little if any courtship took place between the sexes and the relations between husband and wife could be as antagonistic as loving. However, in some Highland societies, adolescent boys and girls did mix together in the *turnim het* or *sing-sing*, where the young people touched noses and foreheads while singing nasal, droning songs as a flirtatious prelude to marriage.[4] The Sambia males of the Highlands were not romantic though, regarding women as "polluting inferiors,"[5] whom men should distrust throughout their lives. This was despite the fact that women made the significant contribution to their clan's wealth, which sustained the feasts, ceremonies, and exchanges.

A hard life lay ahead for many young girls, both Highland and coastal—the acceptance of forced intercourse, constant labor, and economic responsibilities. According to the anthropologist Margaret Mead, in her study of Manus Islanders, as young women entered married life in their midteens, they appeared to her "cowed young girls"[6] resigned to their condition. Customs in different parts of the Islands differed according to the locale. In some coastal groups "love magic"[7] was practiced where a boy with the help of a sorcerer would sing to a special spirit in a girl's body: or free love was allowed frequently as a prelude to the marriage. Men's attitude towards women was generally less hostile in the coastal regions: in New Ireland, for example, women had significant influence as clan affiliation and land ownership was traced through female lineage, and women were involved in significant decision making.

The Third Stage of Learning

This stage was essentially a male prerogative. Full initiation ceremonies for boys, which took place in their early teens, required seclusion from women and other young people. It involved severe ritualistic and physical tests according to the prevailing Kastom. In some Highland regions young adolescents submitted to induced vomiting, cane swallowing, severe nose bleeds from pit-pit pushed up the nostril, and the ingestion of semen and special foods.[8] They were also taught the ancestral bird and flute cults and other phallic ceremonies. Altogether these various initiations accompanied by pig feasts could extend over several years.

In coastal areas, the initiation of boys occurred at about sixteen years introduced by rituals and physical tests. Already skilled in maneuvering a canoe, the young male was thought old enough to join the clan's war parties. Warfare served as a ritualized ceremony and a means of threatening enemies; its final stage, open conflict, was a single-minded enterprise with no quarter was given. Villages were burned, animals and gardens destroyed, and cannibalism practiced. Among prized captives of raiding bands were women of other clans who frequently died as prostitutes. Across PNG the practice of pay-back killings also served to keep past hatreds alive. The third stage of learning ended when the young man was considered ready to assume full clan duties, including marriage as late as twenty or more.

Laying Down Kastom

Thus teaching and learning in traditional society for PNG children took place within a conceptual and interrelated cosmology where spiritual and secular activities were intertwined not separated. The experiences decreed for male and female children existed to "grow the child." As learners, children came to understand how knowledge and skills were created through the dream, vision, and singing of a spiritual world. In building a canoe, for instance, the man will sing the traditional incantations—different verses learned for different stages, his song and adze work coming together.

He does not need drawings or dimensions because for him the significant form is conveyed in the words and music of the incantation. The meaning of the words in the etymological sense is not important—they may be so archaic that their derivation is forgotten: but their semantic meaning—the experience they recall to the user, is an essential factor in his skill.[9]

Indigenous educators today regard the schooling of traditional times as having served their people well, ensuring their clan's survival and the community good. Such Kastom should be prized—as this lamentation from the present Governor-General of Papua New Guinea, Grand Chief Sir Paulias Mantane, tells us.

I wish that my proud father could come back to me now, take me and transform me into one of them so that I would be like them—a colourful, articulate, skilful, proud, confident and brilliant man.[10]

NINETEENTH CENTURY

For much of the nineteenth century and the early twentieth century, schools in PNG offered no more than an elementary education seldom going beyond the equivalent of the first two years of elementary school. The concepts of school and book were introduced through the efforts of Christian missionaries in the second half of the nineteenth century mostly following their country's flag. Before then the country had only sporadic visits by Europeans, Portuguese, and Spanish navigators from the sixteenth century and from sundry explorers, scientists, traders, and adventurers later.[11] None stayed long or ventured far inland.

Australia had a strategic interest in New Guinea to its north and at the urging of the Queensland government Britain established a Protectorate in the southeast in 1884, known as British New Guinea. To Australia's dismay, Germany annexed the northeast naming it Kaiser Wilhelmsland the same year, allowing the private Neu Guinea Kompagnie to run the territory until 1889 when the Imperial German Government took charge. Some dozen Christian missions were attracted to both north and south New Guinea forming a significant and influential group by 1900, about one in five of the total European population of less than 2,000 persons.

The first missionaries, French Marists, landed at Woodlark Island in 1847 and were followed by a small group of Italian missionaries from Milan in 1852. Both groups were defeated by malaria, black water fever, dysentery, and death.

Elementary Schools

The missions who were responsible for all formal education in PNG until the early twentieth century taught a limited number of secular subjects in the vernacular, Tok Ples, or in their homeland language. (See Table 5.1 for full mission list.) The first of these mission schools which opened in 1874 with the arrival of William G. Lawes of the London Missionary Society (LMS) and his family at Port Moresby employed Pacific Islanders as teachers.[12] However when Lawes' LMS colleague, James Chambers, visited him in 1877, he reported back that there was little to show for his efforts beyond the graves of some Islander teachers and their wives and that of Lawes' dead infant son. While the school survived, only "a few children could repeat the letters but no-one could read."[13]

Table 5.1
List of Arrival Dates of Foreign Missions in PNG in the Nineteenth Century

British New Guinea	German New Guinea
British and Australian Protestants, London Missionary Society mission (1874 Port Moresby)	British and Australian Protestants, Australasian Wesleyan Methodist mission (1875 Duke of York Is.)
French Catholics, Sacred Heart of Jesus mission (1885 Yule Is.)	French Catholics, Sacred Heart of Jesus mission (1892 New Britain)
British and Australian Protestants, Australasian Wesleyan Methodist mission (1891 Dobu Is.)	German Protestants, Lutheran Neuendettelsau mission (1886 Finschhafen)
British and Australian Anglicans, Anglican mission (1891 Dogura Plateau)	German Protestants, Lutheran Rhenish mission (1887 Bogadjim)
Australian, Seventh-day Adventists mission (1908 Port Moresby)	German Catholics, Catholic Holy Spirit/Divine Word mission (1896 Aitape)
	French Catholics, Society of Mary mission (1899 Shortland Is.)
	German Protestants, Liebenzell mission (1914 Manus Is.)

Source: Compiled by author.

Mission Relations with Government

In 1885, the British special commissioner presented Pacific Islander teachers attached to the LMS with 11 adzes, 6 axes, 24 handkerchiefs, 13 knives, 89 boxes of matches, 2 tomahawks, and 40 yards of mosquito netting. The government justified its aid to mission education on grounds that official visitors occasionally used the teachers' cottages, that the Islanders were sometimes useful as interpreters, and that their salaries were extremely low.[14] In 1887, the commissioner took a further step paying out £400 for a large native schoolhouse for the LMS. The German administration in New Guinea also funded mission schools in its protectorate provided they taught German. As well, both governments helped the early missionaries through land grants for schools and assistance with transport, stores, and the transfer of teachers' salaries from the home mission.

In 1890, the British Administration negotiated an arrangement establishing spheres of influence among missions as a means of limiting rivalry and proselytism, though the Yule Island Catholics were not permitted to join formally. Another British initiative came in 1897 when William MacGregor, the lt. governor, enacted Ordinance No. III, making school attendance compulsory. Children from five to thirteen must attend for three days a week if they lived within two miles of a mission school or risk a fine. MacGregor's move was not popular with all missions, some thinking it pressured them to open additional schools. Nor did the initiative find much favor with the Colonial Office who described the forcing of pupils into mission schools, "as practically a measure for compulsory conversion."[15] Responding to his critics the administrator insisted that the Ordinance was there only if the missions wanted to use it.[16] Its value was as a threat not as an enforceable edict, and in 1907 it was amended reducing the compulsory distance to one mile and applicable only where schools taught English.

MacGregor greatly valued the educational work of all his Papuan missions. On his return to Britain, when questioned as to whether missionaries did more harm than good, he pointed out that the state had never been in a position to pay for the education of the children of British New Guinea. "Missionaries, therefore, are performing without cost to the state, one of its great functions, a labour which of itself is more than enough to justify their presence."[17]

Mission Settlements and Their Enrollments

Towards the end of the nineteenth century, missions introduced the "settlement model" as a means of better controlling and retaining children. Missionaries had soon discovered that establishing schools was easier than enticing children inside. For example, the Neuendettelsau mission school having been well attended at first had soon emptied; and when its missionaries had called at the front of their parents' huts to collect the recalcitrant, "the pupils slipped away at the back, clearing through under the grass roof."[18] Charles Abel, of the LMS, reported the same problem. While he could attract young children to his school, they were harder to retain: "Our laws become irksome, and they longed for the freedom of their native life. It was just this freedom which was so harmful to them."[19] Missionaries quickly discovered that the villagers wanted something in return for their children's attendance, iron tools, cloth or glass beads; and it was common to reward children in class with tobacco which all smoked, and small knives and mirrors.

Once a class was gathered, there was promise aplenty as was evident to MacGregor when he inspected the mission school at Dobu. "No teacher ever had before him a more bright eyed and intelligent looking class," he reported.[20] Most classes though contained mainly or exclusively boys, the extent of the disparity dependent on the locality. Missionaries generally encouraged the enrollment of girls who were seen as more docile and readily trained, and a civilizing force in later life, though boys were thought a better investment overall for a mission given its aim of graduating preachers and teachers able to cope with the vicissitudes of bush life. At school, girls were usually taught separately from boys having their own classrooms and share of the playground.

A hierarchy of races existed in PNG in the nineteenth century. As quinine had become available as a preventative against malaria, more European children remained for elementary school, and missions began to offer boarding places and day school tuition for Europeans. Whites, and the children of Japanese nationals, were at the top of the educational hierarchy. Next in line were the so-called mixed-blood children where one parent was a European and, beneath them in status, were the "non-Indigenous coloreds" like Chinese and Malays. "Native coloreds" were located at the bottom.

Over time the missions' headquarters became independent settlements, essentially theocracies, operating boarding schools, orphanages, and reformatories, all teaching at an elementary level. Schools within mission compounds taught in the mornings and organized child labor activities in the afternoons. Visits from parents and relatives were strictly regulated, as was personal behavior and dress; and Kastom ceremonies like dancing, singing, and initiation rituals were banned. A curfew was in place with lights-out at 9 P.M. Missions also attempted to limit their students' contacts with other Europeans, officials, traders, or miners in the vicinity. It was not long before government became concerned at the implications of the settlement concept, its officers complaining that missionaries took things too far, being unable to distinguish their own rules from the laws of the protectorate. Late in the nineteenth century anthropological and rational studies fostered new attitudes, and the settlement model was rejected as a denial of people's basic rights.

South Sea Islander Teachers

Protestant missions made extensive use of South Sea Islander converts some of whom came to PNG after laboring as kanakas in Queensland forced out by the White Australia policy. Perhaps they had two or three years at school, and some catch-up studies at night. En route to their mission station, Islanders were mostly kept below decks in the schooners until the landing when they were unloaded to fend for themselves among hostile people—in some instances they were poisoned or speared to death. Typically treated as servants by the missioners, Islanders were paid a miserable sum in money or kind worth £10 a year, and many were forced into petty trading to survive. In more remote stations lacking company and supervision, they fell foul of the villagers and local magistrates. Nonetheless the Islander teachers were the mainstay of the Protestant and Anglican missions carrying the burden of teaching and local preaching; along with their wives, they also taught other skills informally: Polynesian dancing, singing, and weaving, and the planting of new crops.

Missioner heads too were not impressed by their Islanders' teaching skills. After the Anglican priest, Arthur Chignell, toured his diocese out of Wanigera for the first time in 1908, he described them "as ill-instructed and incapable as any body of men who ever handled a piece of chalk or flourished a duster."[21] Similarly, the Catholic Superior at Yule Island held a negative view of the Protestants' helpers: "They are not trained and they differ little in morals or training from the savages amongst whom they live."[22] Not only were they bad teachers, the Superior thought, but they were ignorant in religious and all other matters. Indigenous children also feared the Islanders for their habit of bellowing at them, and banging the table with a stick, scaring them witless. In fact Chignell thought his children, charming and talented, "much more quick and capable than their [Islander] teachers."[23]

European Teachers

The early missioners were preachers first and teachers second being selected largely for their religious zeal, piety, and willingness to serve. As Herwig Wagner has written of the Lutheran activity, "formal Western education was not an indispensable prerequisite for evangelistic work."[24] However all missionaries who stayed for long normally engaged in some teaching activity. The heads of missions like Chalmers of the LMS, who had learned Latin and Euclid, were mostly well educated by the standards of their day, however most of their assistants had little schooling. Given that their own homelands had not as yet established national education systems, LMS and Protestant missionaries were church or privately educated up to the age of eleven or twelve years, and several had entered apprenticeships before they answered the call, "New Guinea for Christ."[25] Among Anglicans, a few senior missioners had a taste of postelementary education, and some of their staff had prior experience as teachers and nurses. While Catholic missionaries mainly received their schooling in a religious house entering as young novices, with the priests better taught than the lay brothers and most of the sisters.

Lady Missioners

In addition to their contribution to home and mission life, the wives of missioners frequently helped out in teaching and supervising teachers, and they were quick to form study groups among local women introducing wifely skills and good husbandry. Life was hard for them, maintaining a household under dangerous conditions in an inhospitable country, health and loneliness at the forefront. James Chalmers took his wife Lizzie to the fever saturated coast of Saguana, itself little more than swamp land, where she taught in a school noted for the quality of its English teaching; and she managed her husband's classes during his numerous excursions. Alas, she joined the ranks of several women to die on station after a debilitating illness in 1900.

At least Lizzie was spared the anguish of learning of Chalmers' death in 1902, killed on an expedition up the Fly River, along with another priest and ten students, whose body parts were mixed with sago and eaten. The Goaribari people suffered severely under retaliation, at least 24 killed and much property lost. Chalmers' own western mission descended into chaos, teachers were stoned by villagers and driven away, and some churches burned. While at his old Saguana base, parents would not find food for mission staff and kept their children out of class.[26]

The health of the sisters teaching at the Sacred Heart of Jesus Mission had become a concern for MacGregor, and he reported in 1887: "It is most regrettable that these ladies suffer so much from sickness. Several of them have died; many have suffered a great deal. Of course they bear all this without complaint, and they are ever ready to die at their post."[27] He was worried about excessive zeal among young missioners promoting a martyr complex. The administrator thought that their living conditions poor, those in charge of them lacking knowledge of tropical hygiene, and recommended that the Sacred Heart appoint a medical missionary to care for them and save valuable lives. MacGregor publicly applauded the role of European women in the protectorate under his charge: they should be cherished he believed, and given good food and frequent leave of absence in a milder climate as a restorative.

Training Teachers

The first Europeans who professed teaching skills had learned their craft on the job. Theirs was a generation which attended school before the nineteenth-century educational revival had introduced the monitorial system and the pupil–teacher apprenticeships, although a flood of books on new procedures had begun to circulate by the late nineteenth century. So far as indigenous teachers went, local training had begun in Lawes' school in the late 1870s, when promising students were trained as preachers and in basic teaching skills. Similar training was followed in missions across New Guinea, for example the Lutherans at Neuendettelsau offered their converts a three-year program in preaching and teaching the gospel.

Father Louis-André Navarre, the Superior at Yule Island, had a particular interest in the teaching of his beloved catechism producing a manual to guide the mission's priests, brothers, and sisters. His staff were directed to learn the local language as their first duty and speak in lively fashion and not stammer as they explained the catechism point by point.[28] Where classes were large, missioners should make use of monitors and provide rewards like medals and coloured ribbons for good behaviour, cleanliness and modesty. After a period of regular attendance, they should allot children guardian angels and form associations for them like the Children of Mary Solidarity. When the priests complained to him that they were too advanced in learning to merely teach the elementary grades, Navarre reminded them that Jesus had chosen to work with the poor and the lowly, and they should look to the future.

As up-to-date literature including training manuals started to circulate, and new staff arrived, PNG trainers learned more of the use of picture charts, the importance of moving from the known to the unknown, and the value of the Pestalozzian object lessons whereby real objects were brought into the classroom to stimulate learning. By the end of the century, the Anglican mission was attempting to recruit teachers who had experience as pupil teachers in Britain; however, the missions found few trained people willing to come. In 1883, the New Britain Methodists called on their Australian home base for more trained teachers else they must abandon some of their hard-won station schools. "Send us a supply of young enthusiastic and well trained men and the battle will be fought manfully and a victory soon achieved over the Devil and his Institution in this land where for ages he has reigned supreme."[29]

Mission School Room and the School Day

The settlement mission school was open for three or four days a week, usually mornings only, allowing out-of-school time for gardening and food gathering. A typical school building was a frame of wooden posts, a rectangular entrance, woven grass walls and a palm leaf roof. Windows were cut into the sides for light and ventilation, and closed by woven shutters. The condition of mission schools varied considerably. While some were clean and airy, Chignell was depressed by the one awaiting him at his Wanigera headquarters. His was a gloomy building, the benches were roughly hewn from the broken hulls of discarded canoes, and the master's table knocked together from bits and pieces of a Sydney meat company's packing cases. The classroom chair was a kerosene box. In more remote stations, the day schools opened for a couple of days in the church or the teachers' verandah, or were assembled under a shady tree.

Between 6:30 A.M.–7:00 A.M., a tolling bell brought children together for washing and a hygiene check. Called to attention, the seventy or so boys and girls formed separate lines as they marched into their class's section of the schoolroom, turning left or right on command, and squatting down on order. This marching and drilling at the start of the school day, known as Swedish drill, was regarded as a valuable educational principle inculcating discipline and obedience—one mission went so far as to drill its boys with "toy wooden bayonets."[30]

Inside the classroom, pictures, maps, object lesson charts, and spit slate rags hung from the walls. The children usually sat cross legged on the floor of beaten earth or matting, with the teacher sitting on a wooden rostrum or on a chair in the middle of the room listening to the various classes recite. After standing to greet the teacher, the day began with a prayer followed by a hymn and a bible reading. Classes then went into their detailed routines of memorization and repeating words and tables and in better equipped places some writing exercises. Children would then collect their slates, chalk sticks, and rags usually handed out by a classmate. A midmorning break was usual, children playing native games in the yard, and a few schools offered classes after a lunch of boiled taro or local food, introducing handicrafts and gardening.

With the school day and team sport over, students boarding in the missions were kept busy at small tasks until bed, mission settlements applying the principle that the devil finds work for idle hands. Punishments were common for bad behavior, from insolence to worse, included the deprivation of benefits, exclusion from class, physical labor, and beatings. As a last resort, there was the threat that a boy's fathers would be hauled before the resident magistrate and fined or imprisoned.

The Elementary Curriculum

A feature of early mission education was the decision by most missions to teach in the local language, Tok Ples. Protestant missions argued that this way their congregations could access the bible for themselves; likewise Catholic missions used the vernacular or pidgin in their catechetical instruction and prayers. Textbooks in the vernacular, some hand copied, had begun to appear by 1880, alongside imported text books. Some more advanced children had access to a primer containing the alphabet and numerals, a catechism, the Ten Commandments, hymns, and moralistic sentences. Eventually local language grammars were available in printed form, either published overseas or on the missions' own printing presses.

The curriculum of advanced classes, mainly designed for catechists and teachers, added extra subjects like geography, sewing, nature study, and the language of the home mission. A few schools also devised new subjects for the curriculum. LMS children, for example, were taught a catechism in English based on the government Ordinances in British New Guinea: "They are taught obedience to those in authority over them."[31] The catechism's question-and-answer format told children they must not destroy valuable rubber trees and must maintain their roads.

At Yule Island, the Catholic curriculum was a particularly narrow one, teaching religion, reading, arithmetic, and singing. Sensitive to the charge that Catholic missions produced ignoramuses, who knew little of the material world, Navarre, the Superior, conceded in principle that secular learning did have a place provided it did not go beyond its usefulness or introduce harmful content. He also suggested that his staff keep records of students' progress at weekly and half-yearly intervals, a step forward in school assessment procedures.

All missions encouraged physical education especially games like football, cricket, and ball sports, including rounders for girls. Team activity was depicted as having its own educational rationale. It was thought to compensate PNG children who had been denied their traditional activities, to lead to rivalry of a friendly kind, and to build character. At Kwato it took four years of student labor in filling in a swamp for a cricket pitch. It was put to good use when Kwato's Papuan eleven had a notable victory over the officers and men of a visiting British warship, HMS Torch.

Teaching Methods

Reading was taught by learning the alphabet followed by meaningless sets of letters; then there were individual words to learn and, finally, words in short sentences. Biblical injunctions were repeated in class; moral tales were read in unison; and for those seniors who could read independently, there was the bible reading class. Arithmetic, as a subject, was basically counting and the four operations, a few pupils going further if their teachers knew more. It was a dull and uninteresting topic, with the multiplication table, weights, measures, and money equivalents chanted and sung. Writing on slates was commonly available beginning with prewriting exercises of curves and loops modeled on British copperplate, though much of it turned out the crudest of copy. In some remote places boxes of wet sand and dirt were used to trace numbers and letters in place of slates: by the turn of the century, the technology of pen and ink had appeared in the better equipped places.

Religious education was not an exciting topic either though at Yule Island, teachers attempted to keep their classes alert by showing a picture or two, keeping their lessons short—about fifteen minutes, and by singing and short breaks taken outside. Nevertheless, content must be repeated and revised constantly, children reading the catechism in unison and singing the drills until word perfect.

A few individual missionaries trialed more advanced teaching methods. In 1888, missionary teachers at Hanuabada were using colored alphabet cards as flash cards, mechanical toys were introduced as teaching aids, and shells and insects were brought into the classroom for the object lesson. When the pace of learning faltered, a class at Mailu station would stop to give, "three hearty British cheers."[32] Such imaginative teaching was one of the hallmarks of the LMS missionary, James Chalmers, a naturally boisterous and noisy character, who thought learning should be as natural as play. He organized his classes in line, hands on the shoulder of the child in front, letting them prance around the classroom singing their alphabet and multiplication tables: at strategic points sweets were distributed.[33] Anglicans also introduced new ideas from Europe, employing the Gouin method to teach English, a late-nineteenth-century French invention that treated words in sentence form and as part of a sequence around a theme.

Post-elementary Education

Missions first introduced a form of post-elementary schooling when children left the mission school to enter classes for catechists and teachers. Industrial training for older boys was also available in some places. The educational justification for this semiskilled training was the religious example of Jesus as a carpenter, and the percept of labor as a virtue in itself, indeed many accepted that PNG children had more to learn from an industrial education than the three R's in a school. Of course industrial work brought a tangible return to the missions adding to their income and capacity for self-reliance.

The best known of the Papuan-based industrial training was run by Charles Abel, the LMS missionary at Kwato, whose settlement managed plantations, boat-building, and metal workshops in a largely English speaking environment. Inspected in the early 1900s, the British Administrator reported:

At Kwato may be seen sheds full of whizzing wheels and hissing straps and circular and vertical saws, besides a planing machine and a lathe—all this machinery as well as the engine and the boiler, being conducted by Papuan youths without any brief from Euro-peans. The needle work of the girls is said, too, to be of superlatively good quality.[34]

Abel's Papuans learned their skills in his classrooms and on-the-job. The clergy-man himself wanted the LMS to move extensively into industrial missions: without such training, he argued, Papuans were doomed to remain gardeners, fishermen, and servants of the white settlers. Not all missionaries though approved of this level of industrial work, opponents thinking Kwato and other centers diverted attention away from evangelism and basic education. As Kwato continued to expand, the LMS was split over its value, and eventually Abel broke from the Society.

Another industrial complex at the Sacred Heart of Jesus Mission supported forges, tanneries, saw-mills, agriculture, and silk production developing its own two-year vocational program teaching carpentry and metal working. By 1899–90, the mission had holdings of over 1,000 hectares of plantation, with its graduates receiving a gift of cattle on their return to their villages. Mission industrial enterprise similarly flourished in German New Guinea under an administration with a reputation for economic development and forced labor: the Rhenish mission, for instance, was directed by the authorities to recruit trade teachers as missionaries to build up its industrial training.

Elementary Schooling at the Close of the Nineteenth Century

Working inside their own enclaves on the mainland and islands, missions boasted around 10,000 under instruction in elementary classes by the end of the nineteenth century. That they taught mostly religious doctrine in the vernacular language, except at some head station schools, seldom perturbed them. As the Neuendettelsau mission explained in 1901, its syllabus was "in keeping with the low cultural level of the natives, [and] extends only to what is covered in the lowest form of an elementary school."[35] Nor did the German administrators expect much skilled labor from the ranks of any mission school graduates: "The scope of the training offered does not make it possible to employ coloured persons for clerical duties or simple business transactions."[36]

The main issue of contention that had emerged in elementary education was language, with both administrations wanting their homeland language taught extensively. Achieving this was difficult because there were non-English speak-ing missionaries in British New Guinea, and non-German speaking missionaries in German New Guinea. Further, the missions preferred to teach in the vernac-ular. The two governments harbored suspicions that the foreign missions in their territories deliberately avoided teaching English or German for political reasons, and that they feared it would open their congregations to external influences and reduce their own power.

Given the sphere of influence policy, and the failure of the colonial govern-ments to provide funds for mission schools keen to upgrade beyond the elementary level, there was little incentive for missions to improve their secular schooling. Nor was there much demand from the Europeans around them. Junior officials, settlers, miners, or traders were more against the spread of education than in favor of it, except insofar as their own children were concerned. Missions started or closed schools as they pleased; few if any standards of attainment applied, and their assistant teachers continued undereducated and ill-trained.

TWENTIETH CENTURY: THE FIRST HALF

British New Guinea passed to Australia under The Papua Act of 1906, making that country the dominant power in Papua's economic and educational progress. The same year, an Australian Royal Commission was instituted to recommend measures likely to encourage white settlement. So far as education went, the commissioners wanted the teaching of English made compulsory in mission schools, attendance enforced at English teaching mission schools, and young male Papuans trained in plantation labor and semiskilled industrial work. They were not though prepared to fund these educational plans, consequently there was little change on the ground up to the outbreak of World War I.

Primary Education

It was the German government which took the initiative in primary education in the early twentieth century. While its missions maintained some effective schools at headquarters, like the Neuendettelsau mission at Finschhafen that ran a German School for Natives offering a three-year curriculum, Lutheran village schools were much less impressive. Many children away from the center received their bible study, counting and perhaps writing, under volunteer teachers who received no pay. A mission administrator has explained the arrangement.

In the good old days we had a similar school system in our own dear fatherland, only that the old village schoolmasters there could not carry out their work without remuneration, and that often men were chosen to teach school because they were unfit for other work—perhaps crippled in one hand or with some other physical handicap.[37]

In one of these village schools, a traveling missionary found the class sitting unsupervised under a tree reciting its lessons, the teacher having taken an unexplained day off.

In 1913, Imperial Governor Albert Hahl signaled the government's intention to require that the Protectorate's mission schools register and follow a syllabus laid down by the government. Attendance would be compulsory. In return he promised to substantially increase the subsidy the government paid missions teaching the German language.[38] Money aside, the proposed reforms were not received with enthusiasm by the hitherto unregulated sector.

It was also German colonial policy to establish its own government schools as soon as possible for teaching German and patriotic duty. To pave the way, the administration organized a Scholars Association in Rabaul, its School for Natives opening at Namanula[39] with twenty-seven indigenous males enrolled in two classes for a six-year curriculum in 1907. The new school offered twenty to twenty-two hours of instruction on four days a week, taught in the language of the Blanche Bay district, a requirement soon dropped in favor of German. By 1914, the School for Natives had around 120 pupils, graded in classes according to their date of enrollment, the final standard corresponding to the third and fourth year of an official German primary school curriculum.[40] While many children made reasonable progress led by their German trained teacher, there were problems related to irregular attendance, and skin and eye diseases were prevalent.

A second government primary establishment, the School for Europeans, opened in April 1909,[41] with seven boys and three girls under a German trained woman, teaching a 30-period week and a superior curriculum: "German, arithmetic, religion, history, geography, nature study, drawing, gymnastics, singing and civics."[42] Its syllabus was considered similar in content and level to that of a one teacher school in Germany, although its natural science and social science subjects made allowance for conditions in the tropical colony. By 1913, the school accommodated 11 boys and 2 girls, 7 of them German, 3 Malays and 3 Chinese. That year, the school celebrated the Jubilee of the Kaiser's reign and on Christmas Eve "a Nativity play was presented at the school by the boys and girls, to the great delight of young and old."[43]

Post-elementary Education

When the School for Natives was established in 1907, a trade school annex also opened which took in promising three- or four-year graduates of mission schools who were taught printing, carpentry, metal work, and book binding. The print shop published the official *Amtsblatt* (Government Gazette), the code of laws for the Protectorate, and around fifty-thousand official forms (of ninety different types) annually, as well as undertaking private jobs.[44] By 1914, the youths were continuing to sew and bind books, produce school equipment including desks and wall lockers, and maintain vegetable gardens. They were also expected to keep the school and dormitory grounds pristine. On 1 October that year, the first group of pupils graduated, twenty-three young men being taken into Imperial Government service as junior clerks, artisans, printers, and assistant teachers.

In 1914, the German New Guinea administration went a step further, preparing a three-year plan to open up new land, expand agriculture and medical services, and extend government schools, elementary and post-secondary. By now there were government schools in Rabaul, and in the German island protectorates of Saipan and Truk, and a new industrial school was planned for Rabaul teaching skills for the building industry. As well, another four elementary and

trade schools were planned on the mainland, with the aim of replacing all non-
local colored employees in government service over the next six years by German
speaking graduates.

Australia Takes over Education in German New Guinea

German government education was shut down in 1914 with the outbreak of
World War I. At Britain's request that German wireless stations in the Pacific
be silenced, Australian forces occupied Rabaul in September, its few hundred
Europeans surrendering after sharp resistance by German and indigenous
troops. The war over, the large German Lutheran mission at Neuendettelsau
was saved from dismemberment by its association with the Australian Lutherans who combined with American Lutherans to fund its New Guinea enterprises. Similarly the Rhenish mission was taken over by the American Lutheran
Church. These stratagems ensured that the pattern of relying on foreign based
missions for education in PNG continued.

No mercy however was shown the German government schools.

In Namanula there are a number of picturesque villas where the higher German officials
used to live. The European hospital, the Government Printing Office and the now
deserted schools are also situated here. The teachers from the school have been
deported, the white children have been taken away by their parents, and the Kanaka boys
who have been brought here from every corner of the Bismarck Archipelago to learn
German, handicraft, and agriculture, took advantage of our arrival to disappear, mostly
to Rabaul, where they have been employed, and they seem to be exceedingly happy.
Boys are always the same, whether white or black. In fact, Namanula is in no respect
what it was a few months back.[45]

The ex-German territory in New Guinea was put under a League of Nations
Mandate in 1921. Though the League laid down no conditions for indigenous
advancement, Australia was told that the well-being and development of its
people was a "sacred trust,"[46] and it should report annually on their progress.
Now effectively under Australian control, the country was divided into two,
the Territory of Papua, and the Territory of New Guinea.

Primary Schools: The Territory of Papua 1918–1940

Australia happily accepted responsibility for the two territories but was
unwilling to spend more than was necessary to maintain a small European outpost and settler community. To find some funds for local education, the Papuan administrator, J. H. P. Murray, introduced a head tax on indigenous
workers, the Native Taxes Ordinance of 1918, its revenue to be applied to general and technical education, and other direct benefits for indigenous people.[47]
Murray kept the money in a Native Education Fund applying it to subsidize
mission schools provided they taught an approved curriculum in English and

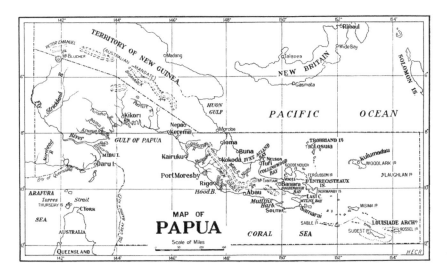

Map of Papua. Native Education. *Papuan School Reader* (Port Moresby: Government Printer, 1928), 158.

arithmetic, and subjected themselves to inspection.[48] Missions received five shillings for every student they presented up to a total of £250. In addition, the LMS school located in Port Moresby received £1000 annually to pay for trained primary and kindergarten teachers, and other schools including the Catholic mission on Yule Island and the Protestants at Kwato received direct grants some of which they diverted to industrial or agricultural training.

One outcome of the Murray funding initiative was that it laid down standards for mission schools if they were to gain subsidies. Standard 1, for example, demanded students read a simple English text which included some words of more than one syllable and speak a short English sentence about an object brought into the classroom. Writing skills covered the formation of letters and the copying of a few lines from the reading book. Arithmetical skills called for mental arithmetic, easy addition, subtraction, short division, and the multiplication tables to six times twelve. Standard 2 increased the English level a little—it was to be equivalent in standard to Brook's *First Reader* of the Australian School Series and included a simple dictation passage, the writing task was to present copy in half-text size, and arithmetic was extended to the twelve times table and an understanding of money, measures, and weights.[49] These Standards provided the basic content for the Syllabuses for Native Schools, and they were extended to Standard V in the prewar period.

Missions enrolled children from their headquarters' schools for the examination. These were children who had moved from the vernacular to English and who seemed likely to be successful. Still the numbers sitting were quite small.

By 1926, the four mission churches eligible for government assistance claimed a pass rate of around 80 percent for 1,173 students taking Standards 1–4. While the English results were seen as satisfactory, outcomes in arithmetic were less satisfactory: for example a boy who could measure timber accurately could not estimate his own height. The government inspector put this down to inadequate teaching methods, attributing them to "incompetent coloured teachers."[50]

Murray justified his decision to fund mission schools directly by the number of their graduates joining the government workforce. In the mid-1920s, the Government Secretary's Department was employing five clerks with typing skills at a salary of £7 a month, ex-students of the LMS Port Moresby school, and other school leavers in private employment proved themselves well able to repair tractors or cars and maintain and drive them. In 1933, the government announced the appointment of Nansen Kaisa, a graduate of the LMS at Fyfe Bay, as a government tax collector: "This is believed to be the first instance in which a native has been placed in a position of financial responsibility."[51] Murray accepted that the increasing numbers of native clerks and others was "a result not believed possible a few years ago."[52] While the standard of the graduates was admittedly good, the government believed many of the best educated were retained by the missions, not the purpose behind the government subsidy.

The First Papuan Readers

The view that the local scene should inform learning in schools had been recognized in principle for many years, but a lack of school materials inhibited progress. In 1928, the *Papuan School Reader*[53] prepared by the Rev. W. J. Saville of the London Missionary Society was published. Pocket book in size, and somewhat inaccurately described as "the first Papuan Encyclopaedia," its pages reproduced a set of flags, the Union Jack and Australian ensigns, black-and-white maps of PNG and of Australia and its region, and drawings of people, objects, and models. It also included a daily prayer set to music and short moral exhortations: learn what is good, work hard, play well, do not take what is not yours, etc. Lesson 35, Our School, described a model classroom.

Of their own country, the *Reader* told the Papuan child:

Before white men came and lived here, people of one part were always fighting with people of other parts. The natives of Papua were very savage in those days. They killed people with spears, bows and arrows, and stone clubs. There was no law and order. Now the Government keeps law and order, and punishes those who do wrong. We can go anywhere in our canoes now, and we are safe. We can walk inland and the people will give us food.[54]

The textbook proposed that teachers take children outside to observe the weather and the community life around them and show them how to make

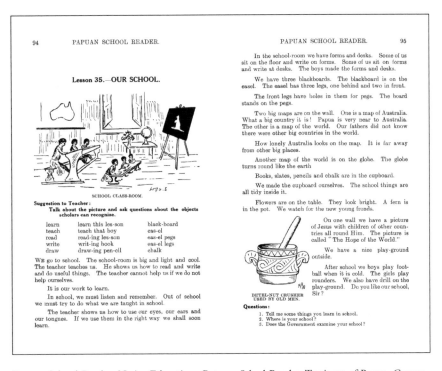

Papuan School Reader. Native Education, *Papuan School Reader*, Territory of Papua, Government Printer (Port Moresby: Government Printer, 1928), 94–95.

useful handicrafts in class. However the suggested treatment for the written text was much more mechanical: teacher talks about the pictures, then reads the text aloud; difficult words are written on the blackboard, explained, and pronounced distinctly; the teacher and class read the text aloud together; and the lesson is completed by questions from the teacher about the content and some short written answers are demanded. Readers were bought in bulk by the government, and their use was compulsory in Standards 4 and 5 in government-assisted mission schools.

In 1932, a set of four *Junior Papuan Readers* was published as the content in the 1928 text was considered too difficult. The extract from the lesson, A Day's Hunting, is taken from the level three book.[55]

Nonformal Education at Primary Level

In 1929, Murray approved publication of a weekly English language newspaper, *The Papuan Villager*, edited by the government anthropologist, F. E. Williams. The newspaper, a mix of news items, illustrations, and simple stories,

30   PAPUAN JUNIOR READER No. 3.

The men went to a mountain not far from our village. Long grass was growing all over the mountain. Near by was a big river.

A great number of wallabies live in the long grass, and wild pigs lived close to the river.

When the men came to the mountain, they put fire into the grass. The wind made the fire burn the grass very fast. The fire and the smoke frightened the wallabies and they began to jump away.

The men shouted and the dogs barked. The men threw their spears at the wallabies and killed many of them.

Lesson XXII.—A DAY'S HUNTING.
PART 2.

| club | shot | nearly | which |
| cuscus | hunt | ended | climbed |

THE dogs caught a big wallaby. Three pigs ran away from the fire. A man shot one of them with his gun, and the other two were killed with spears.

One small pig did not run fast and a man killed it with his club. Another pig was caught in a net.

A boy saw a cuscus in a tree. He climbed up the tree and pushed the cuscus down with a stick. It fell to the ground and a man killed it.

THE BLIND MAN AND THE LAME MAN.   31

The hunt ended in the afternoon, and the men picked up all the animals which they had killed. They had five pigs and nearly a hundred wallabies.

These were put on long sticks and spears and were carried to the village. There they were cooked over the fires by the women.

That night the men were very tired, but all the people in the village were very happy.

Lesson XXIII.—THE BLIND MAN AND THE LAME MAN.

bullock	pity	each	ago
arrived	plan	present	also
lame			

NOT long ago, there was a great feast in our village. Many pigs were killed and two bullocks were also killed for the feast.

Papuan Junior Reader No. 3. Native Education, Territory of Papua (Port Moresby: Government Printer, 1932), 30–31.

drew on government admonition and Indigenous content. Its raison d'etre, it declared on publication, was to encourage Papuans "to learn the white men's language"[56] and enable them to communicate and work well with their "masters." It seems its sales were principally to Protestant mission schools, the LMS, the Methodists, and the Anglicans being the most interested, and some went to the Seventh-day Adventists. Before long, the paper took on an English Protestant slant. This account of Father Christmas arriving at Lawes College won Lekie Tom a five shillings prize.[57]

It was time for us to go into the school-hall for our parcels. So we all went and sat down. Father Christmas was throwing our things down from the top and Mrs. Searle looked at the names of them and gave out to whoever's name it was. Oh! Friend we enjoyed them very much. When the parcels were finished, Father Christmas came round to us and gave out writing-pads and pictures for us to hang up on the walls of our rooms. When it was finished we all said, "Thank you very much."

The newspaper also told PNG children of the activities of King George V, Edward, the Prince of Wales, the Duke and Duchess of York, and Lord

Stoneham, Australia's governor-general. News of Australia appeared regularly, as did pictures of its native animals, of the Royal Australian Navy, and of Aboriginal desert tribes. *The Papuan Villager* also encouraged their student readers to play cricket: "You have to thank the missions a great deal for teaching you to play."[58] Here the achievements of Australia's cricketers and the great Don Bradman were popular. Finally, Williams always found space for a good word for the mission educators telling his readers it was the missionaries who had brought schools to PNG. "You have to thank the missionaries for them—men and women who have come from Australia and England to spend the best part of their lives teaching you."[59]

Primary Schools: The Territory of New Guinea 1918–1940

In the Mandated Territory of New Guinea the Australian administration decided not to subsidize mission education; rather it would establish its own government school system based on a tax on native labor similar to that applying in Papua. In 1922, an Education Ordinance was introduced authorizing the establishment of government schools, school management procedures, curriculum content, standards of attainment, and teacher-training qualifications.[60] There were several reasons behind the government's action: There was a precedent for government schools from German days; the influence and language carried by German staffed missions must be countered; New Guinea was more economically advanced than the south and thought better able to absorb school graduates; and, lastly, Australia had to report to an external body, the League of Nations, on the territory's social and economic progress.

The initial Australian government Elementary School opened in Rabaul in 1922. It soon moved to nearby Kokopo, close to the Sacred Heart of Jesus mission, the plan over time being to develop it as a high school. Initially the Elementary School boarded about 40 boys, aged 5 to 10 years, most of them from the islands and said to include unwanted children, and others sent by their village headmen anxious to learn the white man's secrets. Just getting the children to Rabaul was an achievement: they were buffeted in schooners, or put under sophisticated work boys in interisland steamers with their minders shouting an incomprehensible language at them and feeding them from unfamiliar enamel bowls and iron pots. When they arrived at Rabaul, many wanted nothing more than to return home. "Me no like go 'long see-kool (school); me no like go; see-kool 'e no good place; me like go back 'long place belong me."[61]

Their unheeding headmaster, William Colin Groves, a graduate of the University of Melbourne and trained teacher, had been seconded for the task by the Victorian State Department of Education. Working out of a disused military hospital, Groves learned Tok Pisin for communication as his pupils spoke over a dozen tongues. School was a strange world indeed for the newly made-over students who spent hours hunched over desks engaged in learning activities essentially meaningless to them. "The whole atmosphere," Groves declared, "was non native," although carers were employed, a matron and a doctor, several of the class became "spiritually sick" and were sent home.

The Curriculum

English was introduced as the language of instruction in Groves's school from the beginning, and reading and writing proceeded with considerable success. The short essays in Table 5.2 are descriptions of a scene taken from picture charts by two boys who had been in the school for just two years.

Groves's pupils had less success with their oral English. If the teacher dictated a sentence, "Did you go for a walk?" most of them could write it down correctly but when asked a follow-up question, for example, "Where did you go?" the boy replied almost invariably in Tok Pisin, "Me bin go along Vunapope."[62] Groves thought the guidelines given him too prescriptive and isolated from the children's experiences.

In 1924, the three government schools were consolidated at Malaguna just outside the Rabaul boundary, the elementary school which had adopted a Torres Strait curriculum for the basic subjects thought better able to accommodate indigenous life. English was now correlated with manual and craftwork, and gardening. Children made fish traps and baskets and blinds using native materials, the skills taught them by locals. Even so, Groves considered his school a failure. Various reasons were given: Its location was unsuitable; the soil being too poor for cultivation; the institution was too close to Rabaul, where boys came under the sway of their wontoks;[63] there were frequent changes among European staff; and the new curriculum did not adequately replicate New Guinea conditions. Groves also regretted the absence of any working relationship with the missions in his four years there.

When Groves revisited Rabaul in 1932–1934 and attempted to trace his Kokopo old boys, he found several had entered the government's Technical School as advanced students or assistants or had become teachers. Others were

Table 5.2
Two Essays by Grade II Students at the Kokopo Elementary School 1924

This is a very nice picture. I can see three baby ducks and one mother duck. They are swimming in the water. There are many reeds growing in the water. The mother duck is white and the baby ducks are brown. I think the mother duck has a long neck also.
Harry Soup, of Aitape

This is a very large dog. The skin of the dog is black and white. There are many sheep in the picture. They are standing in the grass. The dog is near the sheep. I think the dog is near the sheep. I think the dog is running at the sheep. They are also in the picture. This grass is green. There are some flowers too.
Joseph Ritako, of Manus

Source: Australia. *Report to the League of Nations on New Guinea, 1923–1924,* 21.

indentured to Europeans and a few were clerks working for government departments. Two had been sent to Australia for a couple of years which improved their English but Groves thought little else. "No more than half a dozen of them," said Groves, "have any real understanding of English, the teaching of which was one of the main aims of the system at the outset."[64] Unhappily, several of them had spent time in prison or had died.

The Role of Kastom in PNG Schools

By the 1920s, enlightened voices were beginning to penetrate PNG. Under anthropological and social theorizing, the denial of traditional culture in favor of mission sanctioned values lost currency. The "blending of cultures" theory of the government anthropologist, Williams, which recognized good in PNG culture as well as bad, raised questions about the motivation of missionaries and settlers who wanted to remake the indigenous population after their own image. The issue was how to recognize and teach the best qualities of traditional culture in schools? Groves, New Guinea's most thoughtful educator, suggested that four principles apply: Education must be employed as an agent of natural growth and evolution within the native community; it must aim to serve the mass of natives rather than a select few; it must be founded upon native life and institutions acting to an extent as an agent of cultural preservation; and it must adapt native life and institutions in conformity with modern ideas.[65] To breathe some life into his beliefs, Groves cited two examples of exemplary practice. The first was a school run by the LMS in 1922 in Port Moresby where he found all 200 children or so in class taught by a young Australian woman whose whole approach was "native ... the use of the local native language, the material of the curriculum, the blackboard illustrations, the stories and reading topics, and even the songs. 'This little pig went to market'—a native market near the village." Groves's second example was drawn from his visit to the Lutheran Mission Training School at Logaweng. After a tedious morning of the three R's, students sang an old Markham Valley war chant, the words changed to convey a Christian message. "In that peculiarly primitive song," said Groves, "I felt that there was something almost priceless—something of the true genius of the New Guinea people."

POST-ELEMENTARY EDUCATION—TECHNICAL AND VOCATIONAL SCHOOLING IN PAPUA AND NEW GUINEA 1918–1940

Most of the Takis money Murray had made available in Papua in 1919 was spent on industrial and technical education; not on primary education. The LMS school in Port Moresby used government funds for its workshop: by the late 1920s it was training 36 boys in the use and care of tools and carpentry, some finding work on leaving with European contractors.[66] Training was more advanced at Yule Island where the pupils were organized under a scheme proposed by the government's technical adviser learning carpentry and iron working skills—again, some of its graduates were employed by government departments. Kwato continued with its ambitious industrial projects, and the LMS school at Fyfe Bay employed a qualified European trade instructor obtaining results said to stand comparison with training in Australia.

In ex-German New Guinea, missions were not subsidized for their industrial training, however several maintained major training programs as an integral part of their settlements. A report in 1929 described the Methodist mission establishment at Salamo whose training enterprise was housed in a large two-storied cement and fibrolite building and boasted twenty benches for wood workers, and workshops for boat-building, and tractor and launch engine repairs. It undertook its own electricity generation.[67]

In 1922, the government opened its own Technical School at Rabaul. Initially under the Public Works section, it taught 25 male students, mainly ex-mission graduates and employed teachers on loan from Australia. The school day at Rabaul began with physical exercises, followed by an hour and a half for English and arithmetic, before training began in carpentry, boat-building, motor maintenance, driving, and plumbing. The sole native craft was rattan work for coal and wastepaper baskets taught by a Chinese. In the afternoons the boys were given set tasks largely unsupervised. Mixed race youths, considered more advanced, were selected and indentured as fitters and turners, and carpenters or were put to work at the government printer. In effect, the technical school operated as a European technical workshop, with the expectation that its graduates would replace the territory's semiskilled "Asiatic" workers.[68]

A year later, a School of Domestic Economy was also founded in Rabaul, its aim to graduate 30 to 40 young men annually as wash boys and cooks. To help defray expenses, the students prepared a daily lunch for the general public at a nominal fee and assisted with public laundry. As this group of students was already indentured, they were returned to their employers on graduation. However, educational outcomes were considered negligible, the employers unhappy with the teaching, and the school was closed after two years or so.

Later in the 1930s, the government developed a teacher-training arm at its Malaguna Elementary School training indigenous teachers in the subjects of "personal, domestic and village hygiene, native arts and crafts, elementary agriculture, the reading and writing of English, and simple arithmetic."[69] However, plans to extend the program ended abruptly in 1942 with the Japanese occupation of Rabaul.

Equity and Race

The white settler population as represented by the *Rabaul Times* did not welcome government education, thinking the mission effort in education more than sufficient. Watching things with a skeptical eye, only the technical school in New Guinea was rated "a slight success."[70] It seems most whites wanted the government initiative in the north halted and the government schools disbanded. White attitudes towards the education of indigenous children were apparent when the administration proposed sending seven New Guinean students from the Technical School to Australia for two years of higher training in 1928. The opposition was immediate, settlers radioing the minister in Canberra to have the proposition squashed. After the plan was abandoned, the Rabaul paper reported: "We learn with pleasure that the seven natives who were to be sent to Australia did not go owing to representations made by the Citizen's Association."[71] The settlers' underlying objection was that New Guineans would mix with other artisans in Australia and come to believe they should receive similar salaries. Here, settler unease was reinforced when 3,000 laborers in Rabaul and surrounds, including most police, went on strike early in 1929.

Racial theories were also to blame. While Dr. W. M. Strong, the chief medical officer of Papua, held the theory that the capacities of the Papuan and European overlapped, thinking the best Papuans superior to the worst Europeans,[72] he believed that Europeans as a whole were the superior race, a view he thought most residents shared. Lt. Governor Hubert Murray agreed with him and made an additional point. As two Papuans had already trained as priests, Murray supposed they could succeed in law and medicine, but he preferred to spend his spare funds on teaching English more widely not on higher education. There was a color bar in white society in PNG, he declared, which would prevent their social acceptance. "It would be unwise," Murray argued, "to give the Papuan first class education unless the way to advancement is to be fully opened to him."[73]

Murray thought Australians, as a whole, more discriminatory in racial matters than Europeans like the French or the British in the West Indies. In Australia the virulent white Australia policy was enforced, and the country's Aboriginal people were badly treated. Similarly indigenous people in PNG were regarded as perpetual subordinates by many whites. Papuan males must dress in lap-laps with bare tops, and it was an offense for a man to wear western clothes unless approved by his master. Some employers made a point never to say "thank you" or "good day" to a laborer, only speaking to issue an order, and locals were expected to use "masta" or "misis" in reply. Where whites gathered, derogatory jokes circulated proclaiming the inferiority of blacks.

The Eve of World War II

Prior to World War II, the government was operating two education systems in PNG: it subsidized mission schools in Papua and funded government schools in the mandated territory of New Guinea. Murray's plans for Papua met little opposition as they acknowledged mission supremacy; however, the government system in the north proved more difficult to encourage and expand. An inquiry in 1929, led by B. J. McKenna, director of Education in Queensland, recommended that the New Guinea government extend its system of schools in the townships along with technical schools, leaving rural schooling to the missions. These modest plans were shelved when the Depression reduced the money available from head taxes. In 1934, a second inquiry under the acting administrator, Brig. Gen. T. Griffiths proposed that New Guinea schools be handed back to the missions. This would have meant abandoning hopes for English teaching in New Guinea as the majority of missions remained German or French controlled, and the closure of other schools. Griffiths' recommendation was not adopted.

Not unexpectedly the League of Nations' response to Griffiths' suggestion of handing all education back to the missions had been cool. In June 1939, Mlle Dannevig of the League of Nations Permanent Mandates Commission remarked that, "She knew of no territory under mandate in which native education progressed so slowly."[74] In both Papua and New Guinea, the total cost of education for Indigenous and European schooling was a niggardly £35,000 a year for all educational services, reflecting the low priority schools had in the minds and pockets of Australia's administrators. As yet, there was no consultation with indigenous graduates as to a future for them beyond the ranks of catechist or native pastor, or that of semiskilled worker under the eye of a European. It is fair comment that the Australian administration saw itself as serving white settler interests.

In the broader PNG—Australian relationship, the Commonwealth government had introduced a scheme in 1925, whereby young Australians served two years in New Guinea undertaking some training, then six months at the University of Sydney prior to their appointment as patrol officers. After World War II this training would be undertaken at the Australian School of Pacific Affairs in Sydney. In other training in Australia, the Department of Public Health introduced a scheme for Papuan medical assistants in 1932, allowing six months in Port Moresby and six months at the University of Sydney. Housed in the North Head Quarantine Station to keep them well away from the general population, the Papuans were warmly welcomed at the university. As these assistants were destined for independent work in the villages, their additional training was not seen as threat to white settler supremacy. However, later groups were sent to Fiji to train.

By 1940, the New Guinea administration was teaching 491 indigenous pupils in six elementary schools.[75] One of them, the Chimbu day school near Madang which employed two indigenous teachers teaching 75 pupils was the first government school on the mainland as distinct from the islands of New Guinea. In 1930, the opening up of the Highlands, with its estimated population of one million persons, brought many missions to the area; and by the 1940s the mission schools in the New Guinea Territory were educating 65,589 students, though the quality of their secular schooling was considered weak by government.

TWENTIETH CENTURY: THE SECOND HALF

Fighting between the Allies and Japan began with the bombing of Rabaul in February 1942. The townships of Buna, Madang, and Lae were occupied and heavily bombed, and tens of thousands of U.S., Australian, and Japanese forces were killed along with uncounted PNG victims. Infrastructure, including dozens of schools, were bombed and razed; missionaries, teachers, and nurses executed; and schoolchildren like those in classes at the Lutheran Jabem Secondary School impressed as carriers by the warring armies.

Between 1943 and 1944, in the occupied Murik Lakes area, a Japanese-American army officer who knew pidgin started an elementary school with the agreement of a local "big man."[76] Bribed by a plentiful supply of biscuits, sweets, and tinned food, a class teaching Japanese and arithmetic opened; among its pupils was the seven-year-old, Michael Somare, who would become the nation's first prime minister. Somare went on to complete intermediate schooling, eventually working as a high school teacher after a year's teacher-training at Sogeri Central Training School. The Japanese at Murak Lakes also established a school for twelve- to fifteen-year-olds where local boys received basic army training. Eventually the Japanese drive to the south was halted by Australian troops along the Kokoda Track and at Milne Bay.

The influx of foreign troops on both sides including substantial numbers of nonwhite soldiers poured undreamed-of resources into the country, changing PNG society profoundly. Aroused from complacency by the Japanese bombing of Port Moresby and Darwin, the Australian people realized PNG's strategic importance; and the romantic pictures of "fuzzy-wuzzy angels," caring for wounded Australian soldiers, played on their social conscience—though in truth some locals were on the Japanese side. In PNG itself, the old white settler order was destroyed. The new attitudes in place had enormous educational significance as they encouraged the Australian government to unlock money for schools, the public accepting the money would be well spent. In 1946, the United Nations recognized Australian control of Papua as a Non-Self-Governing Territory, and New Guinea to the north as a Trust Territory, and the Australia government decided to combine the two administrations under the name, the Territory of Papua and New Guinea.

An important outcome of the war was recognition that the nation could only be fully developed by PNG people themselves. In 1944, the anthropologist Camilla Wedgwood, working for the Australian government, put a rhetorical question to her employers: "Are the natives to be educated so that they may gradually be fitted for the responsibilities of self government, and may acquire the skills and experience to develop a native economy independent of white overlordship and control?"[77] Wedgwood wanted a government school system introduced immediately and subsidies for missions ended. Although thought of highly in Canberra, she would have a girls' school at Goroka named after her in 1955, the administration took a more cautious approach appointing the experienced, William Groves, as its director of Education in June 1946.

Primary Education in Papua and New Guinea to Self-Government

From 1946–1947, Groves's first task was to set up a Department of Education. Its first tasks were to oversee European schools operating an Australian curriculum, and Chinese classes teaching English and Chinese, as well as the new government system of indigenous schools in process of establishment. For the first time, professional education staff were appointed to the Territory, Groves utilizing them in the development of radio broadcasts, and audio and film aids for classrooms; he also appointed a research officer in traditional music. As for textbooks, the Department of Education produced some simple vernacular and pidgin texts in cooperation with the missions. The page below is from a government approved Anglican reader in the Mekeo vernacular.

29

Imoi kekele aka Iesu Keliso.

Iesu Betelemeai e maugi.

Iesu ina aka Maria.

Iosepa Iesu ama ipafa'a.

Bulomakau doniki fou Iesu

egai ke kakipo.

Imoi ke ima.

Mekeo Reader No. 1. Territory of Papua and New Guinea (Port Moresby: Department of Education, 1952), 29.

The new Department of Education had the Papuan Readers from the 1920s, and 1930s reprinted with minor revision. Individual staff members and external publishers were also encouraged to produce textbooks and materials based on local needs and conditions. To ensure momentum in education, the Australian government was prepared to increase its subsidies to mission education; however,

Groves was unwilling to accept the status quo in regard to secular schooling. Overwhelmingly, mission village schools offered the 3 R's in the vernacular, with some English words and personal hygiene and gardening, and maintained at best four classes: an infants' class, a vernacular class, and Standard 1 and Standard 2 classes. Few females were enrolled in these early indigenous schools, or in government schools either; the main government school at Sogeri recording 29 girls among its 197 enrollments in 1948, and the primary school at Kokoda, one female among 59.[78]

An Educational Advisory Board was introduced in 1952, with mission representatives. It was charged with tightening standards. Now Groves began registering mission schools, but many hundreds of them failed to meet minimal conditions and were given a period of grace in which to comply. Overall, the government maintained a cooperative approach to missions assisting them with publications and sharing its services: missionaries were allowed to enter government schools and give religious instruction and mission students in industrial centers benefited from training grants under the Commonwealth Reconstruction Training Scheme.

Groves was supportive of missions not least because he intended to construct his government education system on their foundation. Helped by government funds, missions were to teach Standards 1 and 2 in the vernacular as the first rung of Groves's education ladder. The best of the mission students would then move to the academically stronger, government, higher primary or area schools where the foundation for entry to training in technical and teaching skills would be laid. However, progress was at snail's pace: after two years of operation, Groves's government schools were teaching around 2,000 students compared with over 100,000 taught in missions. (Table 5.3 shows the statistics for all schools in the mid-1950s.)

Expanding Government Primary Schools

In 1951, a new minister for Territories in Canberra, Paul Hasluck, a man used to getting his own way, determined to introduce universal literacy, and a target date was set for 1973. By the mid 1950s though, enrollments remained disappointing, except in the flourishing mission sector.

Groves faced two major problems in expanding the government system: first, he did not have a sufficient pool of students, and second, he did not have enough teachers. His policy of relying on enrollments of Standard 2 pupils from mission feeder schools proved an abject failure as his Deputy Director G. T. (Geoff) Roscoe has explained.

What innocents we were! It took some years to learn that native children did not start school at five or six as children did in school in Australia. Neither did they progress steadily from Standard to Standard each year. The native teachers in Mission schools were nearly illiterate, and neither they nor their European supervisors knew anything of

Table 5.3
Educational Statistics 1954–1956

Indigenous population (1954)	1.68 million persons
Nonindigenous population	17,755 persons
Administration schools (1956)	
Primary	131
Secondary	17
Technical and teacher-training institutions	7
Students in all administration schools/institutions	8,686
Mission schools	3,910
Students in all mission schools	157,000
Teachers:	
Administration	48 European/311 indigenous
Mission	452 Europeans/4,917 indigenous
Other:	
Native local govt. council maintained schools	13
Rabaul Asian Secondary School	1

Source: Adolphus P. Elkin, *Native Peoples, in Australian Encyclopaedia, vol. V* (Sydney: Grolier Society of Australia, 1961), 467.

the technique of teaching. Boys and girls grew up in the Village School, and reached adolescence without attaining Standard 2.[79]

Forced to abandon his plan for higher-level primary entry, Groves began recruiting pupils at the preparatory and Standard 1 levels. While the move brought immediate objections from the missions, the initiative was welcomed by many indigenous people. Roscoe told his boss how he had received a delegation of local leaders at Bruin, all of whom wanted a government school. Although the deputy director had given them his stock reply—they already had mission schools—their response was equally to the point: "Tok bilong God, tasol." The local leaders wanted a school where the boys would learn to use tools like a technical school.

Finding the Teachers

Thwarted by a shortage of expatriate teachers willing to work in PNG, Groves took the bold step in 1957 of recruiting underqualified Australians, single men under 20, who had left school with three years of secondary schooling as a minimum. After six months training in Sydney or Port Moresby they would be certificated and employed as teachers in the PNG area schools. Groves focused his recruitment campaign on Australia's rural schools where many young people left school early predicting these young Australian males would gladly answer the call.

The Director of Education does not believe that the spirit of Gallipoli and Tobruk is dead in the young men of Australia.[80]

Canberra also expressed its approval of Groves's idea, at the same time making it clear that it did not expect too much scholarship from those sent to teach "primitive children."

The people in the Territory do not have our cultural background, and in many ways it is rather artificial to indulge in the niceties of educational method and group dynamics, when all the teacher in the Territory is required to do is teach the 3Rs.[81]

The prediction that the Department would find the numbers proved correct— the young men did come and with their partners' help would kick start a comprehensive government system. Over time, many of the pioneers took out correspondence and higher degrees, some rising to senior positions in the Territory and Australia. By 1963, government enrollments in primary had increased to over 40,000, and mission enrollments stood at 109,000. Admittedly a few indigenous educators were critical of what they saw as the imposition of unqualified and ill-prepared staff by Australia, still standards in PNG were minimal with completion of primary education and one year of training a satisfactory base for teaching in many places.

Curriculum and Teaching Methods

Geoff Roscoe, who would succeed Groves in 1958, was a product of the Queensland public school system having served as teacher and high school principal. Viewing himself as very much the practical educator, he had opposed Groves's philosophy of teachers as professionals creating their own curricula suited to local conditions, believing that the new Australian arrivals would be lost without a set syllabus. Unless teachers were told what they should teach, they would fall back on the curricula and teaching methods applicable in Australia. Groves gave in, and Roscoe set about producing his curricula for all levels. So far as European schools were concerned, the deputy turned to the Queensland syllabus in English and arithmetic, and his social studies content came from local history and geography. He also drew on material Groves had used in the British Solomon Islands. One area that gave him some trouble was the preparatory grade.

I guessed it would be harder than teaching numbers to little Australians so I gave them six months to cover numbers 1 to 5. This slow advance was strongly criticized by teachers in native schools near Port Moresby, whose pupils already had some idea of numbers before they started school. On the other hand Mission teachers in remote parts of the Highlands say that they find it hard to cover "numbers 1 to 5" in six months.

Roscoe also had difficulty preparing the ethics and morals curriculum. His first attempt, based on a recommendation from a Mission Conference that he draw on the Ten Commandments for inspiration, was roundly criticized by the missions. After amending it by introducing bible readings, he learned the missions could not agree on what version of the Bible should be used. The eventual product was a syllabus with limited reference to Christianity, though Roscoe believed that promoted behavior acceptable to most teachers. In 1967, the Roscoe curriculum was replaced by an Agreed Syllabus for Christian Education in Primary "T" Schools, which related biblical texts to topics like God, conscience, sin, the cargo cult mentality, and sorcery and magic.

Teaching English and Raising Standards

Hasluck's plan for universal literacy assumed that English would be the norm, the minister believing its introduction would have a unifying effect and reduce uneven economic development. Here he was strongly supported by his assistant Administrator John Gunther who used the rallying cry: "Teach them English, English and more English; this is what they want."[82] As it happened, the employment of young Australians had effectively preempted the situation—schools becoming English speaking from the point the child entered the playground. The school day for many young Papua New Guineans began with the patriotic recital: "Honor my God. Save the Queen. Love my school. Salute the flag!"

In class, English was taught through the phonics and the whole word teaching methods. Children then progressed to English readers drawing on tropical-island settings read aloud several times and learned by heart. Spelling was a continuous activity taught in context and drilled. However, Roscoe himself had private misgivings about the effectiveness of this emphasis on teaching English in remote areas where there was no opportunities for students to use it, and he came to the view that teaching pidgin would be more productive.

Roscoe also permitted use of the New South Wales state curriculum in a limited number of "A" schools set up in urban areas. These schools were open to the children of expatriates, mixed race children, and children whose indigenous professionals spoke English at home. Enrollments in them had a much better chance of entering higher education; however, the "A" school classrooms cost about five times more than "T" (Territory) classrooms: as well, the administration found itself under pressure from members of the indigenous elite seeking to enroll their own children.

The "one-man syllabus" prepared by Roscoe was superseded in 1960, after the Department of Education established a Curriculum Committee under Dr. Ken McKinnon, an Adelaide-born educator, with ten years experience in New Guinea as teacher and educational administrator. Abandoning Roscoe's

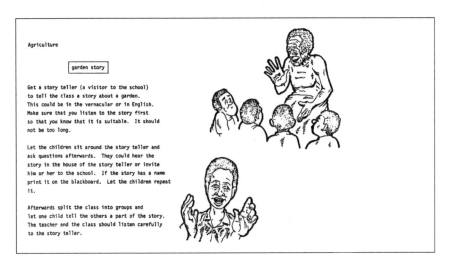

Page from the *Draft Teachers' Guide for the PNG Community Life Syllabus for Grade One.*
David Dufty, with John Cleverley, "Planning Social Studies Instruction," in Howard D. Mehlinger,
UNESCO Handbook for the Teaching of Social Studies (London: Croom Helm, 1981), 117.

necessary but amateur efforts, McKinnon introduced a measure of sophistica-
tion into curriculum planning, producing a substantial primary curriculum in
1963, including the situational method of teaching of English. The Department also trialed a mathematics syllabus drawing on the Dienes method and
new science and social sciences approaches based on the latest concept learning
models.[83]

The pace of change (and its cost) was rapid under McKinnon, some said
beyond the system's capacity to absorb given that most teachers had little more
than primary education and one or two years' training. After government
teachers' colleges relying heavily on expatriate staff opened at Madang and Port
Moresby in 1963–1964, some of the lecturers complained that the McKinnon's
curricula favored the untested ideas of Australian outsiders. For all his teething
problems, he did achieve a breakthrough in curriculum design introducing a
process supportive of best international practice.

Towards Secondary Education

The unwillingness of the Australian government to open fully fledged high
schools was a deliberate decision resulting from the minister for Territories'
social conservatism. Hasluck feared the creation of an elite alienated from its
own people and predisposed to challenge Australian leadership. At this time
government policy was to provide an education up to Standard 5 or 6, then
siphon off the better students into low-level technical or teacher-training. For a
select few, there were places in general education beyond Standard V in the

higher and intermediate schools, including IX–X classes. For reporting purposes, however, the various postprimary schools were designated as secondary.

Precursors of Secondary Institutions

In 1944, the Australian New Guinea Army Unit opened the Central Training School at Sogeri, near Port Moresby drawing on staff already experienced in PNG schools. Its purpose was to extend the education of better-educated village school graduates in post-secondary courses: three-year training for teachers in general subjects including technical knowledge; two-year training for instructors in technical college in subjects like elementary radio mechanics, carpentry, plumbing, improved agriculture etc.; and short-term courses designed to improve the English of medical orderlies. Entry standards among the 112 students enrolled were nowhere near as high as was anticipated: some had only Standard 3, others Standard 4 or 5, perhaps earned some time back and since forgotten. Consequently an important part of the Sogeri experience was the revision of earlier studies going back up to three years for some.[84] One of its innovations of interest was the opening of a Women's Section where a syllabus for girls schools operated by missions, and domestic science course outlines were prepared. The section also engaged in welfare assisting teachers' and trainees' wives.[85]

The Sogeri initiative in post-primary teaching was taken a step further in 1954 when 20 Australian secondary scholarships were awarded, about a fifth of them going to women. They were designed for indigenous students to study in Australian boarding schools on an ongoing basis; and it was hoped that the scholarship holders would remain in Australia to graduate from university, but only two had succeeded by 1967. Even so supporters argued those who had studied overseas would develop social poise, knowledge of English, and work attitudes that would enabled them to compete with Australians in lower- and middle-level occupations.[86] In 1959, an international high school opened at Rabaul, extending upwards the primary "A" school provision for expatriates.

Policy for Secondary and Technical Education

Australia's failure to provide full secondary education was a refrain of members of the United Nations Trustee Council missions visiting New Guinea. In 1956, for example, the mission reported that "everywhere it went it found that a lack of such training prevented New Guineans from participating in the administration."[87] While the 1962 mission led by Sir Hugh Foot praised the Australian effort in primary education, around 40 percent in school, he reported an urgent need for an apex of secondary and tertiary opportunity. Here Foot discounted Hasluck's belief that independence was several generations away.

After Roscoe was replaced by a new director of Education, Leslie W. Johnston, in 1963, the Department of Education accepted the economic argument for educational development. Though literacy was a universal right Johnson believed its spread must be subject to the advantage of the community as whole, with schools in more developed parts deserving priority. His views were bolstered by a survey from the World Bank in 1964, which thought PNG primary education best consolidated not increased. Expatriate teachers and boarding schools should be phased out, local communities made to shoulder more responsibility, and a new curriculum introduced better geared to village life. The World Bank wanted 21,000 new places in secondary, including Forms V and VI, over the next five years, and the whole educational effort informed by research and improved planning.

Two central schools, Sogeri and Keravat on the Gazelle, were chosen for transformation into full high schools. The indefatigable Roscoe had worked on their curriculum, an intervention he justified by an inappropriate mathematics problem he had spotted on a blackboard at Sogeri: "An orchardist plants 1289 trees. 487 are apple trees, 395 are peach trees, and the rest are plum trees. How many plum trees are there?"[88] The first high schools would teach Standards 7–8 as laid down by the Syllabus for Native Secondary Schools, and Standards 9–10 that were tied to the Junior Public Examination of the University of Queensland. Eventually, Sogeri and Keravit became two of four national high schools established across PNG, whose curriculum covered the last two years of the high school cycle, Standards 11 and 12 (Forms 5 and 6).

The government also established its own two-year junior technical schools for boys with five or so years schooling under their belts, teaching skills like bricklaying, carpentry, driving, and boat-building. On completion the boys could enter apprenticeships or find semi-skilled work or be placed in higher level trade training like automotive or diesel mechanics for another two years. Later a full technical school was established at Idubada. It was capable of teaching higher skills and general education, technical drawing, woodwork, and metal work. Missions continued with their own industrial training, their centers at Popondetta, Kwato, and Yule Island among those receiving government grants.

Teacher Education and Tertiary

The PNG teaching force in the 1950s–1960s was slowly upgraded through a registration process which rewarded those missions employing better-qualified staff and by an increased output of graduates with post-secondary and teacher-training. In the period 1946–1954, 179 teachers passed through the centers of Sogeri, Dregerhafen, and Keravat, an inadequate number to meet demand leading the Department to give internal and external recruitment a priority.[89] Two government primary colleges opened in 1963, and another seven church establishments were recognized, and Goroka Primary Teachers College opened in the Highlands in 1965, switching to training secondary teachers exclusively two years later. By the early 1970s around 1,500 indigenous students were in local teachers' colleges, most of whom were taking two years of training requiring Standard 7 or 8 entry.

With post-secondary getting the green light, tertiary education was next in line. In 1964, the Administrative College opened in Port Moresby to train senior-level indigenous public servants. A year later, a report from the Currie Commission (1964) recommended the establishment of a university and a technical institute for the Territory: the University of Papua New Guinea (UPNG) opened in Port Moresby enrolling expatriate and indigenous students in 1966, the latter having to take a preliminary year mainly to upgrade their English; and the following year, the Institute of Higher Technology was established being renamed the University of Technology (UOT) in 1973. In addition to these two institutions there were a number of national and mission colleges catering for specific administrative, technical, and religious training.

The big tertiary institutions found it difficult to recruit students despite scholarships. In 1974, UPNG had 1,780[90] students, two thirds of them nationals, while UOT had 881 national enrollments, and about 6 percent expatriate. Under their Australian vice-chancellors, the two centers were shaped by Australian practices: administrative structures, disciplines, and qualifications. They also attracted many very able academics drawn to PNG by the opportunity of helping establish an institution in a developing country. Despite being accused of reproducing mirror-image Australians, the mix of nationals and expatriates in a free-thinking environment gave intellectual debate in Papua New Guinea an added bite, frequently angering both Canberra and the PNG administration. They were though a massive drain on Education's funds, a university place averaging AUD$5,232 per student compared with an average AUD$62 per place across all schools.[91]

A Unified Mission and Government System

As government had begun to move resources into secondary schooling, it was evident that the patchwork of mission and government schools, each critical of the other and frequently in competition, was failing the country. The deficiencies were shiningly apparent in 1964 when the new House of Assembly with a substantial elected membership sat. Although expected to participate in a government designed by Australia along the lines of the Westminster model, nineteen members of the thirty-eight indigenous representatives were illiterate.[92]

Missions themselves were interested in forging a new relationship with the PNG government if it meant greater funding. After all, the big churches had accepted government subsidies for education already, sometimes against the advice of their ecclesiastical superiors overseas. They also felt threatened by the proximity of self-government in 1973, afraid that some faiths would be favored over others, and that a newly elected government could nationalize the school system. Financial disputes were looming too as the administration was paying its teachers twice the salary most mission teachers received. A unified government-mission system threw them a lifeline.

The Weedon Report of 1969 determined the form the unified school system would take. Under McKinnon's directorship, school governing bodies, District Education Boards, and a National Education Board, all with mission representation, were put in place in 1970. Both mission and government teachers were now paid by government and regulated under a Teaching Service Commission. Mission schools also received direct funding from the state covering most costs. For their part, the mission agreed to admit children of all denominations and allow freedom of religious instruction; these conditions were acceptable to all except the Seventh-day Adventists so that church stayed outside.

Indigenous Perspectives Emerge

Indigenous educators had mixed feelings towards the new unified system they inherited on Independence: some worried it would entrench foreign influence in PNG schooling, others that it represented a form of personal alienation. Nelson Giraure, the articulate senior administrator in the Department of Education, expressed views common enough among his generation. At the heart of his concern was the overwhelming foreign content of the schooling of the 1950s. Wrenched out of his Tolai village culture, Giruane had first of all lost his name, indigenous given-names not being considered suitable for baptism purposes due to their heathen origin. In Giraure's case the Methodist mission named him after Britain's hero of the battle of Trafalgar, Nelson. Initially, Giruare had learned to read and write in the vernacular under Tolai converts for which he was grateful. On moving to the government primary school, however, he was found himself put back to Standard 1 again and forbidden from communicating in his Tok Ples. English was mandatory: all were reminded by the large signs put around around the school. "You must speak English only."[93] Those in default were punished by grass cutting, extra work, or beaten.

The subjects Giruare was set to learning were as foreign to him as the English language, so he spent most of his time passively sitting and listening. Despite the Tolai having a rich music and dance culture, its spirit dances and war songs were banned as evil: instead he was put to learning Scottish highland reels, hymns, and nursery songs like Humpty Dumpty, and Baa Baa Black Sheep. Never having seen a sheep, he confused the word with "ship," visualizing a black boat sailing by. Similarly, he was not taught Tolai carving so his Christmas decorations in Expressive Arts were stick figures of Jesus on the cross and paper cut outs. In social science Giraure learned a little of the Red Indian and Eskimo peoples, and of countries like the United States and Russia. At no time, he said, was he taught about his own people: "The way we lived was considered unimportant." His teachers justified everything they taught him by future examination success which would win him a job in Rabaul. Later he learned that many of his bush kanaka friends had done as well or better by earning money from agriculture and trading.

Remorselessly Giruare's links with his own villagers were broken. At high school he was told by expatriate teachers that his pastime of chewing betel nut was a disgusting habit, the same men who ground their cigarette butts into the ground and blew smoke in his face. During his teachers' college days, he was given collections of European content for his classes and made teach the same way that he had been taught: "I taught European songs. I taught about other countries and about other people. I ignored the local community." Looking back, Giraure regarded himself as Europeanized. It was not that he had too much schooling, he declared, but that it was not of the right kind. His was an unresolved tension, a life torn between two worlds.

Indigenous Educators Take Command

When the country's first major political party, the Pangu Parti, was formed in 1967, it took the opportunity to prepare an educational platform arguing for expanded educational opportunity in the country. There were several ex-teachers among its early members: Michael Somare, later prime minister, Ebia Olewale, the first minister for Education, and the first indigenous director of Education, Alkan Tolo. Self-government was ushered in during 1973, and Independence on September 16, 1975, when a new flag was broken on Independence Hill, Waigani. Designed by a fifteen-year-old schoolgirl, Susan Karike, from the Meii village in the Gulf, it portrayed a yellow bird of paradise on a divided flag of red and black, with white stars.

Flag of the Independent State of Papua New Guinea.

As to her choice of colors for the nation's flag, Karike, the Yule Island mission student reported:

I remember what my father told me. He said that we use a lot of bambang (lime) when we chew betel nut and its colour is white. So my choice reflects that. Yellow and red represent the many wild flowers of that colour that we have in our bushes. I chose black to represent charcoal.[94]

Primary Education after Independence

This post-Independence period was an exciting one. Indigenous staff had new ideas to trial and could draw on a professional education administration at Konedobu, including expatriate Australian and American educators in planning, finance, and research. One major benefit from the new unified government mission school system was the existence of a coherent structure for education across the country. The unified primary schools held around 255,000 students, or 58 percent of the age group,[95] and a five-year National Education Plan was adopted in 1976 to take account of future demand. Entry to Community School (Grades 1–6) was set at age seven, and corporal punishment and beating students were banned. Working together, nationals and expatriates identified major challenges, some old, and others more recent.

A Village-Based Curriculum

Attention was paid to local needs in the 1977 Community Life Primary Syllabus when time was allocated across the curriculum for community activity and local language learning. Teachers were told to bring old people into schools to tell stories, take their children out of class to help with local harvest, collect artifacts from the community, open school museums, and join with local women in making local pottery. At Mt. Hagan, the Holy Trinity Primary School teachers and children learned local stories, picked coffee, cleared gardens, and fetched water. Its pupils also worked in the school garden growing kaukau, tomatoes, peas, and asparagus.[96]

Self-Reliance

Self-reliance, linked with the village-based curriculum, was also strongly promoted by national educators. There was an obvious need to reduce the costs of education in PNG which were frequently tied to costly Australian standards. Educators proposed that community school buildings and teachers' housing follow local standards, that educational supplies be less generous, and staff–student ratios increased. Community school students were told to bring their own food to school or grow it in the school environs.

Decentralization and Provincial Government

Decentralization was another priority issue. While the unified system of 1970 had introduced locally based agencies, these were seen as subordinate to the Department of Education in Port Moresby. Most politicians wanted a school system with its roots in their home regions. On Independence, and under threat of secession by Bougainville, the Somare government established provinces under the Organic Law of 1977 each with its own elected members and complementary administration. As his Minister for Provincial Affairs Oscar Tammur declared: "Every department in our government has to be run as we ourselves wish them to be run. This includes education."[97] In the event, provincial governments were granted power over the community schools subject to their teaching a core of basic subjects.

A good deal of confusion over the roles and responsibilities of the national and provincial ministers for education occurred. Grappling as they were with their newly devolved functions, provinces were not especially innovative. When East New Britain, for example, attempted to introduce compulsory preschools, it ran into problems over resources and legalities. However the North Solomon Education Research Project did introduce vernacular preschools for seven-year-olds known as "Viles Tok Ples Skuls,"[98] successfully. It also gave its community schools a measure of student self-government. These progressive reforms were the exception: Serious differences within provinces emerged between clan, missions, and government over the distribution of education resources, budget control was poor, and there was a general lack of coordination across the country. In some provinces, the examination component in high school selection was as low as 20 percent, in others it was as high as 100.[99] Over time the national government lost some interest in the sector it no longer managed. In the 1990s provincial powers in education were considerably curtailed.

Secondary and Tertiary Institutions

The 1976, education plan established 80 Provincial High Schools (Grades 7–10) holding about 30,000 students, and six National High Schools (11–12). There were also National Technical Colleges (11–12) enrolling about 4,000 students, and the post-secondary Community Vocational Training Centers (7–8 or above) held 5,000. Most of the big issues apparent in primary education surfaced at secondary. Expenditure on school buildings and housing was reduced, educational supplies from government were cut, and class sizes increased. Boarding accommodation would be charged closer to cost, and some vocational centers closed their kitchens over the weekend, forcing hungry students to feed themselves. As with the primary school sector, the national government agreed to pass control of provincial high schools to the provinces, though it retained control over the basic subjects. Overall, the teaching force for primary and secondary remained with the national teaching service.

Dealing with the "Push Out" Problem

In the early 1970s, less than half those who entered Grade 1 reached Grade 5, and only about one third of Grade 6 graduates would find places in high school. Of the minority that did get into high school 15 percent discontinued after Form 2. While these dropouts were partly the result of poverty, most were excluded by the lack of available places higher up the educational ladder. When these young adolescent "push-outs" returned home, they were seen as failures: There was little opportunity for them to use what the schools had taught, their clans would not release land or provide school-leaver projects for them, and physically they were immature, restless, and challenging of authority. Many of them drifted to the towns where they hustled for a living, forming gangs, and living off their wontoks, and the proceeds of petty crime.

In attempts to make children better adapted to village life, the Department of Education introduced a new four-year Secondary School Community Extension Program in 1978, where practical experience dominated the curriculum. It also backed a post-secondary experience offering two years of practical training known as *skulankas*. Individual provinces like the North Solomons introduced school-leaver projects, expanded vocational education, and opened a North Solomon University Center. Individual schools attempted solutions too: Bugandi High School in Lae, for example, ran an "associates scheme"[100] in which 100 of its pupils formed a service core and helped 70 local school leavers clear land for fish ponds and duck farming and continue with correspondence lessons.

The Department of Education also introduced a practical studies subject in its secondary schools in 1977, teaching boys skills in woodwork, building, concreting, and metal work, and girls, home economics. High school parents were also invited to visit their children's secondary schools to observe their learning and help with labor and skills; specially prepared huts complete with pig pens were built for them in school grounds. In technical high schools, staff offered locals short courses in woodworking, concreting, and metal work, with typing and sewing for women. Within the Department of Education itself, staff were directed to save money by sleeping over in B-grade hotels when traveling on departmental warrants, though they complained that colleagues in other Departments still stayed at the best places in town.

Economizing and Self-Help at Tertiary

In the tertiary sector some 2,330 student attended the nine primary teachers colleges in 1976, and 428 were in training for secondary teaching at Goroka. The trainees at Goroka took up work assignments at the hospital and taught at the Corrective Institute, and others built jungle playgrounds for nearby school and tutored early leavers. Universities were also directed to operate more economically, and it was suggested boarding fees be increased. The nexus with Australian salaries was broken in PNG universities in 1973 when lower salary scales encouraged the employment of Filipinos, Indian, and other non-Australian staff. Of all PNG institutions, the Seventh-day Adventist College, Sonoma, was the thriftiest. Pupils were charged a general support fee of K80 a year, and those who could not pay provided equivalent value in extra labor. All students labored 14 hours a week in its plantation, or joined in building or road works. As children grew most of what they ate, very little money went on imported food: in 1970, 60 percent of the college budget had come from overseas funds and, eight years later, the percentage had fallen to 17.[101]

Localization of Staffing

An early move backed by indigenous educators was to press hard for the replacement of whites in teaching and educational administration by Papua New Guineans. By the early 1980s the extent of indigenization was apparent: the community schools were 100 percent localized, lower secondary classes 78.4 percent, and senior classes 9.5 percent. About a third of staff at technical schools was indigenous. Similarly in teachers' colleges, around a third of the lecturers in teachers colleges were localized by 1980; at UPNG the figure for staff was about 20 percent and at UOT between 5–10 percent.[102] Over time national policy shifted to put less emphasis on replacement of expatriates by locals and more on efficiency, with selective expatriate recruitment continuing.

Resistance to Indigenization in Schooling

Towards the end of the 1970s, serious resistance to community activities in schools was apparent. Teachers declared themselves wary of connecting with communities they knew little about, indeed some were scared. Others found the new ideas unrewarding, and both teachers and their students begrudged the time. When asked to assist the local school, some community leaders wanted payment for story-telling, and teaching pottery and wood carving. In secondary, specialist teachers were difficult to recruit for subjects like practical skills, and academic teachers declared themselves too busy to join activities they thought lacked status. Many parents did not support community education either believing formal western schooling a better route for a job in the cash economy. Lastly, budget divisions in the provincial and national agencies queried the need for extra funding for nonessentials.

Indigenous leaders tried a different approach to strengthen the school system in the early 1980s, national parliamentarians passing a motion that education be free for children from Grade 1 to Grade 10 applying from the 1982 school year. However five provinces determined to reject the government offer of funds fearing that the money could be withdrawn later and they would be left with an expanded school system. Alas this "free education"[103] lasted only a year, the government claiming that some provinces had diverted the extra money to noneducation bank accounts, among other reasons given.

The enthusiasm and high hopes apparent at Independence fell away as the educators learned that many clans did not want the community skills promoted in their name. Further, the education that the indigenous elite wanted for their own children was not a community-oriented one as was evident in growing indigenous enrollments in the "A" schools which taught an Australian curriculum: by 1985, nationals made up about a third of enrollments in them, and the proportion was increasing. Under a national budget cut back in the mid-1980s, community education was an early target.

THE PRESENT

How was progress in PNG schooling to be developed in the new millennium? Although experimentation in community education had largely ended, the belief continued that more should be done to move away from western models to better reflect PNG society. This growing nationalism was evident in the viewpoint of seven student teachers from Goroka Teachers College who complained of a foreign takeover of PNG culture in a widely circulated statement.

Rip Kirby, the Phantom and Flash Gordon were all male, all resolved conflict violently, all white, all uninvited in countries not their own, all sure that they know what is right for the nationals, all overcoming nationals who are criminals, incompetents or cowards.[104]

In 1986, a report prepared by Paulias Mantane asked what kind of person the nation wanted for the twenty-first century? The answer was a distinctively PNG solution based on vernacular schooling and a return to the social and spiritual values of the Constitution. Mantane's position was compatible with that expressed in the World Declaration from the Education For All (EFA) conference in 1990 organised by UNESCO at Jomtien, Thailand, where proposals were drawn up for poor countries to universalise primary school education and increase access to secondary schooling by 2000, a target later extended to 2015.

A year after Jomtien, PNG determined to encourage teaching in the vernacular in the early school years and add two years to the community school by introducing an eight-year primary school. Various education sector and international reviews enabled the National Education Plan to be adopted in 1998, accepting that it would take ten or more years to become fully operational (See Table 5.4). International agencies from Australia, New Zealand, Japan, Germany, the European Union (EU) and the UN, as well as the development banks, liked the new proposals and were prepared to back them with expertise and resources.

Various independent, fee-paying primary and secondary schools have continued to operate outside the national plan mainly for the children of expatriates and well-to-do indigenous parents. In primary, some 5,000 students follow an international English language curriculum accessing their own school libraries, air-conditioned audio-visual and teaching rooms, and generous sporting ovals. Independent secondary schools include the Coronation College at Lae, which has a Technical and Further Education section linked with an Australian technical institute. While church schools run by the (SDA) and others operate outside the national plan by choice, others have unsuccessfully requested government recognition for new vocational colleges and teacher training for example under the Accelerated Christian Education (ACE) program.

Table 5.4
National Education Plan 2004–2015

Notes:

- Preparatory (P) and Elementary Grades 1 and 2 are generally taught in the vernacular.
- Primary school teaching changes from the vernacular to English in Grades 3–5, with English dominant by Grades 6 to 8.
- Junior secondary school Grades 9 and 10 can include vocational or other programs suited to the local area.
- Senior secondary school Grades 11 and 12 can offer their own specialities like academic, technical, agricultural, or commercial.
- PET: Pre- Employment Technical Training courses.
- College: the term covers about 60 nonuniversity institutions drawing on Grades 10 to 12 for enrolment like nursing, civil aviation, Telikom, and public administration.
- Elementary teacher training is undertaken by the PNG Education Institute; primary teacher training is available in the government colleges at Madang and the PNG Education Institute, and in five church-owned agencies; and secondary teacher training is offered through the University of Goroka and the Pacific Adventist University.
- Universities: government–UPNG, University of Technology (UOT), University of Goroka (UOG), University of Vudal (UOV): church–Pacific Adventist University (SDA), and Divine Word University (DWU). All institutions can operate open learning departments.
- College of Distance Education and Flexible and Open Distance Education maintain attached centres.

Source: From *National Education Plan 2004–2015, Port Moresby, National Department of Education;* Samuel Haihuie, "Education Development in Papua New Guinea," in David Kavanamur, Charles Yala, and Quinton Clements, eds., *Building a Nation in Papua New Guinea Views of the Post-Independence Generation* (Canberra: Pandanus Books, 2003), 239–245.

Rejuvenating Primary Schools

In 2002, approximately one million PNG children attended school, of whom approximately a fifth were in secondary classes. This enrollment was nearly double the number enrolled ten years earlier, an increase boosted by the popularity of vernacular preparatory grades. Some 40 percent of the total attended church agency schools.[105] (See Table 5.5.)

Curriculum up to Grade 8

The national plan breathed new life into preparatory and elementary grades through access to vernacular or lingua franca languages. Most schools operated for half the day under staff with some local training and paid salaries set at 60 percent of a community teacher's pay. Vernacular dictionaries and grammars, a number surviving from mission days, were rediscovered; framework guides known as shell books which allow for the insertion of vernacular content in reading material are published; and many schools run off alphabet and other

Table 5.5
National System Preparatory and Primary Schooling

Preprimary

Gross enrollment in preprimary	59 percent
Pupil–teacher ratio	35:1
Female-to-male ratio—preprimary	94:100

Primary

Gross enrollment age 7–12	75.4 percent
Pupil–teacher ratio	35:1
Net enrollment rate – female	69 percent
Net enrollment rate – male	77 percent
Survival to Grade 6	59 percent

Private Sector

Primary enrollment	1.4 percent (2000)
Secondary enrollment	2.0 percent

Source: Aid achievements in Papua New Guinea, AusAid, 2006. http://www.ausaid.gov.au/ country/png; Edstats, Summary Education Profile: Papua New Guinea, 2006. http://devdata. worldbank.org/edstats; Efa Regional overview: Pacific Region, UNESCO, 2006, 2, 9–11. http://www.efareport.unesco.org; ADB Performance Evaluation Report: Higher Education Project (Asian Development Bank, 2006). http://www.adb.org/Documents/PPERs?PNG; National Statistical Office of Papua New Guinea, http://www.nso.gov.pg/Pop_Soc%20Stats.

charts using silk screen and home printing. Altogether 250 languages at least have become accessible for classroom use, around a quarter of the national total.

The National Department of Education (NDOE) supports the vernacular and community movement by publishing cultural calendars assisting with the identification of major community events: for instance, the Motu calendar works on the assumption of thirteen not twelve months, with garden planting held in the early part of the year and cultural ceremonies in September. Related themes coinciding with classroom work are suggested.

With the growing popularity of Tok Ples in the preparatory and early primary grades, the worry that the vernacular would hinder English learning is heard less frequently. Nonetheless some elementary schools still prefer to teach all classes in English. From another perspective, some educators have suggested that teaching in the vernacular will further destroy traditional culture by making stories once secret and sacred available indiscriminately, and by denying power to the "big man" of the oral tradition.[106]

The number of subjects in the primary school has also been consolidated, and there are opportunities for provinces to introduce subjects or content of their own. In the basic subjects an outcomes-based curriculum has been

Table 5.6
Outcomes-Based Curriculum Reform from Preparatory and Elementary to Grade 8, 2007

Preparatory and Elementary Grades 1–2 Language, mathematics, culture, and community living
Primary Grades 3–5 Language, mathematics, arts, community living, environmental studies, health education, physical education
Primary Grades 6–8 Language, mathematics, arts, social science, science, making a living, personal development

Source: Complied by author and W. T. Kaleva, e-mail message to author, February 27, 2007.

introduced with learning and skills assessed in a continuous mode and through external examination at Grade 8.

To further stimulate reading, the *School Journal* movement supported by New Zealand aid has taken root with about one in three primary-age children receiving fresh reading materials written and illustrated by Papua New Guineans. The National Education Plan reforms also brought in external consultants who assisted with the creation of new curricula at all levels, and appropriate textbooks. Two major suppliers of textbooks are Pearson Education and Oxford University Press located in Melbourne, who co-operate with the NDOE producing various texts in pidgin and English at preparatory, primary, and secondary levels, and other reference materials including audiovisual media. While the quality and range of text book material is good, texts remain a high cost item as they are published in Australia with small print runs. One way the government helps is through subsidies for dispatching books to schools.

Use of the Mass Media

Certainly radio is the most suitable means of transmitting external educational content, with general news and basic education programs for schools carried by a network of radio stations of the National Broadcasting Corporation in morning broadcasts. Commercial FM stations operate; there is a Christian Broadcasting network; Radio Australia beams a shortwave service to PNG in pidgin; and other radio stations are on the Web or accessible through satellite broadcasting. Broadcasts can be in English, Tok Pisin, Motu, or Tok Ples, however their outreach remains restricted as not all teachers and schools can receive signals, many lack electricity and money for batteries, or else their equipment has broken down and technical repairs are impossible. Solar energy is being utilized as a way around the problem of electricity generation in some townships.

The nation's one TV station, EMTV, provides some primary and secondary school subjects during nonpeak hours, the material produced by the Department's Media Centre assisted by Japanese aid. Otherwise, broadcasts mostly run imported programs. Again, television coverage is limited to major urban centers. A national Internet service supported by Telikom PNG, the government's telecommunication organization, operates a gateway service in major centers like Port Moresby and Lae through work stations and major educational institutions but is not well supported by reliable telephone access. Experiments with audio and visual conferencing in schools are being trialed through the Department, and links among tertiary institutions and research institutions are encouraged by an education and research network.

Other news of educational happenings bad and good are published in English language newspapers like the *Papua New Guinea Post Courier* and *The National*, now available online, and the *Wantok Niuspepa* in pidgin. Taking up hot topics, they are valuable supplements to official education statements, reporting basic educational news like the progress of outcomes based curriculum reform and school innovation.[107]

Secondary Schools

Under the reform plan more students are entering senior studies through Grades 7 and 8, which are offered as part of the primary school cycle. However, numbers drop away rapidly in secondary proper as figures from Grades 8 and 10 for 2004 indicate. Of the 66,907 enrolled in Grade 7, only 34,401 complete Grade 9, and there are just 8,608 in class by Grade 11. The number graduating with a Grade 12 pass, 4,027 in 2004, was quite small.[108]

As in the primary school, an outcomes-based curriculum operates at secondary. (See Table 5.7, below.) There is also an external examination at Grade 10, and a final external examination at Grade 12, supplementing a Grade 11 internal assessment.

Table 5.7
Outcomes-Based Curriculum Reform from Grade 9 to Grade 12, 2007

Grades 9–10
Language and literature, and mathematics compulsory, with five additional subjects chosen from: science, personal development, social science, arts, agriculture, design technology, business studies.

Grades 11–12
Language and literature, and mathematics A or mathematics B compulsory, with two additional subjects from biology, chemistry, physics, economics, geography, history, and visual arts (under review).

Source: Complied by author and W. T. Kaleva, e-mail message to author, February 27, 2007.

Teacher-Training and Universities

The vocation of teaching remains an attractive training option for young people; preschool positions are readily filled, primary teacher-training places in demand, although secondary and lecturer grades are less easily filled. Preparatory and elementary teachers join three six-week training courses organised by their province which they can complete while on the job, or they can train through the PNG Education Institute. In 1991, a two-year trimester Diploma in Teaching was introduced, and entry to government primary teacher-training raised to Grade 12. Unlike many other countries, males make up the majority in primary and above. There are more places available for secondary teacher trainees taking a four-year education degree or postgraduate diploma at the University of Goroka, and at the private Pacific Adventist University. The Divine Word University also plans to introduce secondary teacher training. In-service programs are popular as well, permitting the upgrading of qualifications and training in subjects like school counselling, but these must be paid for.

So far as universities are concerned, the Asian Development Bank Higher Education project substantially funded four universities and the associated higher education bureaucracy over seven years from 1995. However it reported only a marginal increase in the graduation rate in 2006, attributing the disappointing outcome to underperformance in the schools sector characterized by poor governance, "ghost" teachers and high teacher absenteeism. The ADB also wanted the tertiary sector to reduce its costs and generate more of its own income. For a summary list of tertiary educational institutions, see Table 5.8, below.

Table 5.8
Tertiary Institutions 2004

	Total Enrollments	Percentage of Females
Public Universities		
UPNG, UOT, UOG, UOV	6,760	33
Private Universities		
PAU, DWU	1,277	50
Other Tertiary		
Teachers Colleges	2,293	49
Technical/business	2,471	32
Nursing colleges	483	73
Other colleges	1,430	37

Source: ADB Performance Evaluation Report: Higher Education Project (Asian Development Bank, 2006). http://www.adb.org/Documents/PPERs?PNG.

Issues in the Quality of Twenty-First Century Schooling

For parents, the national picture in education is not as important as the local one—the quality of the schooling available for their own children. Life chances for your child may be satisfactory if you attend a good quality urban school, less so if you are at school in an urban settlement, or unsatisfactory if your learning takes place in a particular remote village. Then there are those parents whose children are shut out of class altogether: poverty, school fees, an insecure environment, poor health, and child labor still keep large numbers of children out of school. School performance in PNG, as elsewhere, relates to levels of home prosperity and the availability of resources.

School Fees

Fees remain a major deterrent to attendance. The effort to provide free education in the 1950s was abandoned in the 1960s; however, the early fees were minimal. Today, the fee scale is considerable: up to K$150–250 for primary school, K$700 for secondary 9–10, and K$1,600 for boarding in Grades 11–12. In addition, preparatory schools can charge as much as K$100; and extra money must be found for uniforms, lunch, and books, for example. Some districts provide primary school students with free uniforms and book money or subsidise the fees of individual students higher up the ladder, while a few clans have organised village services groups to pay national secondary school fees for their well-performing children. Outside the education sector, business companies may sponsor students or run competitions paying school fees as promotions for their products, for example, the Lae Biscuit Company. Recognising the seriousness of this long-term problem, a meeting was held in Port Moresby in February 2007 between NDOE, UNICEF, churches and other aid donors, to discuss ways to abolish fees, perhaps over five years. However the government reaffirmed in 2007 that the country could not afford the K$500 million needed.[109]

School Innovation

One test of a lively school system is the level of significant innovation. Promising initiatives occurring in remote areas are finding ways to enroll the poorest children such as that trialed by UNICEF at the Alkena Primary School at the foothills of Mount Giluwe in the Highlands, where many parents with no cash crops were unable to meet school fees, and the viability of the school itself was threatened. A new program, *Nunga Nanga* (Your school, My school),[110] encourages local communities to levy their clans for education in much the same way that bride price or compensation payments are organised enabling schools to admit children across all tribal groups including students who have dropped out.

Other innovations linking both rural and urban schools in literacy projects are National Book Week and National Literacy Week. At Kiunga in Western

Province, for instance, exciting Literacy Week celebrations included two days of dancing, dramas, parades led by the legendary mudmen, and a beauty contest.[111] Nonformal education has also injected new projects and ideas, with more use made of Flexible and Open Distance Education offering "homegrown education."

One urban innovation is the preschool program, Pikinini Care, in the National Capital District. Anita and Nita, twins from a local settlement, had gone with their mother to her Port Moresby market stall since they were babies sleeping in billum bags. Then, in August, 2006, the twins were enrolled in classes under the Pikinnini Care Program held beneath the shade trees of the nearby Gordon Police Station, an initiative of the Royal Papua New Guinea Constabulary and the Correctional Services Department. Anita and Nita are among 60 children under the supervision of two teachers, both prisoners at Bomana gaol: "Yes we tell the kids, don't be like us."[112]

Other children from urban areas are less fortunate as the tale of Jackson John, a fifteen-year-old from a Mt. Hagen settlement reveals. The boy's work is hauling huge bags of garden produce as a "market taxi"[113] in return for a nominal payment, an experience which began at age nine. Market children, he said, had no concept of any right to food, shelter, health, or education: "Our biggest problem is our evening meal." Another sign of outspokenness by disadvantaged groups came in 2007, when children and adults with disabilities marched in the streets of Mt. Hargen urging parents to send their disabled children to school.

The Place of Kastom

The issue addressed by Nelson Giruare and others in the 1970s, demanding that schools teach traditional customs and values, has benefited from the introduction of community programs and the vernacular movement. As part of the NDOE's policy to encourage the valuing of traditional ways, many schools actively promote cultural days with customary dress. This account in the *PNG Post Courier* is from the Gordons Secondary School.

Students from Milne Bay all the way to Wabag and Manus delved deep into their busbus bags and came painted with traditional designs on their faces arms and legs. Their headdresses were a sight to behold. Plumes of bird of paradise, cockatoo and cassowary feathers sat on their heads, something the catwalks of Paris and Milan would have been envious of. But this was PNG, the students had lips painted red with betel-nut and walked the grounds. And the smell of traditional musk was seductively overwhelming. What more could you ask for, the drums rolled and the feet shuffled. It was a day to remember.[114]

Tensions remain between the attitudes of a minority of church leaders over the validation of Kastom in schools. As far back as 1971, the Australian administration differentiated good magic from bad however some Christian agencies remain antagonistic to Kastom, especially initiation ceremonies, naming them unchristian and pagan. Continued suppression of Kastom is thought to encourage cult activities among villagers and schoolchildren with church secondary students among those influenced. In Ambenob, Madang Province, people from villages left their huts to join the cult movement led by Black Jesus and his Queen, girls as young as twelve being recruited. Followers were required to undress before going to worship, with unwilling female teenagers abducted and forced to participate.[115]

The Teaching Force

The dedication of staff is crucial to the quality of education. However poor living conditions, including pay slow to arrive, health issues, and the loneliness of life in remote areas encourage a high attrition rate. Teachers' salaries and allowances are low on the public service scale, and the well-connected or better-trained leave for improved conditions. Dissatisfaction boiled over in 2006 when thousands of primary teachers supported by their union, the PNG Teachers' Association, struck over the failure of government to pay agreed salary increases and increased housing allowances. Major disruption of teaching in primary schools followed, and when staff did return to work disgruntled parents were unwilling to send their children back to class. Despite their elite status, universities are not immune from student and staff disruption either, UPNG, UOG, and UOT have all experienced stop work protests, including the arrest of some union leaders recently, though none as bad as the 2001 sit-in at UPNG when police killed four protestors.

Schools: A Dark Side

For all its dedicated teachers and solid achievement, PNG schooling faces major internal problems. Some rural schools have been unable to accommodate the expanded enrollments demanded by the reform program and have resorted to the open-air classes common a century back. Decrepit infrastructure delays the arrival of school supplies sometimes for months, and when the boxes do arrive they may have been pillaged. In 2006, community schools near Mt. Hagen lost their enrollments as famine hit the region, with no food available for school meals,[116] while Passam National High was closed because its water supply became polluted. In instances of financial dishonesty, schools have found their bank accounts emptied under cheque fraud schemes: such incidents have led the NDOE to sponsor regional workshops for teachers and administrators on topics like Standing Against Corruption Is Your Choice.[117]

Fear of violence, widespread cheating, and nepotism led to the military providing security checks for pupils and teachers taking the Grade 10 examination in the capital of the Southern Highlands Province, Mendi, in 2006. And in the Western Highlands there were reports of ongoing tribal warfare with boys as young as twelve taught to fire sophisticated weapons.[118] In February 2007, the

Lutheran Highlands International School came under heavy attack from warring clansmen during class hours, about 200 foreign and national students and
staff being evacuated, and the school only saved from destruction by police
intervention.[119] In some regions of PNG significant educational decisions are
made at the whim of the "big man" in the district supported by armed guards
and illicit funding. In urban areas, schools report serious drug taking and drug
dealing in their playgrounds.

The Scourge of HIV/AIDS in School and Society

A great contemporary challenge facing schoolchildren, teachers, and parents is
the scourge of HIV/AIDS. According to an Australian assessment, an estimated
5,600 were living with HIV in the 0–14 age group in 2004, and 50,000 in the
15–49 age group. Overall, the infection rate was 1.8 percent. It is thought as
many as 117,000 will have HIV/AIDS by 2025.[120] However, other assessments
suggest a much higher figure with an infection rate of 18 percent suggested by
2010, and 25 percent by 2020, including the loss of a million people.[121] Sister
Tarcisia, head of the National Catholic Aids Office of Papua New Guinea, has
reported that girls face a four to six times greater risk of infection than boys. The
most vulnerable are young married women[122] and adolescent girls in the 14–19
age group, who are subject to infection through early and unprotected sexual
intercourse. For many girls transactional sex is a socioeconomic reality.

Teachers are another group that suffers badly especially in urban area with
many infected and dead. It is estimated that by 2025 over 5,000 teachers will
have died and 8,000 will be living with HIV. Even putting aside the personal
tragedies, the loss of so many will require an increased enrollment in teacher education, this at a time when there will be increasing competition for public funds
from Health, 70 percent of whose hospital beds will be occupied by AIDS
patients. Over 117,000 children are expected to lose their mothers to AIDS.

In 1997, the government established the National AIDS Council, and
Provincial AIDS Councils followed. More recently, District AIDS Committees
have been established in some provinces, and other local groups help children
who have lost one or both parents. NDOE's responses have included the
preparation of an HIV/AIDS policy, rewriting of health and hygiene materials
for personal development inserting more information on reproductive and sexual health, and the introduction of in-service courses and workshops in teachers
colleges. It has been asked to change the time of the lunch hour in Port Moresby schools so as not to coincide with the business lunchtime which brings
out, "a high incidence of men cruising school areas for lunchtime sex, with
offers to pay the girls' school fees for intercourse. For young girls whose families are extremely poor, it can be a difficult proposition to fight."[123]

Different religious doctrines and traditional attitudes have contributed to
making sex and reproduction issues difficult topics to debate in public in PNG.
Women accused of sorcery against AIDS victims have been tortured and

murdered. While the country is advanced in terms of research into strategies to minimise the spread of HIV/AIDS, continued commitment by government is needed to prevent a worse case scenario.

Where Have All the Girls Gone?

When school fees are demanded, poor parents usually invest in boys' education not girls', a situation compounded in PNG by negative attitudes towards women especially in some Highland societies. In 2004, EFA statistics put the female/male ratio at 65/100 in school in the Western Highlands: this contrasted with 80/100 in the National Capital District—while the higher up the educational ladder, the lower the proportion of females in class. Security both in school and out, including the home, remains a major issue in the attendance of girls: girls are disproportionately the victims of physical and sexual abuse, gang rape, physical assault, family violence, and tribal fighting. Given that only one woman held a seat in the National Parliament in 2007, it is difficult to see a female contribution to leadership able to redress the situation nationally.

The extra hurdles that girls must overcome in education lowers their self-confidence. Here NDOE advocates that boys and girls work together in schools, that a balance of sexes be portrayed in curriculum materials, and that mixed sporting teams and coeducational school activities apply. Communities are urged to adjust school timetables to take account of local celebrations and feasts, and the coffee and vanilla harvesting seasons, and schools are asked to be more tolerant where attendance is disrupted by the excessive demands of household duties like laundry, child minding, cooking, and attending to market stalls. Teachers should avoid humiliating punishments that lower girls' self-esteem, and not keep them back after school hours. Where punishment is thought necessary, they can help in the school canteen or tutor younger children.[124] NDOE has begun teaching birth control and family limitation methods to cut unwanted pregnancies in the 15–19 age group.

Another group actively working for gender equality in schools and against child abuse has been UNICEF through its program, Accelerate Girls' Education. The agency supports provincial plans including one which enables young women to return to school after giving birth; in one Highland situation, a student breast fed her baby when the partner brought the infant to school during class breaks.[125] Even so, as Patricia Paraide, senior research fellow in the Educational Studies Division of the National Research Institute, has put it, "girls and women are usually seen as being less important, less intelligent, and less capable than boys and men."[126]

Young People Speak Out

An Open Space Forum held in July 2006 saw young people in the National Capital District encouraged to speak their minds, their views translated and pasted on walls under a project sponsored by the National Department of

Community Development, and UNDP, UNICEF, the World Bank, and nongovernment organisations. Despite having limited or no schooling, the adolescents expressed their home-truths explicitly—horrific stories of individual lives scarred by sexual abuse, drugs, criminality, and early death. These are the stories of misfits, the homeless, and the poor told with the good humour of the young. As a group they were "very genuine, very un-listened to, very frightened about where they might end up, very honest."[127] Despite the rhetoric of politicians and others about the benefits of the future, their overwhelming desire for a job and more schooling remains unfulfilled. In 2006, there were approximately 5,000 monetary sector jobs available for 80,000 school leavers.

Going Forward or Back

Australia has continued as PNG's main aid donor with AUD$332 million allocated for 2007, including a subvention for education. The strong commitment relates to Australia's self-interest as it considers PNG a fragile state whose possible collapse threatens its northern borders allowing increased drug importation, people smuggling, and money laundering. Australia is also experiencing growing admissions to its hospitals in the Torres Strait from PNG HIV/AIDS sufferers. Most recently, the country intervened directly in PNG governance locating Australian personnel in government departments, a move that some local politicians consider threatens national autonomy.

Whether increased Australian assistance will help PNG do more than hold the line in the provision of educational services is debatable. In late 2006, Allan Patience, professor of political science at the UPNG, presented a telling snapshot of conditions.

The education system has all but disintegrated. Literacy rates are plummeting as schools close. Teachers are not being paid properly, or are not being paid at all. The higher education sector is fragmented and grotesquely under resourced. It has long ago ceased being the main builder of human capacity for PNG.[128]

In similar tone, a recent ADB evaluation report has pointed to a breakdown in infrastructure and a reduction in the quality of educational services. Again, in an article in the *Papua New Guinea Post Courier* of January 26, 2007, the NDOE researcher, Patricia Paraide, has suggested: "Papua New Guinea's educational achievements since Independence, with or without donor support, are not usually discussed, possibly because they are viewed as minimal."[129]

PNG pulled back from near bankruptcy in the late 1990s and improved its financial management, and the boom in resources has increased national revenue. Yet it is axiomatic that the quality of schooling cannot stand apart from a society bedevilled by the widespread misappropriation of funds and an overwhelmed police force and justice system. In the early 2000s, public expenditure on education was estimated at only 2.3 percent of GDP, well below that of PNG's neighbors like Vanuatu, Tonga, and Samoa. Happily there has been an

Table 5.9
Millennium Development Goal Performance of Australia's Neighbors

	Goal 1	Goal 2	Goal 3	Goal 4	Goal 5	Goal 6	Goal 7	Goal 8	Unlikely to Achieve
	poverty reduction	poverty reduction	universal primary education	gender equality in education	reduced child mortality	reduced maternal mortality	reverse major diseases	access to water & sanitation	
PNG	x		x		x		x	x	8 Goals

☐ Off track ☒ High absolute levels, off track
Source: Millennium Development Goal–Performance of Australia's Neighbours, How Are the Neighbour? (Melbourne: World Vision 2001). www.worldvision.com.au.

increased budget allocation for education in 2007, and additional activity is evident in some places aimed at regenerating community support by cutting class sizes and reducing fees.

Much hard work still lies ahead. In mid-2006, an international aid agency report rated PNG education against the UN's Eight Millennium Development Goals: the assessment based on UNDP figures was a dispiriting one. (See Table 5.9.)

Certainly the national equity issues expressed by indigenous educators at the time of self-government and Independence are no longer to the fore. There is less interest and confidence in the pursuit of the common good as represented through institutions like schools and colleges, more now hold the view that social benefit accrues to those with access and power. Substantial improvement in PNG schooling will depend on the renewal of faith in the importance of good schools and on the will of agencies, including those outside the control of Education itself, to recognise the sector's social importance. Certainly times that change for the worse can change for the better under the influence of inherent Papua New Guinean values like openness, fair play, and national spirit. A substantial infrastructure of human resources and material development exists in Papua New Guinea: there are many good schools, fine teachers, and competent administrators and, among the population, a strong and genuine desire for more and better schools.

A DAY IN THE LIFE OF A UNIVERSITY STUDENT

Chris Jambahavi is a final-year male student studying to be a mathematics teacher at University of Goroka, Papua New Guinea (PNG).

Goroka is the headquarters of the Eastern Highlands province. It is a small town of 60,000 people. The climate is cool (18–24 degrees Celsius) all year-round. We think we have the best climate in the world—everlasting spring. Goroka is also the home of the famous Asaro mudmen.

I come from a family of ten, including my parents. My parents are not formally employed in the public sectors but they are subsistence farmers in the village. I'm now twenty-five years old and I hail from a village called Tangori in Wewak, East Sepik Province. My language group is Boiken and I speak the Duo dialect. I speak it fluently together with English and Pidgin.

I am enrolled in the four-year Bachelor of Education degree program majoring in mathematics and this is my final year. I decided to become a secondary school mathematics teacher because I love the job by admiring my past teachers. I specifically decided to become a mathematics teacher because I like dealing with numbers, abstract and concrete ideas, etc. Some of the courses I studied here at the University of Goroka are briefly stated below:

- Calculus
- Geometry

- Linear Algebra
- Ethno Mathematics
- Ordinary Differential Equations
- Inferential Statistics, etc.
- Methods of mathematics teaching
- Education courses

I'm also planning further studies to continue on to Honors or Masters in Education at overseas universities and, if possible, I would like to attend other Universities in PNG.

A special day was Thursday (November 15, 2006). As a day student (I live off campus), it is quite difficult for me during the semester to get to the university. Today, I had to wake up early in the morning to prepare myself before going to the university to attend classes. My class starts at 8:00 A.M., so I had to wake up at 6:30 A.M., and get myself prepared. Sometimes, if I wake up late, I don't make breakfast because it's quite a long distance to travel and also it's not easy to catch a bus with the other students and those going to work. I live in the western end of Goroka town and the university is located at the northern end of the town. I had to first of all, catch a bus into the center of town, and then change to a bus to the university.

Here is my daily schedule:

8:00 A.M.–10:00 A.M.: Mathematics class

My lecturer's teaching style is not perfect and it's quite hard for me to understand him in lectures and tutorials, making it very hard and tough. He likes giving plenty of notes and exercises. It takes me one or two days to read and understand the materials he meticulously prepares for the topics. The lecturer's teaching style is "chalk and talk" type and he does not vary his teaching style.

9:00 A.M.–9:10 A.M.: 10-minute break

Get myself relaxed. Check the notice boards for new notices for the day. Back to continue class 9:20 A.M.

10:00 A.M.–class ends

10:10 A.M.–12:00 noon

In the Computer Laboratory typing my major research project titled "Teacher Perceptions about Mathematics Teaching at Upper Primary Schools." There were fifty-four computers installed last year and now only forty-six of them are working. Therefore, in order to have access to the limited computers, I had to be one of the first people in the queue to enter the laboratory. Every student is allowed to use the computers for just two hours and when the two hours is over the next group of students enters the lab and so on until 10: 00 P.M. I am quite happy with my computer skills. Although it is a luxury, I have a flash drive which comes in handy for saving work. Not many students here can afford flash drives. Most save their work on the students folders provided through the net. The use of computers is a new phenomenon here at the university as computer usage by students has been introduced only in the last few years.

The major project is a challenge. I had to write up a research proposal in the first semester. In the second semester, I went to collect the data at four schools, I analyzed the data, and I am now in the process of writing the report. I had given my draft to my lecturer to comment on. It has not been easy but I am happy that I have a feel for the research.

12:00 noon–1:00 P.M.

Buy scones in the canteen at the University of Goroka and have it together with cold water. Sometimes, I have biscuits or go without lunch. With luck, other boarding students will share their lunch with me.

1:00 P.M.–3:00 P.M.

In the Library doing research on the Discussion part of my major project report. We have a big double-story library here at the University of Goroka but it's empty; there aren't enough books and resources available. There are no computers, internet access, or CD-ROMs available in the library so I can access the latest information on relevant topics. The library does have a computerized catalogue system. What I normally do is type in the keywords that I am looking for in the computer and search to see whether there are any books or journals on the topic I am interested in. Sometimes, it's very disappointing to see the books and resources we have here are so outdated.

3:30 P.M.–4:30 P.M.

Had some fun with friends playing soccer in a small oval at the university. The university doesn't have a proper sports field. I like playing sports and I do get myself involved in many sports. It's very sad for me to say that the university sporting facilities are very poor. I feel that the University is not supporting the students in sporting activities in terms of making funds available for sports, etc. There are no volleyball and basketball courts that the students can participate in playing volleyball, basketball, and other sports.

5:00 P.M.

Caught the bus to go home. It takes about twenty to thirty minutes for the bus ride home or one hour walking. It costs me Kina 10 per week for bus fare alone, which is very difficult for me as a student. If I don't have any bus fare, I have to walk home or sometimes to minimize costs, I have to walk if the weather is fine. It's cool climate here in the Highlands of PNG, so we do experience rain anytime of the day.

6:00 P.M.–7:00 P.M.

Had evening meal combination of rice, kaukau, sweet potato, greens, and tinned fish. In the Highlands, kaukau, sweet potato, cabbage, broccoli, and carrot are the typical foods that we enjoy.

TIMELINE

60,000+   Arrival of first wave of inhabitants in New Guinea from the north bringing their educational practices. PNG males commonly experience three learning stages in childhood and adolescence; females: two learning stages.

700+	Trading with other societies outside New Guinea, probably including India and the East.
1526–1527	Jorge de Menes, Portuguese explorer, names southern PNG, *Ilhas dos Papuas* (land of frizzy hair people).
1545	Spanish explorer, Ynigo Ortz de Retes, names northern PNG, Neuva Guinea, after the coastline of Guinea in Africa.
1828	Dutch annex the western half of New Guinea.
1847–1852	French and Italian missionaries occupy missions for short periods in east New Guinea.
1871–1908	London Missionary Society arrives in Torres Strait, and William Lawes opens first school in PNG at Port Moresby in 1874. Major Protestant and Catholic European-based missions and the Seventh Day Adventists establish themselves.
1884	Britain and Germany proclaim protectorates over the south, British New Guinea (Papua), and the north, German New Guinea (Kaiser Wilhelms-land and Islands).
1885	Government provides "presents" for the Pacific Islander teachers of the LMS.
1888+	Innovative elementary teaching methods and the Gouin method of teaching English attempted.
1897	Ordinance III in British New Guinea authorizes compulsory attendance at mission schools.
1906	Britain formally passes control of British New Guinea to Australia under *The Papua Act*.
1907	The German government opens the School for Natives at Namanula, East New Britain, which includes trade training.
1909	The School for Europeans opens in Rabaul under German auspices.
1914	World War I: German New Guinea surrenders to Australia which governs the Territory of New Guinea under a League of Nations Mandate from 1921. German government schools are closed.
1918	Territory of Papua New Guinea: Native Taxes Ordinance raises taxes for Native Education Fund and provides subsidies for mission schools and their technical training divisions, subject to inspection.
1919	Examination Standards for 1 and 2 primary schools gazetted.
1922	Territory of New Guinea: Education Ordinance authorizes government to establish a school system. A Technical School opens at Rabaul and an Elementary School at Kokopo.
1928	Publication of *Papua School Reader* followed by *Junior Papua School Reader* in 1932.
1930	Opening up the Highlands of New Guinea–one million people.
1936	*Native Education and Culture-Contact in New Guinea A Scientific Approach*, written by William Groves, head teacher at the Elementary School, Kokopo, which develops the "blending of cultures" theory in the context of schooling.
1942	Japanese invade PNG and surrender in 1945.
1944	Sogeri Central Training School established.
1946	The Mandated Territory of New Guinea passes to UN Trusteeship Council as a Trust Territory. Australia governs Papua and New Guinea under a single administration from 1949.

1946	Groves appointed director of Education; Department of Education established.
1952	Educational Ordinance of 1952 establishes Education Advisory Board, including representatives of missions, to tighten educational standards.
1958	Department of Education in Port Moresby drafts plan for universal primary education within fifteen years. New curricula prepared by Geoff Roscoe.
1962	United Nations Visiting Mission on the Trust Territories led by Sir Hugh Foot criticizes lack of secondary education under Australian policy.
1963–1064	Government teachers colleges founded at Madang and Port Moresby.
1964	World Bank Report recommends 21,000 secondary school places. Currie Commission supports the establishment of university and higher technical institutions.
1966–1967	The University of Papua New Guinea founded at Port Moresby, followed by the Institute of Higher Technical Education, and later the University of Technology, at Lae.
1969	Weedon Committee recommends a unified system of government and mission schools with community representation and a Teaching Service Commission. Proposal is instituted by Ken McKinnon, director of Education, in 1970.
1971	Department of Education invites senior Papua New Guineans to discuss the aims and objectives of primary education, the meeting recommends schooling be more relevant to the needs of PNG society, including the cultural heritage.
1973	Self-government allows control of Education by Papua New Guinean leaders. Five-year planning for education sector under way for 1976–1980.
1975	Independence under Michael Somare as prime minister, Oscar Tammur as minister, and Alkan Tololo as director of Education, brings vigorous discussion of educational priorities especially related to dropout problems, community education, and self-reliance.
1977	Transfer of authority over the basic school system to the newly formed provincial governments, subject to controls laid down by the national government.
1983	Establishment of an Office of Higher Education independent of the Department of Education.
1986	The Mantane Report emphasizes the importance of community education and the use of the vernacular.
1990	Government accepts the UNESCO Declaration of Education for All, the Jomtien statement, and introduces a major Education Sector Study in 1991, which identifies areas for reform engaging international agencies, aid donors, and national and provincial task force operations.
1996	The National Education Plan is completed in 1996 is adopted early in 1998. It introduces three-year elementary school teaching in the vernacular, followed by a six-year primary school as the basic structure, with further opportunities to enter secondary, technical, and tertiary institutions, including teachers colleges and universities. Postschool education is supported by open learning and adult literacy programs.

2001   National Higher Education Plan II aims to increase access, quality, and range of services, including the application of science and technology.

2004   Enhanced Cooperation Program with Australia allows direct on-ground assistance in PNG governance in addition to Education Sector funding.

2006   Aid agency report notes PNG's slow progress towards the UN Eight Millennium Development Goals.

NOTES

John Cleverley thanks Chris Jambahavi, a graduating secondary mathematics teacher from the University of Goroka for his contribution to this chapter; Dr. Wilfred T. Kaleva, Head of Department of Mathematics and Computing, University of Goroka, for providing access to school curriculum and other materials, and advice. He also thanks Hilda Wayne, Assistant Communication Officer, UNICEF PNG, for supplying material on UNICEF's projects and photographs.

1. Statistical data draws on colonial administration reports, periodic PNG government publications including National Department of Education, and National Statistical Office of Papua New Guinea, and compilations by international agencies. See, e.g., ADB, UNDP, UNICEF, UNESCO, and author estimates.

2. Hilda Wayne, e-mail message to author, January 2, 2007.

3. Compilations are based on anthropological accounts of village life in PNG.

4. ABC Programmes for Schools, *"And I love her" Papua New Guinea* (Sydney: Australian Broadcasting Commission, 1975), 35.

5. Gilbert H. Herdt, *Guardians of the Flutes Idioms of Masculinity* (New York: McGraw-Hill Book Company, 1981), 160.

6. Margaret Mead, *Growing Up in New Guinea a Survey of Adolescence and Sex in Primitive Societies* (London: Penguin Books, 1963), 157.

7. ABC Programmes, *"And I Love Her,"* 36–37.

8. Herdt, *Guardians of the Flutes*, chap. 7, 203–54.

9. G.T. Roscoe, "The Problems of the Curriculum in Papua and New Guinea," *South Pacific* 10, no. 1 (1958): 15.

10. Paulias Mantane [1974], quoted in John Waiko, *A Short History of Papua New Guinea* (Melbourne: Oxford University Press, 1993), 130.

11. For histories of PNG, and documentary readings see, e.g., Brian Jinks, Peter Biskup, and Hank Nelson, *Readings in New Guinea History* (Sydney: Angus & Robertson, 1973); and John Waiko, *A Short History of Papua New Guinea* (Melbourne, Oxford University Press, 1993), for an Indigenous perspective, and historical accounts from early missioners.

12. Compilations from letters and publications of pioneer missionaries and administrators.

13. Chalmers [1877], quoted in Diane Langmore, *Tamate–A King: James Chalmers in New Guinea 1877–1901* (Melbourne: Melbourne University Press, 1974), 4.

14. Great Britain and Ireland. British New Guinea (BNG). *Special Commissioner for the Protected Territory. Report for 1886* (London: HMSO, 1887), 23.

15. R. B. Joyce, *Sir William MacGregor* (Melbourne: Oxford University Press, 1971), 180.

16. Papua. Administrator. *Annual Report on British New Guinea 1896–7* (Brisbane: Government Printer), 12.

17. William MacGregor, *British New Guinea: Country and People* (London: J. Murray, 1897), 92.

18. Karl Tremel [1889], quoted in Herwig Wagner and Hermann Reiner, eds., *The Lutheran Church in Papua New Guinea The First Hundred Years 1886–1986* (Adelaide: Lutheran Publishing House, 1986), 38.

19. Charles E. Abel, *Savage Life in New Guinea* (London: London Missionary Society, 1901), 192.

20. Macgregor, *British New Guinea*, 32.

21. Arthur Kent Chignell, *An Outpost in Papua* (London: Smith Elder, 1915), 104.

22. Louis-André Navarre to the Special Commissioner August 5, 1887, BNG, *Annual Report*. 1887, 25.

23. Chignell, *An Outpost in Papua*, 110.

24. Wagner and Reiner, *The Lutheran Church in Papua New Guinea*, 50

25. James Colwell, *The Illustrated History of Methodism* (Sydney: W. Brooks, 1904), 465.

26. Langmore, *Tamate*, 129

27. Papua. *Annual Report* BNG 1897–8, 54.

28. Louis-André Navarre, trans. Sr. Sheila Larkin, *Handbook for Missionaries of the Sacred Heart Working Among the Natives of New Guinea for the second impression 1886* (Kensington: Chevalier Press, Kensington, Sydney, 1987), 55.

29. The Australasian Wesleyan Methodist Missionary Society, extracts, C66, October 1883, 376. http://www.papuaweb.org/dib/bk2/documents-ng (accessed February 25, 2007).

30. F. Lenwood [1915], quoted in Langmore, *Missionary Lives*, 154.

31. Papua. *Annual Report* BNG 1895–6, 35.

32. F. Walker [1888], quoted in Langmore, *Missionary Lives*, 154.

33. Langmore, *Missionary Lives*, 154.

34. Papua. *Annual Report* BNG 1905–6, 19–20.

35. Imperial Government. *German New Guinea (GNG) Annual Report for 1900–1.* In Peter Stack and Dymphna Clark, trans. and eds. *German New Guinea: The Annual Reports* (Canberra: Australian National University Press, 1978), 214.

36. Imperial Government. *GNG Annual Report 1902–03*, 238.

37. Imperial Government. Draft GNG Annual Report for 1913–14. In Peter Sack and Dymphna Clark, trans. and eds. *German New Guinea, the Draft Annual Report for 1913–14* (Canberra: Australian National University, 1980), 128.

38. Peter Smith, *Education and Colonial Control in Papua New Guinea a Documentary History* (Melbourne: Longman Cheshire, 1987), 32.

39. See Imperial Government. *GNG Annual Report 1907–08*, 281; and 1909–10, 298.

40. Imperial Government. GNG, Draft Annual Report 1913–14, 146–52.

41. Imperial Government. *GNG Annual Report 1909–10*, 312.

42. Imperial Government. *GNG Annual Report 1912–13*, 361.

43. Imperial Government. GNG, Draft Annual Report 1913–14, 147.

44. Imperial Government. *GNG Annual Report 1912–13*, 361.

45. Government Gazette British Adminitration 1915. In B. Jinks et al., *Readings New Guinea History*, 216–17.

46. Interim and Final Reports 1920. In B. Jinks et al., *Readings New Guinea History*, 226.

47. Hubert Murray, *Papua of Today or an Australian colony in the making* (Westminister: P.S. King, 1925), 267–68.

48. J. H. P. Murray [1920], in B. Jinks et al., *Readings New Guinea History*, 120.

49. Government Gazette, 1919. In Smith, *Education and Colonial Control in Papua New Guinea*, 58–59.

50. Australia. Prime Minister's Department. *Report on the Council of the League of Nations on the Administration of the Territory of New Guinea. Annual Report 1935–6* (Canberra: Government Printer, 1937), 12.

51. *The Papuan Villager* 5, no. 4 (1933), 27.

52. H. W. Champion, Native Education, appendage, Hubert Murray, *Native Administration in Papua* (Port Moresby: Government Printer, 1929), 49.

53. See Native Education, *Papuan School Reader*, Territory of Papua (Port Moresby: Government Printer, 1928).

54. *The Papuan School Reader*, 158–59.

55. Native Education, *Papuan Junior School Reader No. 3*, Territory of Papua (Port Moresby: Government Printer, 1932).

56. *The Papuan Villager* 1, no. 1 (1929), 1.

57. Lekei Tom, *The Papuan Villager* 4, no. 3 (1932), 32.

58. *The Papuan Villager* 4, no. 9 (1932): 1, 2.

59. *The Papuan Villager* 2, no. 6 (1930): 1.

60. Australia. Governor-General. *Report to the Council of the League of Nations on the Administration of the Territory of New Guinea 1921–22*, 88.

61. William Colin Groves, *Native Education and Culture-Contact in New Guinea: A Scientific Approach* (Melbourne: Melbourne University Press, 1936), 71, 72.

62. Australia. *Report to League of Nations on New Guinea, 1922–23*, p. 26.

63. "Wontok" literally means people who speak the same clan tongue. Therefore, it designates clan or family association and membership.

64. Groves, *Native Education and Culture-Contact*, 73.

65. Groves, *Native Education and Culture-Contact*, 82, 83.

66. See Champion. In Murray, *Native Administration in Papua*, 46–51.

67. William Edward Bromilow, *Twenty Years among the Primitive Papuans* (London: Epworth Press, 1929), 305–10.

68. Australia. *Report to League of Nations on New Guinea 1922–23*, 89.

69. Groves, *Native Education and Culture-Contact*, 163.

70. Rabaul Times (January 25, 1919). In Loch Blatchford, John Cleverley, and Richard Pearse, Report on the Australian Influence on the Development of a National System of Education in Papua New Guinea 1946–1983, chap. I (Canberra: *Report for the Educational Research and Development Committee, 1987*), 33–34.

71. S. W. Reed [1943], quoted in B. Jinks et al., *Readings New Guinea History*, 285.

72. Commonwealth of Australia. *Territory of Papua. Annual Report 1933–34* (Canberra: Government Printer, 1935), 14.

73. Commonwealth of Australia. *Papua. Annual Report 1937–38*, 21.

74. Mlle Dannevig [1939], quoted in Smith, *Education and Colonial Control*, 131.

75. Australia. *Report to the League of Nations on New Guinea 1939–40* (Canberra: Government Printer, 1941), 41–43.

76. Michael Somare, *Sana* (Port Moresby: Nuigini Press, 1975), 2–6.

77. Camilla Wedgwood [c. 1944], quoted in L. Blachford et al., *Australian Influence 1946–1983*, chaps. 1, 5.

78. Australia. Department of Territories. *Annual Report of the Territory of Papua for the period 1947–8* (Canberra: Government Printer, 1949), 25–27.

79. Roscoe, "Problems of the Curriculum," 9, 16.

80. Roscoe [1980], in Loch Blachford et al., *Australian Influence 1946–1983*, chap. III, p. 37.

81. Department of External Territories internal discussion paper (1960). In Lyndon Megarrity, "Indigenous Education in Colonial Papua New Guinea: Australian Government Policy 1945–1975," *History of Education Review* 34, no. 2, p. 50.

82. John T. Gunther, The People, in chap. II, J. Wilkes, ed., *Australian Institute of Political Science, New Guinea and Australia* (Sydney: Angus and Robertson, 1958), 58.

83. Ken Mackinnon, Curriculum Development in Primary Education: The Papuan New Guinea Experience, in E. Barrington Thomas, ed., *Papua New Guinea Education* (Melbourne: Oxford University Press, 1976), 49–56.

84. Camilla Wedgwood [1944], in Smith, *Education and Colonial Control in Papua New Guinea*, 150.

85. Commonwealth of Australia, Department of External Territories. *Territory of Papua. Annual Report 1947–48*, p. 84.

86. John Lee [1967], in Smith, *Education and Colonial Control in Papua New Guinea*, 228.

87. United Nations Visiting Mission to the Trust Territories in the Pacific [1956], in Blatchford et al., chap. III, p. 6.

88. Roscoe, "Problems of the Curriculum," 8, 14.

89. Smith, *Education and Colonial Control in Papua New Guinea*, 205.

90. Office of Information. Education, *Papua New Guinea Facts and Figures*, 4 (Port Moresby: Konedobu, 1976), 7, 8.

91. Ian J. Howie-Willis [1980], in Blatchford et al., *Australian Influence 1946–83*, chap. III, p. 37.

92. Donald Denoon, *A Trial Separation: Australia and the Decolonization of Papua New Guinea*, 2005 (Canberra: Pandanus Books), 27.

93. Nelson Giraure, The Need for a Cultural Programme: Personal Reflections, in Barrington Thomas, *Papua New Guinea Education*, 62, 63.

94. Issac Ranpi [2003], quoted in Susan Baing, *Social Science Outcomes Teacher's Book Grade 7* (Melbourne: Pearson Longman, 2005), 221.

95. Education, *Papua New Guinea Facts and Figures*, 4.

96. See John Cleverley, "Trends in Education in Papua New Guinea," *Current Affairs Bulletin* 52, no. 3: 16–25.

97. Oscar Tammur [1978], quoted in Blachford et al., *Australian Influence 1946–1983*, chap. X, p. 20.

98. Robert Litteral, Four Decades of Language Policy in Papua New Guinea: the Move towards the Vernacular, Radical Pedagogy (2000), ICAAP, 3. http://radicalpedagogy.icaap.org/content/issue/1.litteral (accessed January 18, 2006).

99. Interim Report, Ministerial Services Unit [1978], in Blatchford et al., *Australian Influence 1946–1983*, chap. VIII, p. 31.

100. Cleverley, "Trends in Education in Papua New Guinea," 16–25.

101. Roger S. Hunter [1983], in Blatchford et al., *Australian Influence 1946–1983*, chap. VIII, p. 21.

102. A Statistical Review of the Education Sector 1982, in Blatchford et al., *Australian Influence 1946–1983*, chap. VIII, p. 10.

103. Department of Education. Education. *Annual Report 1982* (Port Moresby: Government Printer, 1984), 10–12.

104. Sean Dorney, *Papua New Guinea People Politics and History Since 1975* (Sydney: ABC Books, 2000), 288.

105. For statistics, see: Aid achievements in Papua New Guinea, AusAid, 2006. http://www.ausaid.gov.au/country/png (accessed December 12, 2006). Edstats, Summary Education Profile: Papua New Guinea, 2006. http://devdata.worldbank.org/edstats (accessed 27/10/2006). Efa regional overview: Pacific Region, UNESCO, 2006, 2, 9–11. http://www.efareport.unesco.org (accessed January 20, 2007). ADB Performance Evaluation Report: Higher Education Project, (Asian Development Bank, 2006). http://www.adb.org/Documents/PPERs?PNG. National Statistical Office of Papua New Guinea, http://www.nso.gov.pg/Pop_Soc%20Stats (accessed March 6, 2007).

106. Eileen Honan, "Schooled Literacies? The use of vernacular literacy practices in Papua New Guinea communities," *Prospect* 18: 3, 36–50.

107. "Thirty attend teacher in-service," Bougainville Update, Papua New Guinea Post Courier On-line (PCOL), http://www.postcourier.com.pg, June 28, 2006 (accessed July 2, 2006).

108. ADB Performance Evaluation Report: Higher Education Project (Asian Development Bank, 2006), app. 4, p. 32.

109. "Deputy PM banishes idea of free education in PNG," Viewpoint, PCOL, March 20, 2007. (accessed March 24, 2007).

110. "Community pays." Rural education, PCOL, July 28–30, 2006 (accessed August 5, 2006).

111. "Mudman in mud bath for literacy," PCOL, September 13, 2006 (accessed September 14, 2006).

112. "An opportunity to learn," Focus, PCOL, August 20, 2006 (accessed September 5, 2006).

113. "Living off the bags," Focus, PCOL, February 1, 2007 (accessed February 2, 2007).

114. "All eyes on me ...," Culture show, Gordons Secondary School Cultural Day, PCOL, September 29, 2006–October 1, 2006 (accessed October 3, 2006).

115. "Cult irks villagers," Viewpoint, Mamose Post, PCOL May 25, 2006 (accessed June 1, 2006).

116. "Relief supplies arrive in Pangia as schools shut down," News, PCOL, October 24, 2006 (accessed October 24, 2006).

117. See resource details, Coris, Transparency International, http://admin.corisweb.org/index.php (accessed December 15, 2006).

118. "Children learn to use guns," News, PCOL, November 23, 2006 (accessed November 29, 2006).

119. "Clansmen threaten to destroy school," PCOL, February 26, 2007 (accessed March 6, 2007).

120. Impacts of HIV/AIDS 2005–2025 in Papua New Guinea, Indonesia and East Timor, AusAid Public Affairs Group, Canberra, February 2006. http://www.ausaid.gov.au/publications/pdf/hivaids (accessed March 3, 2007).

121. Miranda Darling Tobias, The HIV/AIDS Crisis in Papua New Guinea, Issue analysis no. 81, The Centre for Independent Studies, February 8, 2007, 1, 9, http://www.cis.org.au (assessed February 15, 2007).

122. See response, "The HIV/AIDS Crisis in Papua New Guinea," *Child News Health*, February 14, 2007, http://www.news-medical.net (accessed March 3, 2007).

123. Tobias, HIV/AIDS Crisis, 9.

124. Thomas Webster, "Accelerating Girls' Education in PNG," *PCOL*, August 11, 2006–August 13, 2006 (accessed August 22, 2006).

125. "Give Teenage Mums a Second Chance," Viewpoint, *PCOL*, June 30, 2006–July 1, 2006 (accessed July 2, 2006).

126. "Gender Equality Vital," Focus, *PCOL*, September 15, 2006–September 18, 2006 (accessed September 20, 2006).

127. Fr. Brian Bainbridge (2006). In Hilda Wayne, "Young Life, Expressions that Hold Hope," *PCOL*, July 20, 2006–July 22, 2006 (accessed July 27, 2006).

128. Allan Patience, "The Other Disaster on our Doorstop," *Sydney Morning Herald*, June 1, 2006, 17.

129. Patricia Paraide, "Education's Practical Strategy," *PCOL*, January 26, 2007 (accessed January 26, 2007).

130. Chris Jambahavi, A Day in the Life of Chris Jambahavi, attachment, e-mail message to author, November 27, 2006.

BIBLIOGRAPHY

Books

Abel, Charles E. 1902. *Savage Life in New Guinea*. London: London Mission Society.

Barrington Thomas, E., ed. 1976. *Papua New Guinea Education*. Melbourne: Oxford University Press.

Brammall, J., and Ronald J. May, eds. 1975. *Education in Melanesia*. Canberra: Australian National University and Council on New Guinea Affairs.

Brown, Paula. 1995. *Beyond a Mountain: The Simbu of Papua New Guinea*. Honolulu: University of Hawai'i Press.

Brown, Paula, and Georgeda Buchbinder, eds. 1976. *Man and Woman in the New Guinea Highlands*, American Anthropological Association no. 8. Washington: American Anthropological Association.

Chignell, Arthur Kent. 1915. *An Outpost in Papua*. London: Smith Elder.

Cleverley, John F., and Christabel Wescombe. 1979. *Papua New Guinea Guide to Sources in Education*. Sydney: Sydney University Press.

Firth, Stewart. 1982. *New Guinea under the Germans*. Melbourne: Melbourne University Press.

Groves, William Colin. 1936. *Native Education and Culture-Contact in New Guinea A Scientific Approach*. Melbourne: Melbourne University Press.

Herdt, Gilbert H. 1981. *Guardians of the Flutes Idioms of Masculinity*. New York: McGraw-Hill Book Company.

Kavanamur, David, and Charles Yala, and Quinton Clements, eds. 2003. *Building a Nation in Papua New Guinea Views of the Post-Independence Generation*. Canberra: Pandanus Books.

Langmore, Diane. 1989. *Missionary Lives Papua 187 –1914*, Pacific Island Monograph Series, no. 6. Honolulu: University of Hawaii Press.

Mead, Margaret. 1963. *Growing Up in New Guinea a Survey of Adolescence and Sex in Primitive Societies.* London: Penguin Books.

Sack, Peter, and Dymphna Clark, eds. and trans. 1978. *German New Guinea: The Annual Reports.* Canberra, Australian National University.

Sack, Peter, and Dymphna Clark, eds. and trans. 1980. *German New Guinea: the Draft Annual Report for 1913.* Canberra: Australian National University.

Smith, Peter. 1987. *Education and Colonial Control in Papua New Guinea A Documentary History.* Melbourne: Longman Cheshire.

Wagner, Herwig, and Hermann Reiner, eds. 1986. *The Lutheran Church in Papua New Guinea The First Hundred Years 1886–1986.* Adelaide: Lutheran Publishing House.

Waiko, John D. 1993. *A Short History of Papua New Guinea.* Melbourne: Oxford University Press.

Reports

Annual Report on British New Guinea, 1886–1906, Special Commissioner for the Protected Territory. Brisbane: Government Printer.

Australia. Prime Minister's Department. Report on the Council of the League of Nations on the Administration of the Territory of New Guinea. Annual Reports (Canberra: Government Printer).

Commonwealth of Australia. Territory of Papua. Annual Reports (Canberra: Government Printer).

Papua. Annual Report for the Territory of Papua (Brisbane: Government Printer).

Unpublished

Blatchford, Loch, John Cleverley, and Richard Pearse. Report on the Australian Influence on the Development of a National System of Education in Papua New Guinea 1946–1983 (Canberra: Report for the Educational Research and Development Committee, 1987).

On-Line

ADB Performance Evaluation Report: Higher Education Project (Asian Development Bank, 2006). http://www.adb.org/Documents/PPERs?PNG.

Edstats, Summary Education Profile: Papua New Guinea, 2006. http://devdata.worldbank.org/edstats.

Efa regional overview: Pacific Region, UNESCO, 2006, 2, 9–11. http://www.efareport.unesco.org.

National Statistical Office of Papua New Guinea. http://www.nso.gov.pg/Pop_Soc_20Stats.

Papua New Guinea Post Courier On-Line. (Port Moresby National Capital District). www.Postcourier.com.pg/.

Chapter 6

SCHOOLING IN SAMOA

Eve Coxon

The small, "developing" state of Samoa consists of just under three thousand square kilometers of land in the South West Pacific and comprises two large volcanic islands and seven small atolls, two of which are populated.[1] Samoa's population today numbers approximately 180,000, virtually all Polynesian with a common language, culture, and Christian religious affiliation. Forty-eight percent of the population is female and around 40 percent are under the age of twenty years. The majority of Samoans live a semisubsistence lifestyle in the 330 small *nu'u* (villages) positioned around the coastlines of the two main islands; over three-quarters of the population live on the island of Upolu with about 25 percent of the total population living in or near the capital of Apia. Two-thirds of the villages have fewer than five hundred people living in them. Each village has a high degree of autonomy under a village *fono* (council) made up of elected *matai* (chiefs) who head the *'aiga* (extended families), which own the village and associated lands. Regarding social, political, and economic practices within the village, the control of land and distribution of resources, election to titles and offices, ceremonial occasions, and related functions are all structured by the *faaSamoa* (Samoan way of life). Over 80 percent of Samoa's land is still held by customary title under *mata'i* authority, and agricultural production absorbs about 60 percent of the paid and unpaid workforce. Almost 40,000 people live in the capital of Apia, or in nearby villages. Apia developed as a trade center in the mid-nineteenth century, prospered as a port town, and became the seat of government. Today, Apia is largely a service center, containing government offices, educational and health facilities, retail stores, a large produce market, hotels, and restaurants, with some small industry and manufacturing concerns found mainly on the outskirts of the city.[2]

Although identified by the United Nations as one of the world's "least developed countries," Samoans are relatively well educated, with only 13.5

percent of the population having had fewer than eight years of schooling. Although a good performer in terms of the global push for universal primary education (UPE), as propounded through Education For All targets and the Millenium Development Goals, only 10 percent have any tertiary education. "As with almost all aspects of life in Samoa, education is strongly influenced by Samoan culture."[3]

The development of formal schooling in Samoa has followed a sequence common in the "developing" world. The historical processes of missionization, colonialism, postcolonialism, and the educational aims associated with each, followed similar general patterns and had similar causes and effects in Samoa as elsewhere. However, this chapter takes the view that the actual working out of these processes, and their educational consequences, depended very much on sociocultural structures specific to the context in which they occurred. It also contends that it should not be assumed the Samoan people and their institutions were overwhelmed by these introduced processes—resistance, negotiation, accommodation, and manipulation meant that subsequent social, political, and economic changes were not just imposed.[4] This has held true in the past ten to fifteen years also, with the need for small developing states such as Samoa to deal with the agenda of the international development agencies, which fund much of the education development that takes place in their countries. The creativity with which Samoan people have exercised, and continue to exercise, their collective agency in articulating cultural continuity within change, and particularly their mediation of the global process of schooling demonstrates well the interaction of local "tradition" and global "modernization."

BEFORE THE NINETEENTH CENTURY

The indigenous settlement of Oceania and how the diverse societies concerned survived and flourished has been the subject of endless speculation by western academics and others since Europeans first arrived in the Pacific. Of course, Pacific people themselves have their own explanations of how they came to be where they are. These are recorded through their oral traditions and, when combined with recent scientific information, have enabled "prehistorians" to reconstruct—at least in outline form—the story of the original human expansion across, and settlement of, the Pacific. We know from this that both Samoa and Tonga were settled approximately 3,000 to 3,200 years ago from Fiji and that they were the first islands in Polynesia to be settled. The evidence also identifies Samoa as providing the basis of the distinctive Polynesian culture and the source of most of the later settlements throughout Polynesia. It was the "cradle of Polynesia." Throughout the many centuries between the first human migrations to Samoa and the arrival of Europeans, it is clear that Samoans also maintained frequent contacts with other Pacific societies, especially Tonga and Fiji, for the purposes of trade and intermarriage, particularly at the chiefly level.[5]

Samoa was first noticed by the European world in 1721 when it was sighted by the Dutch explorer Roggeveen. The next European explorer to come across Samoa was the Frenchman, Bougainville, who named the Samoan archipelago "The Navigator Islands" after encountering Samoans in small canoes far from land in 1768. The next two Samoan/European encounters, by the Frenchman La Perouse in 1787 and the British ship *Pandora* in 1791, ended in violence with a number of French deaths in the former case and Samoan deaths in the latter. Despite the resulting negative reputation attributed to Samoa by whalers and traders, by the end of the eighteenth century, regular visits by ships continued to occur.

At the time of European contact, Samoa had a decentralized system of political authority in which the basic political unit was the *nu'u*, a collectively owned and politically autonomous territory controlled by a number of descent groups termed *'aiga*, each being associated with a particular *matai* title. *Matai* titles were of two kinds: the *ali'i*, who was able to trace the sacred origins of the title genealogically and its links to major aristocratic lineages; and the *tulafale*, whose role was to render service to and oratory on behalf of the *ali'i* title with which it was associated. *Matai* were elected by all adult family members and all, both men and women, who served the title under contention, were eligible for selection. While oral traditions tell of women who held very high-ranking titles and were very powerful chiefs, men were more likely to become *matai*. Title holders were the trustees of *'aiga* lands and other property, and together the *matai* formed a *fono* or council that governed the *nu'u*, making all decisions pertaining to communal matters such as the clearing of forests, hunting, fishing, house building, and preparation for war. Decisions were reached through a "process of debate, negotiation and compromise … in the achievement of consensus."[6]

As well as its cultural and political functions, the *matai* system provided a crucial economic base, the foundation of which was *'aiga* land ownership and tenure, subsistence agriculture, and the availability of basic resources to all. The main crops cultivated were taro, breadfruit, yams, plantains, and sweet potato; seafood provided an important part of the diet, and pigs and chickens were also raised and eaten. Although chiefs had control over the distribution of resources, there was no significant difference in the standard of consumption between the highest chief and others.[7] The history of these times as recorded through oral traditions suggest there were periods of endemic warfare between rival factions led by chiefs who sought to establish claims to paramount titles and lands. Despite this, the documented reports of these first European contacts indicate that the estimated population of 40,000–50,000 Samoan people "had achieved a very abundant comfortable way of life in which everyone was well fed and well housed."[8]

Teaching and learning in pre-European contact Samoa was life-long and part of everyday family and community life. It was concerned largely with passing on the collective knowledge and values, the cultural traditions, of the society in order to ensure its survival. In other words, education's primary objective was continuity. Young people were taught to understand the structure of society, the various social roles attributed to their elders, and their own place within the structure of extended family, village, and wider society. Learning was through listening, memorizing, observing, and doing. Through these processes, learners acquired the knowledge and expertise of the teacher, who was always an elder. Learners were given access to the knowledge deemed appropriate to their age, gender, and status.[9]

The person charged with teaching was accepted by the learner as possessing superior knowledge and unable to be questioned about what was being taught. The core *faaSamoa* concepts of respect (*fa'aaloalo*) and service *(tautua)* were central to the teacher–learner relationship, and a key task of education was to develop knowledge and understanding of the complex forms of social behavior and language necessary to maintain relationships between the different strata of the hierarchy.

The common source of the initial migrations throughout the Polynesian triangle and the subsequent contacts between certain groups within Polynesia means that Polynesian cultures draw on a shared belief system, have similar language structures, and share many aspects of material culture such as weaving, tattoo, tapa making, and woodcarving. The forms of education characteristic of pre-European contact also reflected these shared understandings and practices, as described below:

> The primary locus of learning was the extended family. Within the extended family one learned who one was within that particular hierarchical structure. In other words, one discovered one's position within the family, and the role that resulted from that position. One then learned the skill requirements of that role and most importantly one learned the values of respect and obedience towards those superior to oneself. As one grew, one then learned the role one's extended family had in the overall society and the knowledge base and skills associated with that role. So the site of education also perpetuated the existing social structure as one could not learn the skills or acquire the knowledge that were not available to one's extended family.[10]

All young people learned appropriate knowledge about their cultural traditions and the basics of gender-specific practical skills: for males, fishing, hunting, planting, carpentry, and food preparation; for females, weaving, tapa making, and oil making. More specialized technological knowledge about such things as healing, canoe building, navigation, carving, tool and weapon making, however, was usually the domain of adult groups who performed their tasks under the direction of a *tufuga* (expert).[11] On reaching puberty young boys joined the *aumaga*, the "village of men," the village planters and warriors who were responsible for growing and cooking the everyday food required by the village as well as for visiting groups from other villages. As potential contenders for *matai* titles, they also "learned the chiefly role while sitting in attendance at the village council meetings, waiting to carry out the decisions made by chiefs.

They learned village history, how decisions were made and the precedents for these, and, most important, how a chief should act."[12]

The *aualuma*, the village of women, was the group young girls joined on reaching puberty. This group had a key role in providing hospitality during the frequent *Malaga* (visitations) from other villages. These visits were an important means of building village and family alliances. Also, the *aualuma* was responsible for upholding the dignity of the host village's chiefs and demonstrating its prosperity through the hospitality provided.

The *aualuma* lived together in the large guest house of the village under the care and leadership of the *sao tamaitai* (leader of the women).... The young girls were instructed in how to prepare *ava* and weave *ie toga* (fine mats used in ceremonial exchanges).... Finally, the *aualuma* were instructed in songs and poetry, dancing and the etiquette necessary for entertaining visitors, such as how to decorate the house and prepare bedding in the appropriate way.[13]

Oral traditions indicate that the *aualuma* was both independent and had real power within village society and that, although girls' and women's access to knowledge was limited to certain domains, sisters and brothers had equal rights to the resources of the village. However, the organization of both the *aumaga* and *aualuma* reflected the ranking system of the village and were led by the sons and daughters of prominent chiefs, who were served by the children of lesser chiefs or those without titles. Only the daughters of high chiefs could make the *ie toga*, the sacred mats considered to represent a village and family's wealth and which were central to ceremonial presentations marking alliances with other villages and the neighboring islands of Fiji and Tonga. The production of these mats allowed for creativity in design and provided a means of recording family and village history.[14]

The hierarchical nature of chiefly society was central to the life-long education processes of precontact Samoan society and formed the basis of more specialized and elaborated knowledge structures and processes. What was defined as important knowledge, to whom it could be taught and how, were all matters determined by those perceived as holding sacred power derived from the gods. Because the hierarchical system was underpinned by genealogy, genealogical knowledge was highly valued and a source of power to those who held it, often chiefly women elders. An associated skill was oratory—practiced by both men and women—that required a deep knowledge of genealogy and tribal history. "Each prime chiefly clan had its orators whose main role was to establish the genealogy of the clan, its links to other chiefly clans, its entitlement to land and other resources and generally to affirm and maintain the high status of the clan."[15]

Other valued holders of knowledge were composers, choreographers, and poets. Genealogy provided much of their knowledge base also and allowed for elaboration of clan histories through song, dance, and poetry.

Unlike Eastern Polynesian societies, Samoans at the time of European contact had neither large places of worship, such as temples, nor an institutionalized priesthood. However, Samoan religion was complex and polytheistic with two main categories of gods, those of nonhuman origin, *atua*, and those of human origin, *aitu*. The powers of these gods were believed to influence human activities, and sacredness—through notions of *mana* and *tapu*—was integral to many aspects of everyday life. The medium for communication between the gods and the people was the *tailaitu*, one of a small group of men and women with the power, by virtue of inheritance or possession, of speaking to or on behalf of the gods. Because the power of chiefs was thought to derive from the ancestral gods, religion was an effective means of social control.[16]

The impact of the first exposures of Samoans to the west had a profound effect on existing knowledge bases, particularly as regards traditional religion. Meleisea reports: "According to a legend, the war goddess, Nafanua, prophesied that a new religion would come to Samoa and end the rule of the old gods."[17] He also comments that some of the first Europeans to spend time in Samoa—beachcombers, whalers, sailors—had begun teaching Samoans about Christianity (referred to as the sailors' *lotu*), and that a Samoan who had traveled to Australia and other Pacific Islands on a whaling ship had begun a Christian cult movement on his return. For the few decades prior to the arrival of Christian missionaries, an acceleration in both the amount and ferocity of warfare between major chiefly clans, arising from the introduction of guns and other weapons, had encouraged many Samoans to search for religious explanations which could reconcile the *faaSamoa* with recently introduced values and practices. Thus, many had already become familiar with and receptive to Christian teachings.

NINETEENTH CENTURY

Missionary Education

When John Williams of the London Missionary Society (LMS), arrived in Samoa in 1830 with the intention of converting the Samoan people to Christianity, he followed the established missionary strategy of seeking the sponsorship of a powerful chief. Under direction from a Samoan who had joined his ship in Tonga, he found his way to the village of a paramount chief, Malietoa Vainu'upo, who accepted the eight missionaries Williams had brought with him for spreading the "Word of God" around Samoa. By the time of his return two years later, Malietoa Vainu'upo had both extended his chiefly rule and become Christian; under his patronage, missionization proceeded rapidly throughout the 1830s. When he was dying in 1841, Malietoa Vainu'upo expressed his hopes for Samoa to continue living according to the notion of Christian peace. His hopes for peace were not fulfilled, however, as within a few years of his death, the first of the six major civil wars that were to occupy the remainder of the nineteenth century broke out. The ongoing struggles over lands and titles, and the wars that went with them, greatly enhanced the appeal of the Christian message and conversions accelerated accordingly.[18]

The LMS mission saw its role as not just a matter of introducing the "natives" to the "true" god, it also required that they be introduced to European "civilization" in order to become fully Christian. The most significant mechanism through which the missionaries aimed to transform Samoan society into a truly Christian community was formal schooling. Protestant Christianity required that rather than a priestly class interpreting the "Word of God" for believers, each individual Christian needed to be able to know it directly, and that required the ability to read the "Word of God" as revealed in the Bible. They wasted no time in translating the scriptures into Samoan and establishing the formal schooling perceived as necessary to achieve their objective of spreading the Christian message and creating a good Christian Samoan society. As argued by Baba:

> The missionaries were concerned with total societal change and both the church and the school played a part in that effort. The islanders were not only converted ... they were also introduced to new and more "civilized" ways of living, based on Christian principles. The school became an agent of change and it taught the package of skills necessary for living in what was conceived ... as constituting a Christian society.[19]

An orthography of the Samoan language was soon developed, and the Bible and other religious writings were translated into Samoan. Samoan people responded enthusiastically to the opportunity to gain the literacy skills of the *papalagi* (European). Because the ability to read and write was very much associated with the superior technological knowledge Europeans were perceived to possess, the desire for literacy can be seen as an expression of the desire for this knowledge. As the demand for learning outstripped the ability of the available missionaries to provide the necessary teaching, Samoans who had already attained some reading and writing skills were engaged as teachers, and despite their limited knowledge and lack of training did much to advance the objectives of the LMS mission.[20]

Village pastor schools were set up throughout the country (the Samoans having refused to follow the usual missionary-instigated procedure of leaving their villages and moving to central mission stations). Because Samoans would not move from their villages, *fono* decisions and *matai* opinion had to be taken seriously by the village pastors and their missionary supervisors, with the result that church structures took on "a distinctively Samoan character."[21] This was true also of the *A'oga a le Faifeau* (pastor school) that was to become the primary agency of formal education and training for subsequent generations of Samoan children.[22] Within six years of the establishment of the original few missionary-run schools, Samoan teachers had facilitated the development of almost two hundred schools located throughout all the inhabited islands. These first schools were described at the time as, "primitive in methods, subjects and teachers, and above all in buildings. They did not aim very high either in scholastic standards."[23]

The process of evangelizing through the development of literacy was further accelerated by the establishment of the Malua Seminary in 1844, seen by the LMS as a necessary means of raising the educational standards of Samoan teachers. Through the combination of general education with theological training, Malua trained a Samoan ministry to be both evangelists and teachers. The curriculum was designed to provide both the religious education necessary "to furnish the students with a sound knowledge of the Bible and Christian doctrines before sending them to the villages to preach and teach" and the secular subjects "essential to the purpose of offering an advanced education." The former objective was met through the study of "church history, biblical or systematic theology and scripture exposition"; the latter through reading, written composition, arithmetic, geography, astronomy, natural history, and philosophy. "The idea was to produce well-educated Samoan pastors and teachers through a course of mental and moral training. The curriculum was weighted in favor of the inculcation of facts, moral habits, right principles and religious feelings."[24] Malua produced pastor-teachers with high social standing who prized their education and wished their children similar training and status, with the result that pastors' families produced future pastors, schoolteachers, government clerks, and the wives of important chiefs; in other words, "The church added an aristocracy of education to the Samoan social structure."[25]

Eventually all the untrained "native" teachers were replaced, and every village had a pastor-teacher from Malua to run its *A'oga a le Faifeau*. Many of the newly redundant teachers then trained at Malua and returned to village schools as pastor-teachers. The competitiveness and selectiveness that still characterizes the Samoan education system today can be perceived in the LMS system established 150 years ago, with the deliberate fostering by the missionaries of *'aiga*, village and district rivalries. In the pastor schools, reading and writing in Samoan, basic arithmetic, religious instruction, and hymn singing were taught with rote memorization as the main teaching method. A Samoan educator describes the process:

A syllabus for the year was printed and circulated by the missionaries throughout Samoa. The pastors' schools were examined at the end of the school year in Samoan Grammar (oral and written), simple arithmetic and scripture. It was expected that every child should have a minimum of 50 marks in each subject for her/him to be promoted to the next class. The examination was held by the *palagi* missionary in charge of each particular district and the results were carefully tabulated and announced ... at a public meeting of villages in each examination centre. Individuals were played off against individuals, village against village, district against district and, to a lesser extent, island against island.[26]

The reconstruction of male and female roles according to Christian and civilized notions was an important part of the missionary project, which was assisted by the inclusion of gender-specific practical subjects in the pastor school's curriculum; males were taught carpentry and agriculture, and females were taught skills such as sewing and cooking by the pastor's wife. These aspects of schooling, and the selectiveness referred to above, were extended to the boarding schools set up by the LMS in the 1890s—a boys' school at Leulumoega and a girls' school at Papauta—for those chosen to train in church service. Leulumoega provided further schooling for the young Samoan men selected as most promising by the *papalagi* missionary, with the best of that group being selected to enter Malua for further training as pastor-teachers and eventual service in the villages. "Suitable" young Samoan women were selected for training at Papauta in both religious doctrine and the domestic arts, seen as necessary for those who would become wives and helpmeets to the aspiring pastors; together they could provide a model to the village of the missionary ideal of the family.

In Samoa, the pastor's house became a very important focus for the training of young women in domestic skills, and in the art of being a housewife. The opportunity to serve in the pastor's house was a great privilege for it allowed one ... to acquire the social skills and graces befitting a good Christian woman. One would then be fit to marry a good Christian man, even a church minister, and bring up a good Christian family.[27]

As other mission groups established themselves in Samoa—Wesleyan missionaries arrived in 1835, followed by Roman Catholics in the 1840s, and Mormons in the 1880s—they followed the pattern laid down by the LMS of establishing village schools with the aim of religious conversion and the introduction of "civilized" ways, and boarding schools for the most able students where they could be trained to serve the church. The Catholic Church also played a key role in establishing schools in Apia. The first was a Marist Brothers' school, founded in 1871, for both Samoan and European boys, but it closed only six years later because of civil wars between Samoan factions. The school reopened in 1888 with enrollment confined to Europeans, with English as the medium of instruction. In 1897, when a German Marist Brother became school principal, German became the language of the school.[28] In 1890, the Sisters of the Mission of the Society of Mary opened Apia-based boarding and day schools for Samoan girls, from both Catholic and non-Catholic families and from every strata of society. They aimed to provide "the very essentials in life—food, clothing, and shelter, but they also offer to the girls a healthful, wholesome environment, educational opportunity, domestic science, suitable social diversion, moral guidance and religious instruction."[29]

By the end of the nineteenth century, there were churches in all villages, mostly under the control of Samoan ministers and preachers. There were also four parallel "native" school systems with a total of 299 schools located throughout the country. Around 10,000 students were being taught in these schools by 470 teachers. Seventy years of missionary education had produced a very high level of basic literacy in the Samoan language and school attendance was a well-established norm of Samoan childhood.[30] Apart from the use of the vernacular, however, what was included in the mission schools had very little to do with indigenous Samoan knowledge. The knowledge of the mission schools' curriculum came to represent what was considered to be important knowledge while indigenous knowledge and skills began to be undervalued. "Traditional" knowledge was not included in that transmitted through schools, and it was in this period that certain aspects of the cultural traditions started to disappear. The knowledge of ʻaiga and village history fundamental to Samoan identity was not taught in these schools, but biblical history was. Poets, composers, and choreographers who had been highly valued in "traditional" society all lost status because their arts were not part of the school curriculum.[31]

In terms of wider social and economic developments, missionary evangelizing had two main effects as its hold on Samoa strengthened. The first was the weakening of chiefly authority. Despite many chiefs' perceiving the new religion as a source of sacred power for themselves, by 1860, when the Christian order was well established, the missionaries had replaced the ali'i as holders of sacred power; although the prestige of the ali'i was still considerable, it was no longer seen as derived from their genealogical links to the old gods. Their mana, and that of all titles, was now by courtesy of the Christian god's grace.[32]

The second major shift was the introduction of commerce and Samoa's initiation into the world economy. "Legitimate commerce" was accepted by the LMS as part of the foundations on which "civilization" should be developed.[33] John Williams's son established the first general store in Apia and, soon after, began exporting coconut oil gathered from around the islands by a fleet of trading vessels. The LMS initiative was soon emulated by those concerned with nothing more than financial profit, and by 1860 over a hundred Europeans were running businesses or practicing trades in Apia; others were using nearby land to grow foodstuffs for sale to visiting ships. At the same time Samoans were being encouraged to produce coconut oil and copra to sell to the traders and/or contribute to the missions, they were developing a taste for the commodities that the growing number of Apia-based merchants imported. These shifts in the local patterns of both production and consumption marked a crucial break from the totally self-sufficient, nonmonetized, subsistence society that had until then characterized the faʻaSamoa. With the 1857 establishment of an Apia office by a German-owned Pacific trading network, and the use of Apia harbor as a fuelling station by the trans-Pacific steamship line, the number of European settlers increased. Apia became the South Pacific's port of most strategic interest to the colonial powers.[34]

Over the last quarter of the nineteenth century, Samoan leaders' concern about European encroachment led to a number of attempts to establish a centralized form of government, the main functions of which would be to control foreign governments' activities in Samoa and to maintain law and order in Apia, while guaranteeing the traditional autonomy of districts and villages.[35] However, intense conflict among Samoans over the relative claims to power of the holders of the paramount chiefly titles made impossible Samoan attempts to stabilize the situation and protect their autonomy.

Changing relationships between the three major powers—Britain, Germany, and the United States—also affected the unfolding events in Samoa, and in 1899 formal colonial control of Samoa was established. Britain was guaranteed unhampered access to Tonga and the Solomon Islands if she agreed to Germany taking control of the western islands of Samoa while the United States took the eastern islands, thereby gaining access to the strategically positioned Pago Pago harbor.

TWENTIETH CENTURY

Colonial Education

German rule over Western Samoa was initiated in 1900 by Governor Wilhelm Solf, who believed that overturning the traditional political structures and subordinating the indigenous elite to the colonial state was necessary for the "development" of the colony. Solf introduced a head tax with which to finance the colonial administration and build roads and government buildings. He established economic policy aimed at increased productivity and favoring the interests of foreign companies. For most Samoans, economic activity was confined to that required for subsistence plus the production of a small amount of copra for sale to German traders. The administration's exclusionary policies combined with Samoan reluctance to work on the plantations led to the arrival of indentured laborers from China. About half of the exports produced went to Germany with the rest going to Australia and New Zealand, from where most imports came.[36]

The German rulers of Western Samoa were content to leave education in the hands of the churches. The only significant changes were the inclusion of German language in the curriculum and the establishment of three "government" schools in Apia: the Leififi school for expatriate and "local European" children in 1905; a school for Samoan children at Malifa in 1908, which the villages around Apia offered to construct if the Government provided the site, materials, and teachers; and in 1909, a boarding school for boys was established at Malifa in response to a request from the *matai* that some of their older sons should attain knowledge of the German language and the training that would enable them to work as government officials.[37] This development established the Malifa Compound as the central location for government education. It also made clear that although Samoans wanted access to western education, they wanted to determine the conditions under which it was provided according to their own education objectives. The following reminiscence illuminates the schooling situation at the time:

My father entered the Marist Brothers School at Matafele in Apia in 1909.... The school was run by German brothers; in fact, Dad still knows many German phrases. When the Leififi school became an English school, which was at the start of the first world war, Dad was switched to Leififi, and attended that school for six years. (Leififi had been a

German school). Most of his school holidays were spent on [the island of] Manono. At Leififi, he learnt English and *faaPalagi* customs, and on Manono it was all *faaSamoa*.[38]

Soon after, the Sisters of the Mission of the Society of Mary extended educational access for girls in Apia by opening an English school (St. Mary's) for European and part-European students, in addition to the boarding and day schools available to Samoan girls.

New Zealand's military rule began the day after Britain's declaration of war on Germany in 1914, in response to a telegram from the British secretary of state to the New Zealand governor general, requesting that New Zealand seize Western Samoa as "a great and urgent imperial service." The New Zealand government's loyal response in sending an Expeditionary Force to Samoa, lowering the German flag and raising the British ensign, constituted the first allied invasion of German territory in World War I. The repatriation of many German planters and the majority of the Chinese indentured labor force almost ruined plantation agriculture because of the lack of both skilled management and unskilled labor.[39] The combination of imposed export duties and a huge drop in world prices for copra added to the economic hardship endured at the time, which many perceived as resulting from the New Zealand military policies. However, it was New Zealand's mishandling of the worldwide 1918 influenza epidemic when it reached Apia on board the *Talune*, in first failing to quarantine the ship and then obstructing those who were trying to help the sick, which did most damage to New Zealand's reputation in Western Samoa. At least 20 percent of the Samoan population died within a few weeks, including many important *matai*.[40]

In 1919, the League of Nations placed Western Samoa under New Zealand's mandate, for governance in accord with the League's "trusteeship" principle whereby "advanced" nations would ensure the well-being and development of "backward" peoples. The New Zealand government established a Department of External Affairs and began the civil administration of Western Samoa. Under the "Samoa Act," passed in the New Zealand parliament in 1921, a Samoan Public Service was created including Departments of Education, Health, and Native Affairs. Legislative government was enacted, and the High Court of Western Samoa established under the civil jurisdiction of the New Zealand Supreme Court.[41]

The development of a national state education system, which was initiated after the 1920 visit of the New Zealand inspector for Maori Schools, aroused some hostility among the mission authorities who questioned the New Zealand government's right to assume control of Samoan education when they provided schooling for 13,000 students while the administration schools only provided for 150. However, they did eventually agree to work with the administration, and while most village pastor schools, now termed Grade 1 schools, continued as before, the recommendation that some village pastor schools should be developed as Grade 2 schools and offer classes up to a New

Zealand Standard 2 (Year 4) level, under joint mission/state management and supervision, proceeded. Villages provided and maintained the school buildings that were staffed with state-trained teachers who taught a state-standardized curriculum including elementary English. Enrollment in these schools, which became known as *A'oga Palagi*, was open to the children of the village the school was in, and from villages within walking distance.[42] For others, the pastor schools continued to provide schooling as recorded below:

The *aoga faifeau* was the main formal school system in the village, and we all attended every morning. There was a government primary school ... in the nearby villages ... but very few from our village attended, probably because of the distance. So the *aoga faifeau* was our main form of instruction. We were taught to read using the *Faitau pi* [alphabet reader] and grouped in classes from 1–6. Other topics taught included *Tala o le lalolagi tele ma le lalolagi laititi* (tales of the world) which was used by all the pastors to teach students our geography.[43]

In the villages that had a Grade 2 school, its classes were conducted in the morning, and the pastor schools operated in the afternoons. Most children attended both. The pastor schools were then termed *A'oga Samoa* in recognition of the fact that Samoan was the only language of the school. The pastors' wives continued to conduct the *Vasega Faitau Pi* (alphabet reading class), for preschoolers in the morning.[44] Leififi School in Apia, which catered to expatriate European and "local European" children—most of them of mixed European/Samoan parentage—was reopened (having been used as a military camp during the war) and closely integrated into the New Zealand system, taking pupils as far as Standard 6 (Year 8) and the New Zealand Proficiency Exam. The Malifa School for Samoan children was also reopened and run along New Zealand lines. When the reopening was announced hundreds turned up, but the school could only take sixty of them. The problem was solved by appointing a committee comprised of the paramount chiefs, Malietoa and Tamasese, and the *pulenu'u* (mayor) of each contributing village to select a representative group of children between the ages of five and ten.[45] However, although there was no shortage of eager students, finding teachers was not so straightforward as the following reveals: "My mother was only 18 when she stated teaching at Malifa School. She and four other women ... were the first Samoan teachers. The teachers' college didn't exist at the time so these five just went straight to teaching because they were good students."[46]

The New Zealand government appointed a superintendent of schools who was responsible for supervising the government schools in Apia, inspecting the Grade II schools, and running classes in English, and teaching methods for village schoolteachers. During the 1920s, two self-sufficient agriculturally based boarding schools for boys—Avele College on Upolu and Vaipouli College on Savai'i—were established along the same lines as such schools for rural Maori boys in New Zealand. A scholarship scheme for a small number of boys to study at St. Stephen's Maori College in New Zealand was also established (and retracted a few years later by the then New Zealand administrator).[47] At St. Mary's in 1925, a notable development for girls who had completed primary school was the introduction of a commercial studies course that included typing, commercial English, shorthand, commercial practice, and bookkeeping. Classes were held both during the day and after working hours for those already in the workforce. The graduates of the course found ready employment with the New Zealand administration or in the business firms increasingly opening in Apia.[48]

Education policies in 1920s and 1930s depended very much on the educational beliefs and understandings of particular colonial administrators and the educational bureaucrats responsible for New Zealand education in Western Samoa (and the other Pacific dependencies). As reported by a New Zealand teacher who taught in Samoa at the time:

In those days, every officer seconded to the education department started off from scratch. Nobody was much interested in what his predecessor had done. Everybody arrived with brand new ideas of his own. It was no wonder there was no continuity of education policy, school organization or teaching methods and it was no wonder the Samoans sat back to see what was going to happen every time a new European teacher arrived.[49]

According to Ma'ia'i there were two schools of thought on "native" education prevalent among the decision makers. Those in one camp saw education as an efficient agency of assimilation (New Zealand's official policy for Maori education) and a tool in the promotion of social and economic "progress." They proposed a form of "adaptation" education that would produce some graduates with the attitudes and skills that would enable them to fill minor roles in the public service, to work in clerical and sales positions in the commercial sector, and to train as primary schoolteachers, nurses, and trades-people. In 1925, Lord Lugard of the Permanent Mandates Commission and a keen proponent of adaptation education in Britain's African colonies, wrote admiringly of New Zealand's policy in Samoa of "deliberately limiting entry for 'advanced education' [meaning Years 7 to 8] to meet existing employment needs."[50]

The other camp believed that the only purpose of education was to fit people to their environment. They saw the educational needs of Pacific people as ordained by their "natural" role as cultivators of the land and believed that western education beyond a very basic level would be both economically and politically counterproductive as it would make them discontent with village life.[51] From the mid-1920s, this became the prevalent view of the New Zealand administration that, under Brigadier Richardson, became increasingly characterized by discipline and repression in dealing with the strong resistance of Samoa people to the "progressive" reforms introduced with the aim of uplifting Samoan society. Richardson's reforms reflected his "unquestioning faith in the inherent superiority of European values and ways"[52] and his wish for Samoans to become "hardworking, efficient producers with individual land allotments, living in remodeled, sanitary villages, educated for good citizenship but not too much in advance of their environment." In order to achieve his aims he set out to repress those Samoan customs he perceived as wasteful of time and resources and attempted to reorganize villages and change the land tenure system so that increased land cultivation and more individualized enterprise would enhance agricultural production for export.[53]

Whichever view was prevalent at the official policy level, the schooling provided by the New Zealand administration during the 1920s and 1930s was extremely basic in terms of curriculum, pedagogy, materials, and physical conditions. The only Samoan language materials available were those that had been printed by the LMS, which were mainly religious but included translations of some more literary works such as those by Robert Louis Stevenson who had spent his last years in Samoa. Classrooms were traditional open-sided *fale* and contained very little furniture with children sitting on mats on the ground. Although the New Zealand education officials and teachers were charged with both training their Samoan counterparts in "modern" teaching methodologies and improving their English, this was not systematically done.[54]

Richardson was overt in his wish to avoid the creation of a western-educated elite that might threaten New Zealand's political authority. To that end, he restricted the teaching of English, promoted the establishment of school gardens, increased the teaching of handcrafts, and instituted the *Fetu o Samoa*, a Samoan version of the Boy Scouts aimed at "making better Samoans with a pride of race and love of country."[55] His approach was sometimes questioned by New Zealand education officials who perceived the educational needs of Western Samoa differently, especially in regard to the very restricted teaching of English. This contrasting view was supported by the prominent Maori leader and government minister in charge of Maori and Pacific Island Affairs, Sir Apirana Ngata, in a parliamentary debate on the matter. Speaking against those who wished to depress the educational aspirations of Pacific Islands people, he argued:

All Polynesian Islands have been invaded in varying degree by outside influences and the future will find the latter more and more pressing and insistent. It would be criminal folly on the part of any administration to base our education policy on the assumption that those influences can be kept out, and to deny the native population the measure of deliberate preparation and support which in these days can be secured only through the best possible education.[56]

Samoan leaders made continual objection to the education policies of the administration—they recognized the objective of stifling their political aspirations even though, under the terms of the mandate, they were supposed to be being prepared for eventual self-government. However, their pleas for the establishment of more government primary schools, secondary education of the type that would enable them to participate in and eventually control the administrative structures of the country, and teacher education, that would upgrade the standard of locally trained teachers went unheeded.[57]

That the Samoan people were well aware of the politics of education was also demonstrated during the *Mau* resistance, when they withdrew their children from the government schools resulting in the temporary closure of many. The Mau was a nationalist movement formed in the mid-1920s, under the slogan *Samoa mo Samoa* (Samoa for Samoans), as a means of resisting New Zealand's increasingly repressive rule. It brought together members of the local European community who had been marginalized, socially and in business, by the New Zealand administration, and Samoans who resented external political rule and the associated trampling on Samoan custom. Their campaign of comprehensive passive resistance employed traditional political strategies as well as more modern techniques such as petitions, protest marches, and nonpayment of taxes.

In the early 1930s, the church systems continued to play the major role in educating girls beyond the very basic primary years. However, this reminiscence encapsulates some of the complexities of the racial divisions within schools and the socioeconomic barriers to educational access at the time:

When I was seven ... my mother found me a place at Saint Mary's School, Savalalo. At the time Saint Mary's was divided into two sections. One accommodated children of half-castes and affluent Chinese and the other was for Samoans and the not-so-well-to-do Chinese. I was in the section for the not-so-well-to-do Chinese.... I was a promising student but I wasn't able to pursue my education into the prestigious commercial school run by the nuns because we didn't have enough money.[58]

Papauta, which was built some distance from Apia and had its own plantation, continued to operate as a self-sufficient community with curriculum subjects including health, village life skills, and childcare. The following account from an ex-pupil illustrates the lifestyle:

My family was honoured that I would be a Papauta girl like my mother, and so was I. Papauta was run by Miss Downs from Britain with the help of ... local teachers. Life at Papauta was very structured.... When we woke up in the morning, we assembled for prayers in the dining room, then we picked up the rubbish. Breakfast was around seven, and by eight we were bathed and ready for school. I remember we ate Samoan food at all meals ... Usually on Saturday we went reef fishing.[59]

In the mid-1930s, the return of the Mau children and the effects of one of the highest population growth rates in the world led to increased pressure on existing schools and increased demands for new ones. Hopes were high that the election of a Labour government in New Zealand in 1935 would mean some progress in education development, especially when a new policy direction was declared for an education system that would ensure that Samoans had a "fuller and broader outlook and [would] be better fitted to take a greater role in the administration of their own country."[60] Also proposed was the provision of long-requested opportunities for secondary and tertiary education. The notion of establishing a secondary school offering a program up to New Zealand university entrance and introducing a scholarship scheme to support a small number of students through university study in New Zealand was advanced, but unfortunately not translated into action.

The demand for more and better education continued however, and despite almost doubling the number of Grade II schools between 1936–39 class sizes were huge. Increased pressures for entry to the Apia government schools led to greatly increased enrollments and both the Leifiifi and Malifa school rolls were over 1,000. These schools continued to enroll by racial classification with the former for European and part-European children and the latter for Samoans. However, it is widely reported anecdotally that in the case of the former, because a European name was accepted as proof of ethnicity, many with Samoan names took on European names so their children could get into Leifiifi. In 1938 a secondary class attached to the Leifiifi Primary school was opened. Although the primary school enrolled only expatriate and local European children, the administration insisted that merit would determine entry to the postprimary class and the first class of twenty-three included sixteen Samoan students. However, the school closed the following year because of the cost. The constraints on educational expenditure, despite large increases in export income and much greater spending on health and prisons,[61] also led to the administration denying permission to many village *fono* who wished to construct Grade 2 schools. A teachers-training institution offering a one-year course was opened in 1939, but the first twenty-five trainees were neither sufficient to meet the demand for teachers nor adequately educated themselves, many having attained only a Standard 3 schooling.

As in colonies worldwide, World War II triggered significant changes—economic, political and social—in Western Samoa. Britain's declaration of war on Germany in 1939 resulted in the New Zealand administration immediately planning "to put Samoa on a wartime footing,"[62] but it was the Japanese attack on Pearl Harbor that really brought the war to Western Samoa. The stationing of 12,000 U.S. troops, one-sixth the population of Western Samoa at the time, generated an unprecedented level of prosperity and "development" introducing Samoans to a new array of imported goods and opening up opportunities for wage employment in businesses, restaurants, laundry, and construction work.[63] This led to further educational difficulties as many Samoan teachers pursued the new and better-paid employment opportunities with the resulting closure of a significant number of Grade 2 schools. The teacher shortage was worsened by many New Zealand teachers, fearing their proximity to the war zone or wishing to join the forces, returning to New Zealand and being replaced with relatively poorly trained and underqualified Samoan teachers. The American forces also took over some schools' facilities, including Leifiifi and Papauta, for the years 1942–45.[64] The following account illustrates some of the difficulties for teachers of the time:

[M]y first year teaching in 1941 was at Nofoalii. The Head Teacher and I were the only staff members: he taught standards one and two with about 12 students while I taught primers one, two and three, with about 30 students. There was no set curriculum. We did whatever we wanted to do. Our resources were a blank workbook, a box of chalk, a pen and nib. During the Second World War I was shifted to Faleasiu because the head teacher there had gone to work for the marines. After a few weeks the only other teacher at Faleasiu also went to work for the marines.[65]

Education for Decolonization

In 1946, the process of developing a United Nations Trusteeship Agreement that would provide the basis for moving to self-government began. When the UN sent a visiting mission to Samoa, the Samoa leaders made clear their objections to the paternalism of the New Zealand administration and demanded that Western Samoa's political future be determined not in Wellington (the capital of New Zealand) but in Samoa.[66] The agreement, announced by New Zealand Prime Minister Peter Fraser in 1947 and endorsed by the UN, emphasized New Zealand's responsibility as trustee to promote indigenous political development and incorporated three main objectives: to establish Samoan custom and tradition as one of the foundations of the future political structure; to confer a substantial measure of political responsibility on the Samoan leadership immediately; and to recognize and accept Samoan aspirations to complete self-government.[67]

In 1945, at the instigation of Prime Minister Fraser, who on his official visit to Samoa the previous year had noted the poor condition of the education system, New Zealand's Director General of Education C. E. Beeby had led a delegation of New Zealand educators to Western Samoa to discuss the educational direction required to produce the future leaders of an independent country. Beeby reported the New Zealand administered schools as:

beyond words, muddled and messy. Many of the classes are terribly large. Even at the Malifa grade two schools there are four infant classes with four teachers in one large room. The Samoan teachers are severely handicapped by their own lack of education and training. Very few had reached a New Zealand standard six [year eight] level of attainment and many had not progressed beyond a standard three level. The school system is handicapped by shortages of qualified staff, lack of equipment and textbooks.[68]

Barrington describes the recommendations of the delegation as representing "a significant move away from the concept of a self-contained folk culture which had dominated education practice" in the attempt to cocoon Samoans from the modern world, to which Samoans had long objected.[69] The education debates of the 1920s and 1930s were dismissed by Beeby who declared:

The question of whether the Samoan should be Europeanised as quickly as possible or whether the Samoan way of life should be maintained and left unaltered is not relevant in the considerations for future education in the territory.[70]

The recognition of both the effects of New Zealand's educational neglect and the political demands of the Samoan leaders led to the conclusion that, rather than aim for the necessarily long-term comprehensive improvement of the whole system, what was needed was a short-term plan for the creation of an "academic elite" by selecting a small group of pupils, on the basis of ability and leadership, for overseas education and training. Until postprimary education of a good standard was provided in Western Samoa, the best of the primary school leavers would be sent to New Zealand secondary schools and then on to further education and training; in this way, both an able and educated public service necessary for self-government and the nucleus of qualified and trained teachers necessary for a secondary system of high standard would be provided.

Over the next few years, the Grade 2 schools upgraded their programs to a Standard 4 (Year 6) level and four Grade 3 district schools were established to take selected students up to a Form 2 (Year 8) level. A scholarship scheme under which young Samoans were sent to New Zealand for secondary and higher education was inaugurated. This scheme arose out of the 1943 initiative of the Samoan leaders to levy a tax (of one pound on *matai* and five shillings on untitled men) to pay for some of their sons to be sent to New Zealand for education. The administration's concerns that selection would not be open to all led to a proposal in 1944 that twelve students be sent from Samoa immediately with New Zealand footing three quarters of the cost and that they be selected on merit. An examination for the 109 candidates was duly held, and four girls were among the twelve students selected by examination who left for New Zealand in 1945.[71] One of those selected to go to New Zealand in 1948 describes her schooling for the two years prior to that:

After primary school at Moataa, I went to Malifa Girls' School. This was in 1946 and I was 14. I qualified as a pupil by sitting the national test to select girls into Malifa ... the classes were from standards four to six. Our class had 23 girls.... Subjects taught included art, arithmetic, and writing. English periods were spent reading poetry and reciting verse. English grammar was emphasized and we had to write this from the board after recitation. In order for us to perfect our handwriting, Mrs King used to make us print with a ruler under our right arm. My writing is still good!

Our teachers were of the old school, strict disciplinarians who believed hard work made us better pupils.... There were no excuses then for being late to school, even if we had to take the long route because the roads were inaccessible on rainy days. Every Friday after prayers and the raising of the flag, we would walk to Maluafou to gather horse manure for the compost heap.... In those days nobody complained; we did as we were told because we were scared of disobeying our teachers.[72]

The assumption behind the Beeby Commission's recommendations was that the Samoan education system must be geared to the priority expressed by those it was meant for—the preparation of Samoan people for full participation in the government of their own country. This view was reinforced by the UN mission's comments on the lack of provision of postprimary education:

From all sides the mission heard complaints, both from Samoans and from Europeans, based upon the inadequacy of the educational system. In over thirty years, the recurring theme was, the educational programme has failed to produce a group of leaders possessing the high professional and technical skills necessary for self-government.[73]

An example of how the Beeby recommendations worked in practice is provided in the following story:

It was at the time that Dr Beeby from the New Zealand Education Department initiated a scheme for teachers to go to New Zealand on inservice training. I was asked to go to New Zealand for a seven months' observation tour of New Zealand schools.... We started off in Wellington at Victoria University where we attended one months' summer school in English.... That's where I realized that my English was very poor!

When I returned to Samoa following this time in New Zealand ... I became Samoa's first female school inspector! ... In those days the School Inspector was like a teacher adviser. We were there to help teachers.... It was up to us to think of ways we could motivate teachers to want to change their teaching styles. Being an inspector really helped develop my *faaSamoa* as well. Every time I went into a village or school there would be a formal welcome for me, and I learnt how to reply. I learnt to appreciate the formal ceremonies and do everything in the correct way.[74]

In 1953, the racially segregated schooling that had existed in Apia since the late nineteenth century was abolished and the Leififi and Malifa schools amalgamated. Also in 1953, the first secondary school, Samoa College, "dedicated to the people of Western Samoa by the people of New Zealand in token of friendship and as a help towards self-government," was opened by Dr. Beeby with fifty-two secondary students provided by the Leififi accelerate school (that had been enrolling upper primary students selected from all over Samoa since 1950) and 170 primary level (Standard 2—Form 2) students selected from village and district intermediate schools, as well as Apia Primary and the mission schools. The aim of the primary department was to develop the students' facility with English so that by the time they entered the secondary department they would be able to cope with English language texts. It was foreseen that, as the village and district schools improved, it would be possible to drop the primary department. This happened progressively until 1961. In 1962, Samoa College became an exclusively secondary school and Leififi Intermediate School (for Years 7 and 8 students) was established for students transiting from Year 6 at Apia Primary and selected students from the district schools.[75] The secondary curriculum on offer at Samoa College was closely modeled on the New Zealand curriculum offering academic, general, and commercial, but no technical or agricultural, courses. Its initial aim was to prepare a selected group for the New Zealand School Certificate examination at Form 5 (Year 11), followed by further selection for higher education in New Zealand, while most students would have access only to two years secondary in preparation for the Public Service, teaching, nursing, police force, and clerical work. Students' progression through the system as it was in the process of restructuring is elaborated in the following narrative:

At the end of my standard four year (1959) there was a national exam to select students for the a'oga itumalo (district intermediate school). The ... District School was only opened three years before and was only taking in a limited number of students because of the shortage of classrooms and qualified teachers. Six of us from Solosolo Primary were selected while most other schools from our twelve village district only had three or four. The district school had three levels ... Form One E was the new entrants class. There was an exam at the end of ... year to select students for Form One A at Samoa College.... I was one of three students that got selected from our school for Samoa College.... Samoa College was a far cry from the village and district schools.... Our principal was a palagi man, we had palagi children in our class and we had our own desks ... we were not allowed to speak Samoan and the punishment for speaking our own language was weeding grass for two hours in the hot sun.... The year 1961 was the last year of the primary level at Samoa College. Our class left Samoa College to merge with the Malifa Primary Form two classes to start ... Leififi Intermediate. We were the pioneer students of that school in 1962, the year Western Samoa became independent.... At the end of the year, we sat the Form Two national exam and over half of our Form Two students were selected for Samoa College. I went back to Samoa College as a third former in 1963. In the four years from 1960 to 1963, I went through four changes of schools and three external exams.[76]

During the next ten to fifteen years, Avele College, Vaipouli College, and several of the mission schools also introduced secondary programs up to Year 11 (NZSC), and Samoa College advanced to the Form 6 New Zealand University Entrance (NZUE) level. The state schools were almost entirely staffed by New Zealand teachers and were monitored by New Zealand school inspectors.

The steady migration of rural families into Apia in order to access the new educational facilities available to urban children led to calls for more and better rural education, both to keep people in their villages and to enable rural children to compete on an equal footing with those in the Apia schools for further educational opportunities. The location of New Zealand teachers in Apia and the government provision of schools and teacher residences in Apia, while villages and districts provided their own, were identified as disadvantaging rural children by offering a better standard of primary education to those in Apia government-owned schools. In the attempt to curb the congestion in the

Malifa schools, in 1956 the administration introduced fees for the government-owned schools and, as recommended by Beeby following a further visit to Samoa in 1954, appointed New Zealand head-teachers to the district schools in order to raise the general standard of education in those schools, and particularly the standard of English.[77] In preparation for Independence and the localization of educational administration, the Education Ordinance of 1959 outlined the functions of the minister of Education, the Department of Education, and the director and staff of the Department.

Educational expenditure trebled during the decade after the first Beeby Commission—between 1945–56 Western Samoan education had been granted subsidies amounting to half a million pounds—but in the late 1950s the costs of maintaining both the scholarship scheme and Samoa College became increasingly difficult to meet out of government revenue. New Zealand reduced the number of contract teacher positions for Western Samoa and proposed a severe cutback in scholarship student numbers and the return of a number of students already in New Zealand. However, these measures were avoided by the establishment of New Zealand's first educational aid program, which provided 400,000 pounds to assist Samoan education for the five-year period from 1960–64.[78]

Education for Independence

Western Samoa became an independent state in 1962 with an education system dominated by the organizational, curricular, pedagogical, and assessment prescriptions of the New Zealand Department of Education, with educational administration having the slowest rate of localization of any government department, and with secondary schooling tightly geared to the requirements of the New Zealand external examination system. Between 1945 and 1962, 183 scholarships had been awarded, with sixty-four returnees working in the Public Service, eighty-four still training, and the remainder neither on scholarship nor working for the government. Although the UN visiting missions, Beeby, and the New Zealand directors of Western Samoan education had all expressed the desirability of a universal and compulsory education system as the best means of promoting the democratic political structures they saw as necessary for an independent state, what had developed was a "rigorously selective" system.[79] This was not the result of any deliberately elitist intent, but rather because of insufficient resources—material and human—and a rapidly rising population of school-age children. This view is supported by the 1945 Beeby Report's justification for the selective policies recommended:

In a country that has only a handful of native people with so much as a Standard VI education, we can see no alternative to starting with a selected group who will, in turn, undertake the heavier task of raising the educational level of the whole population. We do not contemplate the creation of an educated elite for its own sake, but merely as a preliminary step in the educating of the whole community.[80]

However, by the end of the 1960s, dissatisfaction with the inherited educational structures was being expressed by educators concerned with the appropriateness of what the schools offered, and by politicians and bureaucrats concerned at the (comparatively) large amount of resources being soaked up by the system. The first of Western Samoa's five-year development plans charged the existing system with not meeting development needs, as offering an unsuitable curriculum and not offering enough education. At primary level less than 80 percent of school-age children were enrolled, the secondary schools could cope with only 50 percent of those graduating from primary schools, only 5 percent graduated from Form 5 (Year 11) and 1 percent entered tertiary-level education. But despite the poor performance (as measured by external examination success) of those who did proceed from primary to secondary, the demand for increasing amounts of "academic" education, perceived as enhancing the prospects of joining the escalating migration trend in search of wage employment (either internally to Apia or externally, primarily to New Zealand), made increased provision politically imperative. An attempt to redress urban/rural inequities in access to Samoa College was also signaled in the 1966 Development Plan's intention of making Leifiifi Intermediate, from where most Samoa College entrants came, an accelerated intermediate program for the whole country. Rather than continuing to draw almost all its students from Apia Primary, academically able students from rural primary schools would have access to the "superior" educational experience offered which would include an intensive English program.[81]

Throughout the 1970s, the major educational thrust was towards the expansion of school opportunities at every level of the system, through the construction and equipping of school buildings and the provision of teaching personnel and resources. Government commitment to a countrywide school building program, often initiated and financed by village *fono*, meant that by 1980 all Samoan children had access to nine years of primary schooling. In 1979, the director of Education reported that a number of villages that used to share primary schools had put their resources and energy into developing their own schools because of their wish to manage their children's schooling themselves. It was noted that although this proliferation of small schools was against Department of Education policy they were obliged to "succumb to the wish of the people in each village," and the number of primary schools would therefore be likely to continue to grow "because of this demand from the people."[82]

In 1967 the position of director of Education had been localized through the appointment of one of the original group sent to New Zealand on scholarship for secondary education, who then went on to become the first Pacific Islands woman to be awarded a PhD. As director, she was increasingly concerned about the relevance of what schools offered and in the early 1970s introduced Samoan language and culture into schools at all levels. One of those selected to work as a Subject Organizer in Samoan Language reflected as follows:

Teaching Samoan in schools was a very novel step at the time, but it gave my life a whole new direction. I started to develop my knowledge and love for the *faaSamoa* and the Samoan Language. [The Director of Education] had formed a group of subject organizers and selected some pilot schools to test the teaching of Samoan ... a very different way of teaching from teaching English [which was] a very repetitive method. Teaching Samoan was different because the children already knew how to speak Samoan. Our job was more a language enrichment programme: to make sure their Samoan was grammatically sound, to enlarge their Samoan vocabulary and to tell them the stories and legends which we had heard as children. Not so much *Little Red Riding Hood*! At an inspectors' meeting we discussed how to teach Samoan from the standard classes right up to high school level, and the meeting was followed by teachers' refresher courses on how to teach Samoan to Samoans.... But very few teachers wanted to teach Samoan. They would say ... "Why are we teaching Samoan? But they were Samoans! This was a new beginning for us all."[83]

By the end of the decade, Junior Secondary schools had been established in most districts (either by converting the Grade III district schools or building new schools) and offered a three-year alternative secondary program to those students who had not ranked highly enough in the national examination, held at the end of their primary schooling, to gain access to the senior secondary schools. The aim of these schools was to establish closer links between formal schooling and the rural life to which most students would return.[84] Senior secondary places in both government and mission schools increased but remained highly selective. In 1979 two-year primary and three-year secondary teachers' training programs (for the preparation of junior secondary teachers) were instituted to cater for growing school enrollments, to improve the quality of classroom teaching, and to decrease the dependence on overseas teachers.

Educational statistics for 1979 show that the government system comprised 132 primary and twenty-two secondary schools, two secondary-level vocational schools, and the teachers' college. The mission systems comprised twenty-one primary and seventeen secondary schools, and two secondary and two higher vocational schools. Eighty-six percent of primary students were enrolled in government schools, with total primary school enrollments numbering over 42,000: 51 percent boys, 49 percent girls. Seventy percent of primary school teachers were women. Secondary enrollments totaled only 9,700, evenly divided between boys and girls, with 60 percent in government secondary schools and the other 40 percent in mission schools. Fifty-three percent of secondary teachers were men and 47 percent were women. Of the 221 students enrolled in primary teacher training, nearly 60 percent were female, and of the forty-three enrolled in secondary training, 63 percent were male.[85]

Diminishing opportunities for emigration, the desire to curtail increasing urbanization, and the recognition of the limitations of economic modernization in providing wage employment for all led to calls (again mainly from politicians and educators rather than from parents and students) for an education better suited to the Western Samoan context. The main thrust of reform in the early to mid-1980s was in the areas of curriculum and assessment, particularly at primary and junior secondary levels, with efforts to construct more relevant curricula and an assessment system better suited to local needs. At the same time, however, there were pressures on the senior secondary system to provide more places. Parents pushed for more opportunities for their children to have access to external examination classes because of rising demand for school leaver credentials—the junior secondary leavers' certificate was losing currency and the NZSC (School Certificate) was increasingly demanded as the minimum requirement for skilled and semiskilled employment and further training. NZUE (University Entrance) provided the opportunity to higher education through the scholarship schemes provided primarily by New Zealand and Australia.[86]

A major restructuring of the education system, initiated in 1987, attempted to meet these divergent demands for a more relevant schooling that could provide an education suited to those who would return to village life at its completion, while preparing others for either employment in the modern economy or further education/training. Curricular and assessment prescriptions were to be localized and access to senior secondary places both broadened and made more equitable. The intended restructuring had been justified as necessary in order that "young Samoans be enabled to meet the challenges posed by the changes in Samoan society and culture." An overtly expressed ideal of equal opportunity underlay the changes proposed at each level of education.

The policy statement was endorsed by Cabinet and implementation began in 1987. However, a change of government in the 1988 general election, in which education had been a central campaign issue, led to most of the 1987 changes—the major ones being the abolition of the national end-of-primary exam, the entry of all first-year secondary students into junior secondary schools, and expanded entry into senior secondary—being undone. Year 8 students sat the reinstated National Exam at the end of 1988, and when secondary schools, both junior and secondary, opened for the 1989 school year, they had reverted to the pre-1987 structure. The year 1989 was a year of educational confusion with the turnabout described by one prominent Samoan educator as "devastating to the morale of teachers." He claimed that it was not just a return to the pre-1987 situation, "it took us back to the 1950s. It felt like all the hard-won gains over more than 20 years had been lost."[87]

A notable development in tertiary education occurred in 1984. Although the University of the South Pacific (USP), established in 1968, had provided in-country higher education for Samoans, including transitional courses to prepare students for three-year undergraduate degree programs, this proved nonviable. In 1984, the government established a National University that initially offered the University of the South Pacific's Foundation Year program, which was later phased out and replaced by a University Preparatory Year (UPY). Plans for National University of Samoa development led to the following three objectives being set down:

- the maintenance, development, and conservation of the Samoan Language and Culture;
- the meeting of Samoa's manpower needs; and
- the provision of continuing education and adult education short courses that would benefit the local community.

The Early 1990s

In 1990, the Samoan state education system consisted of 139 primary, twenty-two junior secondary, three senior secondary schools, and an amalgamated (primary and secondary) teachers' college, all administered within the Department of Education (DOE) that was headed by the director of Education. A group of twenty-three school inspectors operated as field administrators facilitating liaison between central management and the primary and junior secondary schools in the twenty-two educational districts. Their function was to monitor school management and educational programs, supervise staff performance, and organize the staffing of schools and transfer of teachers.

The financing of education was shared by parents and the state with village and district communities owning and bearing responsibility for their own school buildings, furniture, and equipment, and the state paying for the salaries of teaching and administrative staff and providing some stationery and curriculum materials. Each primary and junior secondary school was managed by the village or district that owned it. A school committee, made up of village people appointed by the village *Fono* in the case of primary schools or representatives of each contributing village in the case of junior secondary schools, was responsible for the setting, collecting, and expending of annual fees. School fees, supplemented by funds raised through community activities, were used to construct new facilities, maintain existing ones, and provide furniture, equipment, and resources. The schools on the Malifa Compound and the three state senior secondary schools were funded directly from the government budget and owned and administered by the Department of Education.

In addition to the state schools, there were sixteen mission and two private primary schools, six mission junior secondary schools, and one private and eleven mission senior secondary schools. All were administered by their own directors and management boards, and self-funded except for government grants received from time to time, in money and/or kind. The nonstate system included an early childhood sector, a number of community schools for "special needs" children and, at the post-secondary level, a technical center administered by the Catholic Church and a privately owned fine arts school.

About 1,200 preschool children were enrolled in the various early childhood institutions located throughout the country. With no government provision for preschool centers, all were provided through community organizations—mainly church and village—or by private providers. It was estimated that up to one hundred centers existed, but exact figures were hard to ascertain because of the rate at which they were both established and disestablished. The number of early childhood teachers working in the centers and the extent to which they were trained was also hard to ascertain. Some teachers had enrolled in the USP's certificate course through its continuing education program and some organizing bodies also offered certificate level training.

Approximately 38,000 students, 48 percent of them female, were enrolled in the eight-year primary system, which comprised 157 schools—139 government, sixteen mission, and two private. Although under the Compulsory Education Legislation introduced through the 1991 Education Amendment Act, all children from the ages of five until fourteen or until the completion of Year 8, were required to attend school unless exempted by the director, the enrollment figure above represents only about 85 percent of all primary-age children. Primary schools were staffed by teachers almost all of whom had been trained at the Western Samoa Teachers College, with approximately 75 percent of them being women. The overall teacher–learner ratio within the primary system was about one to twenty-seven, but this disguised extremes arising from a proliferation of very small village schools and some very large urban schools. The three state primary schools on the Malifa Compound—Apia Lower, Apia Middle and Leififi Intermediate—had a total enrollment of around 4,500. The primary curriculum covered the following subject areas: Samoan, English, mathematics, science, social studies, music, art/craft, and physical education. Samoan was the language of instruction in the first three years of primary schooling with English taught as a subject in Years 4 to 6 and English the medium of instruction in all subject areas except Samoan in Years 7 and 8. The culmination of the eight-year primary cycle was an examination covering English, Mathematics, science, social science, and Samoan. The main function of the Year 8 National Examination was to rank children for selection into secondary schools.

Secondary education covered a five-year cycle from Years 9 to 13. The cycle was divided into a three-year junior secondary program and a two-year senior secondary program. The state system consists of twenty-two junior secondary schools and three senior secondary schools one of them a single-sex boys' college. The junior secondary schools offered Year 9 to Year 11 programs. Two of the senior secondary schools, Avele and Vaipouli Colleges, offered Year 9 to Year 13 programs and the other, Samoa College, offered a four-year program that excluded Year 11. Total enrollment in state secondary schools approximated 8,500. Another almost 4,000 secondary students were enrolled in the eighteen nonstate secondary schools, which offered the same programs as the state schools.

Students at morning assembly at Avele College, a senior secondary college in Samoa, in 2006. Photograph by the author, Eve Coxon.

Entrants to the state senior secondary schools were selected on the basis of their achievement in the Year 8 examination with approximately 360 Year 9 entrants winning places in these schools each year. The highest achievers went to Samoa College, the next group of achievers from Savai'i was offered places in Vaipouli College, and the next group of male achievers from Upolu was offered places in Avele College. The majority of Year 9 entrants, approximately 2,000 annually, entered the twenty-two junior secondary schools that offered a three-year program. For most of those enrolled in junior secondary schools, their schooling terminated on the completion of Year 11. A few were offered Year 12 places in the senior state or mission schools. In total about 70 percent of the appropriate age-group numbers were enrolled in the junior secondary years, but only about 60 percent of that number completed Year 11. Approximately 25 percent of the total age-group numbers proceeded to the senior secondary years with only 15 percent completing the five-year cycle.

English was the medium of instruction and examination throughout the secondary system, with Samoan being a subject of study. The subjects constituting the junior secondary core curriculum, and examined at the end of Year 11, were Samoan, English, mathematics, science, and social science. Optional

Year 10 students of Samoa College in a mathematics class, in 2006. Photograph by the author, Eve Coxon.

subjects were home economics, industrial arts, agricultural science, and business studies. Music, art/craft, and physical education were included but not examined within the junior secondary program. The senior secondary curriculum offered the following subjects: Samoan, English, geography, history, economics, accounting, science, biology, physics, chemistry. Except for Samoan, all the above subjects were included in both the Year 12 and 13 examinations, and shorthand/typing and human biology were at Year 12. Students did between four and six subjects with chances for further education being determined by the results aggregated from English and their three best subjects.

Student progress through the secondary system depended on three examinations, the first being the Junior Secondary Schools Certificate Examination (JSSCE) held at the end of Year 11 to provide certification for terminating students, with a minor selection role for junior secondary students who wished to proceed to Year 12. The Western Samoa Secondary Schools Certificate Examination (WSSCE) provided certification for Year 12 students and determined selection for Year 13. This examination was set, administered and marked locally by trained examiners, with some assistance from New Zealand, under the supervision of the Fiji-based South Pacific Board of Educational

Assessment (SPBEA). Year 13 students sat the Pacific Senior Secondary Certificate Examination (PSSCE), a regional examination coordinated and administered by the SPBEA with the participation of selected examiners from Western
Samoa.

Performance in the PSSCE determined students' entry into tertiary education, with the most successful students gaining entry into the University
Preparatory Year (UPY) at the National University of Samoa (NUS) or another
of the small autonomous tertiary institutions, which included the teachers' college, a polytechnic, a marine training school, and a school of nursing. Additional locally available post-secondary facilities were provided by the University
of the South Pacific (USP) extension center, which offered both pre-university
and university level extra-mural courses, and USP's regional school of agriculture, located a few miles from Apia. In 1993, approximately 1,500 individuals
were enrolled in the various tertiary programs available.[88] Another two to three
hundred were undertaking tertiary studies on scholarships usually to USP, New
Zealand, or Australian institutions.

In the early 1990s, the Samoan economy was devastated by two cyclones—
Cyclone Ofa in 1990 and Cyclone Val in 1991. They had equally devastating
educational effects as 85 percent of school buildings and virtually all school
equipment and teaching materials were destroyed. The necessity for rebuilding
the education system within a climate of economic decline, combined with
reduced government expenditure and community spending power as a result of
the structural adjustment policies encouraged throughout the "developing"
world by the international finance institutions (e.g., cuts in public sector
expenditure and higher levels of indirect taxation), had the effect of making
Samoan education more dependent on aid-funded development.

The immediate contribution of "disaster relief" in the wake of the cyclone
destruction led to an extensive rehabilitation of school buildings. A number of
projects in various aspects of education were initiated through the official aid
programs of Australia and New Zealand, most notably in teacher education
and the development of teaching and learning programs at the local polytechnic and university, while Japan provided USD$20 million for the building of
a new national university campus. At the primary level, Samoa participated
in the regional UNDP/UNESCO-funded Basic Education and Life Skills
program.

However, whereas these projects were all subsector specific, in 1994 a New
Zealand–funded project concerned with the education sector as a whole and
aimed at addressing the perceived fragmentation of the education system
began. The project, the goal of which was "the raising of the quality and relevance of education in Western Samoa and improvements in equity and efficiency," was initiated in response to a request from Samoa subsequent to a
World Bank Education Sector Review undertaken in 1992. The project's three
main objectives were a comprehensive policy framework, a strategic plan, and a
management information system.

The 1994–1995 Education Policy and Planning Development Project (EPPDP)

The World Bank Education Sector Review (WBR) highlighted the difficulty of rehabilitating the education system given the severe economic conditions and recommended that the rebuilding of the system take place within a long-term development strategy, which would address deficiencies in quality, equity, relevance, and efficiency that long predated the cyclones. A number of specific policy recommendations and implementation strategies aimed at redressing the problems outlined were detailed in the WBR. Prior to the second cyclone, however, the minister of Education had already begun working towards a comprehensive education review. She asserted her belief that Samoan education's greatest need was for the development of clear and acceptable educational policy through consultation with teachers, parents, and community members. She attributed the problems in the wake of the 1987 changes largely to a lack of such consultation, noting that "although theoretically politicians make policy, in practice educational bureaucrats do and it is those who manage and run schools who must implement it." She saw it as essential that the relationship between the various groups involved be worked on positively, and that they all be involved in policy development, as desirable change would not happen otherwise. The minister described the WBR as "OK but they don't go far enough," commenting that "ideas about, and expectations of, education are more powerful in determining what governments and others can bring about than the World Bank seems to think." The Samoan government requested New Zealand assistance in facilitating a contextual analysis of the WBR recommendations and the development of a policy framework that would either incorporate the World Bank recommendations or formulate alternatives. The unease with both the content of the WBR recommendations and the process by which they were arrived at were encapsulated in the following comment from a prominent Samoan educator:

I've seen the World Bank at work before. It doesn't make much difference to them what country they're in, they just see much the same problems—not enough resources, bad management, poor standard of teaching etc.—so impose the same solutions all around the globe. But just because the problems are the same doesn't mean the reasons and answers are—many of the factors involved here are unique; they're the result of what's happened before.[89]

The body charged with analyzing the recommendations of the WBR and developing a comprehensive policy framework, was the Policy Planning Committee (PPC), a group made up of senior ministry officials, other key educators from the government, and nongovernment systems and two New Zealand–funded consultants. Having reflected on why the attempt a few years previously to restructure the education system in ways that were intended to improve the quality and relevance, and reduce the inequities of the existing system, had met such strong resistance from the public, they agreed that the success of the EPPDP required the development of a process within which (in the words of one member):

Policy issues must be debated thoroughly by all groups of Samoans in order to develop a vision—they have to focus on the critical issues in order to develop policies that are socially and politically appropriate.[90]

It was agreed that the ongoing fallout from the previous policy failure and the accumulation of educational problems since made it crucial that the EPPDP succeed.

In laying the foundations of a policy development process that would ensure this, the following steps were taken: a set of principles about the nature and process of policy itself was arrived at; context-specific definitions of the key terms/concepts—quality, equity, relevance, efficiency—that would provide benchmarks for the policy process and some philosophical understandings about the relationship between education, development and culture were developed; a set of broad goals to guide the education sector were defined; and the means whereby dialogue with interest groups could proceed were established.

The principles that guided the policies and strategies informing the development of Samoa's education sector over a ten-year period (mid-1995–2005) started from the position that the aim of a new policy framework was to improve existing educational delivery for all learners and placed a clear focus on both the educational mission of learning institutions and the need to protect and enhance the professionalism of teachers. Although it was agreed that global trends in education must be heeded, it was viewed as fundamental that the policy process be firmly planted in the local setting; that context-specific education policies should be crafted according to a process of analysis whereby problems and their solutions would be considered within political, economic, social, and cultural conditions in which the education system existed. It was accepted that the process of identifying both those aspects of the current system that needed to continue, and the problems within the existing system that pointed to the need for new solutions, must be an inclusive and consultative process consistent with *faaSamoa* decision-making processes.[91] The policies and strategies developed through the process included the educational sub-sectors of early childhood, primary, secondary, and post-secondary/tertiary education.

The PPC was clear about both the importance of early childhood education (ECE) and the likelihood that constraints on government resources would mean no direct funding for the country's various centers for the next ten-year period. The existing decentralized community-based system was seen as best served through a range of support systems to be developed by an ECE Working Party. This body was charged with addressing concerns about the fragmentation and lack of regulation within the existing system by advising on the need for operation standards, regulatory and quality assurance mechanisms, pre- and in-service teacher education programs, curriculum guidelines, and information on learning activities appropriate to the developmental levels of preschool children. These would be developed in ways that could support ECE in providing a sound foundation for future learning through a service that enhances the role of family, community, and village.[92]

The most fundamental problem identified in Samoa's primary school system was that of congestion in the government-owned and managed urban schools, and the underutilization of many rural schools. The overall teacher/learner ratio of one to twenty-seven concealed extremes in class sizes of over seventy in the Malifa Compound schools—the concentration of more than 4,500 children in the four compound schools meant large numbers of children sat on the floor in overcrowded classrooms—and fewer than ten in some rural schools. Many small schools were overstaffed because of teachers' lack of pedagogical skills in individualized and small-group teaching, and the unavailability of the resources necessary for multigrade classrooms.

There were also a number of problems that applied to rural and urban schools alike: Facilities were generally poor with equipment either nonexistent or very run down; curriculum materials and textbooks, particularly those written in the Samoan language, were not readily available in the quantities required; the absence of a systematic bilingual methodology, and teachers who lacked bilingual facility, meant most children were linguistically disadvantaged; an overreliance on rote-learning methods, and a general lack of creativity in classroom approaches, limited learning possibilities for teaching and learning in most subject areas; numeracy skills and literacy skills—in both Samoan and English—were low, particularly among boys; and instructional times for the various subjects were not clearly laid down, with the result that some teachers concentrated on the subject areas they were most comfortable with and neglected others.[93]

The PPC's deliberations on how to upgrade the whole of the primary system centered on the reasons why parents bypassed their village schools to bring their children into Apia at great inconvenience and cost, travel as well as considerably higher school fees. The belief of the many parents from outside the Malifa zone who enrolled their children in the Malifa schools, that their children would be disadvantaged by attending their local schools and conversely advantaged by attending the compound schools, was founded on the historical evidence that schooling at Malifa offered the best opportunity for educational success; this belief was held despite the very evident educational limitations for all children attending these seriously overcrowded and quite dilapidated schools. The policy solutions arrived at—with the general aim of upgrading the quality of the primary system thereby providing an equitable and relevant learning experience for rural and urban children alike, and the specific aim of reducing Malifa enrollments by about 50 percent—included the establishment and enforcing of new zoning regulations for the Malifa Compound and a planned process for reducing each of the Malifa schools' enrollments to a maximum number of 750 with no class exceeding forty children. Staffing allocations were to be in line with established base teacher–learner ratios as follows: single-grade classes to be staffed on a ratio of one to thirty (maximum forty); dual-grade, on a ratio of one to twenty-five (maximum thirty); and multiple-grade classes to be staffed on a ratio of one to twenty (maximum twenty-five).

Other measures proposed for upgrading the whole primary system, which it was hoped would persuade parents that their children would get the best possible education in their local primary schools, focused on the provision of high-quality material and teaching resources to all schools; consolidated curriculum and a strengthened focus on literacy and numeracy; the establishment and monitoring of instructional times for each subject area and at each level; the lessening of the rote-learning and spoon-feeding teaching methods, which were still common, and more emphasis on active and interactive pedagogies; and a move away from assessment based on formal written testing towards more useful formative and summative processes by which to measure student progress, diagnose learning needs, and evaluate teaching programs. The strengthening of literacy and numeracy skills was to be supported through a national monitoring program and benchmark testing in literacy (in Samoan and English) and numeracy at Years 4 and 6. The development of individualized and small-group teaching techniques, able to enhance learning for all children but especially necessary for multigrade teaching, were proposed as one major focus of in-service teacher education programs, with the other being workshops on the production of materials suitable to the learning needs of children at different developmental stages and based on relevant themes and topic. A comprehensive program in the development, production, and distribution of high-quality readers, with a particular emphasis on Samoan language readers, was also proposed.[94]

The inequity and inefficiency of its dual stream structure was seen as the central problem for secondary education with the junior secondary schools offering the vast majority of students—particularly rural students—inferior educational opportunities, such that 75 percent of the total age group did not get beyond Year 11. Given the minimum legal employment age of seventeen, which Year 11 students would not have reached, this signified a serious constraining of life options, especially for rural students. This was further exacerbated by employers' preference for employees with some senior secondary schooling, and a raising of entry qualifications for tertiary institutions to at least Year 12 standard. With access to senior secondary education both extremely limited and highly selective, the fact that a disproportionate number of students gaining access to the state senior secondary schools received their primary schooling at the Malifa primary schools suggested a further constraint on equitable access for rural students. Furthermore, although girls as a group did better than boys as a group in the Year 8 National

Examination, because one of the three government-owned senior secondary schools was a single-sex boys school, only about half as many girls as boys gained access to places in these schools: a clear case of gender-based inequity. Other key problems that could be generalized across the secondary system were identified as follows:

- The overall teacher/learner ratio throughout the secondary system was one/twenty, but this very favorable situation disguised large variations in teacher utilization. Staff might teach as few as fourteen out of twenty-five instruction hours per week or as many as twenty-two. Class sizes covered a wide range depending on the subject and the size of school. Attrition among secondary teachers was high.
- Although rebuilding programs since the 1991 cyclone had resulted in well-constructed classroom buildings throughout the country, facilities such as libraries, science laboratories, home economics and industrial arts rooms were either non-existent or inadequately supplied.
- Having three external examinations in a five-year program was a problem both in terms of equity in that they were used to limit access through the system, and pedagogically in that they dominated classroom activities.
- The secondary system was widely considered to lack relevance to village life and labor market needs with too much emphasis, particularly at senior secondary level, on the expectation of future white collar or professional employment. Because of the low status of, and lack of resources committed to, applied subjects at junior secondary schools, and their unavailability at senior secondary schools, students left the secondary system with limited ability in practical skills and were unable or unwilling to respond to employment opportunities in the trade and technical areas.[95]

It was clear to the PPC that a secondary education characterized by quality, equity, relevance, and efficiency required a fundamental rethinking about the provision, organization, and expectations of secondary education. There was a very urgent need to increase both access to senior secondary education and to raise the levels of achievement of senior secondary graduates in order to meet raised demands at the postsecondary level. The policies required to improve the quality of the education offered throughout the system, and to redress present inequities between rural/urban and female/male students, resulted in extensive deliberation of the alternative ways in which these needs could be met, with a consensus for the current dual secondary structures to be progressively merged into one five-year, single-stream, comprehensive secondary system in which the same curricular and assessment requirements applied to all students. The policy proposal was for the retention (at least in the medium-term) of selective entry into the three senior secondary schools, and the progressive upgrading of the junior secondary schools to four-year then five-year schools. The solution to the inequity in the access of girls to the government senior secondary system was for Avele College to become a coeducational school offering places to girls through a gradual change process, starting with admission to senior secondary classes, which did not displace large numbers of boys was the best approach given the school's long tradition (in rugby competition, for example) and that any concern, especially among the Old Boys Association, would therefore be more easily circumvented. It would also alleviate the concerns of parents of younger girls, if older girls were already there to give them guidance and support.

The secondary school curriculum emphasis was for the development of the core academic subjects—language (Samoan/English), mathematics, the sciences, and social sciences—and the provision of a comprehensive program of optional and supplementary subjects for all students, so as to support and shape the merging of the present dual-stream system into a single-stream system, and the eventual merging of the JSSCE and WSSCE. To this end, during Years 9 to 11, every student was to complete courses in the core academic subjects, at least two optional applied subjects and the three supplementary subjects of art, music, and physical education, with achievement in both core academic and optional applied subjects determining access to Year 12 places. Senior secondary students also would be offered a comprehensive range of academic and applied subjects from which to select the required number of subjects for WSSCE and PSSCE, both academic and applied subjects being equally valid in the examination program and the selection processes for higher education. The proposal included a comprehensive review of secondary curricula with the aim of strengthening and broadening existing courses and developing new curricula as required. The need to achieve a proper balance between imparting knowledge and developing skills, values, and attitudes was identified as a focus of curriculum developments at all levels, and across all subject areas, of the secondary system.

The inevitable state of flux in the secondary system as a consequence of the junior secondary schools upgrading process, and the continued need for a selection process, were seen to require the retention of the existing examination system in the short term, but with an expanded range of examinable subjects including Samoan language and the applied subjects. It was felt that the historical resistance to these subjects was largely attributable to the fact that they did not provide access to the credentials offered by senior secondary and tertiary programs. The need to review and rationalize the examination system was also taken into account, however, and it was proposed that the merging of the JSSCE and SSCE, to be pursued through curriculum developments, would include the eventual abolition of one or other of these examinations. The decision on this would be based on the effect of medium-term policy developments on secondary school retention. While the terminating year for most students was then at Year 11, it was hoped that the effect of the junior secondary upgrading could mean that within a few years Year 12 would be the terminating point for a majority of students. It was also asserted that moves towards internally assessed components of external certificates should be extended, and skill in the use of both formative and summative assessment/evaluation measures be promoted through preservice and in-service teacher programs.

In terms of providing the physical resources that would enable the delivery of the single-stream comprehensive curriculum, facilities needed to be developed in all secondary schools. The postcyclone rebuilding program funded largely by New Zealand had made available well-constructed surplus classrooms in most schools. It was decided that these would be fitted to provide every school with a well-equipped science laboratory, and a well-stocked and properly organized library with reference materials for all subjects and the general reading materials needed to develop language skills. The expense of resourcing all schools with the facilities required by specialist subjects led to the proposal that the wishes of communities regarding the provision of applied subject facilities be surveyed and the resource commitments required by both central and school-based management structures assessed, so school communities could make decisions on the optional school-based applied subjects they wished to offer their students according to the resources available.

Other policies aimed at addressing the existing variation in staffing levels and teacher workloads across the secondary system, and between subject areas within schools, included formulae for staffing based on size of school, with a general expectation that all teachers would teach around 80 percent of total teaching periods with reductions for those with extra responsibilities and external exam classes. It was also proposed that in order to ensure the maintenance of quality across subjects no teacher should be expected to teach a subject s/he had not qualified in and teaching times for every subject were to be standardized.[96]

The PPC identified the critical issue for the development of postsecondary education and training as the scale and range of institutions and facilities—the need for optimum use of the scarce resources available given the small population base, while building a system characterized by quality, equity, relevance, and efficiency and encompassing university, polytechnic, vocational, nonformal, and on-the-job training. Policies aimed at developing a coordinated and complementary, rather than fragmented and competitive, postsecondary system were to be provided through the establishment of a national body to be charged with ensuring limited resources were not dissipated through unnecessary course duplication; secondary school leavers would have the subject knowledge, skills, and attitudes required for further education and training; and graduates of postsecondary courses who were entering the workforce would have the knowledge and skills required by the labor market.[97]

The Education Policy and Planning Development Project was effective in its production of a coherent policy framework, well-supported with detailed plans and statistical data. It provided Samoan decision makers with clearly laid out policy directions and strategies to guide the change process through two five-year implementation stages. Importantly, it also ensured a coordinated approach to the acceptance of aid donor funding through the identification and design of projects in accordance with policy priorities of the Samoan government for the ten-year period. Also noteworthy, given the strong global trend of the time towards a managerial approach to education, was the extent to which teaching and learning issues were centered in the processes and outcomes of EPPDP, a reflection of the Policy Planning Committee's collective professional commitment to the grounded educational interests of Samoan students and teachers. Perhaps the most significant aspect of this major initiative was that, although facilitated through external assistance, it was locally driven by people who live the *faaSamoa* and consciously explored the relationship between education, culture, and development in the Samoan context at that historical time. Research presented shortly before the completion of the EPPDP by Samoan educator Dr. GauGau Va'afuti Tavana, which included the identification of the core Samoan cultural values that should guide the philosophy and practice of Samoan education, illuminates this relationship. He stated:

Samoan cultural values are held as central to the individual and collective identity of Samoan people and guide all facets of their way of life.... The core Samoan values identified in this study as essential to an authentic Samoa educational system are: respect for the elders and the *matai* system; deep and active care for one another; interdependence; communal collaboration; consensus in decision making; and, productivity for the welfare of the larger Samoan society.[98]

During the implementation process, a series of three-year corporate plans were developed in line with the policies and strategies, and every year an annual plan, reporting on progress towards and difficulties in reaching planned achievements, was presented to Parliament. These provided the basis for a number of public forums and departmental meetings to review and evaluate the various programs and projects contributing to the reform process. Thus "the public at large and the stakeholders were kept abreast with progress made and provided with the opportunities to contribute to strategic discussions and debates."[99]

THE PRESENT

In terms of internationally recognized measures of educational development, Samoa is doing well. In 2003, the Asia Development Bank reported that Samoa was making significant progress towards achieving the Millenium Development Goals (MDGs) established in 2000 as the means of measuring global development. It reported that Samoa was close to meeting the MDG educational targets having already achieved universal primary education and made considerable improvements in secondary enrollments—the highest of all Pacific island countries—and that gender disparities in education and literacy rates had been eliminated.[100] Furthermore, subsequent to Samoan participation in the global Education for All (EFA) conference at Dakar in 2000, an EFA Action Plan was developed with the commitment of meeting all EFA targets by 2015, most of which were already included in Samoa's own strategic plan.[101]

The importance placed on education by the Samoan government can be seen in the high level of national expenditure allocated to it: around 20 percent to 22 percent in each of the five years from 2000–2005. However, as the most significant area of public policy in a small state with constrained resources, decisions about education—who gets what, how much they get, etc.—continue to be the subject of much contestation and debate. Despite the undoubted achievements arising from the staged implementation of policies and plans over the past ten years, there is widespread public concern about continued disparities of educational provision and outcome for different social groups, particularly between rural and urban children and perceived problems with the management of some government schools. Much media attention is paid also to the educational and cost-effectiveness of aid donor activities, and there appears an increased desire for Samoa to assert its control over its own education system.

Because of the need to evaluate the outcomes of its ten-year program of education reform as laid out in the two documents produced from the EPPDP (see above), *Education Policies 1995–2005* and *Education Strategies 1995–2005*, and the need to develop policies and plans for the next ten-year period, in the past three years education in Samoa has undergone intensive and widely based reviewing—initiated both by the Samoan Ministry itself[102] and by the aid donors engaged in education projects. An interesting development in the 2005–2006 policy and planning process aimed at determining policies and strategies for the period 2006–2015 was the Ministry's decision not to accept the proposed external assistance from the donors. Instead, a taskforce of key local educators was set up and teams of writers across the various subsectors, forty-five in total, appointed. Together they undertook a widely participatory process of community consultations, writing workshops, and public forums, based closely on the policy development process of the previous decade, before the final document was produced. This section draws on the information provided by the reviews of the 1995–2005 reform program, and by the policy and planning process undertaken in 2005–2006, to provide a summary of the current state of education across key sub sectors and what the focuses are for future developments in each.

Early Childhood

Early Childhood Education in Samoa has come a long way over the past decade reflecting the recognition of its importance by communities throughout Samoa. In 1998 the National Council of Early Childhood Education of Samoa (NCECES) was established as an umbrella body to publish minimum standards and guidelines for the many private, community-based, and church-run ECE centers located throughout the country. These set out what is required to ensure a healthy, safe, and stimulating learning environment for preschool children and are monitored by the NCECES board comprised of twenty-nine members, representative of the many different interest groups involved in early childhood education. This wide representation has encouraged over 120 centers, involving approximately 350 teachers and caregivers in the delivery of programs to nearly 5,000 children, to register with the Council. All three- to five-year-old children, both urban and rural, now have access to a registered ECE center. Over 50 percent of registered centers have their own buildings, with about 40 percent operating in church halls, and a few in private homes. While not all centers yet meet minimum standards there is acceptance of the need to do so, and steady progress towards them.

In addition to the establishment of NCECES and the appointment of a Ministry-based ECE coordinator in 2000, Ministry support to the various non-government and community efforts is in the form of training support and a small grant to each registered center. Because there are insufficient trained ECE teachers to meet existing needs, untrained teachers are encouraged to train at certificate level, and those with certificates are encouraged to upgrade to diploma level through either the University of the South Pacific or the program offered by the NUS since 1999. MESC support over the next ten years will be aimed at the improvement and standardization of ECE teacher salaries, better preservice and in-service training, and collaboration with NCECES in monitoring the quality of ECE offered nationally.[103]

Primary

In 2006, there was a total primary school enrollment of just over 40,000, 49 percent of whom were girls, representing 94 percent of all children between five and nine years of age, and 96 percent of those aged ten to fourteen. The activities of the previous decade aimed at upgrading school facilities and generating more interesting learning programs, thereby improving conditions for both teachers and learners, have succeeded to a large extent. Repetition and dropout rates have reduced over the past decade and are now insignificant. A total of 1,260 trained teachers, most qualified at certificate level but an increasing number with NUS diplomas, staff the 159 schools that now make up the primary system—140 government, thirteen mission, and six private schools. The congestion in the Malifa Compound schools has been reduced with enrollment numbers according to targets. While overall teacher–student ratios have grown, the lowest ratios are in Savaii and rural Upolu schools, which are most likely to have dual- and multigrade classes.

The primary curriculum continues to cover five core subjects: Samoan, English, mathematics, science, social studies, and three supplementary subjects: music, art, and physical education, through twenty-six themes. Many of the themes themselves and the associated teaching and learning materials—print and audio, in Samoan and English—were developed with Australian assistance provided in the years from 1998–2004. These materials and the in-service training and professional development provided have contributed to more active pedagogies, varied assessment methods, and a more child-centered approach. They have also been well integrated into preservice teacher education programs.

With assistance from the Asian Development Bank, European Union, and the Japanese government the facilities of nineteen primary schools have been upgraded, and loan money has enabled reconstruction and equipping of another six. The Ministry's policies for the next period identify the need for further such upgrading and the development of new teaching procedures within national frameworks for both curriculum and assessment. Two areas nominated for focused attention are the Year 8 examination, especially its continued delivery in English, and boys' lower achievement levels.[104]

Secondary

By 2005, the main thrust of secondary education development in the previous decade—for a five-year single-stream, comprehensive system for all students, which would provide more equitable and relevant senior secondary opportunities for rural students and girls, thus enabling a higher proportion of students to complete the program—had achieved much. Parents, teachers, and students all report positively on the more lively, varied, and engaged secondary learning environments today's students are able to access. Enrollments have increased by almost 20 percent with 52 percent of the enrollment being girls and much of the increase at Years 12 and 13. The number of students sitting the Year 13 regional examination (PSSCE) has more than doubled. This increase has been facilitated by the upgrading of many of the schools that previously had offered their students only a three-year program terminating at Year 11. By 2006, the number of government schools offering the full Year 9 to 13 program had increased from three to fifteen, and all but one of the other nine government schools offered classes up to Year 12. In addition to the twenty-four government secondary schools in 2006, there were twelve mission and two private secondary schools.

During the late 1990s, the Year 11 examination was abolished, the single-sex boy's government school became coeducational, and outcomes-based curriculum statements in a range of subjects—Samoan, English, mathematics, general science, biology, chemistry, physics, agricultural science, social science, geography, history, business studies, economics, accounting, design technology, food and textiles technology—with clearly stated learning objectives at each level, began development, as did the integration of those subjects previously excluded from senior secondary examinations at Years 12 and 13. The pace picked up with curriculum developments after 2000 with further statements produced in visual arts, performing arts, music, physical education/health, and computer technology, all of them covering Years 9 to 13 and included in mainstream assessment processes as part of the senior secondary certification processes (SSCE and PSSCE). The new curricula, and a full range of associated teaching and learning resources, had been introduced to all secondary schools by the end of 2004, following an intensive three-year program of in-service teacher education in their use and in appropriate classroom assessment procedures. Simultaneous with the New Zealand-assisted curriculum, resources, and in-service teacher development program, an Asian Development Bank loan funded a school reconstruction and equipment program—with a focus on libraries, science laboratories, and applied subject facilities—in the twelve government secondary schools, which now offer the full five-year secondary cycle.

However, the one area in which the Ministry has not been successful, and one that is well recognized as crucial to their objective of raising the quality of the restructured secondary program, is the provision of a graduate teaching force. Although the secondary teaching body of around 700 enables the established teacher–student ratio to be met by most schools, many secondary teachers are qualified to teach only in the junior secondary years, and there are significant shortages in certain areas: the sciences, mathematics, and some of the applied subjects. Teacher development and provision will be a key focus for the next ten-year period, as will another ADB loan financed school building and equipping program for another twelve government schools.[105]

Tertiary/Post-secondary

The National University of Samoa (NUS) further established itself as the hub of tertiary education during the late 1990s. By 1998, not only had the former Nursing School become the NUS School of Nursing, and the former Teachers' College amalgamated into NUS as the Faculty of Education, NUS by then occupied a Japanese-funded and impressively constructed and equipped set of buildings on the Le Papaigalagala Campus on the outskirts of Apia. As well as the University Preparatory Year, nursing and teacher education programs, NUS offered a Bachelor of Arts with majors in Samoan studies, English, history, and mathematics, and a Bachelor of Commerce with a major in accounting and a minor in management. Certificate programs in commerce, science, computer science, and Diplomas in accounting and mathematics were also available. Overall, NUS's enrolled students of approximately 1,000 were two-thirds women and about 40 percent were in employment and completing work-related qualifications part-time. There were sixty-five full-time academic staff involved in the delivery of the various courses, and twenty part-timers contributing to the commerce programs.

The last few years have been mainly concerned with consolidation of existing programs and courses but have included the development of a research-focused Institute of Samoan Studies, a four-year Bachelor of Education, and sports science and performing arts programs in association with New Zealand tertiary institutions. The major development in Samoa's tertiary sector in 2006, advancing the policy direction for a rationalized and collaborative tertiary subsector, was the merging of Samoa Polytechnic (into which the School of Marine Studies had merged some years before) into NUS. Samoa Polytechnic, now known as the NUS Institute of Technology, offers certificate and diploma courses through three Schools—of Business and General Studies, Technology, and Maritime Training—and short-term training courses tailored on demand. The NUS student body now numbers about 2,500.

In addition to those who gain places at NUS, a significant number of mainly part-timers continue to enroll in University of the South Pacific courses. Tertiary scholarships to overseas institutions also have been maintained at around 300 across various level and types of programs.

Another recent and major development in the tertiary/technical-vocational/ nonformal education and training area aimed at overcoming fragmentation and lack of regulation of what is on offer by a wide range of domestic and international providers, was the 2005 establishment of the Samoa Qualifications Authority (SQA). All providers of programs and courses in these areas will have to comply with the registration and accreditation standards prescribed by SQA. SQA's role includes the development of pathways between senior secondary and technical and professional education.[106]

A Cross-Cutting Issue: Samoan Language and Culture

Both the 1995–2005 and 2006–2015 policies and planning processes have responded to widespread community concerns regarding the dilemma inherent in a situation whereby, although virtually all Samoans speak Samoan as mother tongue and all schools teach Samoan language, culture, and history, English has become the language of educational opportunity and economic advancement. Given that the Samoan language is fundamental to the cultural identity of Samoan people, the policy makers in both time periods upheld the need for language and culture to be integral to education structures and processes at all levels.

The 1995 policy framework proposed the establishment of a Language Taskforce made up of representatives known for their expertise in culture and language and working at every level of the education sector, from early childhood through to tertiary, to consider matters pertinent to the educational aim of producing bilingual individuals fully literate in both Samoan and English. However, as pointed out in the 2006 policy document, although the policy intent was for additive bilingualism (the development and maintenance of both languages), much of the language practice of the previous ten years has been geared to transitional bilingualism. This means that Samoan is used to support the development of English, to the point where English becomes the dominant language of education, thus reducing the status of Samoan language in the eyes of both teachers and learners. The concern about this practical effect of language practice in education institutions, which has constrained the use of the Samoan language in learning and its usefulness in academic, social, and economic advancement, has given rise to government approval for the estab-lishment of a Samoan Language Commission, and a set of policies aimed at an education system "committed to the advancement and maintenance of Samoan language status" as well as the development of bilingualism.[107]

Of interest here, is the continuing role played by the pastor schools, the *A'oga a le Faifeau*, in teaching Samoan literacy skills—reading, writing, and oracy—and *faaSamoa* cultural values and protocols to many of today's young Samoans. In 2001 over 20,000 young people between the ages of three and nineteen participated in the various pastor schools still operating throughout Samoa.[108]

The schooling and wider education system in Samoa shares many character-istics of such systems in small, developing countries elsewhere, insofar as it continues to be shaped by missionary and colonial systems and to be impacted by present-day forces such as globalization, aid dependence, and internal and external migration. However, as for wider development, educa-tional development in Samoa is necessarily a process shaped first and foremost by political-economic and sociocultural forces unique to Samoa and the historical and cultural agency of Samoan people. It is clear that despite early attempts—by missionaries and colonizers—to depress the educational aspira-tions of Samoan people, and the very severe material and human resource constraints on educational progress in postcolonial times, the belief of Samoan people themselves in the benefits of a better-educated population have enabled the very real achievements recorded here. This clear desire for "western" schooling should not be assumed as indicating Samoan people's wish to abandon "traditional" beliefs and institutions for what is "modern." Rather, it indicates the recognition that tradition and modernity, continuity and change, are not dichotomous processes—that an education system that is shaped by and accommodates the lived traditions and practices of the socio-cultural context in which it exists will allow them to mediate and indigenize global modernity in ways that maintain their cultural integrity. In the words of a Samoa writer, "Samoan development cannot be transplanted from else-where. It is a process of transformation that should be anchored in local structures and values."[109]

DAY IN THE LIFE OF A SAMOAN JUNIOR SECONDARY SCHOOL STUDENT

My name is Teuila Lameta. I turned fourteen in October this year (2006) and am in Year 9, the first year of secondary education, at one of the govern-ment colleges in Samoa. Secondary education in Samoa is from Year 9 to Year 13. My family lives in a village that is about five kilometers from my school and about five minutes from the capital and only town, Apia. My mum drives me to and from school each day. Today is the first day of Term 3.

School starts at 7:45 A.M. and finishes at 1:45 P.M., supposedly. The finishing time is not always kept, and throughout the year there are many occasions where school finishes two to four hours early. We have a total of forty weeks of schooling divided into a three-term year that begins early February and finishes early December. Our school has about 850 students this year. My school fee for a term is seventy tala, the equivalent of about twenty-five U.S. dollars and this includes all my stationery. School textbooks are provided without charge.

6:00 A.M. Today is another typical school day for me beginning at 6:00 A.M. when I am up, well almost, until the cold shower shakes me out of sleep. I am dressed in my bright red/orange tunic and bright yellow shirt and sitting down to a breakfast of cereal and obligatory pawpaw by 6:30 A.M. My nine-year-old brother is watching television because he already had breakfast and was ready to go to school. Our family rule is if you are ready, you get dropped off first, so today we will go up the hill first to his school that is about seven kilometers from home.

7:00 A.M. We leave home at 7:00 A.M., a must every day because the traffic is terrible from our side of town. Today being the first day of the third and final school term for government schools, the roads are back to their busy selves with many children walking or packed into overcrowded buses to school. Already the main road into town is thick with the traffic of people going to work and school, bumper to bumper for the first ten minutes of the drive. At this rate, and if my brother gets dropped off first, I will be late, and that means detention. Cleaning toilets and picking up rubbish in my school is definitely not a cool start to a school term, particularly when one is dying to catch up with friends after the holidays, not to mention the substandard, filthy, unhygienic state of our school toilets! I struck a compromise with the nine year old, trading chores for the chance to be dropped off first today.

7:30 A.M.–7:45 A.M. Whew! Made it with fifteen minutes to spare. Many of the students were already at school. By and large, the majority of students jostle for seats on the early morning buses that also carry the workers, and some from the rural villages will have caught the six o'clock buses or earlier. My classroom is on the second story in the junior block. My friends and I catch up briefly on what the two-week school holidays were like. "Boring, nothing much, stayed at home, minding younger siblings, never-ending house chores," were the common events with a few having made it to a movie or two. Being Monday and the first day of term, we go to a whole-school assembly. Each week, we have school assembly three times a week on Monday, Wednesday, and Friday.

Assembly is held in the open space outside on the parking lot, where girls sit on the left and boys on the right. Mostly it is an enjoyable time. A talented song leader stands to lead the whole school in traditional songs, chants, or church hymns. The traditional songs and chants are accompanied by varying clap beats to the rhythm of the song and the hilarious actions of the song leader. Sometimes, this ends with everyone collapsing in laughter, until the staff arrive and begin the serious business of the day. A hymn is sung followed by a prayer led by the deputy principal. On other occasions, the prayer is led by one of the prefects. Following the prayer, we stand to attention as our national anthem is sung and flag raised. Finally, the notices are given by the deputy principal. First up, the five classes, one from each level, on rubbish duty are noted. Duties are allocated to a set area of the school and must be done before and after school each day of the week. Our school, like all government and mission schools in Samoa, does not have caretakers or cleaners—we are it(!) and fair enough too at USD \$25 per term. The second notice reminds us of this very thing—pay your school fees, and those sitting the national examination at Year 12 and the regional examination at Year 13 are also reminded to pay their examination fees. The final notice reminds us of expected behavior in and out of school—the bit about not being in uniform around town by 4 P.M. and hanging out around the bus terminals is stressed. Interschool fighting at the bus terminals is a serious issue, though, thankfully our school is not involved.

8:00 A.M.–10:40 A.M. We have class periods one to three, each of fifty-minutes duration. Considering it was the first day of term, all teachers are prompt and set us immediately to work mainly on revision of last term's work. Before any of this, our form teacher welcomes us, takes the attendance roll, and wishes us a good day. The attendance roll is also taken at the beginning of each class to stop students from skipping class or school. Today, our first class is Mathematics and our teacher presents us with task sheets, gives the instructions, and we complete the work individually. The work is marked during class with the teacher asking different students for the answers and showing us the working out if an answer is wrong. Our second class is Samoan language in which we spend the entire period responding to teacher questions about the holidays. Our third class for this morning is Physical Education and, because it is raining, we spend the time in class on our own doing individual reading. Normally, Physical Education involves playing a game of soccer, rugby, or netball.

10:40 A.M.–10:55 A.M. is lunch time. Most days, I take a homemade lunch of sandwiches to school and a daily liter of water. Once a week, I may take five tala (about two U.S. dollars) to spend at the canteen. Today, I meet up with my friends at the school canteen and, once they have bought their lunches, we go to the Samoa *fale* (an open house without walls). Lunch is eaten while we play handball before the bell signals the next classes.

11:00 A.M.–1:45 P.M. We have three more classes beginning with science, followed by English, and social science. The pattern is the same for all classes today—revise what we supposedly learned last term. By the sixth period, it is pretty useless, with the teacher now asking us to copy notes into our books. The bell rings for school to finish. Our classmates who are monitors hurry us out to the nearest exit, so they can get going with the cleaning and sweeping.

2:30 P.M.–4:30 P.M. My mum picks me up after picking up my brother from his school. It will be just me and my brother at home after school today, as our nana who usually stays with us has gone to her house for some church event.

Once home, I make a sandwich before practicing my music piece on the piano for the recital later tonight. Music school is twice a week after school since I was six years old. Recitals are a final part of our music performance assessment—kind of like the finale for the year except, this year, it is being held before we have school exams. Now that I am in secondary school with the increased workload, music has not been easy to keep up with this year, so there's an added nervous stress to this year's recital.

Sometimes, after-school activities for my brother and me involves going to the pastor's school. Now that I am at secondary school, I have "graduated" to Youth that takes place on Fridays or Saturdays. If we have a special event like a production, then Youth will take place at least three times a week and almost daily nearing production day. Our youth group is an extension of pastor's school but at our age, it focuses firstly on spiritual growth in our relationship with God and as well on life skills. This includes focusing on values, decision-making, communication, cooperation and building trust, safety, and leadership skills. In 2007, the program is going to extend to helping us with academic skills and enterprise skills. Youth is so much fun because much of the activities are interactive and use multimedia. About twenty of us attend the same secondary school.

6:30 P.M.–9:00 P.M. The nervous faces and chatter of performers of all ages and the high expectations of the audience add to my rising butterflies. Finally, my turn comes and I go onto the stage with my heart beating louder than my playing. I had practiced for at least two hours a day for the last six weeks and it paid off. I actually enjoyed it.

After the recital, we were treated to a McDonald's meal, which I was told was well-deserved by my two home supporters, mother, and brother. At home, I ironed my uniform and packed my bag for the next day. I thanked the Lord for giving me the strength to go through today.

TIMELINE

To 1820	Dominant mode of education is traditional indigenous (from c. 3000 before the present).
1721	Dutch explorer Roggeveen is the first European to sight Samoa.
1830	John Williams of the London Missionary Society introduces Christianity and formal schooling to Samoa.
1844	Malua Seminary established to train Samoan ministers as both evangelists and teachers.
1871	Marist Brothers' school opens in Apia for both Samoan and European boys; closed 1877.
1888	Marist Brothers' school reopens, for European boys only.
1890	Sisters of St. Mary open a day school and a boarding school for Samoan girls in Apia.
1890s	LMS boarding schools for selected boys (Leulumoega) and girls (Papauta) opened.

1900	Germany annexes Samoa.
1905	German administration establishes Samoa's first "government" school: Leififi School for expatriate and "local European" children.
1908	A second government school, Malifa School, opened for Samoan children.
1909	A government boarding school opens at Malifa for the sons of chiefs.
1919	The League of Nations places Samoa under New Zealand's administration.
1920	New Zealand inspector of Maori Schools visits Samoa and initiates development of a national state education system.
1921	The "Samoa Act" passed in the New Zealand parliament establishes the Department of Education located on the Malifa Compound and headed by New Zealand appointed superintendent of schools.
1920s	Two government agricultural boarding schools for boys open: Avele College and Vaipouli College.
1925	St. Mary's establishes a commercial studies program for female primary school leavers.
1938	The first government-provided postprimary class for twenty-three selected students is established at Leififi.
1939	The first government-provided teacher-training institution offering a one-year course to twenty-five trainees is opened at Malifa.
1945	New Zealand Director of Education C. E. Beeby leads a delegation to Samoa to explore the education developments needed for self-government. The first group of Samoan scholarship students enter secondary schools in New Zealand.
1953	Racially segregated schooling abolished; Leififi and Malifa schools amalgamated.
1953	Samoa College opens with a secondary curriculum modeled on New Zealand's and taught by teachers recruited from New Zealand.
1959	Education Ordinance formalizes the role of Ministry and Department of Education.
1962	Samoa becomes an independent state. The dominance of New Zealand education structures and processes is increasingly questioned.
1967	First Samoan, and first woman, is appointed as director of Education.
1970s	Expansion of upper primary schooling; introduction of Samoan language and culture into the official curriculum; establishment of three-year junior secondary schools in most districts.
1979	Two-year primary and three-year secondary teacher-training programs initiated.
1984	National University of Samoa established.
1987	Department of Education initiates significant education restructuring; changes reversed by newly elected government in 1988.
1991	Education Amendment Act makes eight years primary schooling compulsory.
1994–1995	A policy and strategy framework is developed to guide educational reform for next ten years.
2005	Samoa Qualifications Authority established.
2006	A further ten-year policy and strategy framework developed.

NOTES

1. In 1997, the nation-state known as Western Samoa (distinguishing it from the eastern Samoan islands known as American Samoa), dropped the "western" and became Samoa.

2. Eve Coxon, "The Politics of 'Modernisation': Education Policy-Making at the Periphery," in *Education Policy: International Series in Comparative Policy Studies*, ed. J. Marshall and M. Peters (Oxford: Edward Algar, 1999), 515–35.

3. Asia Development Bank (ADB), *Equity, Quality, Relevance, Efficiency. Draft Education Sector Review. The Independent State of Samoa* (Samoa: Education Sector Project II, July 2004), 2.

4. Diane Mara, Lita Foliaki, and Eve Coxon, "Pacific Education," in *The Politics of Teaching and Learning in Aotearoa-New Zealand*, ed. Coxon et al. (Palmerston North: Dunmore Press, 1994), 180–214.

5. Malama Meliesea, *Lagaga. A Short History of Western Samoa* (Suva: University of the South Pacific, 1987), 42.

6. Malama Meleisea, *Change and Adaptation in Western Samoa* (Christchurch: Macmillan Brown Centre for Pacific Studies), 14–19.

7. Malama Meleisea, *The Making of Modern Samoa* (Suva: University of the South Pacific, 1987), 50–51.

8. Meleisea, *Lagaga*, 26.

9. Mara et al., 182.

10. Ibid., 184.

11. Meleisea, *Lagaga*, 33.

12. Peggy Fairbairn-Dunlop, *Tamaitai Samoa. Their Stories* (Suva: Institute of Pacific Studies, 1996), 6.

13. Ibid., 7.

14. Ibid., 9.

15. Mara et al., 182.

16. Meleisea, *Lagaga*, 35–37.

17. Ibid., 52.

18. Mara et al., 185.

19. T. L. Baba, "Education in Small Island States of the Pacific: The Search for Alternatives," in *Equity and Diversity: Challenges for Educational Administration. Record of Proceedings of the Sixth International Intervisitation Programme in Educational Administration* (Palmerston North: Massey University, 1986), 83.

20. Mara et al., 188.

21. J. W. Davidson, *Samoa mo Samoa: the Emergence of the Independent State of Western Samoa* (Melbourne: Oxford University Press, 1967), 36.

22. Lonise Sera Tanielu, "O le A'oaina o le Gagana, Faitautusi ma le Tusitusi i le A'oga a le Faifeau: Ekalesia Faapotopotaga Kerisiano Samoa (EFKS)," (PhD diss., University of Auckland, 2004), 142.

23. Tanielu, 75.

24. Ibid., 145–46.

25. Davidson, 36.

26. Tanielu, 147.

27. Mara et al., 188.

28. Stephen Lui Filipo, "O le Aoga Katoliko mo Tagata Samoa," (EdD diss., University of Auckland 2005), 50–51.

29. Fairbairn-Dunlop, 159.

30. Mara et al., 188.

31. Ibid., 189.

32. Meleisea, "Change and Adaptation," 20–22.

33. Davidson, 38–39.

34. Michael C. Howard, Nii-K. Plange, Simione Durutalo, and Ron Witton, *The Political Economy of the South Pacific* South East Asian Monograph Series, no. 13 (Townsville: James Cook University, 1983), 79.

35. Davidson, 47.

36. Howard, 78.

37. Fanaafi Ma'ia'i, "A Study of the Developing Pattern of Education and the Factors Influencing that Development in New Zealand's Pacific Dependencies," (Master's thesis, Victoria University, 1957), 172.

38. Fairbairn-Dunlop, 50.

39. Albert Wendt, "Guardians and Wards," (Master's thesis, Victoria University, 1965), 34.

40. Michael J. Field, *Mau: Samoa's Struggle for Freedom* (Auckland: Polynesian Press, 1991), 49.

41. Wendt, 36–37.

42. Felix M. Keesing, *Modern Samoa* (London: Allen & Unwin Ltd., 1934), 416.

43. Fairbairn-Dunlop, 86.

44. Tanielu, 6, 148.

45. Ma'ia'i, 171.

46. Fairbairn-Dunlop, 48.

47. J. M. Barrington, "Education and National Development in Western Samoa," (PhD diss., Victoria University, 1968), 11; Fairbairn-Dunlop, 181.

48. Fairbairn Dunlop, 161, 181.

49. G. Irwin, *Samoa: A Teacher's Tale* (London: Cassel & Company, 1965).

50. F. J. Lugard, "Education in Tropical Africa," *The Edinburgh Review* 242, no. 493 (1925), 17.

51. Ma'ia'i, 315.

52. Davidson, 11.

53. Hempenstall, 78.

54. Angus Ross, *New Zealand in the Pacific World* (Wellington: New Zealand National Party), 292; Tanielu, 68.

55. Cited in Keesing, 421.

56. Cited in Mara et al., 194.

57. Mara et al., 193.

58. Fairbairn Dunlop, 99.

59. Ibid., 87.

60. Cited in Barrington, 55.

61. Barrington, 68–70.

62. Peter J. Sluyter, "Frontline Samoa. Western Samoa: A Mandated Territory's Part in World War Two," (Unpublished research essay, University of Auckland, 1988), 4–5.

63. Sluyter, 7.

64. Fairbairn Dunlop, 55.

65. Fairbairn Dunlop, 74–75.

66. Davidson, 186

67. C. G. Powles, "The Status of Customary Law in Western Samoa" (Master's thesis, Victoria University, 1973), 57.

68. Cited in Barrington, 180.

69. Barrington, 80.

70. Cited in Ma'ia'i, 225.

71. Ma'ia'i, 216–18.

72. Fairbairn-Dunlop, 116.

73. Cited in Barrington, 208.

74. Fairbairn-Dunlop, 75, 78.

75. Lonise Tanielu, "Education in Western Samoa: Reflections on my Experiences," in *Bitter Sweet. Indigenous Women in the Pacific*, ed. A. Jones et al. (Dunedin: University of Otago Press, 2000), 56.

76. Ibid., 54–57.

77. Clarence E. Beeby, *Report on Education in Western Samoa* (Wellington: Government Printer, 1954), 31.

78. Barrington, 185.

79. Ibid., 186.

80. Cited in Ma'ia'i, 225.

81. Department of Economic Development, *First Five Year Economic Development Plan 1966–70* (Apia: Western Samoa, 1966).

82. Legislative Assembly of Western Samoa, *Annual Report of the Ministry of Education for 1979* (Apia: Government Printer, 1979).

83. Fairbairn-Dunlop, 79–80.

84. Department of Economic Development, *Third Five Year Economic Development Plan 1975–79* (Apia: Western Samoa, 1975), 237–38.

85. R. Murray Thomas and T. Neville Postlethwaite, (eds., *Schooling in the Pacific Islands* (Oxford: Pergammon Press, 1984), 224, 227.

86. Legislative Assembly of Western Samoa, Annual Report of the Ministry of Education for 1985 (Apia: Government Printer, 1985).

87. Pers. comm., November 1990.

88. The summary below of the main characteristics of each subsector draws on an education review carried out by the World Bank in 1992; see World Bank, *Western Samoa: Rebuilding the Education System* (Education Sector Review, East Asia Region, 1992); and research undertaken by the writer in the early 1990s, which contributed to the development of a ten-year program of education reform as documented in Evelyn Coxon, "The 'Politics' of Modernisation in Western Samoan Education" (Unpublished PhD diss., University of Auckland, 1996).

89. Eve Coxon, "Education Policy-making at the Intersection," in *Global/Local Intersections: Researching the Delivery of Aid to Pacific Education*, ed. Eve Coxon and 'Ana Taufe'ulungaki (Auckland: Research Unit in Pacific Education, The University of Auckland, 2003), 72.

90. Ibid., 74.

91. Ibid., 77.

92. Department of Education, *Education Policies 1995–2005* (Apia: Government of Western Samoa, 1995), 15.

93. Ibid., 16–17.

94. Ibid., 16–19.

95. Ibid., 23–24.

96. Ibid., 25–29.

97. Ibid., 33–34.

98. GauGau Va'afuti Tavana, "Cultural Values Relating to Education in Western Samoa: A Conceptual Analysis of the Perspectives of Samoan Social Leaders," (PhD diss., Brigham Young University, 1994), 15.

99. 'Ana Maui Taufe'ulungaki and Abel Nako, *Samoa Education Sector Evaluation Study* (Suva: Institute of Education, University of the South Pacific, December 2005), 12.

100. Ibid., 14.

101. Ibid., 30–31.

102. In 2003, the Department of Education and Department of Sports and Culture merged to become the Ministry of Education, Sports and Culture (MESC).

103. Taufe'ulungaki & Nako, 31–32; Ministry of Education, Sports and Culture, *Strategic Policies and Plan 2006–2015* (Apia: Government of Samoa, 2006), 18–19.

104. Ibid., 32-33; Ministry of Education, 19–21, 39; ADB, 10–12, 26, 43.

105. Taufe'ulungaki & Nako, 34–36; Ministry of Education, 21–22, 43; ADB, 27–28, 38.

106. Taufe'ulungaki & Nako, 36–38; Ministry of Education, 25–29, 54; ADB, 83–84.

107. Ministry of Education, 34–35.

108. Tanielu, 232.

109. Noumea Simi, "Putting People First," in *Sustainable Development or Malignant Growth?* ed. Atu Emberson-Bain (Suva: Marama Publications, 1994), 275.

BIBLIOGRAPHY

Coxon, Eve. 1999. "The Politics of 'Modernisation': Education Policy-Making at the Periphery." In *Education Policy: International Series in Comparative Policy Studies.* Edited by J. Marshall and M. Peters. Oxford: Edward Algar.

Department of Education, 1995. *Education Policies 1995–2005.* Apia: Government of Western Samoa.

Fairbairn-Dunlop, Peggy. 1996. *Tamaitai Samoa. Their Stories.* Suva: Institute of Pacific Studies, 1996.

Field, Michael J. 1991. *Mau: Samoa's Struggle for Freedom.* Auckland: Polynesian Press.

Meleisea, Malama. 1987. *The Making of Modern Samoa.* Suva: University of the South Pacific.

Ministry of Education, Sports and Culture, 2006. *Strategic Policies and Plan 2006–2015.* Apia: Government of Samoa.

Tanielu, Lonise. 2000. "Education in Western Samoa: Reflections on My Experiences." In *Bitter Sweet. Indigenous Women in the Pacific.* Edited by Alison Jones, Phyllis Herda, and Tamasailau M. Suaalii. Dunedin: University of Otago Press.

BIBLIOGRAPHY

Alcorn, Noeline. 1999. *To the Fullest Extent of His Powers: C. E. Beeby's Life in Education*. Wellington: Victoria University Press.

Ali, Ahmed. 1980. *Plantation to Politics: Studies on Fiji Indians*. Suva: University of the South Pacific.

Austin, A. G. 1961. *Australian Education 1788–1900: Church, State and Public Education in Colonial Australia*. Melbourne: Isaac Pitman.

Austin, A. G., and R. J. W. Selleck. 1975. *The Australian Government School 1830–1914*. Melbourne: Pitman.

Barcan, Alan. 1980. *A History of Australian Education*. Melbourne: Oxford University Press.

Barrington Thomas, E., ed. 1976. *Papua New Guinea Education*. Melbourne: Oxford University Press.

Barrington, John M., and Tim H. Beaglehole. 1974. *Maori Schooling in a Changing Society: An Historical Review*. Wellington: New Zealand Council for Educational Research.

Beresford, Quentin, and Gary Partington, eds. 2003. *Reform and Resistance in Aboriginal Education: The Australian Experience*. Perth: University of Western Australia Press.

Brammall, J., and Ronald J. May, eds. 1975. *Education in Melanesia*. Canberra: Australian National University and Council on New Guinea Affairs.

Butts, R. Freeman. 1957. *Assumptions Underlying Australian Education*. Melbourne: Australian Council for Educational Research.

Campbell, Craig, and Geoffrey Sherington. 2006. *The Comprehensive Public High School: Historical Perspectives*, Secondary Education in a Changing World. New York: Palgrave Macmillan.

Campbell, Ian. *A History of the Pacific Islands*. Brisbane: University of Queensland Press, 1990.

Caton, Hiram, ed. *The Samoa Reader: Anthropologists Take Stock*. Lanham: University Press of America, 1990.

Clammer, J. R. 1976. *Literacy and Social Change: A Case Study of Fiji.* Leiden: E. J. Brill.

Cleverley, John F. 1971. *The First Generation: School and Society in Early Australia.* Sydney: Sydney University Press.

Cleverley, John F., and Christabel Wescombe. 1979. *Papua New Guinea Guide to Sources in Education.* Sydney: Sydney University Press.

Connell, R. W., D. J. Ashenden, S. Kessler, and G. W. Dowsett. 1982. *Making the Difference: Schools, Families and Social Division.* Sydney: George Allen & Unwin.

Connell, W. F. 1993. *Reshaping Australian Education 1960–1985.* Melbourne: ACER.

Coxon, Eve. 1999. "The Politics of 'Modernisation': Education Policy-Making at the Periphery." *Education Policy: International Series in Comparative Policy Studies.* Edited by J. Marshall and M. Peters. Oxford: Edward Algar.

Denoon, Donold et al., eds. *The Cambridge History of the Pacific Islanders.* Cambridge: Cambridge University Press, 1997.

Ewing, John. 1970. *The Development of the New Zealand Primary School Curriculum 1877–1970.* Wellington: New Zealand Council for Educational Research.

Fiji Education Commission. 1969. *Education for Modern Fiji: Report of the 1969 Fiji Education Commission, Fiji Legislative Council Paper no. 2.* Suva: Government Printer.

Fiji Islands Education Commission/Panel. 2000. *Learning Together: Directions for Education in the Fiji Islands.* Suva: Government Printer.

Fogarty, Ronald. 1959. *Catholic Education in Australia, 1806–1950.* 2 vols. Melbourne: Melbourne University Press.

Fry, Ruth. 1985. *It's Different for Daughters: A History of the Curriculum for Girls in New Zealand Schools, 1900–1975.* Wellington: New Zealand Council for Educational Research.

Groves, William Colin. 1936. *Native Education and Culture-Contact in New Guinea: A Scientific Approach.* Melbourne: Melbourne University Press.

Jones, Alison, Gary McCulloch, James Marshall, Graham H. Smith, and Linda T. Smith. 1990. *Myths and Realities: Schooling in New Zealand.* Palmerston North: Dunmore Press.

Kavanamur, David, Charles Yala, and Quinton Clements, eds. 2003. *Building a Nation in Papua New Guinea Views of the Post-Independence Generation.* Canberra: Pandanus Books.

Kociumbas, Jan. 1997. *Australian Childhood: A History.* Sydney: Allen & Unwin.

Lal, Brij. 1992. *Broken Waves: The Fiji Islands in the Twentieth Century.* Honolulu: University of Hawaii Press.

Langmore, Diane. 1989. *Missionary Lives Papua 1874–1914.* Pacific Island Monograph Series, no. 6. Honolulu: University of Hawaii Press.

Lingard, Bob, John Knight, and Paige Porter, eds. 1993. *Schooling Reform in Hard Times.* London: Falmer.

Linnekin, Jocelyn. "Contending Approaches." In *The Cambridge History of the Pacific Islanders.* Edited by Donald Denoon et al. Cambridge: Cambridge University Press, 1997.

Mackey, John. 1967. *The Making of a State Education System.* London: Geoffrey Chapman.

Mann, Cecil W. 1935. *Education in Fiji.* Melbourne: Melbourne University Press.

Marginson, Simon. 1993. *Education and Public Policy in Australia*. Cambridge: Cambridge University Press.

Marginson, Simon, and Mark Considine. 2000. *The Enterprise University: Power, Governance and Reinvention in Australia*. New York: Cambridge University Press.

McCallum, David. 1990. *The Social Production of Merit: Education, Psychology and Politics in Australia 1900–1950*. London: Falmer Press.

Macintyre, Stuart, and Anna Clark. *The History Wars*. Melbourne: Melbourne University Press, 2003.

McLaren, Ian A. 1974. *Education in a Small Democracy*. London: Routledge & Kegan Paul.

Mead, Margaret. 1963. *Growing Up in New Guinea a Survey of Adolescence and Sex in Primitive Societies*. London: Penguin Books.

Meleisea, Malama. 1987. *The Making of Modern Samoa*. Suva: University of the South Pacific.

Meleisea, Malama, and Penelope Schoeffel. "Discovering Outsiders." In *The Cambridge History of the Pacific Islanders*. Edited by Donald Denoon et al. Cambridge: Cambridge University Press, 1997.

Miller, Pavla. 1986. *Long Division: State Schooling in South Australian Society*. Adelaide: Wakefield Press.

Ministry of Education, Sports and Culture, 2006. *Strategic Policies and Plan 2006–2015*. Apia: Government of Samoa.

Norton, R. 1990. *Race and Politics in Fiji*. Brisbane: University of Queensland Press.

O'Donoghue, Thomas A. 2001. *Upholding the Faith: The Process of Education in Catholic Schools in Australia, 1922–1965*. New York: Peter Lang.

Openshaw, Roger, Greg Lee, and Howard Lee. 1993. *Challenging the Myths: Rethinking New Zealand's Educational History*. Palmerston North: Dunmore Press.

Selleck, R. J. W. 1968. *The New Education*. London: Pitman.

Sherington, Geoffrey, R. C. Petersen, and Ian Brice. 1987. *Learning to Lead: A History of Girls' and Boys' Corporate Secondary Schools in Australia*. Sydney: Allen & Unwin.

Smith, Peter. 1987. *Education and Colonial Control in Papua New Guinea A Documentary History*. Melbourne: Longman Cheshire.

Tanielu, Lonise. 2000. "Education in Western Samoa: Reflections on My Experiences." In *Bitter Sweet. Indigenous Women in the Pacific*. Edited by Alison Jones, Phyllis Herda, and Tamasailau M. Suaalii. Dunedin: University of Otago Press.

Tavola, Helen. 1991. *Secondary Education in Fiji: A Key to the Future*. Suva: University of the South Pacific.

Teese, Richard. 2000. *Academic Success and Social Power: Examinations and Inequity*. Melbourne: Melbourne University Press.

Theobald, Marjorie. 1996. *Knowing Women: Origins of Women's Education in Nineteenth-Century Australia*. Cambridge: Cambridge University Press.

Thomson, Pat. 2002. *Schooling the Rustbelt Kids: Making the Difference in Changing Times*. Sydney: Allen & Unwin.

Waiko, John D. 1993. *A Short History of Papua New Guinea*. Melbourne: Oxford University Press.

Whitehead, Clive. 1986. *Education in Fiji Since Independence: A Study of Government Policy*. Wellington: New Zealand Council for Educational Research.

INDEX

ABOUT THE EDITORS AND CONTRIBUTORS

Craig Campbell is an associate professor in the history of education at the University of Sydney. He has published in the associated fields of youth history and the rise of universal secondary education. His most recent books, the first cowritten with Geoffrey Sherington is *The Comprehensive High School: Historical Perspectives* (2006), while the second is coauthored with Raewyn Connell and others, *Education, Change and Society* (2007). He is currently researching the recent history of school choice and the Australian middle class.

John Cleverley is an honorary professor at the University of Sydney. His fields of study are comparative and international education and the history of education. He undertook research in Papua New Guinea at the time of its independence. With Christabel Wescombe, he has published a guide to sources on education in PNG. He has written extensively on education in Australia and China. His latest book, *In the Lap of Tigers* (2000), is an account of the Maoist experimental university in Jiangxi.

Eve Coxon is a senior lecturer in education and development at the University of Auckland in New Zealand. Her broad research focus on education policy encompasses global/local intersections in education policy development in Pacific islands countries, and educational equity for Pacific communities in New Zealand. She is currently conducting research into recent shifts in modes of educational aid delivery to Pacific countries.

Gregory Lee is an associate professor in the history of education at the University of Waikato in New Zealand. His major research and teaching interests are in the fields of postprimary education, rural and middle schooling, church and state relations in education, and curriculum history and politics.

His most recent research work appears in *The Death of the Comprehensive High School: Historical, Contemporary, and Comparative Perspectives* (2007) with coauthors Howard Lee and Roger Openshaw.

Howard Lee, after teaching twenty-five years at the University of Otago in New Zealand, was appointed professor of policy and leadership studies in education at Massey University in 2007. His areas of research and teaching include comparative education, curriculum history, assessment, educational history, and policy analysis. He has cowritten two books, two monographs, and numerous book chapters, reviews, and articles in refereed journals. In 2006, he received an "outstanding thesis supervisor of the year" award from the University of Otago.

Geoffrey Sherington is professor in the history of education at the University of Sydney where he has taught for many years. He is the author of numerous books and articles in the history of education as well as the history of Australian immigration, including child migration. His latest book is a study of the comprehensive public high school in Australia, coauthored with Craig Campbell. He is currently working on two projects: the history of public universities in Australasia, and the middle class and school choice.

Carmen M. White is an associate professor of anthropology at Central Michigan University. Her scholarly interests include comparative education and the comparative analyses of "race," ethnicity, gender, and class as interlocking variables in inequality across societies. She has published in such journals as *Comparative Education Review, Harvard Educational Review,* and *History of Education.* She is writing a book on narratives about racial difference and disparities in educational attainment in Fiji.